The Trees and Fields
Went the Other Way

The Trees and Fields
Went the Other Way

EVELYN EATON

HARCOURT BRACE JOVANOVICH, INC.

NEW YORK

B
Eaton

Printed in the United States of America

A portion of this book appeared originally in *The New Yorker* in a slightly different form.

The poems by Evelyn Eaton appeared previously in *Love Is Recognition,* Dragons Teeth Press, 1971. The quotations from *Black Elk Speaks* by John G. Neihardt are used by permission. The lines from Francis Brett Young's epic poem "The Island" (Heinemann, 1955) are used by permission. The lines from "Provide, Provide" and "Build Soil" are from *The Poetry of Robert Frost,* edited by Edward Connery Lathem. Copyright 1936 by Robert Frost. Copyright © 1964 by Lesley Frost Ballantine. Copyright © 1969 by Holt, Rinehart and Winston, Inc. Reprinted by permission of Holt, Rinehart and Winston, Inc. "To Her Images" is reprinted by permission of Charles Scribner's Sons from *To Mix with Time* by May Swenson. Copyright © 1963 by May Swenson. The poem "Liszt and the Russian Soldier" is from *Toward Montebello* by Warren Carrier. Copyright © 1961 by Warren Carrier. Reprinted by permission of Harper & Row, Publishers. The quotations from *The Land of Little Rain* and *Earth Horizon* by Mary Austin are used by permission of the publisher, Houghton Mifflin Company. "Aspasia the Structurist," copyright © 1967 by Eleanor M. Scott, from the book *Alpha Omega, A Newport Childhood and the Last Poems,* by Winfield Townley Scott, is reprinted by permission of Doubleday & Company, Inc.

Library of Congress Cataloging in Publication Data

Eaton, Evelyn Sybil Mary, 1902–
The trees and fields went the other way.

1. Eaton, Evelyn Sybil Mary, 1902–   I. Title.
PR6009.A8Z527   1974   813'.5'2 [B]   73-17100
ISBN 0-15-191152-5

First edition

B C D E

For my grandchildren
Marty, John, David and Ricky
and their parents, Dick and Terry

The Trees and Fields
Went the Other Way

When Prince Lee Boo was taken from the Pelew Islands in 1793 and brought to England as a hostage for his father's good behavior, he was confused by houses because he had never seen one. At Portsmouth, he remarked, he was "put into a little house which was run away with by horses; most agreeable, the trees and fields went the other way."

The Prince alighted in London for the rest of his short life, but I am still in a little house, whisking through the century, astonished by what I see of the fugitive countryside. I set down these impressions for my grandchildren, whose little houses are more likely to be little rockets.

Still, I believe we are all of us Lee Boos.

Sometimes my mother could be teased or wheedled into telling fortunes by a method she said she learned from a gypsy. There were gypsies in England, gypsies in Canada, of the proud Romany kind. They appeared without warning on the outskirts of towns like Fredericton, in dark top-heavy caravans, holding the center of the street, the drivers looking straight ahead, the lean mongrels between the wheels looking straight ahead. Now and then abrupt laughter from behind window slits and curtained doorways derided the watching world. Passers-by went carefully, children stood well back from the pavement's edge, at a safe distance from the long snaky whiplash that could, and did, take the skin off a dog if it came too near.

When they had quite gone by one shivered, suddenly diminished, bereft of a rightful, half-remembered magic, disenchanted.

My mother laid out the cards in a circle of seven threes:

> For you
> for your home
> for love
> for money
> for the future
> for the inevitable
> for your wish.

For you, my mother said.
For me there was the accident of birth.

Nineteen sixty-eight, the year I began these jottings, was the year that we went to look at the moon and discovered the earth, not brown as I had vaguely imagined, or, in moments of despondency assumed, gray and slimy from pollution.

In spite of all that we have done to it, in spite of all we do, the earth still turns, blue-green, luminous, a shimmering pendant against the starless dark, each giving substance to the other.

Now that we have seen it, hanging before us, mysteriously expectant, it is easier to think of the accident of birth as a planned first landing, or perhaps re-entry, most probably a mission, controlled and monitored from Somewhere Else.

The flame of the spirit fired the flesh.

Preparation over, thrust and propulsion over, there came the lonely time, borne through darkness to a meeting already missed.

It was the third attempt. There were two abortive launchings, two scrubbed operations.

One went into orbit flawlessly the first time, circled, waited, then went on without the Other.

We will be far apart, a quarter of a century, half a continent perhaps, if we make it safely.

There are accidents, trajectory errors, interactions of gravitational forces, wasted fuel. Even when the first objective is accomplished, and the long coasting flight begun, there can be accidents.

We may never meet there this time.

Still, it was programmed as a double mission.
I shall look for him.
Remember ... remember ...
Think the way back ...
LISTEN ...
Contact ... gather ... collect ...

There is nothing to be done now, in the sheltering warmth of the capsule coasting earthward.

It is over now to those who monitor the splashdown.

Normal? Caesarean? Emergency? D.O.A.?

Endure ... endure ...

Approach the blue-green planet, face again the blank-out, survive ... survive the annihilation of another

BIRTH.

Part One

It was the Other they expected.

When the doctor said, "You have a healthy child, a daughter," my mother retorted furiously, "You mean a son!"

"*Voyons, petite dame,*" he said in his heavy Swiss French, "I have brought enough into the world to know the difference."

It had been a long, hard night, a difficult birth, without anaesthetic and with forceps, but it was only then that my mother cried convulsively.

When they brought me to her she looked and turned away.

I saw that look, that turn of the head often in my childhood, and the too-bright smile that followed.

Babies in the first few days of life are comic reproductions of all that went to make them . . . little peasant, little squire, little rabbi, little Indian chief . . . race, nationality, rank, all there on the pillow, astutely summarized.

Instead of the fair-haired, blue-eyed Anglo-Saxon son my mother craved and expected, I was a startling throwback to that Micmac or Malecite whose genes were in my father . . . a black-haired, black-eyed, sallow-skinned daughter, with very little bridge to my nose. (Later, when I was twelve, after being thrown from a horse, my nose was rebuilt, with a bone graft from a rib.) It was forty years before I discovered that we had these Algonquin genes and understood for the first time that I did not have to belong to the Anglo-Saxon world, and a lot of other things about my fundamental instincts, passions and fears.

All I knew as a child was what They told me, that I was born in Switzerland, on December 22, 1902, at Montreux in a villa by the lake. I never learned why my mother happened to be there on that important day, instead of in England with her husband, or in Canada with her parents. I only knew that there was something strange and distasteful about this Swiss occurrence, some unfunny joke. I thought because I was born in a wrong place and time there must be something wrong about me.

Older cousins yodeled, tweaked my hair, and asked me questions about cuckoo clocks. My sister told her friends: "She's Swiss," as they ran away to play without me. Grownups smiled the peculiar smile they kept for Santa Claus and the Easter bunny, but those were make-believe and I was real.

Parents held no discussions with children, or even among themselves. It was "Not before the servants, dear!" "Hush, think of the neighbors, dear!" when anything important came up.

If They had told me frankly what was in their minds . . . "You look too Indian. It's all right to have a little Indian blood, a long way back, like Pocahontas on your mother's side . . . we're proud of that . . . but . . . well . . . it's a pity you're a girl, a boy could carry it off better. . . . You're some sort of a throwback, dear. You don't look like a little English girl. . . ."

I would have agreed that I didn't. I might have muttered that I didn't want to, and why not a *Canadian* girl?

If anyone had added kindly, "Still, it's not your fault . . ." I might have borne one childhood desperation better, the loneliness, bewilderment, the ache, what Katherine Woods, the translator of Saint-Exupéry's *Le Petit Prince,* describing her own childhood called "the stigmata of the rejected."

It was more than being unwanted. To be wanted, to be loved, one must be lovable. I never felt my envelope, this time, was lovable.

Rejection by one's species is hard to accept or to understand but it lacks the peculiar anxiety and dread that I grew up with, of being altogether *other,* universally alien, a frog among birds, the only frog in a world of birds, or a bird among frogs, the only bird in a world of frogs. A frog who admired birds, a bird who admired frogs.

I Ching might say "No blame," but still it was a predicament, a communications problem. People didn't talk of "paranoid" or "inferiority complex" when I was growing up, but the conditions existed, the stronger for being unrecognized, unpigeonholed. Eccentric aunts and uncles, who would now be on the couches of psychiatrists, lurked in every family.

If my father, or any of his generation on the Eaton side, had lifted the mysterious veil of something *wrong* with us, if they had brought our Algonquin heritage into the open . . . that is, if they knew of it . . . or described the Indian way of life . . . but they had lost the red man's road themselves by then; they were trying to be English, more English than the English, like other "nice" Canadians, treading the pavement, not the forest trail, in a world of racial snobbery, colonial patronage, upper-class false values, talk of "funny foreigners." I once heard an English colonel on a golf course in Belgium remark at the top of his bluff voice, "I say, this wouldn't be a bad little course if it weren't for all these foreigners!"

The Belgians with me smiled. Those were the days when we still sang in church: "Bless the Squire and his relations, And keep us in our proper stations."

There was another kind of song in another kind of church the year that I was born.

Indians for the most part were forbidden to dance their sacred dances or sing their sacred songs. Bonfires were made of all their holy things. Everything was done to discourage and degrade them, but here and there, on far-off reservations in the Midwest, remnants of the Algonquin faith persisted.

Dressed in a few makeshift buckskins over the ugly, awkward clothes the conqueror imposed on them, supervised and spied upon by ignorant white agents, the priests, the peace-keepers, the dancers went through the Eight Days of the Sun Dance to the triumphant end, with dignity and power, releasing ancient blessing to the tribe, to the country, to the world.

The year that I was born, a young man named Hawkan was priest-director of the Sun Dance held by the Arapaho in Oklahoma.

"If we shall make any mistake," he prayed, "have pity upon us, for we are yet children. May our road be straight and give us peace of mind."

Through the flowery English of the white translation I can hear my Indian friends today murmuring, "The road is not soft, the road is hard. It is not easy. The Grandfathers want it that way."

At the beginning of the Great Eight Days, Hawkan (was *he* perhaps the Other?) stood with his pipe to address the Great Spirit Mystery:

"Our Father, your birds which we shall imitate are white, and have power for long flight, and drink the sweet-water [snow]; may we accordingly! We ask these things with pure hearts."

Through the foreign words the aspirations of the upward journey shine.

"I know that I am young, but this is the way you showed me, and it is the desire that this lodge about to be made shall be the painting for all people, that this race may continue and that all people may continue."

Even in his bitter captivity, the Indian held to the concept of the brotherhood of man, so much talked about, so little demonstrated among his conquerors.

With what delicate understatement, or perhaps the interpreter softened the meaning of the Arapaho words:

"We are young in the ways of our forefathers, and *old things have to a certain extent gone out of existence,* and we are under obligations to call upon you for your sympathy." Then he asked that the substitutes they were obliged to use, now that they had nothing, might be acceptable, that the world and all the peoples in it might continue to be blessed.

That included me, a little Algonquin offshoot, thousands of miles away.

For your home, my mother said.

It was sixty years before I sat with my brothers and sisters in the Sweat Lodge and heard the ancient chants and prayed the ancient prayers, and knew that I had come, however tardily, home . . . or, if not home, at least to a familiar inn.

. .

Some day the way must be found, surely soon it will be, to overcome the problems of re-entry, the initial conditioning, infantile amnesia, slow development of childhood, an impaired and sometimes totally destroyed understanding of the mortal mission. We are the damaged, in the hands of the damaged. The wonder is that so many manage to survive the destructive processes about them, and even in their maimed condition, now and then by flashes re-establish contact with the Source.

Grandfather Eagle, Grandfather Light-of-the-Earth, help us to keep our hearts in the presence of the Great Spirit, and the presence of the Great Spirit in our hearts.

Deadened minds, thickened, made suspicious, as e e cummings says, of "everything which is natural which is infinite which is yes" and still more of "i thank You God" reject such precepts, but the half-mutated, who escaped with partial maiming, use them to *remember, listen, think* the way through.

Freeing themselves, they help to free us all.

My formative years were distorted. I thought it was my fault. I squirmed, evaded, tried to hide raw feelings, and myself, in corners, aware with a child's intuitive certitude how "tiresome" it was of Evie, carrying some dark Something, to arrive as a second daughter instead of a first son, and on top of that to be set apart from *nice* English people born in proper British places.

It did no good to protest that I was tiresome without a choice, that I didn't plan or control the orbit that had taken me off course, that I was merely present, helpless in the capsule at the splashdown, as much a victim of disaster as the rest.

No one could foresee, in the early nineteen hundreds, the importance of birth certificates, passports, quotas. Some of us learned later that third-dimensional man in the twentieth century consisted of body, soul and papers, with, at frightening moments, papers the most important of the three.

The French told an *à propos* story about a merchant who died in the desert and was eaten by vultures, and how his heirs could never inherit the estate because those tiresome birds neglected to sign the menu in triplicate and get it notarized.

When eventually I reached the United States I was grateful to the Swiss quota for not being filled, and to my mother for not arranging the splashdown in Peking. If she had, I should not have been able to become an American citizen—there was no Chinese quota.

Born in Switzerland of Canadian parents, brought up in England and Canada, "finished" in France, married to a Polish citizen of the Free State of Danzig, I celebrated my first Fourth of July as an American, in Cheng-tu, to Chinese firecrackers. This made me a run-of-the-mill do-it-yourself Melting Pot.

In reality I was none of these things, nor ever had been, inside my over-coat. Inside my overcoat, the apologetic masquerade I showed to the world, I was an alien from another place, though sometimes I felt like an early American, a native daughter returning to the reservation on what was left of her once free land.

I was two weeks old when they brought me to England, and christened me in Sandhurst Chapel. Immersion of infant girls was not an accepted part of military worship, but my father was teaching at Sandhurst then, and I suppose baptismal facilities were a part of the equipment available to faculty. No one held it against me. No one teased, for Sandhurst was essentially English, and being christened there should have made up for geographical indiscretions two weeks earlier.

Four-year-old Helen saved me from the embarrassment of being named Sybil. She did not like me, but even disgusted siblings can sacrifice personal animosity to a sense of the appropriate. Sybil, we both agreed later, was for fair-haired, blue-eyed rosebuds, not for a papoose.

"I have a baby sister. Her name's Evelyn."

"Oh no, darling. Her name is Sybil. Dear little Sybil."

"I HAVE A BABY SISTER . . ."

Helen, destined to become the Lady Dashwood whose face and exploits flitted through the London *Tatler* and the *Sketch* between the wars, was already sure of herself, and as usual got her way. To placate her I was christened Evelyn (loudly) Sybil (murmured) and Mary (noncommittally tossed in for near to Christmas).

Evelyn Sybil Mary Eaton.

Mother of all living things, Witch and Sorrow.

Shortened to Evie.

Helen-and-Evie.

Eve.

I didn't get my Indian name for seventy years.

Why do the destroyers, the diminishers, the tamperers mislead us about the most simple things? For example, why do Freudians and psychoanalysts tut-tut ponderously over MOTHER's nursery shortcomings, when the first shock does not come from her? The doctor holds us upside down by our squirming legs and spanks us roughly. After that the hospital nurse gets hold of us. MOTHER's turn comes only third, when the other two great forces have curdled our egos. Yet the doctor and the nurse are never blamed for our later quirks and criminal tendencies. It is always MOTHER who failed to bare her breast quickly enough, or was clumsy with a bottle. It's HER fault if I kick the Dean today, strangle the cat or lie about my income tax. We only claim our praise-worthy achievements and mothers seldom get the credit for these.

To my mother, in this life, I owe a habit of courage, taken lightly. She was a brave woman, in almost constant pain, who managed to ignore it. Her back was injured in childhood, when she tried to climb a forbidden fence, slipped and was impaled on iron spikes. It was several hours before she was found, still weakly screaming.

"A sort of whispering scream," she said. "Inadequate. I hope you children know how to scream properly. Only please don't practice."

She was injured again in a hunting accident, when her horse was crowded at a fence. Most horses carrying sidesaddle fell to the right, or tried to, the legend went. Horses were trusted to make an intelligent effort to save their riders. This one didn't. It fell to the left, crushing my mother beneath it, and had to be killed before they could free her.

After that she spent the major part of her time "resting." But if there was a gathering, especially in England, that promised to be "fun," by which she meant socially important, she would rise and get to it and be the center, the life, the star, the fire, of whatever happened to be going on.

Naturally "the cicadas grinched." People accused her of being a fraud who only fell ill when there was some dull duty to be done. They pitied my father for having a selfish, extravagant wife.

"Beautiful," they conceded—it would have been difficult not to—"but bone lazy, never does a stroke of work."

My mother's reasonable answer ran: "I save my strength for what I enjoy. If I didn't rest so carefully, I wouldn't be able to do the important things."

As for strokes of work, those were the days when a houseful of servants was taken for granted; there was a governess for the children and we had Aunty Nell, my mother's sister, who lived with us and did everything a "resting" mother couldn't do. For a long time I thought that every family consisted of the Mummy, the Daddy and the Aunty Nell. "Where's the Aunty Nell?" I said when I fell down and hurt myself in other people's houses. "I want the Aunty Nell."

Later, whether it had something to do with her accident or was the result of the 1918 flu, my mother, a witty conversationalist, with a passionate love of music, became progressively deaf, of the sort of deafness that does not allow silence.

"Turn off the radiator," she would beg, in summer when the radiators were silent. "What is that pounding in the cellar? Oh, please don't make that screeching noise!"

She wore an ungainly hearing aid fastened to the front of her dress as though it were an elegant touch, attainable only by her. She used it as she might have used a fan, to flirt with, to attract attention, to mock, to repudiate. She made a game of saying what she wanted to say, and then with a half-smile ostentatiously turned off the switch. Often she closed her eyes in order not to lip-read answers she did not wish to understand. She was an expert lip reader. Sometimes at the silent movies she laughed at the most tragic or romantic parts, because she caught what the actors were really saying to each other. The talkies when they came along didn't amuse her as much.

Luckily her voice never changed to the harsh tones of the always deaf. People read aloud to each other in those pre-television, pre-radio, pre-record-player days, when a "good book" was the usual form of home entertainment. My mother only read to us when we were sick, but I was an accident-prone child, always with some new "hurting place." She read *The Oxford Book of English Verse* to me, and when I could recite enough of her favorite poems from it gave me the copy for my birthday. I was seven.

There was no censorship of reading in her house, no age-groups or special books for children. We were let loose among the classics and encouraged to read anything we could haul down from the shelves. Shakespeare, Dickens and Scott, Kipling as his little red books appeared, Surtees' vulgarities and autographed first editions of Meredith, Francis Thompson, a special edition of Whitman's *Leaves of Grass,* which I could read if I washed my hands, French "yellowbacks," and poets like Baudelaire. Thanks to several Mademoiselles I was bilingual.

The only books not on those shelves were what my mother called "sheer trash," the second-rate, the mediocre, the badly written. I owe my early involvement with right words to her. She had a fastidious ear and a flair for style in everything, furniture, dress, music, words. She would have agreed wholeheartedly with the quip in *My Fair Lady:* "The French don't care what they *do,* so long as it is pronounced properly."

Besides, if you could get a tiresome child to be a bookworm you had it made. Books were the baby-sitters then.

My father believed in doing things "when the time is right." In this, as in other ways which I didn't recognize then, he was strongly Indian.

When the time was right he taught me to swim by dropping me into the lake, headfirst, in all my clothes, and paddling the canoe a little ahead of me to shore. He taught me to dive by climbing to the highest perch of the diving board and hurling me off his shoulders. He placed a five-foot-high table on top of the wharf at our summer camp at Glen Logie, and decreed that no child who didn't dive three times from it before breakfast should have any break-fast. It was my favorite meal. After a while I grew competent in the water, in a reluctant sort of way, and then eagerly amphibian.

When the time was right he gave me a briefing in theology. Napoleon, he said, was a wicked man, and so he had gone to hell, but he was also a great military genius, who wouldn't tolerate inefficiency. Nowadays the central heating of the lower regions worked properly, and the demons were trained to bring iced drinks on little trays, and hell was altogether a fine place to be, if only for the racing.

"Grand race tracks there, Eve."

Hell was where he was going and he hoped it was where I would wind up too.

"Yes, Papa," I said, never doubting that it would be.

"But it's difficult to get to. Have to work at it."

"Yes, Papa."

We were living in Kingston, Ontario, at 20 Barry Street, a semidetached red-brick house overlooking MacDonald Park, with the lake only half a block away. Every Sunday we walked back from Saint George's Church, across the park, while my father dismissed the parade, and then rode after us with his groom. The Royal Canadian Horse Artillery paraded to church in full regimentals, blue-and-gold uniforms, black busbies with white aigrettes, six matched horses to each gun, the band preceding them, mounted too, and my father with his drawn sword riding at the head, giving the salute, or, in the absence of the Colonel, standing on the steps of the church to receive it. It was a colorful way to attend Divine Service if we had to. In those days we had to, though the reasons for doing so were never explained or discussed, nor was God ever mentioned in the home. God was not even one of those subjects "not before the servants, dear." Sunday, on the other hand, was dismally observed, and omnipresent when it came.

Some Sundays things happened to break the monotony.

The regiment sat in the right-hand gallery. The cadets of the Royal Military College, at which my father taught, also paraded to church in their scarlet uniforms, but more tamely, on foot. They sat in the left-hand gallery. We occupied the third pew from the front, where my father by tilting his head could see the men in both front rows.

When the hymn "Fight the Good Fight" began, he drew himself up, dropped his hand to his sword and shot fierce glances upward, left and right. They were understood. A roar of masculine voices drowned out the choir until the third verse. Then there was silence from both galleries, and now we could hear the little boys in their starched surplices piping shrilly:

"Faint not nor fear, His arms are near."

Father nodded, satisfied. No man under his command, no cadet he instructed, would so far forget himself as to have any truck with fainting or fearing, or dare to sing such unsuitable words in the Major's hearing. Nor would the Major's family. We stood with sealed lips until the verse was over, then the roar resumed:

"Run the straight race Through God's good grace"—a different matter. My father loved racing. He entered every race he could on anything that had four legs. His jockey colors were orange-and-blue, his dream was to ride in the Grand National. It was "very mete, right and our bounden duty" to sing about racing, and quite as it should be that God had the good grace to approve of it.

One morning there was a particularly harsh reference in the sermon to Eve and her transgressions. "The wickedness of Eve, Eve ignobly this and Eve sinned that."

"I *never!*" I muttered indignantly. "I didn't . . . I didn't . . ." and was shushed by Helen and the Governess. "Nobody ever takes my side, nobody stands up for me," I thought in a black fury. My father caught my eye and winked.

"Iced drinks for two," he whispered across Helen's head, and I subsided, filled with pride and purpose. "Hell, hell, hell," I murmured ardently, and was shushed again.

My father expected instant obedience on the double from all his world. That morning after church when he rode up behind us on his favorite charger, Blue Miracle, he called to me and I ran to him nervously. I waited at the curb while he dismounted, gave the reins to the groom and stood for a moment looking down.

We started together toward the house. Suddenly he stopped and swung half around to face me.

"Mother Eve," he said.

"Yes, Papa?"

Normally we called him Father or Daddy in the Edwardian way, but we were going through a determined French Governess time of "ton Papa" and "ta Maman" which he seemed to have accepted—he was fairly co-operative with governesses. The only time I remember him rebelling was when we had a German Fräulein just before the war broke out. He bribed me with a quarter to sing *Deutschland, Deutschland* unter *alles,* instead of *über.* I was delighted. The Fräulein cried.

"Yes, Papa?"

"Always hold your liquor like an Officer and a Gentleman."

"Yes, Papa."

He strode on and I trotted beside him, breathless in all the constricting clothes a girl-child wore then. He stopped again.

"Mother Eve."

"Yes, Papa?"

"Always ride straight to hounds."

"Yes, Papa."

He tweaked my hair, and said "Scat!" and went on alone to the house and the heavy Sunday dinner waiting for him. Next day he left on a mystery called "maneuvers" and I didn't see him for the rest of the long summer.

When he came back we were never alone. In front of other people he teased me, but the Sunday conversation wasn't mere teasing. I was eight and the time was right for him to give me those directives, two sound precepts. They helped me on rough roads and sticky places. I memorized them, in case he should talk of them again, but he never did.

Now and then he looked at me reflectively and I thought he must be remembering "iced drinks for two," and the road to hell, as I was. Or perhaps he had something to tell me for which the time was not then right. Perhaps he was wondering if he should talk to me about our Indian ancestry. Perhaps he was thinking of the son he would never have, the son who tried to arrive that year, and crashed stillborn, making it impossible for my mother to expect another.

Whatever was in my father's mind as he looked at me, it went unsaid.

One of my earliest disturbing memories, disturbing because nothing else in my dull Edwardian childhood had this magic shimmer to it, was to watch my parents skating together, waltzing to the music of the regimental band. After the first few turns they circled alone, with the other skaters staring at them from the sidelines.

It was an open-air rink, lit by flares, and in my memory by the moon and the stars. It cannot have happened often, but it completely took over certain tunes. "The Blue Danube" has never evoked ballrooms in Vienna to me, always this winter scene, those winter sounds, the whirring scrape and spurt of skates, the two skimming figures, turning, turning, separating, meeting in long geometric sweeps, while I stand there, freezing, on my awkward double-runners, cheeks burning, eyes smarting, beating my red-mittened hands together in a spasm of possessive pride.

Before and after these rare skating frenzies my mother rested more completely than usual. Sometimes the doctor came.

My father would have danced well in the Sun Dance, or in Cry-Dances, as I have been privileged to do. I wonder if he ever did? I know he attended a Sweat Lodge in Labrador where Grandfather Reindeer came, and thousands of hoof marks were found in the snow and on the roof of the igloo in the morning. It is in his diary, the year he was on an expedition making maps of Labrador. But the diary also shows that he attended chiefly out of curiosity, and very much from the white man's point of view, although obviously impressed and sympathetic. I wish he had lived long enough to tell me the things he cared about. I never met my father, only his overcoat, his "British Warm," and not the lining of that. Exteriors were all that mattered, all there *was* to man. We were expected to conform to the facts of existence, as nowadays many struggle to "maintain the image," but at least it is known to be only an image.

In Kingston, in 1909, I kept a notebook in which I copied lines from the poets I liked, clues to the Great Puzzle. My father also was keeping a notebook, found among his papers when he died. In it he copied "passages from the poets which dear Mynie says are good," beginning before their marriage. Notes in the margin showed that he could not agree with her, he had no ear for poetry and pretended to have none for music, though he played the violin well as a boy, and still practiced sometimes, surreptitiously, in the cellar. His first violin was made for him by his father, from an exquisitely grained piece of walnut. It had an excellent tone. Grandfather Eaton was, among other things, a fine cabinetmaker.

After some years of struggle with his notebook, my father gave up, about the time that I was reaching Whitman:

> The open air I sing, freedom, toleration . . .
> The common day and night—the common earth and waters . . .
> The democratic wisdom underneath, like solid ground for all.

Nothing common was allowed us, nothing for *all*. We were protected from the solid ground by boots covered with rubber galoshes. As to open air, freedom, toleration . . .

My father went to his barracks or to his classroom, and I to my school-room and my nursery meals, rice pudding made with an egg, a too-full glass of milk, listening to my betters, adjusting to their norms. Frog among birds.

Next to the Royal Family and God came the Fitz Randolphs of New Brunswick, in that pecking order. The Eatons didn't count. They were rarely spoken of. They lived far off, in Nova Scotia. This was a little *wrong,* though not as wrong as Switzerland. New Brunswick was the proper province, especially Saint Andrews and Fredericton, in summer, where Grandmother lived.

It never occurred to me that I had another grandmother, and uncles and aunts and cousins. Mother and Aunty Nell were Fitz Randolphs. . . . My mother might be called Mrs. Eaton, but that was irrelevant. She was a Fitz Randolph . . . descended from Edward Fitz Randolph. Edward the Pilgrim, who came to the United States when it was still a good sound British Colony.

Americans developed later, regrettably I gathered, and even then:

"Never so English as when they rebelled!" Aunty Nell explained, and further pointed out how sad it was that an English colonel, who had taken vows of loyalty to the King, and also a salary from him, should so far forget himself as to wait until England was "embroiled in a foreign war with France," and then treacherously stab her in the back. "His name," she added solemnly, as though this made it worse, "was George Washington."

Edward the Pilgrim was "Roman Catholic under Elizabeth," which brought a strange picture to my photographic mind, but when he landed he "turned Puritan and married a Puritan maid." So he might as well have stayed in Warwick Castle and turned Protestant there, if he was going to, Aunty Nell said, and have kept the family estates for his descendants.

Before this unsatisfactory Edward, there was William the Conqueror, from whom we "descended directly, since he was the son of Robert le Diable." The logic of this reasoning escaped me, although I became more interested in it when I learned French and understood that we were descended directly from a devil. It gave me a claim on hell and a better chance of joining my father there, when the time was right.

I was always hoping, even expecting, the time to come right, when the world around me would change or disappear, and I would stand free—again —under an open sky, preferably at night beneath the Milky Way. Later the moon would rise over a body of water, perhaps the sea, but first there would be silence, darkness, stars, *rightness* around me. And then I might find hell, a merry place, full of fine horses and fairy-tale beings who knew me. And my father, off and on from maneuvers. Sometime. When the time was right.

Meanwhile Aunty Nell and others continued to fill in the family background. Another Edward, Fitz Randolph of course, "gave away an old meadow which the family didn't need, to Princeton. Nassau Hall is built there, with commemorative gates."

"Commemorative" sounded to me like the iron curlicues on fancy entrances, cemeteries or Buckingham Palace. With Fitz Randolph on them, enhancing the Family Importance.

Later came the loyalists, "our immediate ancestors," who escaped from New Jersey in the United States to Nova Scotia, where they spent the first winter in tents. Years of bitter hardship followed, until my grandfather left Nova Scotia (which probably accounted for its becoming an inferior place) and moved to Fredericton, in New Brunswick, where he restored the family fortunes and made his own out of lumber and wholesale merchandise.

It was too late for the older generation, those in tents or on "lands from the King," who did not live to see the first A. F. Randolph & Sons over the door of the imposing brick building he constructed in Fredericton, which is now the office of Beaverbrook's *Daily Gleaner,* but it was nicely in time for his children, my Aunty Nell, my mother, my uncles, Alan, Robert and Charles.

It was also in time for Helen-and-Evie and their cousins. We loved to go down to the office . . . it wasn't polite to call it a store . . . and get ice-cream cones, home-made with real cream, two for a nickel, and play the trick of the door advertising cereal. "Use Force" it said, but if you did you fell on the floor, because the door opened easily. The cereal's name was Force. The pun was explained to me. I thought it clever of my uncles to put that sign on the door. Force was my favorite breakfast food, sold there among other good things . . . but we were never to say that our grandfather was a grocer, especially in England, even though the word "wholesale" made it almost all right. We were to say that our grandfather was the Honorable Archibald Fitz Randolph, given the improbable occasion when we would be asked. I never was.

Meanwhile, it is strange to reflect, across the land, from Wyoming to Labrador, remnants of the Algonquin nation—Micmac, Malecite, Arapaho, Cheyenne, Passamaquoddy, Mohegan, Shawnee, Cree and others whose tribal names are in danger of being forgotten—were struggling to exist, and to conserve the ancient wisdom.

Here and there children related to me were being taught, *loved* into learning why Manitou, the Great Mysterious Spirit of All, allowed the White Man to take the land, and to treat it and the Indians so cruelly.

"It was because we forgot."

"What did we forget, Grandmother?"

"We are guests in the House of the Great Spirit. We should behave accordingly."

"But . . ."

"Listen, or your tongue will make you deaf."

Mother Earth belongs to all. She cannot be divided up or owned by anyone. The Indian takes only what he needs, and asks forgiveness of the deer he kills. He does not waste, he uses all. The Indian goes through life without an ugly trace left of his path. The Indian knows the powers of animals and plants. They are his brothers, so too all that lives. The Indian shames a boaster by his silence. The Indian must dance again, and sing and pray in joy.

"All this we forgot. We fought among ourselves. The White Man came. A punishment. But one day he may learn. When the White Man learns humility the good times will return."

"That is old people's talk. In school They say . . . to succeed Indians must be 'smart' and 'get ahead,' make money, forget that we are Indians, behave like whites."

But Hawkan and others like him, a handful, kept the flame alive, in secret, in the government-built shacks, and danced when they were allowed to, blessing all the world.

Like many wealthy Canadians in Queen Victoria's reign, especially those of United Empire Loyalist descent, Grandfather Fitz Randolph took his family "Home" to England every two or three years, on one of the great steamers of the White Star or Allen or Cunard lines. My grandmother was fond of Mr. Handel's music and liked to hear the latest news of the court. The Royal Family was so much a part of our lives that when Queen Victoria died, a cousin, I think it was my cousin Guy, deeply interested in this incredible event, asked innocently if we would now have to sing "Send him Edwardious," instead of "Send her Victorious," in the national anthem.

Fitz Randolphs were well educated. Grandfather Fitz Randolph took his family abroad. It was always desirable to go abroad, though of course there was naturally no place like Home, *England,* especially if one lived in Canada.

Grandfather led his little brood through Italy, France and Germany, before leaving the daughters in Munich to be finished. There they acquired a taste for Wagnerian opera and a weakness for Prussian officers, which lasted until World War One put Wagner and Prussians into the category of things "not done."

After she was married, my mother kept up the family traditions and took us Home once a year, "by boat." It had become the fashion by then not to mention "steamers" or "ships." Air travel was still decades away.

That was how it was that Helen-and-Evie were brought up as much in England as in Canada, with intervals at sea. It was these intervals which filled my dull Edwardian childhood with excitement and something to live toward. The sea, like darkness, like the Milky Way, like There, was mine, mysteriously moving, gray, green, black, deep, phosphorescent (with the luminous blue sheen we saw in 1968—the sea which makes the planet look the way it does in space).

The boat was mine too, its bells and bangs and creaking walls, portholes and white-coated stewards, all the bustling importance of what grownups called "the crossing." (How was the crossing? Did you have a good crossing?) My bunk, my chicken broth, the decks I trotted around, the nautical clothes I wore, white middy blouse, black sailor tie, reefer with brass buttons, sailor hat . . . ashore or afloat, Helen-and-Evie wore sailor hats with black bands lettered in gold: H.M.S. *Majestic,* H.M.S. *Olympic,* H.M.S. *Mauretania,* H.M.S. *Empress of Britain,* all those vanished boats, whose names were borne by more and more successors, bigger, grander, but not in the same way *mine.*

We wore the hatbands of whatever His Majesty's Ship our boat to England happened to be, and the H.M.S. which took us "back" not "Home" to Canada. Canada didn't count. My father's regiment, the Royal Canadian Horse Artillery, was Canadian, we lived where he was stationed, which was mostly in Canada, we were Canadians, all but tiresome Evie born in Canada; still, I "collected," as Jane Austen puts it, that there was something unnecessary, even inferior, about Canada, and that boats sailed westward only to sail eastward again for Home.

Nelson, I was made to feel, had his good eye trained on our nursery, through his telescope from the top of Trafalgar Square, but it was the Army I heard invoked about me all day long. Soldiers' daughters always this, soldiers' daughters never that. Soldiers' daughters ate everything on their plates. Soldiers' daughters smiled at iodine dolloped on grazed knees and never made a fuss at the dentist.

Soldiers' daughters held up their heads, threw out their chests, breathed deeply through their noses, kept stiff upper lips and went through other dislocating exercises. Their anatomy was different from mine. It was one of those secrets I anxiously tried to conceal, as I would have hidden my foreign nativity, given a chance, "a fair start." I was so busy presenting a blameless overcoat to the world, I hardly noticed what other people were hiding beneath theirs . . . that even Helen, for instance, sometimes winced.

Helen was no help to me. Four years older than I, a cherished only child, she intended to go through life as she had begun. *Cherished only child* was how she thought of herself, and how she succeeded in being treated most of the time. She ignored me. There was this composite Helen-and-Evie, dressed alike, in clothes becoming only to her, appearing together on occasions, but there the distasteful matter rested. Grownups with their unrealistic points of view might say to her "Take care of Evie" when we set out for a children's party. Her reply was a rebellious wail, "*Need* Evie come?" Some grownup answered absently, "Yes, dear. Now run along with Nannie."

The question she raised remained in the air between us. Sibling trauma had not been defined yet. Even if it had, I doubt that identifying it would have helped much. Ours was a simple case of one-sided adoration. I thought Helen the most beautiful, the most brilliant, the most magically satisfactory sister in the world. I was never tired of staring at her, of creeping near to overhear what she was saying, of hiding in the cupboard to listen to her practicing the piano. "Spying on me!" she called it indignantly, and so it was. I only knew that Helen and Helen's music were a part of the painful magic that could sometimes set me free, to grope toward where I belonged, where those who *liked* me might be hiding.

When I was six I wrote the first of my "tiresome" poems:

> God made me in a bitter hour
> but sent this special grace to me
> that I should grow beside a flower
> which is my sister's face to me.

I wrote an even more tiresome one when I was eight. I don't know how it got to the Montreal *Star*. I think McKinnon, our fat, kindly cook, God rest her soul, who used to rock me on her lap and feed me forbidden tidbits, who sat up at nights with me when I had whooping cough and nearly died, when there was nothing much to do for whooping cough but "nursing care" and taking you to the gas tank to inhale the fumes, or on the lake, for the sake of the dampness in the air . . . I think she must have admired the poem, copied it out and sent it in to the paper. McKinnon and I were friends, with a deep, tacit alliance. Well-brought-up children never went into the kitchen; well-trained cooks rarely came out of the kitchen, so our rocking, which I remember as a steady comforting warmth, had the zest and perils of conspiracy.

McKinnon launched me as a published poet. The poem appeared in the adult section of the *Star*, over my name and the hitherto dignified family address. It began:

> I have kissed burning lips and loved many faces.

My father read the statement at breakfast, and put down the paper with a rustle. Helen's wails could be heard rising: *Need* Evie? *Must* Evie? *Stop* Evie!

But after such a promising beginning, I threw the situation away.

> Now I turn alone into the night.

I was sent to spend the morning in the spare room, as a punishment for "writing to the papers." This was a vulgar thing to do. Didn't I know the old saying, my mother asked, half seriously, that *nice* people were only mentioned three times in the papers, when they were born, when they married, and when they died?

Nothing was said about poems or poetry. In this way she ducked the issue of having encouraged me to read and to admire *The Oxford Book of English Verse,* to love certain poems, to recite them . . . now tacitly I must understand that is was *wrong* to write them. The poets, evidently, were not nice people.

"Nice people," I thought sourly. "Little ladies," Nannie said. Little ladies held their forks in the proper way, remembered their manners, kept on their gloves and their hats and their tight shoes even in the woods. Little ladies led tedious lives. I never wanted to be a lady, I was never asked if I cared to be a lady, I never consented to being a lady.

Well, when I was grown-up I would not be a lady. I would be a poet. There were poets in feminine overcoats in *The Oxford Book of English Verse.* It was just a little harder for them, that's all. Somewhere I would find someone to read my poems to. I longed to discuss them, to have them taken seriously. . . .

The subject was dropped. Ignoring Evie-the-poet, the family felt, would be the best way of discouraging me.

Next year it was whooping cough, McKinnon's nursing and my third poem:

> Then, tenderly Death
> let my pain-wracked body cease
> its woeful throbs . . .

The family shrugged and said I would outgrow it.

All my irrelevant childhood I was watching for signals, picking up sounds which those around me never seemed to hear, listening, listening for news from There, from the Other, searching my elders' faces for signs of recognition, of direction to the Source.

But never asking questions, not even about the surface daily perplexities. The important precept in Edwardian schoolrooms was: "Never ask a question unless you are quite sure you cannot find the answer for yourself." In practice this boiled down to: Never ask a question unless you want to be considered tiresome. You might end up in the spare room for asking what They called a "rude" one, but you would never get an honest answer. Grownups were always condescendingly amused, or holding back something, or annoyed at interruptions.

It was safer to accept the silly challenge and to live with the unsolved problems, picking up the odd clue here and there, from adult talk and speculation, or from books. But books were confusing too. Just when they seemed on the threshold of explaining something, there were little stars called asterisks which everyone skipped over without comment. Judging from the way Miss Alden behaved when she encountered asterisks, they were tiresome, like Evie. They were concealing something nice people, little ladies especially, would never inquire into . . . asterisks, in fact, were merely decorations on the page to nice people. Not that it did much good to consider them. You could always get a general idea of what they were hiding, but then you were no better off. The Bible, on the other hand, went into many details. One could learn a lot from the Bible and be commended for reading it too. It was frequently quoted in church.

"The Lord delighteth not in any man's legs, neither in the strength of a horse." Then what about church parade? one wondered.

I wore my stuffy heavy clothes, and ate my starchy heavy food and filled my mind with irrelevant answers I "found for myself."

Thus, I collected, Navy offspring were never mentioned, though the Navy figured so prominently on our hats. Civilians were inferiors from whom no one expected the behavior required of an Army child whose father "wore the King's uniform" and was trained to go to war.

My father had a closet full of uniforms and didn't need, so far as I could see, to wear one of the King's. I decided that his dress uniform, with the most gold braid and the big black busby with the white aigrette on top that made him nearly seven feet tall, must be the one he borrowed from the King. I was never allowed to borrow other people's clothes, especially Helen's, but that was "different."

My father wore this dress uniform on occasions like the King's birthday or the Opening of Parliament in Ottawa, when we had to stand at attention and watch (and listen to) the salute. Soldiers' daughters loved The Guns and never put their fingers to their ears.

Soldiers' daughters never had to ask silly questions; they thought things through for themselves. So, it was my father's duty to be trained for war. But war was a thing of the far, bad past. There would "never be another conflict between the great nations." Napoleon was the last wicked tyrant who tried it, and Nelson at Trafalgar settled all of that, with some help from the Iron Duke (whatever that was) at Waterloo.

"*Vaterloo, Vaterloo, Vaterloo, morne plaine,*" I learned in French Literature from Mademoiselle, and:

"Half a league, half a league, half a league onward," I learned in English Literature from Miss Alden. Poets repeated things endlessly, but when little girls did it was tiresome.

"England," Miss Alden explained, "watches over all the world to make sure the natives everywhere are keeping the King's Peace. It's expected of Her."

So, under our Navy hats we were in the Army. England was Home for all right-minded people, no matter where they lived, or if they never went there. Natives and lesser breeds without the law were lucky to be watched over, and one day would grow in grace and think so. Peace belonged to the King. My father was in the King's service. Most children's fathers were civilians. My father was better than any civilian because he was trained for war. War was "unthinkable in this day and age," though we all had a battle line on Sundays.

> God of our fathers, known of old,
> Lord of our far-flung battle line,
> Beneath whose Awful Hand we hold
> Dominion over palm and pine. . . .

It went to a rollicking tune and was one of those hymns the men in the galleries were allowed to sing.

Every day Miss Alden read to us out of sound pro-English books as we lay on the floor for our midday rest, making sure that our backs grew straight.

"It used to be a blackboard strapped across the shoulders," Miss Alden said. "You are lucky little girls to have the floor. 'If drunk with sight of power we loose Wild tongues that have not Thee in awe . . .'"

It might have been fun to loose them, but it was beyond my aptitude for successful misbehavior. I had all I could do to maintain the honor and well-being of my current liner. They had begun to call the boats we went Home in "liners" then.

"'The liner, she's a lady,'" Miss Alden read. "And remember," she added darkly, "England expects that every man this day will do his duty."

But it turned out that Lord Nelson was really thinking of soldiers' daughters doing theirs.

Since "Have you done your duty?" meant "Have you been to the bathroom?" in my nursery language, I was both resentful and embarrassed.

And "Why didn't he say so?" Helen asked, surprisingly impertinent.

For which we both had to learn "Oh, where are you going to, all you Big Steamers, With England's own coal, up and down the salt seas?" "putting in the expression" as one did in music, when one had "mastered the notes."

We were on a steamer, sailing toward Home, when King Edward the Seventh died. The news came "by Marconi," and threw "everyone on board" —the first-class passengers—into pleasurable consternation. The pleasure was for drama in dull sedate lives. Now we could wallow in a permissible public emotion, an upsurge of national pride, with a nicely tempered sorrow. (It was hard to feel much affection, let alone genuine grief, for Edward the Seventh.)

The consternation "everyone" shared was how to get suitable black clothes in mid-ocean. National mourning would begin at once and be complete. Widow's weeds for women, black mourning suits for men, black dresses for girls, black suits for boys. It would last six months, and then give place to light mourning, ending in lavenders and whites. We would shop for mourning in London, but meanwhile we could not land on English soil unless we were swathed in black.

The twenty-two trunks we traveled with were in the ship's hold. One by one perspiring stewards brought them to our cabins, to be searched despairingly.

Miss Alden had a neat black suit, neat black shoes, thick black stockings and gloves, a black straw hat. She would be all right. Helen had a black velvet dress, but the sleeves were short. She could, however, wear a pair of my mother's long black kid gloves, and one of our winter black velour hats. Evie had nothing black except her shoes and stockings and the velour hat, but there was her winter overcoat, of black sealskin. That would do for Evie, buttoned to the chin.

It was a heavy fur coat, almost too hot in winter—the Canadian winter—and we would be landing in the "hot weather." I started to murmur.

"I should *think*," Miss Alden said, "that any little discomfort at a time like this would be borne in cheerful silence. No *nice* little girl would choose this moment of great national sorrow to make a peevish fuss."

That left Mother and Aunty Nell to be outfitted. This was more difficult. They had plenty of fashionable clothes, among them their "landing suits," one brown, one silver-gray, but nothing black. It was no use eying Miss Alden's suit, though both of them did. She was far too thin, a suitable governess shape. It was no use canvassing the passengers, who were having the same crisis. Black was "not being worn" that year.

I do not remember whether we landed in Southampton or Liverpool. I do remember that the boat train was held for several hours while some of the passengers scoured the place for mourning, and I waited, sweating in my fur coat. Mother and Aunty Nell came back with the last two black garments to be had, available for obvious reasons. One was a voluminous serge dress, such as an elephantine housekeeper might wear in a Dickens nightmare. The other was an ultra-fashionable satin hobble skirt with a black lace blouse. They tossed for it. Aunty Nell won and took the serge.

The hobble skirt was very tight. Fiery-faced and heavily perspiring in my hot sealskin, I watched my mother begin her national mourning in a series of kangaroo leaps toward the boat train, Aunty Nell striding ahead of her, saying "Mynie, come on! Come on!"

They were to look like that around London for the first week or so, with their trunkfuls of becoming clothes unworn. In those days there was no buying off the rack, no ready-made clothes, for nice people. Where the poor got what they wore I don't know. But people like us had "little dressmakers," who made our clothes to order for us, as there were bootmakers, hatmakers, glovemakers, and what Aunty Nell called her "little face-woman" who came once a week with creams and lotions "to do the face" in secret. All these arrived by appointment and were closeted with us for hours of ponderings, decisions, fittings. It was a trying business to contrive to be "fit to be seen," even when there was no crisis. But now there was no black cloth to be had in London anywhere, and all the little dressmakers were booked for weeks ahead. Most shops were closed. The streets were depressing. Men, women, children, even babies in their prams, went about in unrelieved black. Here and there those already in mourning, with proper outfits made for them by "little dressmakers" before the crisis, looked unexpectedly chic, and a little smug, but also disconcerted to find themselves suddenly demoted from their special status— "in mourning you know, for their uncle, four months ago now, I think"—and reduced to the general condition. But at least their clothes seemed to fit. Unlike ours. Our choice was to stay indoors in comfort or go out about our business, looking as unhappy as we felt.

There were a few light moments. I remember my mother trying to hop into a hansom cab in her hobble skirt. Aunty Nell took the high step in stride and filled the foot space completely with *her* skirts. "Come on, Mynie, come on!" Mynie hopped and panted and hopped. Then a passing stranger gravely took off his hat, handed it to me to hold, and lifted her in to whistles and hoots from the crowd, bowed, took up his hat and went his way.

It seemed an odd way to grieve.

A generation later, when George the Fifth died, Helen, then a lady-in-waiting at his court, mourned for just six weeks, in a fetching little Spanish mantilla, and was not allowed to dine in a public restaurant for the period of court mourning. Otherwise there were no restrictions. People went about in whatever they normally wore. Yet I think the mourning was more sincere.

Times and absurdities change.

Undernourished, impoverished, penned into reservations in forgotten corners of their own land, children half my age knew twice as much as I did, and would not have to discard most of what they learned before they could travel the good way. They were loved into learning, and some of what they knew I am only beginning to discover now.

At eight, if I had been an underprivileged, scorned Indian child, ignored and neglected by the white world . . . that part was important . . . I would have known a number of the crucial things there are to know while we are in this life. I would have been taught from babyhood my place in the scheme of things. Instead of the Royal Family and the Fitz Randolphs, I would have absorbed from those around me the existence of a great creative force pervading everything, human beings, animals, trees, the universe. If I had been among my father's Micmacs and Malecites, I would have heard of this Great Creator as Manitou, and the journey to It the one Glooscap undertook and left to us to follow. If I had splashed down with the Iroquois I would have called It Orenda, with the Sioux, Wakan. I might have called It Grandfather Sky, and I would certainly have known Mother Earth and the Four Old Men.

I would have understood that no one can own or sell the Earth, our

Mother. I would have understood that one must not disturb the balance of nature. I would have learned patience, from long hours of waiting, silently, sitting on the ground, for ceremonies to begin. I would have entered the Sweat Lodge in my father's or my mother's arms, and learned a hard discipline, administered with loving warmth. For always, everywhere, I would have been sure of being loved, of being a part of my tribe and my community. When I fell down, the nearest adult would right me, and act as my parent. Older people too would tell me stories.

I would have been taught to watch my younger brothers, the animals, and to observe every change of the surrounding earth, the sky. I would have been taught to keep silence, not because anything I might have to say would be sure to be boring, "tiresome," but because the world was full of mysterious and lovely sounds. "Be silent, or your tongue will close your ears."

I would have been taught that before the coming of the white brothers, my people had a rich and beautiful religious life full of dances and ceremonials and special sacred objects, and that we now preserved these things in our hearts, our minds, and as best we might among ourselves.

I would have been taught how to behave as a grateful guest in the House of the Great Mystery, and how to enjoy my visit, and my journey to the World of the Beyond. I would have been taught to live.

Yet it would not have been teaching of any formal sort. I would have absorbed it gradually, from cradle board to adolescence, and some of it would surely stick, even if the white world got me into its corrupting power later.

In summer we had Mademoiselle, in winter Miss Alden, each laboring to destroy our confidence in what the other taught. In summer Bonaparte was the great military genius who unified all France and would have conquered the world but for perfidious Albion, who captured *l'Empereur* and turned him into a defeated but romantic Eagle on Saint Helena. It was a long time before I discovered that Saint Helena was an island, and not a saint undergoing some unusual torment.

In winter, Napoleon was the wicked tyrant who "fell at Waterloo," entangled in his underwear, I supposed hazily, since my English history book stated: "Napoleon's combinations failed and fell apart, whereas Wellington's held fast." My own combinations, summer and winter, were made of scratchy wool, lightweight and heavyweight, inconveniently buttoned, with a slit through which one could do one's duty. They never failed and fell apart, but I could imagine Napoleon's predicament. And since he was, in French lessons, the *Empereur* who turned into an Eagle, this was probably his way of retreat from the whole embarrassment. "Oh, for the wings of a dove," we sang in church. The wings of an eagle might be better, especially if Saint Helena was fond of eagles.

It required some agility to move from French to English history, from

French to English perspectives and loyalties, but there was one thing on which Mademoiselle and Miss Alden were wholly agreed, the desirability of *apprendre par coeur* and *learn by heart*. It used to be "by rote," and in these more scientific days "memorizing." Most of what I was forced to memorize I thankfully forgot as soon as it seemed safe to, but now and then an apt line lingered, making sense among the generalities. Sometimes it was a mistaken line— Gray's *Energy* in the Churchyard, and from the same interminable poem a felicitous description: "The short and simple animals of the poor."

"Annals," Miss Alden corrected testily, but that meant nothing to me, and probably the poor wouldn't have known what they had either, whereas short and simple animals we both could recognize. My alley cat with no name and only half a tail was short and simple, so was my dog, "part cocker spaniel" we always explained, just as we had to confess that he had come to us named after an American President, Taft.

Anyone with an ounce of right feeling and all those loyalist ancestors would have understood at once that it wasn't done to call a dog after an *American* President. Helen's dog, a pure-bred British bulldog, with nothing short and simple about it except its temper and its brain, had the insipid name of Binky.

There were also some short and simple goldfish, and Helen kept a canary in her bedroom window. It is amusing to reflect that birdseed in those days was more than half marijuana. The little yellow singers trilled ecstatically from their bow windows up and down the street because they were high on pot. Nowadays, with all the harmful drugs removed from the birdseed, canaries do not sing so fervently and sometimes will not sing at all. Dispirited chirps are all they care to emit, which is why they have gone with the bow windows. Parakeets and lovebirds are in the cages now, but mostly people have aquariums.

It is amusing too, to look into old family albums and illustrated periodicals of the turn of the century and to realize that most of those pompous-looking paragons were addicts, hooked on a habit-forming drug. Everyone, from Queen Victoria down, took laudanum, a heady mixture of opium and alcohol, the trusted household remedy. They gave it to children on lumps of sugar, even to babies on their pacifiers. Much of the time they must have been taking trips, which explains a lot about the Victorian era and aura . . . the vapors and fainting spells of the ladies, the rages and eccentricities of the gentlemen, and some of those mysterious "declines." They were junkies.

In my childhood, paregoric, a camphorated tincture of opium, was liberally ladled out for pain, and as I was always more or less in pain, with earache, stomach ache, sprains, cuts and general allergy to my surroundings, I was opiated quite a lot, which might account for my poetic output at a precocious age. Certainly so much paregoric must have had some effect, if only on my choice of morbid subjects. Death, Betrayal, Murder, Madness and the Pangs of Unrequited Love were what I mostly wrote about, from the point of view of an old cynic who had not long to endure life in this world.

Often I used to wonder why Helen-and-Evie didn't go like other children to Canadian public schools. English public schools were superior, and different, as I came to understand later. English public schools were private establishments for the custodial care of the upper and upper-middle classes, or, as my mother called them unthinkingly, "nice people."

Nice people's children didn't go to school in Canada, except in some cases to private boarding schools like Miss Edgar's in Montreal or Miss Ganong's in New Brunswick. This apartheid from which I dimly suffered meant that I had very few children to play with, and only when there was a party at their house or at mine, and then there was always a barrier of collective resentment to climb over. Helen-and-Evie were labeled "stuck-ups" even though we had not stuck ourselves up onto that uncomfortable ledge but were put there, because, the official excuse ran, our education once having started in the English way must be continued along English lines. Our education certainly was not Canadian. There was never any reference to Canada in our schoolroom. English history, English literature, English geography, French history, French literature, French geography, some patronizing references to the United States before 1776, when it "passed beyond the pale," but of Canada, nothing. Indians, of course, were never mentioned, except in connection with Kipling's India, where they were "natives."

Lake Ontario, unpolluted then, was at our doorstep, the forests, cool and heavy with the scent of pine, were all around us, and, especially in New Brunswick in the summers, beauty, space, grandeur, the House of the Great Spirit. . . . We turned our backs to the lake, hatted and gloved we kept out of the woods, we walked on pavements, listening to Miss Alden talk of things at Home.

We were small-town people, I suppose, living a small-town life, but more frustrating, more restricted than the lives of the other citizens of whatever place we were in, partly because we moved so often, to wherever my father was stationed, but more because of a negation of where we were in favor of an otherwhere Home. . .not the otherwhere of There, either. Merely England.

Never in all my childhood from anyone about me did I hear a hint, a whisper of what we were doing on the earth, what we were supposed to do. No one spoke to me of what the Indians call "the Great Mystery." They didn't have redskins in England. No one spoke to me of nature, except in terms of not getting wet feet or dirtying my dress. There was no nature in England, I almost said, but it is true to a certain extent. England was more a large park, preserved for the few. Canada had space.

It was hard to get into the country from Kingston. There were no scenic drives, few cars. The roads were dirt tracks. We got about on foot, on bicycles, on horseback, or in the family carriage, which was an actual surrey with a fringe on top. In winter we had a low open sleigh with buffalo robes and straw to keep our feet warm. It was painted red, the horses wore silver bells, but it was not romantic like the song. It was just the way we went to the dentist or on other commonplace errands when we had to. I used to come back half frozen, usually with an earache. "Sleighbells in the snow" means to me paregoric and hot oil in my ear, and a throbbing eardrum, and lie-still-Evie-don't-get-it-all-over-the-pillow.

When the weather was fine and my mother drove out to pay calls she sometimes took me with her, to give Miss Alden a rest. I was always eager for any escape from a "nice brisk walk" hatted and gloved across the park. Besides, I loved motion and speed, like Louis the Second of Bavaria, who was my favorite story-book King, because he used to order the royal coach to take him at a gallop through the forest at night. "Naturally," I thought, but They declared him insane. Coaches, They said, were meant to go at a decorous trot full of people on official errands. I liked his other eccentricity too, making the royal orchestra play for him alone and play him to sleep. Music, They said, was for court occasions, a background for formal gatherings on little stiff gilt chairs.

Poor King Louis, born out of his time—a mistaken entry, a trajectory error, a missed rendezvous—and there he was, in the wrong century. Nowadays he would be normal enough, considered a square . . . a little run in the car to cool off before bedtime, and then turn on the radio and go to sleep to it. . . . What is insane about that? Except that the music on the radio nowadays is mostly Muzak. So he strangled a footman and squashed another behind a heavy door because they were spying on him for his enemies? That kind of violence is twentieth-century too, almost old-fashioned in 1970. Nowadays he would be considered rather a quaint mild mugger, square and limited.

My father's horses were "prize horseflesh," equivalent of a high-priced car. We went at a spanking four miles an hour, slowing to a walk for each incline up or down. It was the fastest progress possible, except in a train. The first time "giving full rein to his passion" appeared in print, it must have seemed the ultimate image of frenzied urgency.

What I remember thinking of horses in my childhood never happened . . . galloping a bare-backed, unbridled Royal Grey through forests and open country under stars. Actually I only rode sedately on a stodgy brown cob beside a groom holding my leading rein, round Rotten Row in London, chiefly to be seen "in the right place," or on a hired hack in Fredericton, without the groom, just for exercise. Later I hunted with the Berks & Bucks, and the Old Berkeley, but it was still not exactly full rein . . . not the Indian horse of the Sacred Horse Dance described in John Neihardt's *Black Elk Speaks*.

> They will appear, may you behold them,
> a horse nation will appear!
> Neighing they come!
> Prancing they come!
> May you behold them.

My horse pricked up his ears and raised his tail and pawed the earth, neighing loud and long to where the sun goes down. . . . Hey-hey! Hey-hey! all the horses neighed, rejoicing with the spirits and the people.

When the horses and the men were painted, they looked beautiful; but they looked fearful too.

The spirit horses of the red people, the great mysterious immortal Horse . . . that was how I thought about horses, about riding, and that was how I rode, in my dreams.

I have a painting of the Spirit Horse which I found in a trading post. White lightning streams from mane and tail and hooves. The sky full of white stars churns back from its feet. One night after death I want to ride, or at least to see, the Great Spirit Horse like that.

"I do hope Mrs. X is not at home," my mother would murmur, taking out her card case as the horses stopped, and turning up the corners of three cards to show they were delivered in person, one for my father, one for herself and one for Helen. It was only the eldest daughter who could be Miss Eaton and have a card turned up at the corner to be handed by our coachman to Mrs. X's maid. On the other hand it didn't matter if Evie's gloves got dirty, so I was allowed to hold the reins while we waited for the coachman's report.

Usually Mrs. X was "receiving" in her drawing room behind a little table with a fringed lace cloth. There would be fragile cups and saucers and plates of paper-thin bread and butter for me to be awkward with. I was sure to spill tea or upset the sugar bowl. The most I could hope for was not to trip over my own or someone else's feet and fall and break the china.

All this went through my anxious mind as we climbed down the slippery small steps of the carriage, or squeezed through the narrow half door at the side of the sleigh. Then the coachman would drive off to circle the block until we came out again, for the horses could not be "kept standing." Still less allowed to lie down. In summer there were flies "to drive them mad and make them run away"; in winter it was too cold.

"Don't keep the horses waiting," we reminded each other, like characters in a Jane Austen novel. Horses were chancy, unpredictable things . . . not like parking the car and comfortably enjoying a visit.

Strict rules governed calling. They are described in *Cranford* and remained essentially the same in my mother's calling days. You must never stay more than a quarter of an hour, and never mention anything interesting, so absorbing that you might forget the passing of the time and be carried away, or rather *not* carried away from Mrs. X's drawing room promptly "for the horses' sakes." You must repay a call within the week, and you must concede one day a fortnight when you would be at home, "receiving." My mother's day was every second Wednesday from three to five. On other days you could use "a social lie."

"Not at home," I used to hear her blandly tell the parlormaid, who repeated it to Mrs. X's coachman, when the X's came to return a call. But if I claimed to be out when I was manifestly in, that wasn't a social lie, that was a "downright" lie, typical of Evie-being-tiresome.

"Be sure your sin will find you *out*," the minister urged on Sundays, and my photographic mind saw a stalwart footman, or a trim parlormaid, at the door of my soul, reporting "Miss Evie is not at home." I watched him accept Sin's card, properly upturned at the right-hand corner, and bring it to me on a tray where I was safely "not receiving."

Sleigh bells in the snow. On Christmas Eve we drove out to deliver presents and met half the town driving by in sleighs like ours, waving and shouting. The bells jingled, the horses' breath and ours smoked in the pale afternoon light, the runners squeaked as they slid over hard-packed snow. We wore layers of winter clothing—red woollen overstockings, red woollen mittens, scarves, fur caps with earflaps, fur overcoats—and still I got a frostbitten cheek the last time we delivered Christmas presents in Kingston.

No, it was not romantic, but solitude was, when I could find it, and escape was, when I could risk it, around any handy corner where I might find the Other waiting for me. He would call me by the name I never heard, the name I would recognize, my remembered name. We would laugh and sing and kick off our shoes and walk, and make sense together, eternal sense from There.

Perhaps I would never have to go back to 20 Barry Street, or Fredericton or Montreal, or sail again for Home. Perhaps. Next time, surely, *perhaps*.

I don't remember when I first began to hear my father talk about his land "in the wilds of Ontario" and the war through which it had come to him. I was confused about that war. It was later than Napoleon, yet Napoleon was "the last wicked man who tried it"—war, that is. This war was different. It had several names, none of them related to Canada. It was called the South African War, the Boer War, and my father also called it his guerrilla warfare. My geography book showed a picture of gorillas swinging through the jungle and I got the notion that my father slugged it out with a band of large black monkeys, probably swinging as they did, only more expertly, through the trees.

I considered this clever of him but not remarkable, since he was a superb skater, swimmer, all-round athlete, horseman of the French *haute école,* against whom mere large monkeys would not have a chance. If they tried to overwhelm him with the weight of numbers he could resort to one of his devices, like the treacherous electrified jar with pennies at the bottom which a child could have if he would put in his hand to pick them up. My father enjoyed practical jokes and liked shocking people. He drove one of the first Stanley Steamers in England, hissing about the narrow roads, making horses

34

shy, and what was worse, he encouraged my mother to drive it, to the horror of the local Colonel Blimps.

Later I discovered that he inherited his penchant for "devices" from his father, born in Truro, Nova Scotia, where his branch of Eatons, after being tarred, feathered and flung out of Connecticut, in 1779, for remaining stubborn loyalists, went to settle on the stony strip of land presented to them by the King whose cause they had upheld.

Besides being part Algonquin, my grandfather Eaton was an engineer turned reluctant farmer on the family grant, where he spent most of his time inventing contraptions to make farm work more interesting. One year he hoisted his horses onto a sort of carrousel connected to the well to draw water and spray it on the fields. Ingenious lesser devices fed and watered them while he went about his research.

Later he hoped to escape from the farm by recovering pirate gold. He formed the first company to raise the hoard Captain Kidd was supposed to have buried off the shore of Oak Island. He did succeed in raising one bar of bullion before the tackle broke and the rest of the treasure disappeared, lost in the shifting bottom or swept into the bay.

Grandfather Eaton persisted. When the first company went broke he formed a second, and sank more time and more machinery into the sea, leaving the hard routine of the farm to his wife and children, of whom he had thirteen.

My father, the eldest of the seven who survived the rigors of this childhood, left home as soon as he could. When he was sixteen he was sailing before the mast on a tea clipper out of Digby Harbor to the Indies, and when he had saved enough money from his voyages and work of many kinds ashore, he put himself through Royal Military College (in Kingston, where he afterward taught and where we lived) and into the Canadian Army. His two brothers followed him, and by the time of World War One, three Colonel Eatons were serving their regiments and no farming Eatons were left on the grant King George the Third made to the family. The farm, which had never succeeded as a farm, was sold, and my father was landless except for the tract he owned in Ontario, given to him the year that I was born.

On November 1, 1902, Military Certificate No. 123 was issued to Daniel Izak Vernon Eaton, entitling him to a grant of land, tax-free, on account of his services during the South African War. He was then a young Captain in the Royal Canadian Horse Artillery, who had taken his battery through the bloodiest fighting of that messy mopping-up campaign. For this he received two medals and the only piece of real estate he was ever to own, a grateful country's first attempt to reward her veterans with something tangible.

Because of the leisurely pace of those days, it took five years for the certificate to be applied "on the north half lot 9, Concession 2, Ledger Township, 156 ½-acres District of Thunder Bay, and on the 16th November, 1907, patent issued therefor."

The wording of the patent enshrines a good deal of history. It begins with a flourish that the grantor's great-granddaughter, the present Queen of England and of Canada, Queen Elizabeth the Second, can no longer use in its entirety:

EDWARD THE SEVENTH, by the Grace of God, of the United Kingdom of Great Britain and Ireland and of the British Dominions beyond the Seas, KING, Defender of the Faith, Emperor of India, to ALL Whom These Presents shall come, GREETING:

Know ye, that We, of our Special Grace, certain Knowledge and mere Motion, have GIVEN and GRANTED, and by these Presents do give and grant, under the authority of an Act passed in the First Year of Our Reign, Chapter Six, and entitled *An Act to provide for the appropriation of certain lands for the Volunteers who served in South Africa and the Volunteer Militia who served on the frontier in 1866,* unto   Daniel Izak Vernon Eaton . . .

Neither EDWARD, for all his Special Grace, certain Knowledge and mere Motion—what a delightful ballet that would make!—nor the men who drew up the patent, nor my father, who received it, ever saw this land. They had no idea of the nature of it, or the riches it might represent, but the KING was taking no chances. In 1907 land was valued for lumber and water for fish, so EDWARD, thinking of his large tracts of unexplored territory in these terms, after describing the location of the concession, prudently GAVE and GRANTED it to my father . . .

In fee simple and all Mines and Minerals which are or shall hereafter be found on or under the same as provided by Section Eleven of the Said Act, saving, excepting and reserving unto Us, Our Heirs and Successors, all Pine Trees standing or being on said lands, as provided by Section Nine of the said Act, and the free use, passage and enjoyment of, in, over and upon all navigable waters which shall or may hereafter be found on or under, or be flowing through or upon any part of the said Parcel or Tract of Land hereby granted as aforesaid, and reserving also the right of access to the shores of all rivers, streams and lakes for all vessels, boats and persons, together with the right to use so much of the banks thereof, not exceeding one chain in depth from the water's edge, as may be necessary for fishery purposes. GIVEN under the Great Seal of Our Province of Ontario, Witness His Honour Sir William Mortimer Clark, Knight . . . Lieutenant Governor of our Province of Ontario.

In this way they spoke of land which belonged to Gitchee Manitou, or, if it must be parceled out to humans, to members of the Algonquin race.

There were no roads or railway stations near my father's land. It would have taken him many weeks to get there, and perhaps the most practical way would have been by dog team, in winter, as he had traveled to Labrador. No doubt the reason he never made the attempt was that he never had the necessary free time. Between 1905 and 1909 he was Director of Military Training in Canada, and after that returned to duty with his regiment. Besides, I think he had no serious intention then of turning farmer, with his memories of the childhood nightmare on the farm.

It was only much later that he began to talk about his land nostalgically. He would get to it one day, he said, by dog or any other team, see what was there, set about clearing it himself, and send for us to join him. He spoke of what he would do when he could leave the Army and settle down to farm. Yes, he wanted to farm, he said; it was not the impractical dream of every retired soldier, because he had farmed in the "primeval days," and now it would be better.

He drew pictures of moose and deer and bear, and a sketch of a beaver swimming in the navigable waters flowing through his land, while the Royal Family fished on the bank. The caption beneath it ran: "Portrait of EDWARD's Heirs and Successors, His Majesty King George the Fifth, Her Majesty Queen Mary, His Royal Highness the Prince of Wales, Her Royal Highness the Princess Royal, together with their vessels, boats and persons [persons characteristically coming last] a chain from the water's edge."

The chain is held by the King, who looks a little smug.

My father never saw his land. More than half a century after Military Certificate No. 123 was issued, I was the first Eaton to set foot on it. I did not get there by dog team, or even in a train. I flew in a comfortable passenger plane from Toronto to Port Arthur and drove on two fine roads, the King's Highway 17 and the King's Highway 11, which is also the Trans-Canadian Highway.

My father's land is easy to get to nowadays. There are few pine trees on it and no navigable rivers—Queen Elizabeth the Second is welcome to what wood and fish there are—and it is not good farmland. Still, I think my father would be amused. I think he might alter the expression of the royal faces in the drawing to look more wistful than smug, for his land is in the District of Thunder Bay in Ontario, where over half the claims for the mining of precious metals in Canada have been staked out. Grandfather Eaton might be interested too and get ready with contraptions. There is uranium and lithium all around it, and heaven knows what other undiscovered riches EDWARD by his mere Motion and all that Grace GAVE and GRANTED away.

I have paid the taxes on my father's land for half a century and left it undisturbed, a wilderness, a refuge for animals and birds. I like to think Algonquin feet still cross it unobserved. I see it mostly as it must be in winter, when the snow covers up the trail.

> Under the snow it lies
> the brambly tentative path
> winding nowhere
>
> moccasined feet
> traveling it
> had dignity
> had worth

so much the snow
the tracks beneath the snow
concede.

In all this irrelevant nonpreparation for life in the twentieth century, let alone the Aquarian Age, some things about the early part stand out more than others.

One of these happenings I have by hearsay, one I am not sure was on this plane, the other two I know were three-dimensional.

The first occurred when I was four or five. I heard about it from several people, McKinnon was one, Helen another, and now and then cousins wanting to get my goat. It appeared that I was in disgrace as usual, but this time it was bad enough to be dealt with in an unusual way. Perhaps I wet my drawers or was rude to Nannie. It may have been the time I circumvented the law against direct rudeness by saying: "When I'm grown-up, Nannie, and you call me on the telephone, I shall say 'Hello, Pig.'" Or something else. Anyhow, the decreed penalty was that since I behaved like a baby I should be a baby, for the day.

I was swaddled in a sheet and put on the spare-room bed and fed from a bottle. Helen was allowed to feed me. I was dressed in a bonnet and jacket over the sheet and stuffed into the pram and wheeled into the park where what They called my "little friends" were waiting to play with me. They ran up to the pram inquiringly, and Helen, walking beside it, explained: "Evie can't play with you today. She's just a baby."

They kept it up till night came. But next morning when Helen resumed the taunting she was told that it was over, it was another start, it was all forgotten.

Not by me. I was a humorless child, a Capricorn, with a well-developed sense of human dignity and a growing inferiority complex. I never played with any of those "little friends" again, for which I was punished too. Later that year I ran away, in a bright red reefer coat, visible for miles against the snow. They let me run for a while, then a friend of my father's came after me. I butted headfirst into his legs and looked up startled. When I saw who it was I thought that he had come to help me.

"Where are you going?" he said.

"Away."

He swung me up on his shoulder and brought me back to Them. So I never spoke to him again willingly, nor ate the candy he gave me, nor played with the doll.

The next episode was in Kingston in the winter of 1912.

It was my shop-lifting period. I stole from the stores, partly from boredom, partly because I would not have been allowed to buy the things I stole, nor would anyone have given them to me. My mother would have called them "trash of the worst kind." They were mostly religious objects for Roman Catholics, little images of the saints, medallions, candles and crucifixes. There was a strong anti-Roman-Catholic bias all about us, and especially in our schoolroom. Things that "smacked of Popery" were faintly menacing, like the French Canadians, and therefore to be ridiculed and of course forbidden. Also I had no money to buy anything. My weekly allowance of twenty-five cents was not mine to dispose of. Ten cents went into the collection, ten cents went into a dime bank, to encourage saving . . . it did not encourage me . . . and the remaining five cents were often docked for bad behavior. So to possess something I wanted, I must steal it.

There was a little closet under the eaves out of the schoolroom which was never used or looked into, I suppose because it was only two feet high and shallow. Here I fixed up an altar out of a shoebox, on which I put my loot, and here sometimes, when Helen and Miss Alden were safely out of the school-room, I used to crouch on my stomach—there was not room to kneel—and light the miniature candles and say rebellious prayers to Something, some God of the Forest, some God of the Sea, like the Saki story of the Great Ferret to whom Conrad prayed in the toolshed, to rid him of his aunt. My prayers did not have such a triumphant outcome.

I was not caught in the stores, my loot was not found, nor my hiding place discovered, but for years I bore the psychological scar of having become a thief.

Next to the children's bathroom on the top floor there was a sewing room which was sometimes a maid's room, and next to it a larger room, Miss Alden's bedroom. I was a "nasty, sneaky, prying child, into everything." The sewing room had the only window in the house from which, by craning a little, you could see the lake. I used to go in there sometimes to lean on the sill and look out, a form of escape for a few moments from our schoolroom routine.

Miss Alden's room had no view of anything exceptional, a backyard or two, a row of other houses like our own. I didn't creep in there to look out of the window. I went to look at her things, the photographs of her family at Home, the pincushion with the pins arranged as a crown, the tray with knick-knacks. In those days nice people never went into other people's rooms un-invited, never touched anything that didn't belong to them. In these permis-sive days it's hard to imagine such a strong taboo. I got a tremendous wicked thrill out of "crossing her threshold," but I wouldn't have dreamed of opening one of the drawers or looking into a closet. There was a little jewel case on top of the chest. I opened that and poked my finger among the brooches, pend-ants, keepsakes. My heart beat wildly and I dashed out of the room and rushed into the bathroom to recover.

But I went back many times, and one of the times there was something new in the jewel box, three five-dollar gold pieces lying in a corner of the tray. I picked them up and jingled them together in my hand. I had never seen so much wealth. Now and then, at Christmas or on my birthday, an uncle or godfather would give me a gold piece, but it was generally, in England, a ten-shilling piece, or in Canada a $2.50 one, never a whole five dollars, never three at once, and whatever it was, it was taken from me and put into the bank.

There was a noise downstairs. I left the room clutching one gold piece. All afternoon with it in my pocket I felt feverish and most of the night I couldn't sleep. Would it be missed? Should I put it back? I needed it. I began to spend it, over and over. There was a necklace of cat's-eyes I had seen in a shop window priced three dollars. I would get it for Helen. She would be overwhelmed and at last understand who was her real friend. There was a book of Andrew Lang's fairy tales I wanted, and candy and ice cream. I would be rich for months. But I must be careful when I got it changed. If any of Them saw me with it They would ask questions and ferret out the truth. I must go shopping by myself, but how could I manage that?

There was a better way, a way in which I could openly possess the fortune and spend it under anybody's eyes. I would *find* it. Even They believed in finders keepers. I would find it when Miss Alden was there. Then if she missed her gold piece—though why would she with three?—she would not be able to think that I had it, for I would have my own gold piece, which I found myself, in the snow, on our daily walk.

I waited for a good moment when Helen and Miss Alden were deep in talk, then I lagged behind. I dropped my treasure on the path and ran to Them shouting: "Look what I've found! Come back! Come back!" I dragged Them to where it lay shining. Helen stared, enviously amazed. Miss Alden said, "Well, well!" As for me, I put on such a good performance that by the time we got home I believed it myself, and could pass on to the second part of my triumphant good luck. I began to tell Them what I would spend it on, I bragged and swaggered and tossed the gold piece up and down, too excited to notice Miss Alden's expression. I never did look at her unless I had to.

That night I slept well, and so it went for a week, during which I must have been unbearably smug and patronizing to those not as rich as I.

On the seventh night, as I was reaching up to turn out the gaslight above my bed, the door opened and Miss Alden came in.

"Leave it lit," she said. "I want you to read this."

She put a black notebook into my hands and left the room. Everything turned cold, then fiery hot. I sweated, opening the book with awkward hands.

"Evie is a thief," I read. "For some time I've suspected that she came into my room and pried among my things. Today she took one of the marked gold pieces I had left in the tray of my jewel box. Perhaps she will bring it back. I cannot bear to tell her mother, poor sick woman, or her father. What will *he* say?"

The next entry told of my "Horrid lying scheme pretending to find it in the snow. I could understand a sudden temptation, but this is hardened deliberate deceit." She wrote that it would break my mother's heart to have to hear such news about her daughter, and that she would wait awhile to see if I returned it, "so that at least this sign of repentance can be added to the sad report."

The third entry said: "If Evie were a poor child she could be sent to the penitentiary for this. It is only because her father and mother are the fine sort of people they are with their high position in this community that she will escape the consequences of her theft."

The rest of the pages were blank. I sat stunned, waiting for the door to reopen. When it did I whispered, "Please . . . please don't tell them!"

"I have already told your poor mother, and she is writing to your father. Your poor, poor mother, your poor, poor father."

"*I hate you,*" I cried out inside. "*You didn't need to tell them!*"

"Aren't you going to say you're sorry, even now? Aren't you going to ask me to forgive you?"

I couldn't speak. I took the gold piece from beneath my pillow and gave it to her blindly.

"Don't you realize what it means to be a thief? A thief and a liar?"

I began to sob. She sat down on the edge of my bed. I drew away from her, head against my knees. For a long time I cried, wiping my eyes on the sheet. When at last I stopped and raised my head she was gone.

That night and other nights, lying miserably awake, I thought: *I should be in the penitentiary. I would be if we were poor.* I had disgraced us all and lost the last slim chance I ever had of being accepted someday by the family, let alone being loved.

The big penitentiary was not far from our house on Barry Street. The whole town was conscious of it, especially when there was an escape. Then a gun was fired, echoing loudly across the lake, and telephones rang with a warning: "Two men out" or "One man out," a description and a reward offered for capture or information. A deep-toned bell tolled and kept on tolling until the convict was caught. Once it tolled for a week and people began to complain. Then it stopped. They had found the escaped man, dead from exposure. It was a winter escape, one of the few attempted in below-zero weather. He must have been desperate.

Whenever the bell tolled, especially at night, I would become that running criminal. *I've been out a long time. Perhaps this time I'll get away.* Then the bell would stop and I would know that I was caught again and locked up in my cell.

My mother never spoke to me about the gold piece. My father was away on one of his military missions. I dreaded his return. Sometimes I have wondered whether Miss Alden was lying too, when she said she told Them, or whether They thought silence the best way to deal with Evie. Our daily routine went on as though nothing had happened to disturb it, but for me it was not the same. I looked at Them, I looked at everyone, and at many things, through outcast eyes, "damned from here to eternity" with Kipling's fallen gentlemen, only I was a fallen lady, which was probably worse.

I have always been fond of skunks, because of the second this-dimensional episode with Miss Alden. We were walking in a wood, so it must have happened in New Brunswick—Duck Cove, Shediac or Randolph, the three places we went to in the summer. All I recall is that we met a skunk and I turned and ran, panting out a warning as I went.

"Nonsense!" Miss Alden said. "Don't be such a coward. Come back this instant! It's a dear little pussy cat."

She advanced in the attitude of one about to colonize a creature for its own good.

O valiant skunk! O champion of the outcast criminal!

Miss Alden had to bury her clothes and wash her hair—and all the angular rest of her—in strong tomato juice.

"Why didn't you warn poor Miss Alden?" my mother asked sternly.

"I did," I protested. "I told her. As soon as I saw it, I did tell her."

"Evie is such a little liar. How could I believe her? I didn't imagine. . . . We don't have skunks in England. . . ."

Not the four-legged kind, I mused.

That was the real grievance. Canada, her tone implied, had once more let down the British Empire, instead of following the right example set us by Those at Home.

O brave skunk!

But he hadn't made things easier for me. Miss Alden behaved as though I had deliberately aimed the tail and triggered the lucky shot.

My Uncle Charlie told me a skunk story once that I enjoyed almost as much. He had been skipping Sunday School and coming home with good but implausible reasons. Grandfather Fitz Randolph told him, "Listen to me, Sir! You go to that school no matter *what!* Don't you dare come back for any reason whatever."

One Sunday morning Uncle Charlie overtook a skunk and startled it. Instead of returning home for repairs and a change of clothes, he went on to the school. Pretty soon it had to be closed for the day and some of the children went home reeking. The indignant superintendent complained to Grandfather, who sent for Uncle Charlie and demanded to know what he meant by it, holding his nose as he spoke. "But, Papa," Uncle Charlie protested, "you told me to go to that school no matter *what.*"

It took a discerning skunk, in his day as in mine, to put down an infallible elder.

There was also the skunk who used to come every afternoon at four o'clock to my studio at the MacDowell Colony to ask for a handout. Once I made the mistake of offering him a peanut-butter sandwich from my lunch basket. Up went the tail. I don't blame him, I don't like peanut butter either. Skunks and I disapprove of the same things. Skunks are my people.

I have been unfair to Them, men and women going through the bewilderment of incarnation without knowledge or remembrance of There.

My father was frustrated in his profession by the hatred of an exalted official whom he once court-martialed for stealing regimental funds. (This brush with dishonesty may have made his younger daughter's crooked record more distasteful to him, if he knew of it.) The exalted official, cashiered from the Army, went into politics and rose to be All Powerful, with his knife into the Permanent Corps and the R.C.H.A. in particular. Many people tried to get my father to transfer to the English Army. Lord Kitchener wanted him on his staff. He was offered an English division. But my father was a loyal Canadian and chose to stay, unpromoted, with "his men."

My mother, often in pain, was frustrated in her social ambitions by her deafness and the "accident of birth"—splashing down in Canada as a colonial, instead of in England as an Englishwoman, preferably among the landed gentry. She was also provoked by my father's stubborn refusal to solve the whole problem by transferring to Lord Kitchener's staff, where he would be appreciated and promoted as he deserved, and she and Aunty Nell and the girls could live in London.

Miss Alden? The last time I saw her, at the coronation of Queen Elizabeth the Second in 1953, she was wearing the uniform of the Saint John's Ambulance Corps and was in charge of a group of Pakistani soldiers lining a part of the procession route. Well over seventy, she must have been up since 4 A.M. and have marched some miles with her detachment before they reached their appointed place, opposite the stands reserved for the foreign press.

I too was up at 4 A.M. but I was comfortably seated in the American section for the less-important correspondents, with a wad of soggy newspapers over my head, while Helen and her family performed in the Abbey.

One of my nephews was a gold-stick-in-waiting, my brother-in-law was Assistant Marshal, right-hand to the Duke of Norfolk, in charge of the complicated seating arrangements. Helen sat in proper regalia in her proper place. I, as the only American member of the family, sat in the rain outside. But, unlike the memory I had of the coronation of George the Fifth, everything was televised and broadcast to us in the stands, so that in a sense I was seeing and hearing more than they did from their limited historical places.

Miss Alden was standing stiffly in the downpour, taller than the soldiers she herded and a good deal more robust. Poor shivering Orientals, in the lightest of summer uniforms, they had never encountered the cold and damp of Home. Some of them fainted and were dragged aside and carted away in stretchers. Not those in Miss Alden's charge. I could see through my field glasses that she was rallying them with something out of a Thermos. Hot tea laced with rum, I learned later. She was determined that *her* men should see the Queen they had come so far and stood so long to honor, and she had all of them on their feet and cheering when the coach rolled past.

"Of course, some of them may have seen two queens," she said when we met a fortnight later for tea, and when I ventured, "I didn't know you were with the Saint John's Ambulance Corps," she explained: "I joined it in the war. You see, I was a little overage for the other women's services and I needed to be in uniform so that I could legally resist the Germans if they landed. In peacetime, of course, except for shows like this it's quite a bore."

I could not help admiring her, in spite of childhood trauma. There are facets to everything. In Kingston perhaps she hated her position, or was lonely, or crossed in love, or, since she too gulped down paregoric as we all did, perhaps she was slightly opiated once in a while.

Possibly it was just the Edwardian-Victorian hangover. Women were legally classed with criminals, lunatics and minors, and in spite of such exotic companions had a very dull time. Also there was I for them to deal with, argumentative, restless, clumsy, wrong-behaving, wrong-looking, wrong-headed, underhanded, my mind "full of things no nice child should be thinking," written down in lurid poems which I tried to hide. If it had been the Other they had to deal with, he would have been packed off to a good prep school at eight, there to find his own misery, well known and well described in English books, but at least he would have had companions of his own age to undergo it with. For me there was just the adult world, and Helen, whom the adult world admired and included, excluding me. That I had to be deceitful and wrong-everything in order to survive is irrelevant. That I did survive is due, I think, to the lasting influence of the fourth episode, on whatever plane it occurred. I have never been quite sure of where and when . . . overlapping, perhaps.

I was lying in a hammock between pine trees for my "afternoon nap." Afternoon naps were almost as important as the three English R's, Royalty, Rheumatism and Religion, Church of England kind. Afternoon naps, like nice brisk walks, were undertaken solemnly. But this one was different.

I don't know where it was, I think at Saint Andrews in New Brunswick. The hammock came to a halt and I was unable to make it swing without sitting up to use my feet, which I could not do. I was fastened in securely, my arms down by my sides, the fringes of the hammock spread across me, fastened by safety pins, with straps around the whole. I don't know why I was alone in a wood, if it was a wood. It may have been a grove of trees near the house where we were staying for the summer.

They did not intend to take any risks. I could not wander off or run away. I was still Their captive, but alone, under great pine trees, in my own surroundings. I absorbed this unexpected soothing solitude as a plant without water drinks when the vase is filled.

When later I read of "cosmic bliss" I knew, remembering this experience in the forest, what the two words meant, how it felt to be in the state *pure autre vie, otherwhere,* plugged into the wavelength of the Great Mystery.

Because They didn't want me to fall out of the hammock in my sleep . . . more likely because They didn't trust me, They had placed me in the traditional position of an Indian baby on the cradle board. They didn't know this, nor did I—then. I didn't hold a cradle board in my hands until I was a grandmother. I doubt They ever saw one. Certainly They never knew the Indian way with cradle boards. But I am sure that it was not by accident that I lay swaddled in my hammock, looking up into the sky through great fragrant trees.

An Indian mother carries the child on her back, so that he will face away from her toward the universe, but still feel her nearness, the rhythm of her walking, her love. Sometimes she hangs the baby from a tree branch swayed by the wind. "Rock-a-bye, baby, on the treetop" must have been written with a cradle board in mind. Indian mothers know the truth about There, the Spirit land, and the road to be traveled, the training required, from infancy, to tread it, especially the training in silence.

Words are the windmill machine of the pale-faced, silence is the language of the spirit. Entering the silence is as natural as the act of breathing to the Red People, traveling the Beauty Path of the Great Mystery.

I lay suspended, as one floats, weightless, on the sea; I felt the earth turning beneath me; I breathed the incense of sun-heated pine; I heard the soughing of the breeze-in-leaves. Gradually, yet from always, I *became* these things. Yeats, as he lay face downward, pressed into the grass, had his great experience of the cosmic bliss. He "became the universe," and so did I, for aeons— seconds; now—forever; timeless—immortal. . . .

Suddenly there was a shape at my left shoulder. I saw it against my eyelids before I opened them. I knew, I recognized, the moccasined feet, the fringed leggings, the beaded buckskin, the necklace of colored quills, the proud feathered headdress, but when I looked with my eyes I could only see the face . . . old . . . old . . . wrinkled with laughter, with understanding love.

I stared into the kind wise eyes and would have stretched my arms to him.

He said a word. I hear it in sleep sometimes, and in the Sweat Lodge, chanted. . . . I have sung it myself. I know it perfectly and what it means, but when I wake, or when I leave the Sweat, it is gone. I know nothing.

He set the hammock to swinging gently, then he went as suddenly as he had come, through the forest, or through the air or through the mind, and left me staring at the sky.

Hawkan? The Other? Someone older? No matter. I knew him and he knew me.

When They came to get me I was so quiet, so serene, so glowing with strange joy, They said, "The child must be coming down with something," took my temperature, gave me a dose of castor oil and put me to bed.

I didn't tell Them anything. It was better to be punished for not telling things, like the presence of the General's wife in the drawing room who, I thought, was probably not there, than to talk of a tall man on the stairs, or an Indian in the forest, who knew me.

I believe he was a tribal "old man," maybe a "Grandfather," and until I became hopelessly whitened and lost from the Indian way I think he was sometimes with me to protect, to guide, to teach, and even to join me in my solitary games. Sometimes he played the drum and voices sang around us. I had a background accompaniment of chanting that ran through dull gray days.

The important thing was that he listened. I could talk to him and reach him, however far away, unlike my father, "on maneuvers," or my mother out calling or shopping, or Helen and Miss Alden, at any time. There was no one else, no one to tell important happenings to, or thoughts, or sudden knowledge. That was the deprivation of my childhood, no one to share with. I was well fed, well housed, well taken care of, certainly not underprivileged, but after the mores of the middle class in those days, I was a no-person. I rarely saw my parents, and almost never alone. Helen was lost to me, from before remembrance, somewhere in infancy. There was no one else, except McKinnon, and she was both busy and afraid.

Helen . . . it was a pity They encouraged her aversion. Love is love, a warm cloak about a life, no matter where it comes from. Next to Helen I loved the dog Taft, and more than either I loved the earth, the forests, the sea and my Indian Companion.

I played two favorite games in Kingston, one in summer, one in winter. In summer I had an iron hoop and a wooden stick to beat it with. I drove it faster, faster, until it got far ahead of me. Where it stopped, whanging down to silence as I caught up with it, there the adventure began. That was where I must start from "this time." I looked to the four directions to decide where I should go, hid the hoop, or carried it on my arm, inert, deprived of power, as I walked "to meet my fate."

It was a dim reflection of the splashdown, I suppose, with undertones of reincarnation. Later I learned about the Indian Sacred Hoop of the Nation. Black Elk speaks of it to John G. Neihardt in *Black Elk Speaks:*

Everything an Indian does is in a circle, and that is because the Power of the World always works in circles, and everything tries to be round. In the old days when we were a strong and happy people, all our power came to us from the sacred hoop of the nation, and so long as the hoop was unbroken, the people flourished. . . . The sky is round, and I have heard that the earth is like a ball, and so are all the stars. The wind, in its greatest power, whirls. Birds make their nests in circles for theirs is the same religion as ours. The sun comes forth and goes down again in a circle. The moon does the same, and both are round. Even the seasons form a great circle in their changing, and always come back again to where they were. The life of a man is a circle from childhood to childhood, and so it is in everything where power moves. Our tepees were round like the nests of birds, and these were always set in a circle, the nation's hoop, a nest of many nests, where the Great Spirit meant for us to hatch our children.

In winter I took a toboggan to the small park on the shore of the lake, a block from home, where there was a ruined fort with a deep moat, and a man-made hill on which the tower was built. There was a stone lion at the foot of the hill, green with age, his tail curled on his back; black iron benches, and an old-fashioned cannon from the war of 1812. You could climb on the lion's back if no grownups were about, with due care for your drawers. I was always damaging my drawers.

No one but tiresome Evie would have thought that hill a good toboggan slide. It needed fancy steering between benches, cannon and lion to come out on the flat part of the course. Once I crashed into a bench and cut my head open. I lay in the snow, half-stunned, bleeding, abjectly afraid of what They would say. I don't remember how I got home. I walked it alone, I expect, in pain. I do remember "having to have stitches," and the scolding I got for the state of my clothes. "What were you doing? Never do it again!"

It didn't occur to me to give up the game. I went on dragging the toboggan up the forbidden hill, where I said farewell to Celestial Companions, all sorrowing greatly to lose me, and "descended into hell," standing when I could manage it, lying on my stomach if the snow was too icy, whirled in my chariot on a destined way.

Once down, I started "this time," as I did in summer with the hoop, from where I found myself, where the toboggan stopped, bound to accept the conditions of existence, the luck I drew. Then I climbed in spirals to the top of the hill again, to be welcomed by the Celestial Companions and spend a brief, satisfactory time with them, before I must redescend, "face the ordeal of the Green Lion," avoid the "siege perilous" of the benches, and undergo another round of mortal existence. Evidently danger and life on this plane were synonymous; also it was exile, or an evil enchantment.

In those Kingston years I was reading Andrew Lang's Fairy Books, the *Lilac*, the *Red*, the *Green*, the *Brown* and all the other hues, with their satisfying illustrations, somebody's *Legends of King Arthur*, George MacDonald's *Phantastes*, the Nesbit books, especially *The Enchanted Castle*, and *The Magic Key*, by a second cousin, Beatrice Turnbull. I think it was the only book she wrote. It was my favorite, the story of a boy whose magic key unlocks one drawer of an old cabinet each night. He swallows the pill he finds inside it, follows the directions on a scroll, and gets one gift . . . he is invisible for a day, he can fly for a day, he outruns the fastest runners in the world for a day, and so on, always with superb and logical results. It was a wonderful book. Someone should reprint it.

I was reading all the other prescribed things too, including most of the

Bibliothèque Rose, but there were some books and poems that reinforced my private world. My games reflected a hodgepodge of these with what I heard in church and read aloud on Sundays from *Pilgrim's Progress* and the Bible. I was groping toward some Blueprint of the Cosmic System. When I first heard of reincarnation, in London, in 1921, at a lecture where both Annie Besant and Krishnamurti spoke, it was familiar, recovered knowledge, and I was relieved that something said in public to an audience of Them made sense, even if They made ignorant or snobbish fun of it, or took to it too eagerly as a sort of social endorsement, hard to contest. London was full of people, "seekers," mostly suburban housewives with a sprinkling of old dowagers, who claimed to be Cleopatra, or Napoleon, or Saint John the Beloved.

Helen was busy being "interesting" in *this* life. And I didn't care who I was in past lives . . . obviously someone less evolved than I was in this one, if we build from where we leave off. What mattered was the endless *time* restored to us in which to develop, and the taking away of Injustice.

"Be ye therefore perfect, as your Father in Heaven is perfect," had always seemed to me the most heartless and cruel mockery the Master Jesus was credited with saying. Who could accept a Supreme Creator, a Father, who would give to one of His children imbecility, hopeless deformity, and to another, genius, for the one chance on which a "future eternity" depended?

It seemed clear to me that we must be eternal *now,* immortal *now,* that there could be no such division, logically, as time *and* eternity. Myriad levels in the same eternity, planes, the "many mansions" talked about in church, but not the existence of a temporal part outside the whole. Certainly no Creator who would damn us to eternal punishment in everlasting fire for losing a rigged, an impossible race.

I wanted the elementary courtesy of being consulted about my own existence, some choice, some responsibility . . . if in the penitentiary, I wanted to *know* that I had stolen to get there. Given Justice and a consenting say-so, I would accept the rigors of the splashdown, I would participate . . . would even wholeheartedly co-operate with the Supreme Will. . . . ("Gad! She'd better!" Humorless Margaret Fuller had nothing on humorless Eve.) Otherwise NO!

When Mother and Aunty Nell became excited seekers, I accompanied them in and out of occult and other fashionable circles in the London of the twenties, but I never joined the various groups officially. I was not much of a joiner, not even of the human race.

I do not enjoy talks, discussion groups, lectures—except those I give myself, for a fee, and then it is the fee I mostly like. But I did go to lectures in those days, and to the Theosophical Society Library and took out many books. And in 1923 I did follow Mynie and Nell into *Le Droit Humain,* an international order of Co-Freemasonry, in which I worked, off and on, the rest of my life. Once a Mason, always a Mason.

But in Kingston I was still a child, playing made-up, revealing games.

. .

In a letter sent to me in 1968, Miss Alden recalls far better than I can dredge up from an unreliable memory the stodginess and muddled thinking of those days, from the sentimentality of her description of my father's charger as a "rogue horse" which died a soldier's death, to her need to tell my father a one-sided story which must pain him, and put me in jeopardy of losing the only ally that I had in the family, without my guessing why.

This letter, with all its implications, is in the appendix for anyone who cares to read it.

On August 4, 1914, everything changed.

My father left with his regiment for the war, "unthinkable in this day and age," sailing with the first transports from Quebec. We went with other officers' families to Lake Saint Joseph, from where we could be driven to Valcartier camp each day to be with him until the division embarked.

We stayed in a summer hotel, closed for the season, and there my father sent a battery wagon for us, drawn by six horses, with three men riding postilion as though they were wheeling a gun into action.

The wagon had no springs, the roads were deeply rutted muddy lanes, we sat in deck chairs lashed to the sides, bumped and jolted painfully to and from the camp feeling true blue as well as black and blue, keeping stiff upper lips as well as stiff necks and backs.

Every evening the regimental band played outside the officers' mess, one-steps, two-steps, waltzes, always closing with "When You Come to the End of a Perfect Day," "The Maple Leaf Forever" and "God Save the King." The sun set over the tents in their patterned field, the stars came out, Retreat was sounded—not the disgraceful thing the word implied, this Retreat was only the opposite of the morning Reveille—the battery wagon reappeared and we were jolted back to the hotel. It was for me a long sleepy journey underneath the stars.

I don't know how long we stayed at Lake Saint Joseph. Long enough for Valcartier to assume in memory the essence of chivalry, romance and loss. "Were you at Valcartier?" "Qu'il est triste, le son du cor." Of that regiment spread before our eyes, only two officers and fourteen men returned. My father was not among them.

My mother went to Quebec to see the transport sail. The rest of us returned to Kingston to wait for her to join us, and then to wait for the two or three months of the war to be over. No one thought it could last more than that. Not with the British Empire fighting on the right side. No one, except my father, who had lectured since 1905 on the coming war with Germany, and on the aerial defense of England against attack by bombing planes. My father had his share of clairvoyance.

. .

Presently it began to look as though the war would last, after all. Our hatbands grew heavier and heavier as we prayed for the boats they named, and for the R.C.H.A. in France, as we listened to the war news Miss Alden selected to read to us from the newspapers. The news was old, but we didn't think so then. There was a time-lag of about three weeks, sometimes six, but we thought and talked of the "miracle of modern communications."

The house in Kingston, the last home where we were all together, the last home we ever had in Canada, was sold. Taft and my toys were left behind. He ran after the cab that took us to the station, howling and trying to jump in. Eventually we outdistanced him and all I could see was a black dot in the road, still valiantly following.

I began to cry.

"He'll forget you very quickly," Miss Alden said. "He'll be much happier with the little boy he's going to."

I was never sure that They had found a home for Taft. They never told me any details, the name of the little boy, where it was, when Taft would be going there. They never talked of him again. The little boy joined that other little boy, the hungry one who was always waiting around the corner, whom Nannie knew, and who wanted to eat up my porridge, while I cried from frustration that I could not run to him and give it to him gladly. Instead I had to eat it while he starved. And now I had to think of Taft and wonder if he would be all right, if he would ever forgive me.

We went to Montreal to wait for passage Home. Miss Alden left on an early boat. It was easy for her to make arrangements, she was ENGLISH, we were only British Subjects. Still, our father was fighting for England, and our hearts were probably more or less of oak. We would be able to join her at Home before too long, she assured us.

I was wearing the *Lusitania*'s hatband when she was torpedoed. We had friends on board, grownups whom we knew, but also two "little friends," the daughters of Sir Montagu and Lady Allen of the Allen Line. We had given a farewell party for them in our waiting-for-passage apartment.

I was envious of Gwen, the younger, more adventurous one, who said she could hardly wait to reach the danger zone. She did so hope something exciting would happen when they got among the German submarines. But it was Anna, the shy one, who dreaded leaving Canada, even for Home, who was last seen giving away her lifebelt to another passenger. Both girls drowned. Gwen's body was found sucked into one of the four great funnels. Anna's was never recovered.

Lady Allen remembered that they all jumped together, holding hands, then something struck her on the head. When she recovered consciousness, she was on a raft off the coast of Ireland, and someone was saying "This woman's dead. Shove her overside." She moved and was saved. Later she telegraphed her husband AM SAFE, BUT CANNOT FIND GIRLS.

When the news of the sinking of the *Lusitania* reached Montreal, it was rumored that "German waiters held a celebration party at the Ritz," supreme proof, if proof were needed, of German "frightfulness."

As I looked at the gold letters on my hat, something of the earlier guilt associations made me feel that it was partly my fault, my undoubted wickedness, that so many people died. The *Lusitania* hatband was the last H.M.S. I wore. The fad for sailor clothes faded at about this time.

Two years had passed since my father sailed to "unthinkable" war. If we wanted to spend with him the leaves he still might have, we must give up waiting for a British ship to take us and embark from New York for England. No one now expected the war to end quickly.

The train from Montreal to New York ran through New Brunswick, crossing the road that led to Randolph, my Uncle Alan's home, where my happiest summers were spent. He lived with his married son Guy, Kathleen, his daughter-in-law, and their four children in a rambling wooden "mansion" near the family lumber mills. All around the island, named for the family, there were pinewoods leading to the sea. I could sometimes escape for an afternoon—mornings were given up to lessons with Mademoiselle Tantereille—and wander freely by myself, in the woods or on the beach. I could fling myself down to stare at the sky, the rich deep-blue sky I never saw in England, with wild clouds crossing it. I could even sleep in the open, my body pressed to Mother Earth for food, for peace. Healing, meaning times. Randolph was Home to me.

Alone in my lower berth I watched for the familiar road. Helen was asleep in the next compartment, but I was sitting up with the blind raised. The train slowed for the crossing, the bells rang, I looked down the moonlit strip. . . .

> White in the moon the long road lies
> That leads me from my love . . .

A child goes where its elders take it, helplessly. I remember my nephew Francis, when he was three, climbing into the family car for a short drive, asking, "Are we going to Sandringham?" the seaside place he loved in the summers, as I loved Randolph. In childhood, at any time, you might be told "get in the car," or the train, and arrive somewhere, and that would be that, the inevitable unexplained way things were, in the grip of the elders.

I felt enormous grief, out of all proportion to merely passing Randolph in the night . . . yet what a crossing of roads that did turn out to be! How right I was to grieve.

The sound of a train in the night, a Canadian train's deep roar—not the European piping—nor the diesel whistle—brings back that ageless, heavy sorrow, desolation, the child sobbing into a stuffy Pullman pillow.

It is strange to recall how little red tape there was in those days, even in wartime. Civilians traveled about quite freely, on anything that would carry them where they wanted to go, responsible to no one but themselves. Early in 1916, my mother, my aunt, Helen-and-Evie, sailed from New York on the S.S. *Philadelphia*. No gold-lettered hatband this time. She was an American boat, not very seaworthy, certainly not well equipped for crossing the ocean in wartime.

"Nothing but a riverboat," the Captain was reported to have said. It was also reported that the Captain was "disgruntled because he had been kicked upstairs."

Fascinated by this unexpected tableau, I looked at him searchingly when he next appeared. There was nothing that I could see to confirm it. *How,* I asked myself despairingly, *do grownups always know what has happened to people?* The Captain must have wanted to hide this indignity, as I always wanted to hide what happened to me. Apparently one never could, not even a Captain in uniform with gold buttons and "supreme authority on his ship."

The *Philadelphia* was as unsatisfactory as he complained it was. Even on calm days the waves went over her prow and stern. The only place for walking her one deck—and at sea one had to walk the deck for a measured mile twice a day—was directly amidships. Still, she was neutral and so the safest way to cross.

An outsized American flag streamed over her wake. The stars and stripes were painted the full length of her hull on both sides. At night these were lit by searchlights and lanterns. I thought the flag against the phosphorescent sea so beautiful that I begged to "stay up after dark" to look at it. When They discovered what the attraction was, They shrugged, more in disgust than amusement. Trust Evie, the gesture implied, to admire the Wrong Flag. . . . It was an irritating nuisance to Them to have to be "beholden" to the United States for Their safety, a country which was neutral, when the British Empire fought "to preserve American skins," a country, in the words of its own pompous President, "too proud to fight."

What a deal of scorn I heard about the United States in those days. Still, if America were going to be neutral so long, it would be better for it to stay so until we arrived. "Sitting duck," the Captain called the S.S. *Philadelphia*. Everyone believed the United States "would come in now, over the *Lusitania*," everything "pointed that way" when we sailed. There was no radio to tell us what had happened since, but it did seem likely that we would be sunk as the German answer to a United States declaration of war . . . "at last!" . . . but a little inconvenient as to timing.

"Can't zigzag with this tub," the Captain complained. "No use trying. No use putting out the lights and slipping by."

Orders appeared in the cabins. "On entering the danger zone, passengers will assume lifebelts and will wear them at all times."

There were very few passengers. I remember a Russian Baron, an Italian Count, a Belgian doctor taking hospital supplies to his country, Maude Allen and her manager, Mr. Hast, and one Englishman, named Ernest Bird, who flirted with Helen. So did the Count.

There were lifebelts for each of us, but they were the old-fashioned heavy cork kind. Mine went around me twice. I couldn't reach a table or sit in a chair. If I fell down I couldn't get up until somebody righted me. At night we took them off, though we weren't supposed to, and apologetic stewards rushed in now and then to check and make us put them on again.

I have written about this voyage in *Every Month Was May,* and of how Aunty Nell dressed for disaster in a pair of black-serge bloomers and a yellow sweater, with brandy in one pocket and her passport in the other, and how she asked the purser: "What shall I do if I find myself unexpectedly in the water?" and how he answered, after a moment's thought: "Just be perfectly natural, Madam."

As it happened the United States did not declare war for another year, and we arrived without incident at Liverpool. We docked beside a boat we had traveled on, the *Mauretania,* now a hospital ship, with a great hole in her side. She towered above us; our smokestack barely reached the top of her hull.

It took a long day to disembark. We had been expected to land in Southampton and be examined there. While we waited for officials to look us over, we bobbed in the dirty harbor water, beside the great gray wounded friend, and thought of her sister ship, the *Lusitania,* whose ghost she might have been in her wartime paint.

After that I never could remember the white shining liner I had seen depart with waving friends. I saw the *Lusitania* always gray, battered, listing a little toward the land, with a huge hole in her side.

My nightmares about ships began. When I am tired, coming down with flu, facing an operation, or hounded by fears of defeat or bills I cannot pay, I embark, sometimes over a long rickety plank bridge across a treacherous marsh, sometimes up a steep rope ladder, sometimes from a fisherman's inadequate wharf, but always on a Great Gray Shape which I know is going down. No one knows it but me, and I am powerless to prevent "the others" from embarking.

England was sad and exalted in 1916. Barbara Tuchman in *The Guns of August* describes those war years well. She was not there. Perhaps one would have to be not there, not born then, to write of The Great War to End All Wars with dispassionate pity, insight and authority. All the discoverable facts were available to her by the time she wrote her book, but to us, who were living through them, they were still fragmented, unknown, unknowable, and for the most part, no matter how hard we might try to grasp, to master them . . . inconceivable.

Our world was put to sleep "for the duration" beneath a quilt of patriotic slogans and outworn illusions. What woke and rolled toward us . . . "what rough beast" . . . was another world altogether, which must have been there all the time, tucked in with ours, to smother and devour it.

I was thirteen when we came to England-at-war. Mother, Helen, Aunty Nell, had left their native land, but they were coming Home. England was their country of the heart. It was not mine. I was a displaced person, without that label for it then, taken from the earth I knew, the soil I trod when I got the chance, the trees and fields I needed, the forests to explore, the air I should breathe, the ancestral simplicities, the mysteries I was on the move to discover and those I dimly knew already, the future I might begin to trust, to a cold dark alien town in an alien land.

They might call it Home if They liked, it would not be home to me. But neither was the turning world. There was Somewhere Else, dimly recalled. There was a journey away from a Parent Place. I wondered about others, the everyones. Did they recall it too? There was no sign that they did, nor that they wanted to.

I looked at England, "right little, tight little island," through non-English eyes, and everywhere I looked saw men in uniform and women in mourning. London was full of ghosts, some of them ghosts of the living, all of them solid to me. Once I was standing in the usual wartime queue to take the rare bus, the top-heavy, narrow double-decker kind of those days with an open top. It was November or December, raining as usual. My feet were wet, I was cold, everything was damp and grimy. It seems to me that I was always cold and tired in those wartime winters. I envied the young officer standing ahead of me for his comfortable "British Warm" greatcoat. I was glad that he had it. One was always glad when a soldier on leave had anything good or comforting. Their life-expectancy was short.

The bus arrived and the line began to move forward. The first sodden shapeless bundles were passing to the warmth inside. My turn was almost next, the officer was helping the woman in front of him onto the step. I hung back a little to give them room. An impatient shove, a "Get on with it, do!" knocked me off balance. I fell forward, apologizing as I went, but where there should have been solid khaki shoulders to land against, there was nothing. I fell *through* him, and was directly behind the woman he had helped into the bus. I followed her to the stuffy aisle and sat down shakily, to sort out the dimensions. I always suffered a queasy malaise, like seasickness, after dimensional blurs.

There was nowhere for that officer to go. He was not in the bus, he was not in the queue, for I could see it and the street behind it clearly. He had not climbed on top, for I could see that too, and the conductor was blocking off the stairs, in his black oilskin, saying, "Seats inside! Seats inside!" So why would he leave his companion and go up in the rain? If I went to look I knew I would not find him. I had fallen through him. One moment there was his back in the British Warm, the next an impatient shove . . . the man behind me seeing only wasteful space . . . then the woman's back, the girl's really, for she looked very young, sitting opposite me, dressed in the heavy widow's weeds we mourned in then, with a long black veil about her face.

I looked at her uneasily. Should I lean forward, touch her on the knee, murmur, "Excuse me. I have just seen your husband help you onto this bus." Would it be better to wait until she was getting out, get out too, if it were not very far away from my own stop, follow her and say, "I'm sorry, but I must speak to you. I have just seen your husband. . . ."

Nowadays I would not hesitate, I think . . . I hope. I would speak to her, at the risk of being put down as a nosy old "irrelevant" fool. But then I was bewildered, young and insecure, and stupidly brought up. One didn't speak to strangers about anything. One didn't "meddle in other people's business" at any time. Probably she knew her officer was there . . . but if she knew, if she had seen him, and felt his protecting hands, why did she look so lost, so deep in lonely despair?

"Excuse me . . . I'm sorry . . . your husband . . ."

My stop came before hers. I left without speaking, without even catching her eye. She didn't look in my direction, she didn't look up at all. She stared at her black-gloved hands, not seeing them, not seeing anything, as the bus bore her away.

London was full of women wearing widow's weeds, and sometimes there were men with them, in uniform, but unless they spoke to each other I could never tell, never be quite sure who was there, or in some other dimension.

Khaki, black; khaki, black. After a while one noticed only the exceptions, the grays, greens, browns. Most of the crowd streamed by in mourning. It was only a few more months, just a little while, before my mother too wore widow's weeds with a long veil about her face, and I wore black armbands on the left sleeves of my school uniform, looking, looking, looking, for any sign of my father among the khaki crowd.

He came to me later, and was seen and heard by people with me, but not in the year that he was killed.

Aunty Nell blossomed in wartime London. She came into her own as a valuable executive, an organizer, a great warm-hearted woman, mothering the men in uniform. "One million superfluous women," the *Daily Mail* deplored with its usual brisk candor, speaking of the British casualties. Aunty Nell might not be married, but she was not, certainly not then, superfluous.

She found war work at once, at London Bridge Station, in the Red Cross canteen that took care of the trains of wounded arriving from France. My mother and Helen were busy settling in the flat we had rented in Chelsea, around the corner from Whistler's house in Tite Street, where Belle Douglas, a friend of ours, lived, who helped them find a music master and a piano for Helen and generally to "pick up the threads" of English wartime life.

Aunty Nell took me with her to the canteen, to "do my bit" while I was waiting to be sent to boarding school.

We joined the night shift, the most short-handed. What I saw and heard during those first months in London became a permanent part of subconscious horror waiting to emerge when I am weak. My job was to make tea, wash the cups and mugs, run errands, tidy things away, and when the stretcher cases were carried by, if they slowed down at our counter, to light cigarettes and put them into the mouths of the wounded, those who were conscious and would accept a smoke. I also helped to change the dressings of the walking cases, and it was my responsibility to gather up the old ones, covered with mud and blood and often lice. Men were coming straight from the trenches, in the state that they were in when they were wounded, with only a few hours' pause at a casualty clearing station, and then the rough crossing on a hospital ship, pitifully understaffed, a target for submarines.

We were the first people with time to talk to them.

"Well," we all said cheerfully, "so you've got a blighty" (a wound bad enough to get a man back to England, to "dear old Blighty" from a popular song). "Well, welcome home. Nice cup of tea? Cigarette? Postcard and pencil to write home? We'll post it for you. Well, glad to have you back." And we smiled with all the enthusiasm of the airline hostess of fifty years later. When I saw my first stewardess in a jaunty uniform bearing down on me toothily, I expected her to say "So you've got a blighty!" and gather up my old dressings to throw away.

The last hospital train drew in just before midnight. The last underground ran at five minutes to one. We rarely made it. It was oftener near two before we finished and left the canteen ready for the morning shift. That meant we had to walk home to the flat in Chelsea, a good three miles through the blackout, with only pinpointed torchlights to see by. It was especially difficult on foggy nights and there were plenty of those.

Noël Coward has a scene in his *Cavalcade* of a train nosing into a darkened wartime station, a hiss, a cloud of steam, the dim running figures with the stretchers, then a pause, and then the wounded carried slowly by. It lasts only a few moments on the stage, but when I saw it in New York some years ago, the winter of 1916 in London rose again around me, sharply alive. I felt the old indignant pity for the stupid war-making race of men, the young whose adolescent years, like mine, were frosted in May, the wounded, the lost, the decreed-superfluous. It made it worse to have to reflect that I was one of the lucky, protected children who spent those years on an island which was never invaded. What of the Belgians, what of the French, whose countries were overrun in that war and the war to follow?

"The Germanic tribes," Julius Caesar remarked in 55 B.C., "fall upon their neighbors with unnecessary cruelty, savagery and treachery." It was no new trait, but in 1914 it astonished a civilization grown accustomed to peace.

Aunty Nell was appointed "Lady Superintendent," a title she detested, of the big Canadian Y.M.C.A. Hostel, the Beaver Hut, in the Strand, with its thousand beds and three thousand meals a day for soldiers on leave. Whenever I was at home she took me with her as a volunteer helper.

I was there when the Prince of Wales came to inspect it and won the hearts of all the staff and the men drawn up on parade before him by his simple charm, his prodigious memory for this man's face—"Weren't you at Cambrai a year ago?"—and that man's medal—"Wasn't that for so-and-so in such-and-such an action?" "What is your name?" "I thought so. You were with the Princess Pat's in 1914...."

Oh, innocent, heart-warming, pre-Wally days!

Twenty years later, in December 1936, I was in a taxi passing Buckingham Palace when an official emerged to post the abdication bulletin. The taxi drew to the curb and the driver and I raced to the railings to read it. We came away downcast.

"Abaht time!" the driver said morosely. His King had let him down.

That abdication weekend I went to Helen's country house in West Wycombe. She was, through her marriage, a lady-in-waiting at the court, and knew the latest happenings, but though Wally had announced a few days before that she would "put that Duchess of York in her place!" ... which she did, right on the throne ... still, nothing had quite prepared Helen or any of us, still less the uninformed British public, for the sudden cresting of the crisis.

My small niece Sarah rushed to me, eyes popping:

"Aunt Evie! Aunt Evie! The King is a wicked man! He wants to marry a lady who's already married!"

Sarah was awed and entranced. Remembering the portraits of the King and the Royal Family hanging in every well-appointed British nursery, I knew what a prop had suddenly been cut from the structure of nursery discipline.

Instead of: "I can't think wot His Majesty would say if he could see such goings on, Miss Sarah, and well I never did!" here was Nannie complaining tearfully to Helen, "I'm sure I don't know *how* I'm to bring them up properly, m'lady, not after this, I don't!"

Some publisher missed the bus by not canvassing the nurseries of England for a special view of the abdication. Comments poured from self-constituted authorities not nearly so directly involved as England's Loyal Nannies.

It was while I was working at the Beaver Hut, addressing envelopes and watching Aunty Nell and her staff rescue men on leave from the clutches of fallen women in the Strand, that I met the Donegalls.

Lady Donegall, who worked with Aunty Nell on the Board of the Beaver Hut, was a Marchioness. The only Marchioness I knew was Dick Swiveller's friend in *The Old Curiosity Shop*. I liked to imagine that this stately woman must have spent her youth in a mobcap, struggling up and down steep cellar stairs with heavy pails of water, in a house in a slum, speaking fluent cockney. I knew better, of course. Violet Donegall was an American, the heiress of Twining Teas. But that was how Dickens said a Marchioness behaved and I wanted to believe him. I wanted to believe everything I read in books, especially in novels, which developed truth from fact. Fact was the bulb to the flower, and to me there was more truth, more dimensional truth, in the flower.

Lady Donegall's son, Don, whom she brought with her to the office to help me lick stamps, turned out to be the present Marquess, an Irish way of spelling Marquis. England, of course, spelled it properly. So did France . . . Britannia balancing her trident, Marianne tossing her red nightcap, bent together over a spelling book, doing it properly.

Ireland was a Law Unto Itself, better than a colony, but odd and rebellious. "An Irishman doesn't know what he wants and won't be happy till he gets it," Aunty Nell quoted. Ireland was perhaps a little *free*, or struggling to be free. "A wicked, wrong-headed rebellion. In wartime! We never mention it."

She meant to our Irish friends. All this threw a charming aura around the Donegalls for me. I was reading Yeats, and Stephens' *The Crock of Gold*, discovering the Irish and liking them very much. For one thing the Irish believed in an unseen world, which I knew could be seen at times, and in Ireland those who saw it were accepted in a natural sort of way, as the Donegalls took poets in their stride.

I was used to "Helen's Music" being treated with respect and fond encouragement, while "Evie's Songs of Protest" (the title of a notebook of my poems found in a schoolroom drawer) were "a weakness the child would outgrow." The Donegalls neither teased nor deplored, nor found it strange that I wrote poetry. To them it seemed the normal thing to do if your tastes ran in that direction. They were ahead of the times in believing that people should do their thing. Lady Donegall preferred painting to music or poetry, especially the French Impressionist School, but she was also an authority on French and English literature, and a "noted beauty," according to the *Tatler*. Several established poets had written lines or dedicated books to her.

Moreover she kept four Pekingese in her cottage in Kingston-on-Thames, where I went sometimes for tea, and to walk in Richmond Park among the deer, discussing books and life with Don, and what we were going to be.

He could be anything he chose, if the war was over before he had to go to it, or, if he had to go, he managed to survive. But I could only be married, if

I were lucky, if any eligible husbands came home from the front. It didn't seem likely, and there were already one million surplus women doomed to be old maids, among them surely tiresome Evie.

Then I would give a twist to my doom. I would be an old maid, if I must, while I was in this bewildering existence, while I waited for the Other to return or overtake me, and for us both to continue our flight to a better splashdown, but I would be a spinster like the ones in *Twelfth Night,* who were poets, or singers of poetry:

> O fellow, come, the song we had last night.
> Mark it, Cesario, it is old and plain;
> The spinsters and the knitters in the sun,
> And the free maids that weave their thread with bones
> Do use to chant it. It is silly sooth,
> And dallies with the innocence of love,
> Like the old age.

I would be a free maid and weave my thread with bones, whatever that might mean. It sounded like making poetry.

Don intended to be an explorer, climb Everest or reach one of the poles. He became a gossip columnist for the *Daily Mail,* or was it the *Daily Express?* Whichever did not have Lord Castlerosse. Those were the years when Society courted publicity like stars of stage and screen, and it was "done" for Don to be the English Hedda Hopper. The Souls, the Bright Young Things, Everyone needed him to write up weekend parties. Otherwise if you sat in the House of Lords there were very few things you could do, except take your seat and go to sleep in it. Don couldn't earn his living as a photographer like Princess Margaret's husband, or as a male model like Lord Litchfield today. Things were almost as restricted for a lord as for a lady, but Don's profession took him to every event he cared to go to, from the famous ball in Rome with the naked gilded footmen—one of them died from paint-poisoning, which was a pity—to the maiden voyage of the *Queen Mary.*

I intended to become a poet—I was a poet—I became, among other things, a novelist, with one small book of verse. Dylan Thomas liked to describe himself to audiences as "a fat poet with a slim volume." I could claim to be like him, but only shapewise, to use a repulsive word.

I was grateful to the Donegalls for seeing past the incongruous human envelope of the awkward schoolgirl, to the hermit thrush behind it, struggling to explain the universe in a few uncertain notes.

Now as I watch the confident young doing their thing, a little mixed up together so you can't tell which is which, wearing glorious crazy clothes and singing, when it takes them, as it takes them, and *being listened to* (in spite of loud complaints of being unheard, they are the most heard of any generation), I cannot help wondering, a little enviously, what it would have been like to splash down now, free, with the Other beside me, with an eagle feather in his hair.

It was from the Donegalls' garden on a moon-filled night, with roses, a nightingale and new-mown clover, that I went through my first Zeppelin raid.

Up to then the sky had been a vast expanse of "atmosphere," sometimes blue, sometimes gray, sometimes black; nothing moving through it but the clouds, the birds, the stars, the moon and—not to be stared at directly—the sun. We used to think, in quotes, "the army of unalterable law" and "that inverted bowl we call the sky" comfortably settled in its ways, orderly, unchanging, more or less predictable, what the French call *rangé,* with nothing man-made in it but children's kites on windy days.

Now, for the first time, there was something strange, mechanically directed, in the sky, a long, thin, silver shape, like a pointed finger moving slowly overhead, so beautiful we caught our breath and somebody applauded. I think we must have shown the same expressions as those later faces watching the Apollo missions and the landing on the moon . . . awe, delight, pride in man's achievement, hope. . . .

If the astronauts had suddenly turned lethal weapons on the earth and fired them with intent to kill as many people as they could, we would not have been more astonished, more incredulous, more helpless than we were that night in Surrey when the first bombs fell. Little piddling bombs to those They have now, but the biggest then, *the first.* The idea was new. And there was no defense, nothing to be done about it. The silver shapes came when they wanted to, and cruised slowly, unopposed, above us, taking their own time.

Antiaircraft defense was barely a concept, far from being installed. On moon-filled nights the Zeppelins came and the bombs dropped "at random," as in the second war, a generation away, bombs would also drop at random and the German radio, monitoring British news, would report "the important town of Random was destroyed last night by our precision bombing."

There was no radio in World War One and very little precision. Soon, in daylight, the first enemey airplanes began to arrive over London, guiding themselves by the Thames, up the river, down the river, passing over our flat in Chelsea twice each raid, dumping bigger and better bombs. One of them hit the Chelsea Pensioners' Hospital next door and broke all the windows in our building. It took six weeks to get them replaced and a week before they were even boarded up. It seemed a long time before a gun was installed in Hyde Park which could answer back. It didn't hit anything but it made a loud, reassuring noise.

Later I did see a gun hit something. I saw a Zeppelin downed, broken in half, into two falling fires, with smaller sparks that were burning men spilling out of them. I could not quite believe what I saw. I had fallen in love with the new sky. That there were enemies in it, intent on killing me and vulnerable themselves, was irrelevant, so too the probability that as a woman I would never be able to go up in a flying machine, as I would never be able to vote.

Yet a generation later, in the second war to end all wars, I flew thirty-three thousand miles with a group of war correspondents covering twenty countries, including a mission over the Hump between India and China. And one of my schoolmates, crippled since childhood with polio, flew in the Battle of Britain, ferrying planes from the factory to an R.A.F. base. It was rumored —she never denied it—that she flew at least one mission on her own over enemy territory and dropped her bombs at random.

Grounded again on the sofa, cripple on the earth, eagle in the sky, she became an expert in aeronautics, writing scientific papers for professional journals under a man's name, in order to be taken seriously. By then, too, she could cast a vote, whereas when we were at school together women were still legally classed with "lunatics, criminals and minors."

The twentieth century has seen the coming of age of half the human race.

Heathfield was the school my family chose to send me to, an ultra-snobbish nonsense place known as "the girls' Eton." On the day before I had to climb into uniform and catch the school train, the Donegalls took me to a musical comedy, much as we tried to distract boys going to the front. It was a very up-to-date show, with an actual airplane on the stage, canvas wings, wooden struts and open cockpit faithfully reconstructed from a downed one. The hero in helmet, goggles and dust coat, but breeches, puttees and spurs like a cavalry officer, stepped into it while he and the chorus sang the theme song:

"Going up . . . going up . . .
Like a rocket gone insane,
Sailing in an aer-o-plane. . . ."

We felt—we just naturally *knew*—that airplanes couldn't get off the ground by themselves. They were propelled into the sky like rockets, like an insane rocket...the whole thing was slightly lunatic...and we still *sailed* in them. The concept of flying had not quite come into focus for the general public. We spoke of air*ships,* all our terms were nautical and some of them still are—pilots, charts, navigation, landing, docking, boarding, airports, et cetera.

It was Tennyson, I suppose, who helped to put the sea into the sky. He also tried to prepare us for those dropping bombs with his airy navies grappling in the blue; and Shelley before him had his aery chariots and charioteers flying over cities "flocking to earth" for perfect landings.

The poets, as usual, were ahead of the rest of us as we entered the Aquarian Age. So were the Indians with their Great Birds transporting men.

Heathfield was not in the Aquarian Age, nor even in the twentieth century. It was early Early Victorian. The uniform, which was ridiculously extravagant in wartime, had to be purchased at a special establishment in Knightsbridge, called Swears & Wells . . . all swears and no wells, my mother said when she saw the bill for such items as six Spencers, two Good Sense Corsets, three Vyella Bodices and a garden hat. It was designed, all nineteen pieces of it, in the first years of the old Queen's reign, to discourage female vanity, which it did effectively. So did life at Heathfield, sadistically repressive, socially snobbish, hypocritically pious, like most church schools of the period. It was also High Church. We were "Romans who flunked in Latin."

Most of the girls had titles, there were very few commoners and only three colonials, including "littul Evelyn Vernon-Eaton," as the Headmistress and following her example the rest of the staff called me, inserting a hyphen between my father's first name and his surname. I protested, but Vernon was not a Christian name, They said, it must be part of a hyphened surname. One small hyphen could not take me very far in this world or the next, but it was the minimum token of respect required of a colonial. Eaton was a goodish name, the family name of the Grosvenors, with Eaton Place and Eaton Square named after it. Vernon too was a fine old surname. The two together, hyphened, would look appropriate in the catalogue.

My father's full name was Daniel Izak Vernon Eaton (he used only the initials of the first two), after his ancestor the printer, who in King George the Third's time lived at Three Amen Corner, Ave Maria Lane, in the City of London, where I also had an office in 1936, and where I found the bronze plaque commemorating him. He was four times tried before the Old Bailey for publishing Thomas Paine's *Rights of Man* and "putting it into the hands of the populace at a shilling a copy." Twice he conducted his own defense and was released, twice he employed a lawyer and was convicted of treason. He was put in the stocks, but "the populace brought him refreshments," which was not the idea, so he was hastily removed from the stocks and imprisoned instead. The records of his four trials and his intelligent arguments in defense of Paine's *Rights of Man* are on file at the Old Bailey and the British Museum. His name was never hyphened.

Looking well in the catalogue and doing well, that is, being accepted socially, were two different things at Heathfield. Even Royalty was not automatically acceptable, "completely desirable," if it happened to be *foreign*. Marie of Roumania's daughter, the younger Marie of Roumania, who became Queen of Yugoslavia, was never "in" at Heathfield, not because she was overweight—there were plenty of beefy English maidens galumphing about—nor because she had more knowledge of the world than her classmates—this was effectively hidden beneath her faulty English, as her appealing, friendly charm was hidden beneath the school uniform. No, it was not her fault, of course, but she was a foreigner. It was better than being an American . . . at least she was European . . . and far, far better than being a colonial, but still, it was not quite . . . well, for want of a better word, *English*. But was there a better word than English? Could there be?

There were one or two cases when even being English and possessing a title of the longest sort, *The* Lady So-and-so, in white letters across the top of the black domed school trunk, didn't qualify one necessarily for cozy life at Heathfield.

Eleanor Smith, for instance, in spite of being the daughter of the Lord Chancellor of England, "*The* Lady Eleanor Smith, daughter of Lord Birken-head," was more or less an outcast at Heathfield, not because she disliked the school and openly showed her dislike (she wrote about it devastatingly, later, in her autobiography, *Life's a Circus*), but because she was the granddaughter of a gypsy, married, it was said, to a tinker. While They pointed with pride to the spectacular rise of her father from plain F. E. Smith to earldom and the Highest Office in the Land, "from slum to Woolsack" as the *Daily Express* put it (proof that England was the only *real* democracy in the world), They also implied without saying . . . ("of course I didn't *say* anything, dear") . . . that there was a difference between rising in a sort of upstart way too speedily, and being born at the top, like themselves.

Eleanor was "brainy." All of us upstarts, except the Royal ones, were brainy. We had to be something. Those who were not abnormally bright had to be abnormally rich, profiteers' daughters, of which there was a sprinkling, paying, it was rumored, double fees.

Eleanor and I became good friends for the short time that she was doomed to Heathfield. Both of us were psychic. She saw and heard strange things and wrote of them in her books, but she was better able to distinguish between the dimensions, and rarely as confused as I was. Both of us intended to be writers, and both of us made it. Both of us hated the school and the two activities the school revolved around, games and Guides. In *Life's a Circus* Eleanor writes:

> Nobody asked you if you wanted to be a Guide. I didn't, for the simple reason that I was anxious during this period of recreation to learn Italian. This was thought unnatural, and I was forced to join an affiliation known as the Scarlet Pimpernel Patrol. Within a week, however, I was dismissed in Dreyfus-like disgrace; I had been caught committing an unforgivable sin—powdering my nose. I was more or less "drummed out" of the Scarlet Pimpernel Patrol, and this was one of the few happy days that I can remember during this wretched period of my life.

My experience was different. I couldn't have learned Italian, or Music, or Drama, or Art, or anything appealing or useful . . . these were Extras. I was a "charity child," that is, I was there on a scholarship, and this included noth-ing extra, except the tiresome chores for which I was expected to volunteer.

A Guide welcomes responsibility, according to the Handbook thrust on us, but I joined the Scarlet Pimpernel Patrol to escape responsibility, and also, if I could, to escape Miss Hogg, the Drilling Mistress, a lady so formidable that it never occurred to her victims to make fun of her name. (In fact, I have not used her right name here, but the real one was as short and as descriptive.)

Most of my schoolmates later developed quirks and fixations which they and their psychoanalysts traced to Miss Hogg.

She was short, hefty and overenergetic. She could roar along on her motorbike from her weekend cottage on one of the more ozone-swept cliffs of bracing Sussex to our unbraced corner of Berkshire, fling herself off it, throw down her coat, revealing blue serge tunic, black cotton stockings and thick games shoes, rush onto the playing fields, snatch up a lacrosse or a cricket bat and outrun any girl.

The first time I had to face her I was a new girl, frightened, determined to do my best, the shortest in the front row of the drilling division, lined up by sizes, so that there was no one ahead of me to copy. I knew enough not to turn my head, and I got along all right with the simpler exercises, though Miss Hogg grimaced, beat time and clucked at me. Suddenly she shouted: "As you were!" We stood panting, trying to conceal our lack of wind beneath our flannel blouses, while she looked us over scornfully, balancing back and forth on her pudgy legs. Then she shouted: "Shun! Raise the boom! One-two!"

I decided she must be referring in her hearty way and strong Yorkshire accent to what the Dancing Mistress, in dreadfully refined French, called the "dairy-air." I bent in a low kowtow and gave an upward hitch of the oops-a-daisy kind. There was a gasp and a snigger behind me.

"As you were! If you wish to adjust your undergarments, leave the room," Miss Hogg said acidly.

Boom, it turned out, had nothing to do with bum, it was balance bar. Raising it, one-two, meant that four girls detached themselves smartly from the line, took the heavy bar, climbed with it till it was ten feet above the floor, fixed it in place with wooden pegs, and ran back to their positions. The boom was twenty feet long and about three inches wide. We were required to walk it like a tightrope, chest raised, eyes rigidly fixed on a distant point above the head. When it was my turn to climb the side support, hoist myself up and start along it, I was still unnerved from the mistake I had made, and the public jeer it received. I took three steps, wobbled badly, tried to right myself, and was beginning to get the hang of it when Miss Hogg shouted: "Noel Power-tall!" and I fell off.

"My name's Evelyn Eaton," I said sullenly. It was bad enough to be bruised and shaken from a ten-foot drop to a hard wooden floor, without being called by someone else's silly-sounding name. Miss Hogg raised her eyebrows.

"I cannot imagine any information of less interest to us," she said reflectively. The class laughed. She repeated her comment slowly. This time I understood it. "No will power at all." She added, "Of course, if you played cricket . . ." and left the phrase unfinished. I could feel the cricketers behind me raking my back with scornful looks. "Well," she added grimly, "we must teach fair play to you without the aid of games."

It was her great grievance. She was in top form on the games field with all its opportunities for chivying a victim, and here I was, a colonial, a victim made to order, excused from games "with written consent of a parent and a doctor's certificate," because of an operation after falling off a horse. A rib had been taken from my side and grafted in my nose. It was one of the first experimental operations performed by Doctor Carter of the Polyclinic Hospital in New York, under whom Dr. Blake and other English doctors were trained to rebuild the faces of the wounded. The operation was only a few months behind me, and my nose was beginning to grow normally. A cricket ball or a bang of any kind might undo the whole delicate graft, with Dr. Carter then three thousand miles away.

I had explained this to the school doctor, the school matron and the school nurse, but this deviation from what she called "normal medical practice" annoyed Miss Hogg. She intimated that it was vulgar, dramatic and "typically colonial," a phrase she was fond of crackling at me, to have a rib in the nose. It savored of unhealthy ostentation. It could not be said to fit the school motto: "The Merit of One is the Honour of All." Later this motto was changed, lest any girl should suppose she might have merit, to "Work of One for Weal of All." Weal meant only one thing to my colonial mind, the kind of stripe one got from falling off the boom, one-two. I thought the motto was well chosen.

During the four years I suffered at Heathfield, there were very few days when I managed to escape rude public comment from Miss Hogg. I was, as she liked to remind the class, "charitably received among us, to learn our ways and take back to the colonies *some* of those traditions which are the backbone of our English heritage." In 1945, when I was asked to help "cement relations" between two countries, I thought of Miss Hogg's brand of cement, and how much I owed to it. Earlier than I might have, otherwise, I dropped out from bullying and bluster and sarcasm, especially to the young. I got a valued tribute from a student once: "You never put us down. You're the only faculty I've ever had who says right out 'I don't know' to a question, when They don't know. They always have to pretend They know everything...."

It chagrined Miss Hogg that in spite of all she could do to put me down I was popular, because I acted as a lightning rod for her destructive energies. My schoolmates cherished me as an efficient scapegoat, an obvious irritant drawing away her attention from them. The day they elected me prefect Miss Hogg referred to the "general lowering of the standards of the school, shown by the recent voting," and said that she would make it her business to supervise what she called my "poor qualities of leadership."

It was hard enough to be a prefect without Miss Hogg's supervision. I had reached the lowest point of endurance and come out in a nervous rash, when the Headmistress decided that she must "further a movement dear to the hearts of the Royal Family," and offer the school as an officers' training corps for the Guides. It was still the accepted principle that officers of any organization must "come from our public schools," wearing appropriate ties. Ours were dull green with bright-scarlet and baby-blue stripes.

Heathfield was the girls' Eton, and since our brothers at Eton, and even those misguided enough to be at Harrow, would be expected later to devote themselves to the good of their regiments, so we would be expected to organize companies of Guides "among the lower classes." Nobody said "underprivileged" then, or "disadvantaged." We spoke of the servants, the poor, the lower classes and even the criminal classes. The servants were the only ones whom we were ever expected to encounter, and they were to be dealt with firmly. I remember that my mother was considered eccentric, and even a trifle vulgar and colonial, because when her servants were *seriously* ill she would have the doctor come to see them and even let them rest for a day or two, however inconvenient it might be. She always hoped that no one would find out about this weakness, of which she was uncomfortably ashamed.

Exploitation was praiseworthy, the God of the Church of England had placed us all in our proper stations, upper and lower. Later, the lot of the lower, if they bore it meekly in this world, would be changed for the better in the next, though I think we all expected heaven to be run on much the same lines as England, and God to be an English gentleman.

In the meantime "all that" was far off, and the thing to do was not to be morbid about it, or tiresome like Evie, nor should one talk or listen to a lot of "wicked socialist nonsense" at tea parties or weekends.

The thing to do, while the worst and most atrocious and unnecessary carnage so far in history was just across the Channel—on fine days one could hear the guns—was for little English girls to strut about the playing fields in heavy uniforms, marching and countermarching in a travesty of military drill. That was what mattered.

What mattered to the Headmistress was that there might be a Royal Visit to the School. H.R.H. Princess Mary was High Commissioner of Guides. The formation of a new company would be an occasion for her to inspect it. That was what the Headmistress "envisioned," as we stood in our respectful ranks for weekly mark reading, before she dismissed us to what she called our "good pursuits."

Normally Miss Hogg would have prepared herself and us with unusual fervor and much raising of the boom, one-two, for a Royal Visit, but, as it happened, she was "against the whole occasion." She had not inaugurated the Guide Movement; the Baden-Powells tactlessly thought of it first; it was a new development; it did not exist when Miss Hogg was young; it "formed no part of her experience," and anything which formed no part of Miss Hogg's experience was "not to be given serious consideration," yet here we were, encouraged by the Headmistress, giving it time and thought. Moreover this was an organization claiming to teach fair play without the help of organized games. Miss Hogg found herself obliged to oppose it.

"It will not be the first time that I have run counter to Unsound Views," she said with a shake of the mane.

The Guide Movement formed no part of my experience either, and sunk in the complications of my difficult existence as a frog among English birds, also some poignant sorrows . . . my father's death, the realization that without him we would probably never go back to Canada, for which I was developing a desperate homesick longing . . . I would not have added its straw to my pack, but when Miss Hogg announced that she would have no part in the project, I signed up at once, eager to shed rank and responsibility for six hours a week. I was enrolled in the Scarlet Pimpernel Patrol, because it was considered weak after Eleanor had been drummed out of it, and its members thought that I would "show aptitude and pull the standards up." We all talked like Miss Hogg most of the time. It was infectious.

They were disappointed to find that I intended to remain a tenderfoot, tying only the most elementary knots and wearing no badges of distinction on my blouse. Some of my friends' sleeves and chests were already covered with round woolly emblems proclaiming that they boiled water, drew maps, rubbed sticks or found paths. How? Where? England was a well-kept garden. Any such pursuits as these would get them into trouble if they tried them in the "open air." As far as I was concerned the air in England was closed, had always been closed. Even without the blood and mud of Flanders and France and Gallipoli into which the young men of Europe were being sludged and massacred, I would have found this imitation military marching of school-girls on playing fields, forming fours, unforming them, this company drill, this pseudotraining for roughing it in the wilds of landscaped grounds more than absurd . . . frustrating. If it hadn't been so ridiculous I would have found it sickening, in view of the daily casualty lists . . . what, I wondered, was casual about them? I still don't understand that choice of words.

In a minor way I was daily chafed by English ignorance of anything to do with other lands, especially the colonies. Once the Geography Mistress swept her pointer down the east coast of Canada, taking in Montreal, a good part of Quebec, all the Maritime Provinces, and a large part of the United States, announcing that this was a prairie on which herds of buffalo and what she called *bee*son roamed. Claire Monroe, the other Canadian, and I raised timid hands. Montreal was a city, quite a large city, Quebec was never a prairie, nor were the Maritimes, deeply forested with real forests, mountainous. And there were cities there too. We did not speak for the United States, but in Canada the only *bi*son were now in zoos.

"Leave the room!" was the response we got for this truthful and helpful information, also two order marks which had to be reported at mark reading. We were absent from Geography for several sessions. When we got back the class was "doing India," perhaps more accurately, although I have never felt that I could rely on my acquired knowledge of the Far-Flung East. Certainly when I got to India in 1945, it was not the country we heard about at Heathfield.

. .

For love, my mother said.

> I have been so great a lover: filled my days
> So proudly with the splendor of Love's praise ...

We were reading Rupert Brooke in 1917. Rupert Brooke loved men, women, plates, cups, sheets, blankets, wood, clouds, a great machine, hot water, furs and old clothes, books, grass, roses and honey for tea.

So did, so do, I.

In those innocent days before the Freudian blight, one could have deep, passionate friendships without being branded a nymphomaniac or smirched by the whisperers as homosexual.

I have loved men, women, children, animals, trees, the sea, stones, planes, cars, an Alaskan sea lion, a lynx, passionately, tenderly, but not necessarily, always, *only* sexually. I have also had my share of sex. Most of it was fun and some of it was funny. I think sex should be funny, sometimes, to be right. Sex is a dance, a song, an expression of emotion, of love. There can be love without sex, a wide, tremendous range of it, but not sex without love, at least not for me, and I think not for my friends reared in Edwardian-Georgian nurseries.

The Entente Cordiale, which Edward the Seventh created to facilitate his romance with Sarah Bernhardt, introduced, or reaffirmed, against the heavy Germanic influences of his parents, Gallic, Latin, Celtic standards into England ... *style*. Style would be empty without content, content betrayed to dullness without style. Perfect Content in Perfect Form, we were taught in our Divinity classes, was the secret of the Incarnation. The *way* in which a moment was lived, acts, gestures, silences, especially silences, was the important challenge confronting us.

The Edwardian-Georgian habit of "not before the servants, dear, not before the children, dear, not before each other, dear," had its advantages. It led, if not to innocence, at least to a widespread, comfortable ignorance. I remember that Helen, a week before she married John, asked me what a prostitute was. She could not ask him, or the older generation, her mother, her aunt, or anyone outside the family, so, for once, she turned to me. I, after all, was more sullied by the world than she, I went to a boarding school, where perhaps I had been able to pick up information on asterisked subjects. Remembering those fallen women in the Strand from whom the Y.M.C.A. workers used to rescue falling men and take them to the safety of the Beaver Hut, I replied with conviction: "A prostitute is a wicked woman who tries to get soldiers drunk so she can steal their money from them." The explanation rang true to both of us, and deprived the subject of further interest.

Sinfulness protected innocence, the concept of sin, I mean, and of one's duty to the deity. For instance, English public schools are notorious hotbeds of homosexuality, yet I doubt that there were Lesbians at Heathfield. There were romantic attachments, crushes, "pashes" they were sometimes called, between children in the Third Form and divinities in the Sixth. Crushes were accepted with a sort of amused tolerance, though everyone knew they were sinful besides being silly. They were preached against in Lent as "inordinate affections." Not a mortal sin, but a serious one, which most of us indulged in. The sin lay in the *inordinate*. We knew as Heathfield Girls we must give our affections to God, with a modicum left over for our immediate families. We knew too that in any showdown or conflict of affections God must always come first.

It was difficult for me to give my whole affections to the Church of England God, since I had a standing grudge against Him, but, brainwashed, I accepted the principle in a remote sort of way and left it at that.

"Inordinate affections" explained many predicaments nicely, for example, in literature. We studied Shakespeare unabridged, and thoroughly. He was the great *English* genius. I have sometimes wondered whether we would have devoted so much time to him if he had been less English, less national, sounder on Agincourt and on Jeanne d'Arc.

We learned, when we came to the Sonnets, that very probably Shakespeare, at some time in his life, had an inordinate affection for a mysterious Mr. W. H. who stirred his soul (it was always the soul, never the flesh) and inspired him with some of his best poetry. Since most of us wrote poems to crushes who stirred our souls, this made the lofty Shakespeare seem more like ourselves.

It was the same in history. There was no need to be curious, or furtive, or troubled about the text of anything we encountered in our reading. We knew the terms for everything, and each term had a familiar, innocent meaning, taught to us casually, which we took for granted. Nothing had to be censored, or, if it was, the real reasons for the omissions escaped us. I remember when we gave *A Midsummer Night's Dream,* which I stage-managed ... because as a charity child I could not act, was not eligible for Drama or Diction ... with Jean Forbes-Robertson as Titania and Rosalind as Bottom, Hermia's speech refusing to marry Demetrius was cut to one line:

> So will I grow, so live, so die, my lord.

The speech continues:

> Ere I will yield my virgin patent up
> Unto his lordship, whose unwishèd yoke
> My soul consents not to give sovereignty.

We took it for granted that it was the word "virgin" our audience might be embarrassed by. Words like virgin, womb and bathroom embarrassed everyone. It was natural that "the parents and friends of Heathfield" should be shielded from them. They were coming to enjoy themselves, supposedly, not to be made uncomfortable.

It was still a problem of the soul, the *soul's* consent. "Yoke" meant to most of us two oxen side by side, plodding peacefully, as we had seen them in our illustrated history books. "Sovereignty" evoked nothing more sexual than Buckingham Palace and our being presented at court when we grew up and the war was over.

Rosalind and I took Greek. We translated the fragments "descended to us" from Sappho, and learned that she, like Shakespeare, had an inordinate affection for somebody, a girl called Atthis. In her case it was more excusable. There was no real Christian God for her to give her affections to. "Lesbian" had no connotation for any of us but the geographical one of "living on or coming from the Island of Lesbos."

In this way we were able to study the unabridged masterpieces of the world's literature in several languages, untroubled by a loss of innocence or ignorance. We got the *gist* of situations, love, jealousy, lust, murder, and because nothing was ostensibly withheld or covered over we did no further research, taking for granted the matter-of-fact explanations given us. We read our assignments and went on from there to discuss the beauties of style.

There were limericks and dirty jokes about sex, which we passed on to each other, giggling, but the meaning, the mechanics, the nature of the thing itself escaped us, even while we were sure that we knew all there was to be known about life and death and the Four Last Things beyond them.

> There was a young man of Hindoo
> Who had nothing whatever to do,
> So he sat on the mat
> And married the cat
> And sent the result to the zoo.

> There was a young lady named Starkey
> Who had an affair with a darky.
> The result of her sins
> Was quadruplets, not twins,
> One white and one black and two khaki.

Nice, obvious, cheerful nonsense that didn't trouble us. But nonsense one must never tell to Them, the parents, the grownups, the "friends of Heathfield." We were protective of the old.

At school, as at home, sex was neither funny nor conceded to exist. We discussed it in low voices, by trusted twos and threes around the steam radiator in the gym, the only comfortable place to gather, more or less unchaperoned . . . we were always in danger of Miss Hogg or a passing Power demanding to know if we couldn't find something better to do than coddle ourselves "in that unhealthy way." The English had a thing against warmth or comfort of any kind. Discomfort was a part of their religion. There was no decadent central heating in this richest of rich schools, no heating of *any* kind in bedrooms or bathrooms, and only the rare steam radiator in far corners of main halls. We had "our chilblains" and "our winter colds" as a matter of course, as people now have allergies.

Those moments we could snatch to warm our hands on tepid rusty pipes were bastions of resistance to which we held, from which we would not be dislodged. I spent most of my six Hogg-free hours a week at the radiator with Rosalind de Bunsen, Yvonne ffrench, Marie of Roumania, Eleanor Smith and a flotsam-jetsam of changing hangers-on. We talked about everything forbidden, especially sex. Once a girl came back from a weekend away and gave us to understand that she had lost her virginity. A friend of her brother's home on leave . . . patriotically she could not refuse. . . .

We gazed at her entranced, then someone, it may have been me, blurted out what was in our minds: "What was it *like*? I mean . . ."

"I don't know," she said. "I was asleep."

Her lofty tone implied "Don't you know one *sleeps* with a man?"

Only Marie of Roumania had a dubious expression. Perhaps her faulty English made her uncertain of what she had just heard. The rest of us nodded reflectively. It was what we knew, had gathered from books . . . one *slept* with a man, and during that sleep the mysterious change occurred. It was said to be painful . . . when did the pain begin? Probably when one woke. Before I could ask, "Did it hurt? I mean much? I mean as much as they say?" we were startled by the bell for evening prayers.

Not that Compline changed the train of thought exactly. There were uncertainties and fears about sleep, about beds, in the liturgy. Beds were compared with graves. "Teach me to dread The grave as little as my bed." As a child in Fredericton I got the notion and could not quite get rid of it that to be in right with God one must have an enormous grave, and I was disturbed to note that not even pillars of the church like Grandfather Fitz Randolph had been able to manage this. The cemeteries I walked in had narrow graves, smaller than my bed. It was disquieting.

Bedtime itself was disquieting, a mysterious hour full of quirks, and getting to it safely each day an achievement. We slept alone, in single rooms, or in our dormitory cubicles, behind heavy unbleached curtains tightly drawn. We could be expelled for disturbing those curtains, or even sitting up in bed behind them before the rising bell.

My first year at Heathfield I had a single room, looking across a drab metal roof to a row of grimly prying windows. It was at the head of the stairs. Its name was Holly. All the rooms were named for trees, flowers and the more innocuous saints, also a few poets like Wordsworth, Shelley, Keats. Byron was not considered suitable for a bedroom name.

When I reached Holly at 8 P.M. each day—for we all went to bed at eight, after the Silence Bell, even the eighteen- and nineteen-year-olds of the Sixth Form—I used to feel safe for a moment, after the painful, hazardous day, relieved to be alone and unobserved at last. Then the moment passed and I felt penned in, imprisoned, the old desolate feeling of those wakeful nights in 20 Barry Street when I listened to the penitentiary bell.

After worse than usual days I fell into a heavy sweating sleep and had what I told myself, even as I was having them, were nightmares, only nightmares. Beckoning shapes of horror filled the room. I could not see them in the darkness but I knew that they were there, burning blacknesses that I had summoned through some evil hunger in me. Once I followed a demon with a penny whistle down the carpeted stairs into the entrance hall, across the brick floor to the door, and out of it, running across the games field to the woods. All the way I shook with opposing terrors, terror of the figure I was following and could not break away from, terror that some human would see me and find me and smash the spell.

I woke as I was climbing into bed and the soles of my feet were muddy.

Night was always a dangerous time. The last hymn at Compline quavered: "Let no ill dreams disturb my rest, Nor Powers of Darkness me molest."

Powers of Darkness were on the prowl round everybody's bed. Dying in our sleep was a possibility, almost a probability, against which we prayed in chapel every evening: "If I should die before I wake, I pray the Lord my soul to take."

Now losing our virginity in sleep was another unfair hazard to be dreaded, but at least we were forewarned and there seemed to be a remedy for this one . . . the important thing was to stay awake, no matter how sleepy we might get, *stay awake* near a man.

What Brother Brooke and I had more in mind was romance, enchantment, when, as someone says, the soul seems to be the senses, and the senses the soul, the mood one hears in Ravel's *Ondine,* played by Gieseking or Iren Marik, immortal longings, intimations, shared remembrance of other dimensions, of There . . . for want of a better, less distorted, overused word, LOVE.

In love is another strand of it. Once I was in love with a boy named Desmond. He had flaming hair of a kind I only saw again on Maeve Brennan, the novelist, at the MacDowell Colony, in the winter of 1968. When she came into Colony Hall for the first time with the light full upon her, I said, stupefied, "Desmond!" Fifty years funneled backward and I was in the group round the radiator, back from the holidays, telling that I had lost, not my virginity, but my heart, to Desmond. Then I was in London for the Easter holidays, in my school uniform and ugly hat, gawking, across a drawing room full of suave, secure grownups, at Desmond in his uniform, new and shining . . . eighteen, just down from Eton and bound for the front.

The average expectation of life for a second lieutenant in 1918 was said to be three weeks. Desmond made it for ten days longer. Then he was killed. But not before we had ridden the top of a bus together to Kew Gardens and walked for an afternoon beside the river, holding hands, and walked again in the chaperoned gardens of Heathfield not holding hands.

I transposed the setting of those two walks to one I loved at Randolph, a forgotten path that wound through pinewoods to the sea.

Is it strange we tread again
Our wild wet wood-road to the sea?
Spring birds singing in the rain,
mist and haze fall heavily,
the earth lies open greedily.

Is it strange that I should stand
beside you at the end of years?
The sea is lipping at the sand,
most soothing sound a woman hears,
it has in it the depth of tears.

Love we have snatched this hour's lull
out of our lives' divergent ways,
circling above us one grey gull
drifts . . . drifts . . . is gone beyond our gaze.
This must suffice in after days.

In 1954, generations and a continent away, "Walk" was published in *The Small Hour,* and six years after that, the composer Joseph Wood picked up the book in my studio at the MacDowell Colony and set "Walk" and four other poems for women's choir and piano. Among those he chose was a poem written about the same time, "Midnight." "Midnight" has been set by other composers, and occasionally sung, but the Joseph Wood version is the one I like the best. Few composers marry words to music with his sensitive integrity.

"Midnight" was written when I was unhappy, when I had insomnia and must woo sleep. I was also discovering Ravel and Debussy and staying in a cottage near the Thames. The flowing river healed me, and I was grateful to the owner of the cottage for going away for the weekend and leaving me there alone.

MIDNIGHT

The silver fish of sleep go by
each with a glittering tail, and I
have come down to the river grass
to watch the slow procession pass.

Eleven of the twelve have gone—
I seize the last wet gleaming one,
slipping forward silently
through sleep's dark river to the sea.

Forty years later *The Small Hour* was performed, for the first time, at Oberlin, for the Festival of Contemporary Music held there in January 1960. I flew in for the premiere and when I saw the young choir file onstage . . . with spectacular hair but none like Desmond's, who might have liked to wear his shoulder-length . . . I thought how strange it was that no one there had known him, that he was dead long before most of them were born, that no one on the stage or in the hall knew the springhead of the poems Joseph

Wood had chosen and placed in a new sequence which I would not have thought of. They were written years apart, in different lands, at different times, and here they lived again with new and secret meaning to those who sang and those who heard.

As W. H. Auden said, "The words of a dead man . . . are modified in the guts of the living."

There was a magnificent black girl at the piano. I watched her serious, rapt face as the eerie accompaniment to "Midnight" began. The composer and his wife were beside me, we shared the experience of the premiere together, but I felt strangely alone. Even Joe, who had worked with them for months and brought them to new and felicitous incarnation, did not know the original occasions of the words or what went into them, their *Ch'i*. Desmond should have been there, or someone from that other incarnation in the Europe of the twenties, the Europe *entre guerres*.

Later, in the plane returning me to my this-day world of making a living and trying at the same time to stay alive, I wrote:

ON HEARING A CHOIR SING "MIDNIGHT"

Now the young voices sing
new music to old words
*the silver fish of sleep go
by*. . . . none here know
to whom I wrote of spring,
sleep and the rainwet birds
two wars ago.

Now it would be three or four or more wars ago. We have desperately stopped counting. And those of us who can remember how it was in the world when war was "unthinkable in our day and age" do not talk about those times to the young, nor even, much, among ourselves.

My father was killed at Vimy Ridge, commanding the artillery attack. He was wounded on Easter Sunday, which that year came on April 8, and he died on the following Wednesday, April 11, 1917. The news arrived in three telegrams, over the telephone, all within twenty minutes. The first telegram said: CONDITION IMPROVING. EAGER HEAR FROM YOU. VERNE. The second, which should have arrived two days before, had been held up in the confusion of the attack on Vimy Ridge. It said that Colonel D. I. V. Eaton, R.C.H.A., had been seriously wounded and was in Casualty Clearing Station No. 6. The third said that His Majesty King George the Fifth regretted that Colonel D. I. V. Eaton, R.C.H.A., had died of wounds received . . . et cetera . . . et cetera. . . .

He had longed for three days to hear from us and died the day before the news arrived. We could have been in touch with him. Telegrams and telephones still worked behind the lines.

I was at home for the Easter holidays and alone in the flat that morning. I answered the telephone. I listened to the brisk impersonal voice reading the telegrams, and during the days that followed, of shock, grief, confusion, it seemed to me that They, the Authorities, the King, had taken my father over, that he was now, in some strange, final way, Theirs.

A Cry-Dance would have been more fitting, more consoling to the bereaved . . . any sort of attended funeral, rather than this nothing-but-a-telephone-pad, with messages in my careful best handwriting . . . and no convincing proof that my father was dead.

Later my mother received an official letter, stating that her husband as "the Senior War Casualty of the Canadian Expeditionary Force" had been accorded a military funeral behind the lines, a gun carriage from his old "B" Battery, his own charger, boots reversed in the stirrups, the R.C.H.A. band playing the Dead March . . . but we did not see or hear these tributes, nor, speaking for myself, quite believe in them. Comforting lies, perhaps, for next of kin.

My mother got another letter, a long one in French, in beautiful old-fashioned script, from the Sister-in-Charge of the Casualty Clearing Station, a nun whose convent had been turned into this Emergency Hospital. She wrote that my father's wound, an abdominal one, had been too *grave* for him to suffer much; that he had been conscious, very cheerful, even *exalté,* had talked about us much, wishing for a telegram or letter to arrive, hoping and expecting to be going home to England, whereas, of course, there was no chance of that. The poor man was dying from the first, but she could assure us that he suffered little pain.

I believe that was true of abdominal wounds. It was the agonizing ones that could be recovered from.

He was buried in a small British cemetery at Barlin, a village near Vimy Ridge. In 1930 I visited his grave, and the convent that had been Casualty Clearing Station No. 6, and there I found the *Soeur* who had nursed him, and who said that she remembered him very well. Perhaps she did, for he was memorable and loved by his men.

Larks were singing the day that I went there. It was a small peaceful place, with only three hundred graves, not like the chilling acres of endless rows on rows in the bigger military cemeteries. Next to his grave, with the R.C.H.A. crest and his name, unhyphenated, on the headstone, there is another headstone with a blank where the crest should be, and underneath it: "A soldier, known to God."

I felt alone and resentfully desolate when I got back to Heathfield. Morning and evening my father was prayed for by the snobbish wrong name, among the "souls of the departed." It might have amused him; it irked me. I felt that it was insincere, another way of looking well in the catalogue, another "Heathfield Casualty," one more colonial privileged to die for England, for Home. There was no compassion, no real interest in my father's death, or his life, or his child, facing them. Three days after I got back, in the Current Affairs class, where we were required to read aloud selected news of the week, the History Mistress handed the paper to the girl on my left. This meant that I would be next to read. I had just time to realize that it was an account of the taking of Vimy Ridge by the Canadian First Division, when my turn came. I got through a paragraph and then began to choke.

"Speak up!" she said impatiently.

I tried, but my throat closed on the praise given to the Royal Canadian Horse Artillery. I lowered my head and in spite of angry pride began to cry.

"Next!" she said, giving me zero for the week's assignment. I do not know if then or later she noticed that I was wearing black, if she inquired or anybody bothered to tell her that my father had been killed commanding that attack. The zero stayed, pulling my average down from A to C, which for a scholarship child was serious.

No one spoke to me about my father's death. They prayed for him in chapel, and my obligatory mourning made me stand out everywhere, like an obscene shout, at a time when I craved obscurity, silence, healing peace.

Desmond died a year later, but I did not have to mourn publicly for him, his name was not tolled unctuously out in prayer by indifferent lips. No one remembered Desmond except my friends of the radiator group, and they pretended to forget.

Eleanor Smith revived my interest in gypsies. I told her about the black painted caravans in Canada and the precautions people took when the gypsies were due to pass through town. She introduced me to Borrow's books, *Lavengro* and *The Romany Rye,* and taught me some gypsy sayings. We quoted them in public, and passed notes in class, to remind us of reality. Eleanor was as hungry as I was for some contact with nature, with Mother Earth, with There.

On Saturday half-holidays we got together in a deserted music room to read Borrow. We left out all the "brothers" with which he strewed his pages. We didn't substitute "sisters." As good suffragettes, we felt "you" or "human beings" was a better expression. We used to wonder what men would think if the race was always referred to as "womankind," and it was explained that this included men, or if the press said "woman" has always this or never that, and "women think" when they spoke for humanity. We would have liked the story I heard later of the young suffragette who poured out her woes to Mrs. Pankhurst. "Tell it all to God," Mrs. Pankhurst said consolingly. "*She* will understand."

When I think of Mrs. Pankhurst I think of Dame Ethel Smyth, the composer, who was arrested with her so often. When women were finally allowed to receive the degrees they had earned, Dr. Smyth went back to Oxford and was presented seven times, with her various tutors, until finally she stood forth as a Doctor of Music. I was there on that occasion because a cousin of mine was also receiving her degrees. As the graduates appeared and reappeared each time with more honors and more hoods there was growing applause, until finally Dr. Smyth stood out alone. The last time that I saw her, she was conducting an orchestra on the occasion of the unveiling of a statue to Mrs. Pankhurst, the fourteenth statue honoring a woman, in England, over all the centuries.

She was wearing her academic gown and the colorful hood I had seen her receive in Oxford. As the orchestra burst into soaring chords I glanced at my program and discovered that she was conducting the orchestra of the Metropolitan Police Force, the very body which had so often dragged her and Mrs. Pankhurst off to jail.

"There's night and day," Borrow wrote and I passed on to Eleanor, "both sweet things; sun, moon, and stars, all sweet things; there's likewise a wind on the heath. Life is very sweet; who would wish to die?"

"I would," Eleanor scribbled back, "if I have to stay here much longer."

We spent a lot of time at the radiator discussing suicide and various ways of committing it. I don't know if Eleanor ever tried, but I did later, and bungled, thank the Great Spirit. I would have missed a rich, absorbing life, full of friends and felicitous moments, outweighing sordid struggle and some tragedy. Even those were turned to good. As the Egyptology Professor in the Musée Guimet was fond of pointing out, the lotus emerges from mud and from slime, and passes through dark water to the air and toward the sun.

Roses grow from corruption, but that is hard to remember when your face is in the mud.

I am glad I lived. I would not like to have missed the last fifty years, from 1921 to 1971. It seems to me they have gone crescendo, crescendo, opening space before them, in any direction that we look. It depends on where we look whether we transcend what we see, or are sucked into despair.

My father came to me in Fontainebleau when I was recovering from this attempted suicide, in what I might have thought was only a vivid dream if the woman who was taking care of me had not seen him too. She was a countrywoman whose father had been one of Napoleon's favorite huntsmen when the *Empereur* came to Fontainebleau Forest. When Napoleon's son, the little King of Rome, outgrew his first cradle, Napoleon gave it to this huntsman for his children. I bought it from his daughter for my daughter, Terry, who used it for a year. It was a lovely thing, with a swan's head in cherry wood, but the Pinaults were glad to get rid of it for what they thought a great deal of money, almost what you would pay for a new bed at the store.

Hélène Pinault was the seventh child of a seventh child, born with a caul and second sight. "There was a Monsieur here, in the room last night," she told me, "a Monsieur who knows Madame well. He crossed to where the baby sleeps and looked long at her, and then he came back to look at Madame. He said something, in English, I think." Hélène knew only French. "He was dark, handsome."

She went on to describe my father, even to a characteristic gesture of right hand to chin. There was no photograph of him she might have seen and I had never talked to her about him. She saw him, not in uniform, which she might have guessed or taken for granted at that time in Europe, but in a brown, rumpled suit. "*Ce pauvre Monsieur,*" she said, "badly needed a woman to look after his clothes."

Remembering how fastidious, even fussy, my father was about his uniforms, and how he was always in uniform, I was puzzled. Then she added, "And such a funny hat, with fishhooks and feathers in it."

That surprised me. In my dream I had only seen his face. But I remembered a shabby old tweed jacket he liked to wear on leaves when he went fishing, and how he stuck his extra hooks in the brim of a weather-beaten hat. I was glad that he had come to me in his old coat. Perhaps it meant that he was through with uniforms and wars.

I must stick it out to the end, my father told me in my dream.

It was not my time to die, not in the cards.

I showed Eleanor, at Heathfield, how my mother laid out the cards and she agreed it was the true gypsy way.

"But even if you know some of the secrets, they will never take you in, you have to be *born* Romany," she said, a little smugly.

I nodded, seeing again the dark carts passing by in Fredericton. But if I couldn't be a gypsy like Eleanor, I could be a poet, which was better than the novelist she planned to be.

I did not see Eleanor often after she left school and I left England, but I was present in the theater the night that she and eight others saw the ghost of Pavlova. We were watching Frances Dobell play the lead in Eleanor's *Ballerina.* She was due to enter in the second act, when not Frances came in, tall and awkward in her entrechat, but something small and exquisite, like swansdown, floating and staying in the air for that impossible suspension of time only Pavlova could manage, then drifting slowly, slowly, to the stage.

Eleanor had written *Ballerina* with Pavlova in her mind and heart, but Pavlova was dead.

There was a gasp in the front row. The figure straightened, taller, more lanky, more clumsy, quite incapable of doing what we had just seen. Frances spoke her lines, the play went on. Later, when Eleanor went round at the intermission, Frances apologized. . . . "What happened? How did I get on? Was it all right? I don't remember doing the entrechat at all . . . then there I was . . . I must have blacked out for a moment . . . I'm so sorry . . . I don't know what happened. . . ."

78

But I think she guessed. She was very shaken.

It was the last time I saw Eleanor. *Ballerina* was her pinnacle, I believe, although she wrote a number of other good and interesting books, especially her circus and gypsy novels, which would have pleased old Borrow, and her autobiography, but *Ballerina* had a special *frisson,* reminiscent of those stories we used to whisper to each other around the radiator at Heathfield.

Ascot was near enough to Windsor for Princess Marie of Roumania to eat her Sunday dinner at the Castle, when the Royal Family were there, and spend the afternoon with them.

One day she seemed pensive and upset when she rejoined the radiator group for the last half hour of free Sunday time. In the middle of a discussion about something else she asked suddenly, "What is a tank?"

"A tank," I answered quickly, wanting to get back into the talk, "is a great big heavy machine that goes over everything and squashes it flat."

When I turned around Marie had gone. The bell for silence rang, and I went back to the Sixth Form, where I found her in a corner, crying.

"Whatever is the matter?" I whispered. "Marie, what is it?"

"David called me a tank," she said and began to sob.

"Hush," I said. "The bell's gone. . . . He couldn't have. You didn't hear him properly."

But I knew that he could, that she had. The description was too cruelly apt. I put my arms around her. For some time it had been evident to a few of us that Princess Marie of Roumania was in danger of developing an inordinate affection for Edward, Prince of Wales. Those Sunday dinners at Windsor Castle after dull Heathfield days were too much for her. We also knew that "David" preferred brunettes, dark, slight, sophisticated girls, with blue eyes. "Violet-shadowed" was the term used by the gossip columnists.

We were in a good position to know those tastes of his. He had two inordinately affectionate affairs with sisters of current Heathfield girls. He even visited the school with one of them. They walked for an hour in the rose garden "incognito," spied on by Miss Hogg and most of the Guides.

Our poor blond bloated Princess didn't stand a ghost of a chance with David, but inordinate affection is no respecter of persons. It strikes where it lists, and, as Dorothy Parker points out, the fat suffer as much as the thin, with the added injustice of looking grotesque in their grief. Jane Austen, in *Persuasion,* said it before her: "Personal size and mental sorrow have certainly no necessary proportions. A large bulky figure has as good a right to be in deep affliction as the most graceful set of limbs in the world."

There were footsteps in the hall. We broke from each other, startled. What if Miss Hogg or some other passing Power discovered us in such a disgraceful breach of Heathfield Bearing? Marie blew her nose. When the footsteps passed she broke a rule for which a commoner would have been expelled if she were caught. She went upstairs to her room for a moment of essential privacy.

When we met again she was aloof and shy for a time, then the old easy association came back. The Sunday expeditions to Windsor tapered to an end. Marie left Heathfield for Roumania. We wrote to each other, but the correspondence went through so many censoring hands, and our lives to such different directions, that the letters grew stilted and ceased.

I saw her only once again, in 1934, in a strange encounter. No one, except perhaps an Indian with an expectant "when the time is right," or Marie, or I, would believe it happened.

I was on my way from Cagnes-sur-Mer to Paris for a dreaded operation. She was on her way from Paris to Marseilles, to take home the body of her assassinated husband, King Alexander I of Yugoslavia. Our trains reached Marseilles at about the same time. Mine had stopped at the northbound platform as hers was drawing in.

Millionth chance of a millionth chance, I got up to look out of the grimy window at the compartment sliding to a stop opposite mine. There she was at her window looking out at me. The wonder was we recognized our changed faces. It was fifteen years since we had seen each other.

My train began to move. I stretched out my hands to her. I mouthed, "I know. I know why you're here. I'm sorry." She said something too, then she put her hands to her mouth as though she intended to blow me a kiss. We both had our cheeks to the windowpanes looking back at each other as the trains moved apart. Something startled her. She turned her head. Someone must have come into the compartment behind her, an official to escort her on the next lap of the royal mourner's journey, or perhaps her Secret Service men had seen my face at the window and were afraid of another tragedy. She had been threatened with assassination many times since her marriage to the King of an unhappy, fiercely divided country. Now, as Queen Mother to the new King, young Peter the Second, she would be in more danger than ever. I wondered if she managed to persuade the agitated aides who pulled her back from the window that it was only two Heathfield Old Girls, Class of 1920, in an unplanned reunion.

There was another occasion at Heathfield when I tried to meet a need for compassion, for help, thrust suddenly upon me. I was crossing the entrance hall toward my classroom, at a time when everyone should have been at work, just before the releasing bell rang, when a child I had never spoken to, hardly noticed, in the lowly Fourth Form, ran out of the changing room sobbing and retching in some unendurable agony . . . blindly into my arms. She took hold of me wildly, clinging as though she would fall. We stood together in the center of the entrance hall, part of me filled with pity, part of me quaking in cowardly dread that Miss Hogg or Someone would appear and catch us in "an unhealthy, an indelicate position." We would be publicly disgraced, I would be expelled, probably she too . . . at any moment . . . but the moments passed and my arms remained, steadily holding, sheltering, lifting the terrible wordless grief of this unknown child.

Presently she raised her head and said my name in dazed, wondering tones. I loosened hold, we backed apart, the bell rang. There was the sound of opening doors and advancing feet. I smiled at her and she ran back into the changing room.

We never spoke to each other, nor met alone again. I saw her marching by at roll call and in the chapel in her place. Soon after I left Heathfield. A few years later she was at the Old Vic on her way to becoming a well-known actress. Now and then, watching her on the stage, or reading of her steady great success, I wondered what the devastating wounding blow was that brought her to extremity.

All I knew at the time was the aching soreness in my throat that lasted the rest of the day, and a literal, physical, emotional, mental, psychic sharing. . . . "Bear ye one another's burdens" is not a sentimental admonishment to be kind to people in trouble, like taking jellies to the poor, it is the actual lifting of too heavy karma from another's back. Not that karma is ever too heavy, but sometimes the bearer has a karmic right to have it shared.

There is also cosmic bliss to be shared. We do not hear enough about that.

From the daughters of the cream of England, for I went to school with an absurd elite, I worked my way outward, keeping very few of them as friends or acquaintances. Rosalind de Bunsen was one who persisted in an intermittent friendship over the years. We sang in the Bach Choir together. She had a strong contralto, I a thin, high pipe, no volume and no depth. When Ralph Vaughan Williams took over from Sir Hugh Allen and ran voice tests to weed out deadwood, I was among the first to be weeded.

"I'm sorry. We have too many sopranos. We need more basses."

"I could try to sing bass," I said earnestly.

He looked at me. I was wearing a very becoming red hat. I must have looked quite desperate and ready to cry.

"Oh well," he said, "I daresay you won't do the choir any actual *harm*."

So I stayed, swaying in the front row, with my mouth wide open, as if all the blast of glorious sound came straight from me . . . getting an excellent musical education for a layman. The choir had the right to attend all rehearsals, even those for orchestra alone. We sang with the London Symphony, the Philharmonic and other visiting orchestras. I went to every session. I was conducted, vicariously, as cellist, violinist, pianist, by Goossens, by Gustav Holst, whose *Ode to Death* we premiered, by Vaughan Williams, by others. I missed the Bach Choir when I left England. The rehearsals for Beethoven's Ninth Symphony alone taught me more than years of formal education, about music, about life.

Rosalind was one of the few people I kept in touch with. We seldom wrote to each other, but we were there, unchanged in friendship. It was like reaching the radiator again, with no readjustments required, whenever I got back to England for a visit.

I saw her after the long absence of World War Two, on the edge of a faultless English lawn, at twilight, milking a refractory goat. For a moment I didn't recognize that stately gray-haired woman, with poise and presence, and all those attributes I, and the goat, lacked. The occupation seemed a little odd, a little *outré* for anyone so beautifully dressed, and the setting of her father's country place too noble for the goat, but I remembered that during the war Rosalind joined the Land Army, and gave up her work on the stage for animal husbandry. The goat may have been a relic of that topsy-turvy time. Also, in the years of austerity after the war anything edible was valuable and valued.

Later, in 1959, when I was doing research on Edward the Third and witchcraft for *The King Is a Witch,* I stayed in Rosalind's fascinating minia-ture house in Hadleigh in Suffolk. It was a fourteenth-century weaver's house, Rosalind's first home of her own, and she was as happy, as fulfilled, as Beatrix Potter when, at the same time of life, she finally achieved her independent Hill Top in Near Sawney, and wrote the Peter Rabbit books in it and about it. Rosalind didn't write books illustrated with favorite corners of her home in Hadleigh, but she did bind them in leather and old gold, with a texture of weaving. She had a car to suit the house, a miniature three-wheeled "Bubble," into which she folded her majestic self and me, on expeditions into unspoiled parts of Suffolk, on the trail of witchcraft and Edward the Third. She was tolerant of my transatlantic nonsense that the King was the devil of a royal coven, although she had for many years, on much less evidence, considered me a witch, "a beneficent, pre-Christian witch."

I have not been back to England since, and if I went there now I should not find her.

After Desmond died it was a manless world. I went from my segregated school to my segregated home. No brothers, or cousins or uncles. The nearest male relatives were in Canada. Until Helen began to have dates (which we called "beaux") and bring them home for family approval, we went for weeks without speaking to a man.

Luckily there was Don. He wrote to me at school. Letters were like mail to the jailed. And he came to see me once or twice a term. "Lord Donegall for Evelyn Vernon-Eaton" . . . that little stabbing hyphen . . . was a soothing, welcome announcement, status-bestowing in that snobbish place, but more than that, it was friend and companion coming, co-conspirator.

I had almost forgotten the Other, and given up trying to find him, but I was still looking for a figure, father, brother, even mother or sister figure, *any* figure who would come toward me frankly, who would see me . . . people never saw me, never met my eyes. Even when I closed my eyelids people were always crossing in profile, right to left.

Once I met a bear in the New Hampshire woods who reversed the process, crossing the road ahead of me left to right. I was so startled that when it paused at the edge of the wood to give me a long slow look . . . it was twilight, almost dark, and yet it *saw* me . . . I held my hands out to it, laughing in absurd delight. Perhaps it was the safe response. It ambled off on its affairs, leaving me to feel that if I had followed it would have taken me with it to a honey tree.

This matter of approach is a phobic quirk for some of us. Some people dislike mice. I have a horror of crabs. They scuttle sideways. So do Cancerians, more politely, "Moon Children."

"Ah, Moon of My Delight that knowest no wane. . . ." I feel at ease with the Moon. (I was happier before trespassers turned her into a golf course for the unimaginative.) At one time I followed a cult of Diana.

"Diana, Goddess of the Moon / Will bring us into harbour soon," and she does. It is not the lunar aspect of crabs that troubles me, nor their involvement with the tides. It is the way that they approach the universe.

There was a lobster who loved a crab and was unhappy because his beloved never came toward him frankly. One day he met her walking directly forward and cried out, amazed and joyful, "At last!" "Get out of my way, you fool," she said. "Can't you see I'm drunk?"

Don was a brother figure who appeared to be *seeing* me, and even to like what he saw, and for that I liked him back. I might have worked up an inordinate affection for him easily as we went about together during the dreadful period of my first season among the flappers and the bright young things, but I never did. I think perhaps it was because with Don I could be myself, the weary old disillusioned poet of many other lives.

One thing that kept me from being deadened, permanently spirit-washed, at Heathfield, was that I had other-dimensional experiences, of the kind Elizabeth Bowen describes in World War Two as "strange deep intense dreams." " 'Whatever else I forget about the war,' a friend said to me, 'I hope I may never forget my own dreams, or some of the other dreams I have been told. We never dreamed like this before; and I suppose we shall never dream like this again.' "

My dreams during the earlier war were intense and horror-filled. Sometimes I was running, sometimes flying, mostly through fearful places on the lower astral planes, which I had not heard of then. Later, when I studied the Egyptian and the Tibetan Books of the Dead I recognized conditions, states of mind, figures in the Sidpa Bardo who attacked or befriended me, also the symbolic beings who encountered Dante when he woke from his deep wood. The lights, the sounds, the colors . . . for I dreamed in partial, distorted color

. . . the various stages of tests and challenges of these otherwhere journeyings, which I summed up half a century later in *The Progression,* a ballet-oratorio (composer Joseph Wood) were sharper, more significant than daytime happenings.

There was no one to whom I could turn for reassurance, for enlightenment about psychic experiences, or about anything important. I tried to hold my tongue, even with the radiator group, once I began to realize that people who didn't know what I knew, who couldn't see even as far as that, would be unreliable guides to anything further. If they, unconfused by other planes because they couldn't see them, didn't believe in them, were giving all their attention to this one, how was it they were so inept about their earth? For it did seem to be theirs to make a mess of. They were all-powerful. Life among them was like plummeting down among dinosaurs. One was confronted with a different species, strong, morally right, implacably set up in power and in judgment, who, if they could see or sniff out or come to suspect the heretic beneath my flimsy camouflage, would "soon put an end to *that.*"

George Orwell, describing his schooldays in *Such, Such Were the Joys,* speaks of a "sense of desolate loneliness and helplessness, of being locked up not only in a hostile world but in a world of good and evil where the rules were such that it was actually not possible for me to keep them. . . . This was the great, abiding lesson of my boyhood: that I was in a world where it was *not possible* for me to be good. . . . It brought home to me for the first time the harshness of the environment into which I had been flung. Life was more terrible, and I was more wicked, than I had imagined."

A. E. Housman asked:

> And how am I to face the odds
> Of man's bedevilment and God's?
> I, a stranger and afraid
> In a world I never made.

I did not stumble on those hints of others who were like me, then. All I knew then was that I was different, alien, and yet it was laid on me from Somewhere, by Someone, to survive, and to survive I must say what They might want to hear and hope to hit it right . . . and never, never trust Them.

Mistrust of the older generation is as old as humankind. Young men who came back drained and old from war in 1918 were as bitter and as angry as young men now who refuse to go to war. There was not so much violence in the streets, or mass confrontations, but there were some. Mostly the returning men and the women who loved them said as the brothers and the sisters say today about irrelevant or boring situations . . . "later" . . . and went about the business of patching up their broken lives.

I do not know how it would have gone for me if Desmond had survived. Some of my friends' brothers waited in blue hospital suits in Roehampton to be fitted with the clumsy, heavy artificial arms and legs which were all there was to offer them, no light aluminum or plastics were developed then. Some, blind, went about on a companion's arm, or with a white-painted stick—seeing-eye dogs came later. Some were in mental hospitals for shell shock. Some remained there for the rest of their lives.

Others who had come through comparatively unscathed begged in the streets, wearing bemedaled uniforms and masks to hide the shame of being "an officer and a gentleman" reduced to begging . . . returning heroes of Vimy, Ypres, the Marne, the Somme, the Dardanelles, for whom no jobs, no G.I. Bill of Rights were furnished or thought necessary. Some went back to their parents and lived on them as awkward strangers and dependents, some wrote books and songs of protest like Siegfried Sassoon's war poems, which changed the "lost generation's" outlook upon war and life and marriage. Many of my generation decided we would not be responsible for bringing children into the world until it was a brave new one, safe for democracy. Many of us decided around 1926 the conditions were stable and right, and went ahead with marriages and babies, just in time for the Depression and for sons to be the right age for World War Two or Korea. Our timing didn't mesh with the times. Mine, looking back on it, could not have been more inept.

Part Two

F*or money,* my mother said, laying out the cards.

Money has its feelings, money has its *Ch'i.* Money does not come to those who snub it, any more than people rush to people who delight to put them down. The rude and disdainful are avoided by those they brush aside.

My mother's attitude toward money was Victorian. Money was something nice people naturally had, but never mentioned, "not before the servants, dear," never before the guests.

Nice people "came into" their money from rich parents, who left them well-to-do. Nice people married "well," with substantial marriage settlements. Nice people's wives and daughters, especially their daughters, were not expected to know anything about "the world of affairs." Ladies concealed any interest they might have in the source of their settlements. A girl who understood dividends was in danger of losing her "bloom," Jane Austen's word for the mysterious idiocy which made her attractive to nice men.

My mother agreed pretty well with Jane's Emma and Lady Catherine de Burgh and Aunt Norris about money and the taint of low connections in trade. The trouble was that while she had managed the first requirement of a nice girl by splashing down to rich parents, she had made the mistake of marrying a comparatively poor man, who was killed at forty-six in a senseless war, leaving her his debts and his daughters. My mother had no idea how to handle this legacy. She wrote to her brothers, who still managed the family business, now Randolph and Baker, to send her some money, because there must be plenty "there" and she needed her share of it.

It was impossible for her to understand—it would not have been *nice* for her to understand—that times had changed and there was now no family business to speak of, and what little equity there was did not belong to her but to the business partners of the enterprise. The brothers explained, singly and together, that she and Aunty Nell had long ago been bought out of the company, that they had both received full payment for their equity.

"Equity" was a word my mother associated with King Arthur and the Table Round, a quality. If there was equity, her brothers, who were Fitz Randolphs and therefore the souls of knightly noblesse, would send her what she needed. But, she wrote, she could not wait too long, she needed equity *now.*

More expostulations came. She put them aside with the bills and tried to lose herself in books, the biographies and poetry "everyone" was reading. She did make one concession while she waited for equity to set in. Instead of buying the books and having them bound in expensive leather editions with the Fitz Randolph coat of arms on them, she joined the Times Book Club in Wigmore Street, and twice a week we walked together to the Club to change them and have the new ones delivered . . . it was not ladylike to carry anything through the streets, even a book, though sometimes if it was a special one she had been waiting to read she would let me slip it under my arm and take it with us, pretending not to notice.

Meanwhile non-nice tradesmen sent respectful requests for payment of accounts long overdue, and the brothers wrote from Canada inviting us to stay with them until her affairs could be straightened out and a home for us found within the limits of my father's meager pension.

My mother was outraged. Surely they must know England was our Home. All she wanted from them was to send her what she asked them for, money. Down she sat at her walnut-inlaid desk in the morning room to write another long emotional letter which I copied for her to be referred to later. I addressed the envelopes and took them to the post. Helen, at the height of bloom, must not be allowed to risk dimming it by hearing about bills, duns, money. Even during this trying time of "temporary straits" my mother managed to send Helen to the right weekends at the right times with the right people. Helen was my mother's consolation for the stupidity of the brothers, the provincialism of her advisers, the general unsatisfactory condition of the world. Helen, my mother thought happily, pushing aside another bill or another letter, could be depended upon to do the right thing, turn the right heads without losing her own. She had mothered a perfect daughter, and the brothers were cold-hearted clods if they could dream of dragging us back to Fredericton to live where there would be no suitable young men for Helen.

No one expected me to develop bloom, or keep my foot out of my mouth or do anything *nice*, but I could be shipped off to Paris to be out of the way. Someone could always be depended upon to come through with equity for the really necessary things, like not spoiling Helen's chances with a tactless younger sister who didn't look English. A finishing school was the proper place. I was sent to Mademoiselle de Verez's École Pour Jeunes Filles in Passy, until it became too expensive. Then, we all agreed, I could be finished just as well in a family, and incidentally learn much better French. One of Mademoiselle de Verez's chaperoning teachers took me home with her. Her mother was the widow of Joseph Ollivier, brother-in-law to Émile Ollivier, Prime Minister of France in 1870, and also brother-in-law to Liszt's daughter, Blandine Ollivier. "La Tante Blandine" was often talked about by the two old ladies who were her nieces and their wizened mother who was her aunt. I settled down in an attic room, filled with boxes of letters and memorabilia of Liszt and his entourage, especially "the lady who shared his life," as they delicately referred to the Comtesse d'Agoult, as though there were only one, which for them there was.

I had finished my formal education. To be in Paris on my own, in an indulgent French family, with all the *Ville Lumière*—within reason—to explore, was a heady experience. It colored my life and brought me back to France at crucial times, for love, childbirth, marriage, divorce. Then I could understand the family feeling for England, France became my Home and but for the "goings on of that there Schicklgruber," as the Cockney put it, I might have been living there still, in my favorite *Quartier*. But then I would have missed some complete and crowning fulfillments in Canada and the United States, and I might not have four American grandchildren.

My years in France are covered in *Every Month Was May* and *The North Star Is Nearer,* collections of short stories published in *The New Yorker* between 1946 and 1960, in the great Rossian days. France was also the background of several novels. The France I knew was not the France of the American expatriates or the international set. It was a more indigenous and indigent France of the little underdogs. I went through the Depression there, of the second-class métro, yesterday's bread, the sou-by-sou struggle for survival. Some of these experiences are in my early novels, *Desire Spanish Version, Summer Dust* and *Pray to the Earth.*

In 1922, with Hitler still in the future, I came back to London, reluctantly, confused about money but trying to come to grips with it. My confusion was more than Jane Austen attitudes or Victorian ostrichism. I had a fundamental inability to take money seriously, a hatred and contempt for banks and business as the enemies of poetry.

The redskinned people, and in this perhaps I was a throwback, have no natural affinity with money. They do not have the instinctive kinship with it of the ghetto Rothschilds, the built-in understanding of the ebb and flow of gold, silver, copper, paper, to buy and possess and hold. The great civilizations of the Indians before the white man arrived flourished without money or the concept of money. The Indians did not *possess* material things. One missionary reported of the Paiutes that he despaired of their becoming civilized because "they have no concept of selfishness and persist in sharing all they have." Other agents complained of the backward, unenlightened way an Indian presented with his half acre of land on the newly created reservation would sit in the dust and do nothing, or poke listlessly at the earth . . . after being free to hunt and roam the entire continent.

One thing "the Savages" could not understand and would never subscribe to without compulsive pressure was the notion of accumulating wealth through private property. Especially they rejected the idea that a man or group of men could traffic in the Earth, could buy, sell, fence in, deny the right of others to approach, to hunt or fish or camp or simply to pass over any part of the Earth our Mother.

They felt about the land as we used to feel about the sea, as until lately we felt about the air, that it was common to all, the two-legged, the four-legged, sharing the planet with us, for the wise use of all.

I came back from France the first time with a sheaf of poems, and what Sir James Barrie in one of his plays called "the twelve-pound look," the price of the first typewriters when they appeared on the market. Barrie's play was about a wife who discovered that a typewriter could be the door to freedom from marriage. I was not thinking about marriage or freedom from it, I was thinking about bills. I talked with Aunty Nell—it was impossible to talk with Mother. She lashed out furiously, or told me to write again to the uncles and demand our equity. Helen must not be talked to, must not be troubled by anything sordid. Aunty Nell, though she was older than my mother and unmarried, was less Victorian and far more spunky about flouting what "the world" might say. She agreed with me that if I felt equal to the sacrifice, I might, for a little while, until I got married to a nice young man, which of course I naturally would, she asserted stoutly, staring at me absently, work at something *suitable*. I stared back. Aunty Nell was beautiful, a rich man's daughter, at a time when there were many more "nice young men" about than in England after World War One . . . yet *she* had never married. What chance would there be for me? But I was brought up not to dispute any statement by my elders and betters. We turned to the business of enrolling me in Mrs. Hoster's Secretarial School for Young Gentlewomen with its suitable address in Grosvenor Place.

The six months' course cost fifty pounds. Aunty Nell would lend me this amount, "make the investment," as she put it, and I would repay her when I could. Thus my aunt, a model of integrity, launched me on an attitude toward money that requires a good deal of courage and thickness of hide to live with . . . borrow, invest in the need of the moment, rely on the English system of overdraft and repay when you can . . . when something comes in from somewhere . . . my mother's dreams of equity, or "money from the land," except that I had to earn the something for myself.

Mrs. Hoster, small, wizened, shrewd, had a well-appointed office in the city, staffed with eager students paying her for the privilege of working there, "acquiring actual office experience" during their last three weeks of the course. Since her placement agency got us our jobs for the rest of our working lives, we naturally exerted ourselves to please her during those three crucial pre-graduation weeks. The letters and manuscripts that came out of Mrs. Hoster's Translation and Secretarial Transcription Bureau were tasteful works of art and a hundred per cent accurate. She had a great reputation in the City, and a box at Covent Garden for the opera season, where I used to see her from my shilling perch in the gallery, sitting alone in a black silk dress, flashing diamonds from an old-fashioned tiara.

I made one friend at Hoster's, Helen Dashwood, nicknamed, for some

English reason, Babs, with whom I used to eat lunch sometimes. We shared a bag of cherries, walking through the park or along the river embankment, talking together of our future plans. Babs intended to work for a year, save up her salary and spend it on a trip around the world. Later she did just that and I envied her. Not only because my family would never let me go around the world—I could hardly go around the corner unopposed—but my salary would have to go on bills, and living and paying back Aunty Nell's investment.

We shared other things besides our plans. Her plans, that is. Mine were nothing to talk about. We shared a dislike of town, a craving for the country, for nature. I told her about the Canadian woods, she told me about the beech trees near her home, with bluebells carpeting the ground. I told her about Paris and how I would rather be there, where the air seemed alive with light, and one could *think*. Though even there it was town and people and pavements. London was worse. "The twice-breathed airs blow damp" described London. I read her my poem "Rain."

> Rain on pavements in the night
> walks quietly.
> Her feet are soft and cool and white,
> they do not bruise
> the tired pavement's aching head
> with sharp uneven high-heeled shoes
> and mincing tread.
> The old gray cobbles croon and mutter
> songs to her from every gutter,
> when she passes, sleepily.

She liked it. "I may go around the world," she said, "but you're a great poet." I agreed with her. No sense in false modesty. I told her how much I disapproved of Society and coming out and marriage. She told me she had thoughts of becoming a socialist. I described Heathfield "bearing," she described the repressions of a governess-ridden life.

We were getting along well, until one day we came to our lunch meeting troubled, awkward, embarrassed. We had learned over the weekend that her brother and my sister were engaged to be married. It was a shock to both of us. We had ranted in general against our backgrounds, but we had been reticent about our families. Now all that we had kept apart from our independent lives and from our friendship would be thrust upon us, not only now, but for the future. We did not approve of our nearest and dearest, but they were still dear, and we were bristling in defense. What should have been a bond between us became a barrier.

Babs' brother was the premier baronet of Great Britain, Sir John Dashwood. His country place, of the beech trees and bluebells she invoked nostalgically, was the famous home of the Hell Fire Club and other notorious eighteenth-century goings-on, West Wycombe Park, in Buckinghamshire.

It is one of the great show places of England, now belonging to the National Trust, although the family is still allowed to live there. Sir Francis Dashwood, who was also Lord le Despencer, employed the greatest architects of the period to design it, Robert Adam and Nicholas Revett among them. He brought Italian workmen, plasterers and marble cutters over from Rome and with them the Italian artist Bergnis to paint the great ceilings. The house was stuffed with treasures, which are still there to be enjoyed by tourists, chimney pieces of white Carrara and Siena marble inlaid with jasper, bookcases by Chippendale, doorframes of imported colored marble, a grand staircase of red mahogany inlaid with yellow yew, a tapestry room built for a weekend visit of George the Third, a great hall with paintings by Hogarth, Zoffany and Romney, a large salon, or ballroom, 100 feet long by 40 feet wide, with the ceiling painted to represent the "Banquet of the Gods," based on Raphael's designs for the Villa Farnesina. The façade is 240 feet long, with a colonnade of forty Doric pillars, and above them on the second floor another row of Corinthian columns. It is the only example of a double colonnaded building in England. The west portico is a copy of the temple of Bacchus in Greece, the first attempt to incorporate Greek architecture into an English country house.

Sir Francis was a man of taste and knowledge, founder of the Dilettante Club, which transformed and set the pace for all the arts, but especially for architecture, in eighteenth-century England. He was also immensely rich, and even for those ribald times, excessively lewd. Some of his inventions and devices so shocked John Wilkes, himself no prude, that he could only describe them in Latin, and " 'Tis astonishing," he said on one occasion, "the lengths Dashwood will go, simply to be nasty."

The grounds at West Wycombe were laid out to be both beautiful and pornographic. Daniel Mannix describes them in his book on the Hell Fire Club:

> Even today the garden is regarded as one of the most perfectly balanced landscaping compositions of all time. Lawns as green as emeralds and as smooth as a billiard table led down to the swan lake. There is a little island in the center on which stands a tiny but exquisite Greek Temple. Woods surround the lake on the three other sides. Flowerbeds, studded with Greek statues and fenced by carefully clipped boxwood hedges, spread out to the south of the house, interspersed with little pools and fountains often connected by rustic bridges. Paths of soft moss led to small Greek temples set about the grounds; the Temple of Flora, the Temple of Daphne, the Temple of the Four Winds (a copy of the Horologion of Andronicus in Athens), and the Temple of Music. There was even a canal with gondolas floating on it. There were also Water Gardens, Wildflower Gardens, and Wood Gardens hidden away among the trees where lovers could stroll in complete seclusion or swim by moonlight in the marble pools.

> The lake was so large that Dashwood kept a full-rigged ship on it as a sort of toy for his visitors.

The garden was laid out as a naked woman, elaborate fountains of milk and of water could be turned on to startle the stroller. Embarrassed descendants did away with most of this décor, but the general outlines can still be seen from a plane. There was another temple, later destroyed, which Wilkes describes as follows:

"The entrance to it is the same entrance by which we all come into the world and the door is what some idle wits have called the Door of Life. Lord Bute particularly admired this building and advised the owner to lay out 500 pounds to erect a Paphian column to stand by the entrance."

These phallic symbols and odd decorations were nothing to what Sir Francis did with the ruins of Medmenham Abbey, which he bought to accommodate his Hell Fire Club. Many books have been written about the Hell Fire Club and the not-so-nameless orgies that went on there. It was a licentious age, and also an age of grace and charm and reason, but the accounts which have come down to us of the proceedings of the Hell Fire Club, the Friars of Saint Francis of Wycombe, as the founder preferred to call the group, were tasteless and ugly.

The important thing about it today, to those not hooked on humorless pornography, is the membership, which included many influential members of the government, among them the Earl of Sandwich, who was First Lord of the Admiralty, and the Earl of Bute, who was the Prime Minister, and as the seducer of the Princess Augusta, wife of Frederick, Prince of Wales, controlled her son, King George the Third, from his childhood. Bute hated the American colonists, supported every act against them, including the Stamp Act, and bitterly opposed any attempt, particularly Edmund Burke's, to find a peaceful solution.

The people of England hated him "with a rage of which there have been few examples in English history," Thackeray says, and on several occasions, in spite of his bodyguard of prize fighters, tried to murder him. He was probably more responsible for the inevitability of the American Revolution than any other single influence. In this he was opposed by Sir Francis, a staunch friend of Benjamin Franklin, who also attended the Hell Fire meetings, and by John Wilkes, the people's idol, who was a founding member. It was a practical joke, played by Wilkes on Lord Sandwich during one of the meetings to celebrate the Black Mass at Medmenham, that brought about Wilkes' political downfall, and gave victory on the American question and every other to Lord Bute, Lord Sandwich and the "King's friends."

Other names have come down to us on the records which survived destruction by horrified descendants who burned the contents of the library—the catalogue is a collector's item—and all the records of the club's transactions. . . .

Some of the characters of the Hell Fire Club were: *Bubb Dodington,* Lord Melcombe, enormously rich, the first requisite of membership in the club, and as enormously obese. Another member, the poet Charles Churchill, describes him in one of his amiable couplets about his fellow friars:

Bubb is his name and bubbies doth he chase,
This swollen bullfrog with lascivious face.

But he was the intimate friend of the Prince of Wales and so had considerable political power.

Thomas Potter, the son of the Archbishop of Canterbury, is credited with having corrupted John Wilkes, and was spoken of as "Wilkes' evil genius." He beat his wife to death after exhausting the fortune for which he married her, and made brilliant speeches in the House of Commons, for which he was rewarded by an appointment as Vice Treasurer for Ireland.

Paul Whitehead, the only comparatively poor man to be a founding member of the club, was considered a brilliant political satirist. Sir Francis made him the club secretary and he had charge of the smooth running of the club, the club accounts, and the writing of blasphemous hymns to be sung at the Black Mass. Later he married a half-witted cripple for her dowry of ten thousand pounds, and was unexpectedly good to her.

George Selwyn, "the first of fashionable wits," was attracted by corpses and visited undertakers regularly, especially after public executions, which he always attended, mostly disguised as an old woman. He went to France especially for the horrible execution of Damien, who had tried to kill Louis the Fifteenth, and was given a front-row seat for the torture with red-hot pincers, breaking on the wheel and tearing to pieces by horses.

There is a witty anecdote about him attributed to Lord Holland on his deathbed. "Should Mr. Selwyn call, show him up at once. If I'm alive, I'll be glad to see him, and if I'm dead, he'll be glad to see me."

Hogarth, the painter, was a member and has left us several sketches of scenes at the Hell Fire Club meetings. The Earl of Oxford, Horace Walpole's elder brother, reputed to be a half-wit, was another member, Sir Henry Vansittart, who became Governor of Bengal, the Duke of Kingston, the Marquis of Granby, Sir Joseph Banks, President of the Royal Society, the Chevalier d'Éon, whose sex was indeterminate, but whose enigmatic influence over the King of France, whatever clothes he wore, man's or woman's, was unbreakable, another Vansittart who was a professor at Oxford, Laurence Sterne, the novelist, all were friars or regular attendants at the Hell Fire gatherings. No less influential were the women, Lady Mary Wortley-Montagu among them, who, dressed as nuns and wearing masks, mingled with the regular bands of specially prepared vestal virgins from three of the best brothels in town.

These were the people who had an influence on history out of all proportion to their numbers. Whenever one comes across them it is like plunging into the fetid atmosphere of a small, more ruthless, Versailles.

I knew nothing of West Wycombe when John and Helen were engaged. The eighteenth century was touched on very lightly in my Heathfield History classes. Statesmen's morals were never mentioned. They might have been interesting but were difficult to explain, even under the handy heading of "inordinate affection."

Later I was relieved to learn that John was not descended directly from Hell Fire Francis, but from his half brother, a John Dashwood to whom the estate and the title passed, since Sir Francis had no legitimate sons. Also, on the distaff side, John could claim the poet Milton, which may or may not have added some stability and spiritual values to the strain.

All I knew at the time of the wedding was that Helen was marrying a "nice young man" and would be joining the Establishment, which, in those days we called, a little vaguely, "the world," meaning, as it still does, a few hundred people with wealth and influence. Helen would share, among other things, a diplomatic career. John was in the Foreign Office, a staunch Conservative, Sir Stafford Cripps' right-hand man. Later, both would have positions at the court of King George the Fifth and Queen Mary, John as Marshal of the Diplomats and Helen as lady-in-waiting.

When they married, John was still recovering from his experiences in World War One. He had enlisted at eighteen, risen to major at twenty-two, and commanded the first tank attack. He was blown up and buried alive, rescued only after he had heard the digging party about to give up. Then someone said, "Let's turn a few more spadefuls for the poor bugger," because, luckily for him, he was a popular officer. Ian Hay described him in *The First Hundred Thousand*. John is the original of Bobby Little.

He was also trying to get over the loss of his only brother, a year younger, listed missing in action when he was eighteen. George Dashwood's identification disk turned up in a German grave which was being relocated after the war. No one ever discovered what happened to him, why it was there.

The wedding took place on a December day at Saint Margaret's, Westminster. There were twelve bridesmaids in silver lamé gowns, three flower girls and two pageboys in blue velvet, with agitated nannies prompting them as they carried the long train in. I was the chief bridesmaid, leading the procession, with Babs marching beside me. She may have known who the others were. I didn't. It was bitterly cold and I wore nothing under my gown "in order not to disturb the fit." I shook and shuddered through the ceremony with its lovely robust Bach and the other trimmings Saint Margaret's is famous for, and afterward through the reception, in a horde of supercilious strangers.

Frog among birds . . . If it was hard for me, it must have been worse for Babs. She was losing not only her brother, but her home and even her name. There would be another Helen Dashwood now, the one the "world" would mean when it said her name. Babs, her mother and stepfather, for the Dowager had married again, would have to leave West Wycombe when Helen and John moved in.

Babs would have her job and after it her tour around the world. But what for Helen? It was a waste for her. She might have been one of the world's foremost pianists. The three recitals she gave in London were acclaimed by the critics more than those of Myra Hess, who made her debut at about the same time. She might have been a rich, warm human being. But she was caught in the Victorian steamroller, more a victim of the system than I was. Less educated, that much older, and approved by everybody, all "the world," she could not break free and yet could not be happy, so much of her discarded, so much unfulfilled.

Her wedding was a far cry from mine, in the seventeenth arrondissement of Paris, on a Saturday morning, when the workers marry, an affair of papers, passports, a surrender of principle, not an affirmation of it, a believer in free love standing reluctantly before Monsieur le Maire, with two casual witnesses picked from the crowd.

One afternoon last summer I was talking to a small Arapaho called Charlie Duck, who asked me suddenly: "Are you 'rolled?" I said tentatively, no, I thought not. "I'm not, either," he said wistfully. "I'm 'rapaho but not 'rolled. To get 'rolled you have to have your father and mother fixed up good together, and they have to be 'rolled."

I asked him what was so good about being 'rolled if you could be 'rapaho without it?

"If you're 'rapaho *and* 'rolled," he said, "you get the money."

I checked. Enrollment as an Arapaho requires legal marriage of the parents, their enrollment and the legal marriage and enrollment of the grandparents. It was a question of the division of the tribal money. Poor little Charlie Duck. His world, like mine, was early divided into those who belonged and those, like him, who couldn't belong, through no fault of their own, unless you count karma, not taught in any widespread way on reservations or in British nurseries.

I wrote about West Wycombe as Carre in *I Saw My Mortal Sight,* and as Wycherley and also under its own name in *Give Me Your Golden Hand.* I had some strange experiences at Wycombe, beginning with the first time that I stayed there, in 1923.

Helen put me into a charming little room, done in bright chintzes, with cozy lamps and everything inviting and welcoming about it. I felt a sense of well-being and pleasure, and went happily to sleep.

In the middle of the night I woke, drenched in horror, and lay still in agonized listening for Something about to assault me. I sat up and turned on the light. It made no difference. The room was filled with darkness, the heavy psychical blackness of an approaching horror. Something in the room above me was moving across the ceiling with rough uneven steps. It was coming downstairs, roll, bump, slither, a measured distance between the sounds, but there were no stairs near, only the grand staircase across the great hall. This descent was at my ear, fumbling, thumping . . . something in the closet opening the door.

I screamed, as I had screamed in my dreams at Heathfield, and no sound came. Something reached the bed and seized me by the throat, shutting off my breath, squeezing my windpipe. . . .

I struck at it. I called for help. I sent my astral wail into the universe . . . and suddenly was freed, gasping, strangling, whooping for air, believing I would die before I breathed again, yet thinking lucidly and stumbling to the door. I groped into the blackness of the hall, full of marble statues and massive furniture. I made no attempt to look for lights. Lights could make no difference, as I had just found. With all its dim vastness and shadowed corners full of menacing shapes, it was safer than that small bright room. What I must do was *breathe*. I tried, and waited in agonized congestion, and tried again, until finally I sucked in a little air. Then I sat down where I was, on a marble bench near the wall, and gave thanks that I was going to live.

I spent the rest of the night sitting up, alert on the hard cold bench. I did not dare to lie down, nor to move and risk arousing It again. I didn't want attention from anyone, human or inhuman. I wanted to breathe, endure, somehow survive the night. In the morning . . .

In the morning I went back to the room, with the first sound of stirring maids carrying hot-water cans. I got into bed and turned out the lamp. When a pleasant-looking woman came in I tried to relax, watching her prepare basin and towel for my morning wash. I asked her cautiously (because one must keep one's place, "the servants didn't like it" if you talked to them as though they were human beings) how long she had been at the Park.

"A long time, Miss. Seventeen years, it will be."

"Then you must know . . ." I stopped short, and changed what I was going to say to "Then you must know Miss Babs?"

It was a silly question, but maids were used to foolish, condescending remarks. She answered matter-of-factly, "Oh yes, Miss. I've known Miss Helen almost since she was born." She glanced around her. "This was her own room."

She plumped up the towels, smiled at me respectfully and left. I lay still, thinking.

If this was Babs' room, then why . . . ? I am a friend of Babs . . . wouldn't It know that? But *that Thing* had nothing to do with Babs, with anyone living. It was some primeval foulness from the dead. "The dead and damned. Dead and damned."

My voice was hoarse and raspy when I spoke. I got out of bed and looked in the mirror. There were marks on my throat, bruises, turning purple. I would have to wear a scarf. Perhaps my own hand had seized my throat in a nightmare. I did not believe it, even though I knew nothing then about West Wycombe, the Hell Fire Club, the legends.

Helen was not at breakfast. Later I found her and told her I would like to change my room.

She frowned. "Don't be tiresome. It's a lovely room. Babs always had it. . . ."

"I know she did, but I can't stay there."

"Nonsense. There's nowhere else to put you. And besides . . ."

"Besides, what?"

"Nothing. I suppose you've been listening to the stories."

"What stories?"

"Did something happen?"

"Something certainly did."

"It can't have. There's nothing wrong, and if there is, it doesn't bother women. Babs always slept there and loved it. Lots of guests . . ."

"Does it bother men?"

"One or two crashing bores left in a fuss. But you're just showing off. It *never* bothers women."

"Well," I said, "it bothered me. Can't I change rooms?"

"No. The house is full. Don't be so tiresome."

"Then I think I'll take the train back to town."

"Do."

I did. I don't know what she explained to John and the guests. Probably nobody noticed that I had come or gone. They may have thought I was another ghost. The English habit of not introducing people to each other at house parties made this sort of disappearance easy.

Some years later, when workmen were making alterations, they found a concealed staircase leading to the closet in Babs' room, from a walled-off windowless space above it no one had known was there. When it was broken open it revealed a Masonic temple in miniature, with distorted symbols and some elaborate blasphemies. When I heard of this I wondered whether the gentlemen who fled, inconvenienced, happened to have been Freemasons, and whether my being a member of International Co-Freemasonry, which admits men and women and works the Ancient Scottish Rite, had anything to do with my experience.

Nothing more was said to me. When I next stayed at West Wycombe I was given a room at the far end of the hall.

Certainly the house was haunted. Too many people saw and heard too many things there to doubt it. There were voices and footsteps on the colonnades at night, which might have been amorous guests on the prowl, but there were the same sounds in broad daylight which couldn't be explained away. Sometimes there were wild poundings on the dining-room wall, and doors would open and close when certain music was played, especially water or fire music. There were dogs who growled and whimpered, and one sprang at something, dashed out of the room in furious pursuit and dropped dead in the hall. There were things the children said.

Sarah, when she was five, asked me: "Aunt Evie, do you like him?"

"Who?"

"Him." She pointed where there was nothing.

"I'm not sure. Do you? Tell me what he's like."

She stared, with a see-for-yourself-Stupid expression.

"There. The big black monkey . . ."

"If you don't like him," I said, "say a prayer as you do at night and tell him to go away."

"Well . . ." She sounded doubtful.

"We might say together 'In the Name of God the Father, go where you belong.' "

"Oh . . . he's making faces. . . ." Then, "He's gone. He didn't like us, Aunt Evie."

"No, but we don't like him either, popping in and out. Just tell God the Father when anything bothers you, then we're all right."

I was bothered. I thought of talking to Helen, but I knew she would be annoyed and call me tiresome for putting ideas into Sarah's head. Nannie would think it wrong for Miss Sarah to say her prayers, except in church or at bedtime. John would be furious. He always denied that his home could be haunted. "Protoplasm. There's always a lot of protoplasm in old houses," he used to say when he was faced with audible or visible manifestations that couldn't be explained away to those who were tactless enough to be on the spot to see and hear them.

"Protoplasm," he said firmly, and as he was the host that usually ended the discussion, at least while he was there.

When my mother moved into Mill End House, in the village, she noticed that if Helen went away for a night, John would call up to propose a game of bridge and find it too late to go home when the game came to an end. He would linger and rub his eyes, and ask for another drink, and say it was odd how *tired* he felt, until it became routine and taken for granted that he would stay for the night. Mother had the guest room made ready for him whenever she heard that Helen expected to be away. She thought it was touching that John was so lonely without Helen, but I thought perhaps he was afraid of being alone in that part of the house at night, and too proud to summon the servants. I would have felt the same.

When Sarah was about six and Francis, I suppose, four, we were having tea with Helen when the butler entered, followed by a footman carrying a painting in a massive gilt frame. It had just been discovered in one of the unexplored corners of the third floor undergoing the process called a "turn-out."

"There he is! There he is!" Sarah said as the painting was held up before us. "There's the monkey. You know, Aunt Evie . . . the one that runs about."

Helen looked crossly at me. "Time for Nannie," she said firmly, and rang the bell for the children to be removed to their part of the house, behind the solid, separative door, hung with green-baize curtains to muffle nursery sounds. Distracted by the need to say goodbye to the guests, Sarah said nothing more. She started on her rounds bobbing curtsies. Francis followed, bowing, his hand on his little fat belly, the nearest he could get to his heart.

Nannie appeared, the children left, and Helen told the butler to put the painting back where it was found. We all knew it was the portrait of the barbary ape to which Sir Francis administered the consecrated Host when the Black Mass was celebrated at Medmenham, or West Wycombe, or later in the caves beneath the hill, which can still be seen by tourists.

John drifted in for his tea and nothing more was said about the painting. Once when he was away Helen had a famous spiritualist come down for the weekend and go into a trance to discover what was in the house. Later, members of the Psychical Research Society came to see what they could find. I never heard the outcome or saw the reports. Helen tore them up, I believe. But after that, when she could manage it without disturbing John, she had the house exorcized, first by the Vicar, then by a bishop, and once, I believe, by a Roman Catholic prelate.

The effects were the same, an improvement in the atmosphere, "less protoplasm," which lasted for a time, the sights and sounds would recede, and then they were apt to return. Ghosts, of course, are part of English country life. They do not interfere with social gatherings. The ghosts at West Wycombe liked gatherings, were famous for their own drunken brawls, and Helen's weekend parties were coveted events of the season, the hectic, merry seasons of England between the wars.

In 1970 I went to a powwow on the Wind River Reservation in Wyoming. I was staying with Arapaho friends whose sons and daughters were taking part in the dancing. It was an intertribal meeting for the purpose, among others, of choosing the yearly queen, as whites choose Miss New York, Miss Florida, et cetera, and there is now on the national level a Miss American Indian.

My host's daughter had been queen two years before. The sons had won many trophies for dancing. There was an obvious family and tribal pride in what the Arapahos were doing, but a Crow girl won the contest, tall, more beautiful than pretty, who danced in a particularly dignified and modest way and was dressed in authentic buckskins which did not thump on the eye as some of the more colorful, almost Hollywood, entries did. I would have voted for her if I had been given that privilege and I felt the small but solid satisfaction one has from a confirmation of good judgment in an unfamiliar field. But what interested me most was the dancing, all ages, all sizes, no dancer touching another, though sometimes groups would circle in the same part of the great turning ring, turning always anticlockwise round the room. There were older men with stern, sad faces, younger men with eagle feathers circling shoulders and rumps and eagle feathers in their hair, small boys with bells on their leggings and turkey feathers on their rumps, whirling and stamping. The women were more plainly dressed and danced on the edge of the circle, in groups of threes and fours. Now and then a few, usually older women of obvious tribal importance, advanced against the tide, circling clockwise. While they danced the voting was in progress.

When the queen was finally elected, after several ties and extra dances, she was led to the judges' table, there to be proclaimed. Her name was given and tribe, and age, and the history of her dress, her *coups,* that is, her achievements in the Indian and white worlds, the name of her sponsor, and then it was announced that she would lead the final dance.

She turned from the dais and began a slow, simple step in a wide sweep round the room. The runners-up, now her maids of honor, danced in pairs behind her. As she circled us slowly there stepped out from the crowd, in blue jeans and workaday dresses, her father and mother, her grandfathers and grandmothers, other members of her family, her sponsors, all older people, swinging in behind her, taking up the step. Stocky, independent, proud, dancing with dignity and grace, eyes straight ahead, grave-faced, every part of them cried:

"This is what we have produced, this is what we stand behind!"

Look, look well, oh wolves, Kipling had Mother Wolf cry, showing Mowgli to the pack. This was a *look-well* too.

Watching that display of pride and love and confidence I thought of my own presentation to the world at the court of King George the Fifth, in Buckingham Palace, half a century before.

It was evening then, too, and tribal music playing, and ritual steps taken, toward the King and Queen and backward from the Presence. My name was called, my mother named as the sponsor presenting me. The history of my dress was not given, but the nature of it had been rigidly prescribed. The court was in minor mourning, therefore only whites and silvers and pale lavenders could be worn. Mine was the silver dress I had worn at Helen's wedding, with white kid gloves to the shoulder, the traditional veil and feathers.

The chosen queen of the intertribal powwow *earned* the right to wear the feather in her hair, an eagle feather, which is not lightly bestowed. The three ostrich plumes I wore meant nothing to me. Some long-dead Prince of Wales had the whim to choose them for his emblem along with a motto in German, *Ich dien,* I serve. Possibly women wore them at court to show that they were servants of the crown, but nobody explained them, nor was anything said to me on that cold official occasion except "Take care not to tread on the train in front of you, keep two paces behind." As for dancing . . . if my family had swung in behind me, as these did for *their* girl, how different some things might have been!

What about the runners-up? The Charlie Ducks of the world? Later perhaps they will dance in the general throng, and who is to say what feathers their children or their children's children will wear at what great future powwows?

The thing is, the world should *dance* on these occasions.

There was nothing warm and proud for me, nor, I believe, for the other girls presented beside me that night, only the humiliating certainty that now we would be officially on the marriage auction block and since we were, that year, wartime surplus goods, we must make a special effort to get ourselves disposed of before more seasons passed.

I have written of the glittering visual effects . . . Queen Mary displaying the royal diamonds as no one else was able to wear diamonds, walking toward us with the King . . . and other observations, in *Every Month Was May*. I am glad I went through the experience, if only for its pageantry. Nowadays the traditions are relaxed or changed, and it is not such a frightening ordeal.

What frightened us? Me, I should say. I cannot speak for the rows of sleek veiled feathered heads. First, I suppose, the frog-among-birds syndrome; then the fact that I had not practiced my three deep curtsies and might stick at the bottom or fall over; the train I might step on and tear; the trauma of being out there in the center, in the Royal Presence, stared at, as my name was called, by "all the world"; but mostly, I think, the family dissatisfaction in the product they were launching, and my blind trust in them and their judgment. I had tried my best, but my best, as usual, was not enough, was not like Helen's, who never had to try at all.

As on so many other occasions, the most I could hope for this one was to live through it, and get back to my desk in the morning, for I was "not before the servants, dear" actually working, earning my living as a typist in a secretarial pool, in the City on Threadneedle Street. There I was, bird-among-frogs, and if they, where I worked, found out that I had been presented at court the night before, there would be as much disapproval in the office over parasitical antisocialist goings on as I met with at home over grubbily earning my living.

I existed at that time in overlapping hostile worlds. My days belonged to the sordid realms of trade, the business world in which I betrayed my class. My evenings and weekends belonged to the marriage market, the world of the right people doing the right things in the right way, in which I betrayed myself.

Luckily, or perhaps unluckily, there was a third world, the only world I accepted for mine, the world, the universe, of the poet. There I lived, moved and had my being. There I was what I was, under the grotesque disguise of a girl. For poets were always, or nearly always, men. The exceptions led horribly dull lives. Who, in love with forests, mountains, nature, freedom, would want to live like Emily Dickinson, or, in spite of walks on the moors, Emily Brontë?

If an unmarried girl, *jeune fille,* old maid, was an object of indifferent derision, how much more so an unmarried-girl, *jeune-fille,* old-maid poet? Poetess, lady novelist, woman writer . . . how different from poet, novelist, writer.

"All pity for Miss Dickinson's 'starved life' is misdirected," Allen Tate says in *Essays of Four Decades.* "Her life was one of the richest and deepest ever lived on this continent. When she went upstairs and closed the door, she mastered life by rejecting it." One wonders what the man who wrote that would have felt if because of the way his physical body looked to others he had to live all his life upstairs behind closed doors? The poets I walked with, taken seriously as their equal, such was my superb conviction, were Shakespeare, Shelley, Keats, Rimbaud, Verlaine, Baudelaire and Walt Whitman, besides all those in *The Oxford Book of Verse* whom I read and approved.

The French poets seemed to me more practical and less sublime than the English trio I wallowed in. The French poets appealed to my torn emotional being. With Rimbaud I knew all about seasons in hell. It was where I mostly had to abide. With Baudelaire I would search for a new shudder, having exhausted the old. With Verlaine I would suffer mysteriously and plaintively from the results of inordinate affections. But with Keats and Shelley I would soar into the impersonal sexless universal world of . . . what? Vibration? Light? Cosmic Being? There.

"This is what you shall do," Walt Whitman said.

Love the earth and sun and the animals, despise riches, give alms to everyone that asks, stand up for the stupid and crazy, devote your income and labor to others, hate tyrants, argue not concerning God, have patience and indulgence toward the people, take off your hat to nothing known or unknown or to any man or number of men, go freely with powerful uneducated persons and with the young and the mothers of families, read these leaves in the open air every season of every year of your life, re-examine all you have been told at school or church or in any book, dismiss whatever insults your own soul, and your very flesh shall be a great poem. . . .

I could and did say yes to all of that, until the next encounter with my contemporaries, who saw me otherwise, and were borne out by the mirror, little Evelyn Vernon-Eaton, on the marriage auction block.

"Hello, Evie, written any epics lately?"

"How about a few quotes from the latest sizzling love poem?"

A girl who *worked?*

"I mean to say, what's amusing or chic about work?"

One must be amusing or chic. Helen was both, had always been both.

Still, I was a poet and those who could not see it now would see it later. Cornel Lengyel, in his introduction to a book by Gustav Davidson, *All Things Are Holy,* writes:

"Knowing the shortness of his lease on earth, the poet must decide what he can do with his portion of time. Not what he would, but what he can and must do."

I tried it with female pronouns. "*Her* task as an artist is the transmutation of time, and *she* knows that the purchase price of anything valuable in life is usually life itself."

I was willing to pay that price, and ready to transpose anything said to or about poets into the feminine gender. I did not want to be a man from any penis envy or Freudian put-down, but I did want to be free from arbitrary and ridiculous restrictions. "An unmarried woman must not walk down Bond Street alone." "A girl cannot go into any profession." "A girl can only be a governess or get married." "A girl must be careful of everything she says or does." If I envied men, it was that they could be anything they chose, they could go right out and make mistakes and suffer and write, and no one found them ridiculous because they were "only men, born to be husbands and fathers."

"To preserve *her* own angle of vision and give it durable form, the artist may have to stand apart from or against the current tide."

Yes to that too. I would continue to transpose the pronouns:

"Whether classic or romantic, *she* tends by nature to be revolutionary. . . . For this and related reasons, an original poet may find *her*self an outsider in any age or company."

There were other precepts to add to Whitman's.

"To avoid easy applause, to shun the glare of the limelight, to court unpopularity and risk premature or permanent oblivion, these may be ways in which *she* purchases the privacy which *she* may need for developing *her* particular vision."

Yes indeed. It would not be hard for little Evelyn Vernon-Eaton to court unpopularity, it was already thrust upon her. But I did not want to transpose *her* with *him* so much as to deal in one impersonal all-inclusive pronoun like the French *on,* the Hungarian *eu.* One could, of course, go into the plural: "The majority of artists, though fueled by burning ambition and laboring furiously, earn little lasting glory for their efforts. Though many feel chosen, few are recalled by posterity."

But I, *on, eu,* was different. Fueled I might be, sure of being a great and lasting poet I most certainly was, and as to being recalled by posterity, that was inevitable. There were four notebooks of poems to ensure it. Only I didn't know what to do with them, once they were written in the special *cahiers* with French squared paper I thought suitable for enduring works of genius. It never occurred to me to send them anywhere. From all I had read, poets gathered in the evening to read their works to each other, or went on long walks in the Lake District or on the Moors, wherever those places were. I didn't know any poets to do these things with. Helen knew the Sitwells, they stayed at West Wycombe, but I would have been far too terrified, especially of Edith, to venture into the same room.

The other procedure toward emergence into poetic fame was to be pursued by an editor, as Francis Thompson was pursued "through London's darkest corners of shameful night," by Wilfred Meynell, who, married to Alice Meynell, knew the value of a poet, even of a woman poet. Alice Meynell had landed on her feet, her winged feet. The poems did betray her anguish—

a poet must be anguished—hers had something to do with a Catholic priest. Francis Thompson's anguish had to do with her. Also they were Catholics in a disapprovingly Protestant England. So was Coventry Patmore. It seemed to be his only anguish, which might account for the less turbulent tone of his elegantly despairing odes.

While I waited to be discovered and pursued, the notebooks filled. I was reminded of this stage of what the French call *pas à la page* when in 1963 I was waiting in a stranger's living room for a meeting of the Central Democratic Committee, a Democratic grass-roots organization I had wandered into temporarily. The meeting was in the little hamlet of Olancha in California. My hostess was a simple, earnest woman, a lion in the good fight. We were alone together when she suddenly whirled on me.

"They tell me you're a writer."

I admitted that I was.

"May I ask you a question?"

"Of course."

"Did you ever have anything published?"

I caught back my gasp. I was looking at her as she asked, and I could see, and my ears hear, that this was not a put-down or a wisecrack or a slip of the tongue, nor anything it might have been from someone else. She was respectful, inquiring . . . this was something important to her, something she wanted to know, something she had probably not been able to ask before because she had never met a writer.

"Yes," I said. "I have had things published."

I was glad there was no officious someone there to set her right, no one to explain that being a writer means having what you have written published.

"Poems?" she asked wistfully.

Now I held the key to this tense little exchange. There must be notebooks in this house, scraps of paper, backs of envelopes, in straggly or precise penwomanship, tucked away in boxes, in drawers or jam jars. I found myself looking obliquely for signs of hiding places. Here she had waited, all the years, to be pursued, to be discovered. . . . Meynell lived in England, there was some excuse for his not finding her, I thought a little wildly, while I heard myself answering:

"Yes, I have had some poems published."

There were sounds of committee-arrival at the door and I rushed on:

"You have to send them out, you know, to poetry magazines, and sometimes the local newspaper will print a poem. You can get lists of places from the library, or buy a magazine like *Writer's Market,* and then . . . just send them out. . . ."

My voice trailed away as the first talkative ladies erupted into the room and after that I had no chance to speak to her nor she to me, except to ask if I would take lemon or cream in my tea, an irritating question. I have long given up trying for a little milk, which is how I like it best. I opted for coffee and she smiled at me. I do not think she wanted to talk. Does one chat with a *deus ex machina* when at last enlightenment rips across the sky?

No one told me about the market for poetry in magazines. I had always read poetry in books. Even if I had known about it I would have been distressed at the idea of selling my immortal words about inner holy things to a magazine. A magazine was like a newspaper, and since the episode of the Montreal *Star* I had a prejudice toward newspapers. Yet I wanted my work to be read, "read, marked, learned and inwardly digested." I felt a grave responsibility to report to the world, to share my unique discoveries.

I did not, like Emily Dickinson, reject the world—if she did reject the world. It is a man who says it. Probably she only rejected the double standard. I loved the world, not "the world" my mother spoke of, mine was the world of poetry, the strange lands, inner and outer, which I trod with the poets in courage and despair . . . "putting on the agony, putting on the style," as a folk song has it.

There was also bliss, the emotion a poet knows, pride, joy, humility, when the first copy of a book arrives that strangely bears your name, an extension of yourself, conceived, reared, lived with, written, rewritten . . . rewritten . . . and now in stumbling words, a limping travesty, at best a poor translation of what was rich and magnificent before you set it down . . . still, uniquely yours, the best that you could do with the tools at hand.

The experience came to me, I did not go to it, I was in a sense pursued by a publisher to bring out my first book.

It came about through valiant Aunty Nell, who had taken me in hand with the same zeal she brought to managing the Beaver Hut. She was making it her mission to get me married somehow "in spite of everything." Neither of us probed the "everything," and she was inclined to think that I was at last trying to co-operate. I was working at the Lithuanian Legation, a better-sounding place, which could be lent a certain glamour. I hunted at weekends when the meets were near West Wycombe and I looked my best on a horse, especially galloping off in the distance. I went now and then to the right dances with whatever partners I could manage to scrape up.

Invitations in those days of man scarcity were issued by hostesses to "Miss So-and-so *and partner*." Without a partner, no admittance. Girls like Helen, who always brought two or three of the most eligible, were beamed on and invited everywhere. Girls like me must make do with anything in trousers, the maimed, the halt who trod on my feet, and worse, the penniless who wanted to climb into the great houses.

Observing my situation with her innocent shrewd eye, Aunty Nell began to turn elsewhere on my behalf. The friend of hers, Belle Douglas, who lived in Whistler's house in Chelsea held a sort of salon on Sunday afternoons where "interesting people" came. It was the background to one of the pieces in my second book, *The Encircling Mist* . . . "We move, we move, in such an interesting circle. . . ." Here the talk sometimes turned on poetry. Once it happened that there was a young man there who attached himself to Aunty Nell, in need of the sort of warmth she dispensed, as the soldiers in the Beaver Hut used to come to her instinctively. It turned out that he worked for John Lane, the publishers. In her unworldliness she may have thought she could transfer his interest from herself to a girl who wrote poems, when the most elementary knowledge of psychology, a science no one "nice" studied in those days, would have told her that the last thing an average young Englishman wanted was a bride who wrote anything but the household accounts and social notes. English wives wrote charming notes.

Aunty Nell said nothing to me, but she took my latest notebook to him and he took it to his firm, who gave it to readers. The reports when they came in were good, but John Lane didn't publish much poetry and the book would have to be subsidized no matter who published it, unless it was by someone as well known as the Sitwells. They explained all this to Aunty Nell, and sent her to Walter de la Mare's brother-in-law, Roger Ingpen, who had edited an authoritative edition of Shelley's collected works, and who was the senior partner of a small publishing firm called Selwyn & Blount. Later I had good reason to refer to them as Seldom & Blunder, but one wonderful thing happened to me through going there.

Hugh MacNaghten, the Vice Chancellor of Eton, picked up the manuscript while he was waiting in the office, read it and offered to write a foreword for it. I am still surprised at this. At the time I took it for granted, I was in my "I am a great poet" phase, and found it natural that people should write forewords and do all they could for my book.

Hugh MacNaghten was an old man then, and, though few people knew it, ill with cancer. One might have thought that after a lifetime of teaching hundreds of schoolboys the Latin and Greek classics, he would not have had the energy or the inclination to take on anything more, especially to interest himself in a young unknown girl. But he wrote a charming, thoughtful foreword and even offered to put up some of the money to bring the book out. Aunty Nell decided that she would make a further investment in her awkward duckling niece and do it herself. She was beginning to be excited about the venture, and enjoyed visiting the publisher, especially as Selwyn & Blount had their offices in the beautiful, now vanished, Adelphi Terrace, overlooking the river.

There began a long correspondence between a great classical scholar, an old and ill man, and a stubborn young girl in her teens. Hugh MacNaghten took infinite pains with me. He wrote long letters in his miniature script and his beautiful English about each of the poems.

He suggested changes, he advised books for me to read, he talked as though we had an equal meeting of minds. I wrote back, fighting fiercely for every word. He would then praise those he liked and tell me why, but still beg me to consider changes and I would refuse. In this I think I was right, since the lines had been many times rewritten and were as good as I could make them then.

He ended his foreword with a rash statement: "I venture to think that

Sappho would have liked them." Who could want more than that from a classical authority? Owing to the foreword and because of his prestige the book got off to a good start. *The Times Literary Supplement,* which set the tone for critics, gave it a long column, quoted from the poems and reproduced the foreword, commenting: "But as for Sappho, she would have smiled a little wearily at the white fancies of this Western child."

I went around wrapped in the bliss of achievement. Here was my book, in blue and gray, and lovely rough-edged paper, proof of what I had always known, and others had brushed aside. Now I could afford to be modest and make disclaimers, while I was drunk with pride. I hugged Aunty Nell, gave copies to my mother and Helen, and bought a new notebook for my dedicated life as a poet. Aunty Nell had defeated her own plans by sponsoring the book. Who would bother to compete in the marriage stakes, when she could be a published poet?

In 1960, when I was living in a miner's hut in California, in oblivion and poverty, "the greatest living out-of-print author" as I bravely styled myself, I received a letter from a very English address: "Mrs. Sowerby," it said, "of Humphrey's Homestead, Greatham, Pulborough, Sussex," in an old and distinguished handwriting.

Dear Miss Eaton,

I am not in reach of any book of reference, and don't know if I should address you thus—but the reason of my writing at this moment is that by chance I have pulled out from the shelves of my parents'—Meynells—library a little book of your poems sent to my father in 1923 (!) by his acquaintance Miss Douglas (from the illustrious address 'The White House, Tite Street, Chelsea'). And finding this book confirmed in me a long-held intention to send some word to you, which came to me some five or six years ago when I read aloud to my sister Viola, who was ill, your novel "Flight," and your quoting of our loved poet Conventry Patmore made us both sit up with keen awareness of a sympathetic mind.

Then a little later, in different mood, I *delighted* in the New Yorker account of that inheritance from a thrifty English King!

Now this is very much a letter into the unknown, but if you ever felt inclined to take a day's expedition from Victoria Station to Pulborough, it wd give me great pleasure to see you here. I am no longer young—70—but there are sometimes other members of our family about.

Yours sincerely
Olivia Sowerby

Olivia, with a sister Viola. . . . This was that Olivia Meynell to whom Francis Thompson wrote:

I fear to love thee, Sweet, because
Love's the ambassador of loss

which may have been the last lines that he wrote. Fifteen years before this he had written "The Making of Viola" to the child who became the sick lady who enjoyed my novel *Flight*.

I answered that I would have loved to journey to Pulborough to meet Mrs. Sowerby. I added more about her mother, her father and Francis Thompson, and what these had meant to me in childhood and later, but I was living in California, a long way away. I never heard from her again, but her letter coming so graciously out of the ordered past helped me through a bad time in the present.

It is this sort of delicate continuity, these frail hand-bridges between *Ch'i* and *Ch'i*, which lift the spirit, and which the traditionless generation, who have never read *The Hound of Heaven* or heard of Francis Thompson or the Meynells or Shelley, have chosen to miss, poor things, as though obliterating all that went before them could enrich their lives. No wonder they think they need drugs.

> Ah, did you once see Shelley plain? . . .
> How strange it seems and new!

What I like about Browning's comment is that he goes on to compare the experience with picking up an eagle's feather. When you think Who the eagle is, especially to Indians, and what acquiring His feather means, once more the poet scores.

I never met Hugh MacNaghten. No attempt was made for us to meet. Alas that I have lost his letters. I kept them for many years. No one else ever did for me what he took the time and trouble to do, for a stranger, who was stubborn and young and thoughtless, if not ungrateful. It is an episode I like to recall when people disappoint me, when they are "rude and dumpy" as Nannie used to say. How lucky those generations of Eton boys were who had him for their mentor. He died as unobtrusively as he had lived, a year later, but not before he had seen the manuscript of my second book, *The Encircling Mist*, a collection of prose poems. He did not like these, preferring the short and I suppose artless lyrics of the first book, but he added in a postscript: "The lady with whom I have the honour to live likes two of them very much, and I have the greatest respect for her good judgment."

The first poem began with an enforced compromise:

> The poet sang alone with the wind in his hair.

It should have been:

> The poet sang alone with the wind in her hair.

But that was not what I intended, either. Why repeat the mistake of excluding half the human race? I needed an impersonal, all-inclusive pronoun. There was the plural "their" but I was speaking of *one* poet, behaving in a particular way. I needed something like the French *on*, the Hungarian *eu*.

Pronouns are important. "Want ... want ... want ..." is only an animal grunt. When the pronouns are there the statement changes. Grammar is more than the art of manipulating words correctly. It can throw light on manners, customs, history. Perhaps the Elizabethan woman was so much better off than her Victorian counterpart, in legal rights and equality with men, because in the sixteenth century grammar, like every other subject, was still taught only in Latin, and in Latin the pronoun has no gender, is not divisive because it has no separate existence, it is swallowed in the ending of the verb.

In French, the official language written and spoken in England until Chaucer's time, the *he-she* division is softened, does not stand out so sharply, because in French everything is male or female, house female, palace male, street female, bridge male. Things share with people this absurd absorbing game. But I was not writing in French and who nowadays reads Latin?

I had inherited the rich, flexible language of the great English poets.

I needed the letter S in "his" to suggest the sound of the wind. The wind whispers, whistles, sighs, stirs the boughs, rustles the leaves. The wind is zephyr, breeze, and there is that wonderful strange word "soughing." Besides, if I used "she" in the second line, it would suggest, to me at least, some stammering damsel with a dulcimer, probably under a tree. If I was jarred, the reader would be ... the reader for whom we write, the judge out there, other half of the process of bringing a poem to life. The reader is that Other, infinitely wise, sensitive to our most subtle hints, overcome by our humor, better informed than we are, instantly understanding ... but also inflexibly dense, easily bored and unpredictably fickle. The reader must be led, lured, tempted forward into the poem, not put off by detours. So it remained:

> The poet sang alone with the wind in his hair.
> He sang confusedly, for he sang of love.

My third book, *The Hours of Isis,* did not have to be subsidized. It dealt with an unusual subject in a new way, so it was accepted by the Baskerville Press on a small royalty basis. I had become a Co-Mason in a lodge that stressed the ancient mysteries. We studied the Egyptian *Book of the Dead* as a ritual working which could throw light on our own, as indeed it did. I became steeped in Egyptology and spent my weekends in the British Museum. I even took some lessons in writing and deciphering hieroglyphs.

As I read and compared the Hindu, Egyptian and Gnostic mysteries it struck me that the Hindu Nari or Devanaki, the Egyptian Isis and the Christian Virgin Mary were astonishingly alike. There was even a litany to each of them, written centuries and lands apart, in languages undecipherable and unknown to the other two writers, in which not only the titles bestowed on them, but the actual order of invocation was identical.

The betrayal of Osiris by a traitor, his dismemberment by enemies egged on by the Powers of Darkness, the destruction of his body, scattered to the four winds, his triumphant resurrection to reign over the dead, were not only Masonic, they paralleled the Christian version of the Cosmic Allegory.

I decided to write a Book of Hours like the Duc de Berry's *Heures* for the Virgin Mary, only this would be Egyptian, based on the search of Isis for her dismembered God. Each hour would be divided into three parts: a statement of the theme for meditation—for example, the finding of the right foot; an explanation of this portion of the legend; and a general application to our own lives.

It was a study of the legend and a manual of devotion, illustrated by vignettes from the *Book of the Dead* and paintings by a friend, Jacqueline Hotz.

When *The Hours of Isis* was published I sent it to the greatest authority on Egyptology at that time, a man whose work I revered, and whose knowledge filled me with awe. I wanted to make some return for the inspiration his books had brought to me, and I was filled with astonishment and joy when he acknowledged the gift with an invitation to meet him. He asked me to come to his office in the late afternoon when he would be at leisure.

I was shown into a room which was not so much an office as a private library, with books from ceiling to floor, armchairs and reading lamps and a large desk on which I could see *The Hours of Isis* beside a great tome which I recognized as Sir Wallis Budge's *Osiris*. The sight of them together overpowered me and I could hardly stammer "How do you do?"

"Come here," he said. "I have something to show you."

I went round to his side to look down at the books.

"You know what all this is about, don't you?" he asked. "It's a phallic myth. You know what a phallus is?"

He proceeded to show me. The shock was enormous. Not so the object. I had seen those before . . . indecent old men in the Paris métro exposing themselves at the rush hour in the hope of getting a reaction. Once a sturdy fishwife standing next to me turned the tables superbly by saying loudly: "*Quand on n'a pas de marchandise on n'ouvre pas sa boutique,*" which I suppose can be translated roughly: "If you're short on goods don't open up the shop." The crowd laughed and he edged over to the door and got out quickly at the next station.

What shocked me was that this great man could insult Isis and Osiris by behaving in that way. The book was a serious, original contribution to his own field.

By this time he had seized me and was pawing and nuzzling my breasts. I managed to squirm loose, shaking with rage and shame, and after a moment, during which he probably saw me clearly for the first time, he began to mutter something, excuses, justification. The gist of it was that no nice girl would fill her little mind with phallic myths. A girl who wrote a book about Osiris was fair game, obviously asking for it, which showed how enlightened his own thoughts were toward the God of Music, Healing, and the Last Judgment.

I got out of there somehow, with the book under my arm. I would not have left it with him if it meant having to bite and kick. I was more upset over the sordid insult to *The Hours of Isis* than I was for myself. Even in those days I had learned, or instinctively I knew, how to "go behind the blanket" as the Indians do, leaving the outer shadow to take the brunt of anything unwanted or unworthy to encounter the true self. That man would never meet *me*. What he met, what I left there to confront him was able to take care of the situation. We had a session at Hoster's on how to cope with an employer who took liberties. "Keep the desk or table between you." I had gone round it to join him. "Go at once to the door and throw it open. Most men will take the hint, but if there should be further trouble, scream. Never mind losing the job, you're better off without it." They also showed us how to kick effectively.

But I had not come there as a secretary, nor as a social caller. I had come as a published author of a serious book. It was the *he-she* syndrome again, another hard lesson in grammar.

Cocteau says somewhere about himself and Maurice Rostand, "We believed that we were Byron and Shelley and that this could be achieved merely by talking about Oxford and going down the Champs Élysées in an open carriage in the April sunshine."

In the same spirit but without a Rostand I trotted about London sure that I was Keats, whom I placed above the other two. It needs tremendous bolstering of the ego and sublime transcendent faith to produce even the most minor of lyrics. There is also suffering and hypersensitivity out of all proportion to the results. Now I smile at the forty or so little verses I produced in sixty years. I am glad that they are there to recall when and how they were born, and that some of them are sung where other younger poets may be listening. They brought me a rich harvest of perceptions.

London was exciting in the early twenties. There was the great Russian ballet, with Diaghilev's company, which has never been excelled. There is compensation for the weight of years when one can remember seeing Pavlova and Nijinsky in childhood, and later Lopokova.

There was excellent theater of a kind that has gone out of fashion. Plays like *Dear Brutus, A Kiss for Cinderella,* matinée idols like Gerald du Maurier, and musical comedies from which we emerged light-hearted and brave, singing snatches of melody. There were wonderful tunes which now and then reappear after fifty years and in spite of being distorted and played out of time and wailed without regard for the meaning of the words manage to survive and even appeal to the traditionless generation, misled about "irrelevancy."

There was Fiona Macleod's *The Immortal Hour,* which I must have seen more than a dozen times. Gwen ffrangcon-Davies glided about the stage and through my life. I died with the poor mortal King and rose with the immortal

Midir. The whole theater was filled with emanations from the underworld, and one could see and hear the elementals, the Good People, the Sidhe.

Change of every kind was in the air. Barriers were overthrown. There would be no more war. Art would rule the world. The Gramophone was here. The cinema was the coming medium for new great works. Cocteau was in Paris revivifying everything. Every day there were new discoveries, a new sense of freedom.

In this heady atmosphere it was inevitable. . . .

For the future, my mother said.
For the inevitable
For your wish. . . .

I fell in love. My life in London ended.

I did not drop out, I had never been in. I went away. More and more I stayed away. Now and then I was summoned Home to be "my other daughter," but no one probed, no one observed, no one cared what transformation had come to me. I came, put in my time, and went again across the Channel to France.

Everyone knows that Paris is the place for lovers. It is a cliché which like many others happens to be true. *L'heure bleue* in Paris has a mysterious magic unlike the twilight hour in any other place. The moon over the Sacré Coeur is not the moon the astronauts go leaping on. Paris in spring, or summer or autumn or winter, is the citadel of romance.

We walked a lot together, across the Luxembourg, through the long galleries of the Louvre, along the *quais,* and down the avenues, looking into the faces, individual living faces, passing by. Once a man and woman strolled toward us, shabbily dressed, like us, older, middle-aged, but around them there was such a light of transformation . . . they were like two swimmers drowning far out to sea . . . we smiled, for we were swimming too. Four pairs of eyes met briefly with warm understanding.

That corner of a Paris street is surely haunted. Four ghosts must walk there sometimes, visible to lovers who know the same completion.

Whatever happened later, and much that was horrible, that was even sordid, did, there were those first brief years in Paris to remember. " 'Take what you will, and pay for it,' says God." I was poor and overworked and tired, snubbed, harassed and sometimes frightened. I choose to recall light-hearted laughter at sudden shared absurdities, snatches of songs we sang and hummed, the smell of chestnut blossoms in the spring and later roasted chestnuts on cold and foggy days, the Café Chez Rosalie where when we had a franc or two we feasted and listened to her stories of being Renoir's model; the concerts that we heard, by going without eating, at the Châtelet and the

Salle Pleyel; the bookstalls where we browsed on Sunday afternoons, leaving behind the treasures that we found and yet possessing them; the night clubs like Bobino where I sold cigarettes and perfume and candy now and then for extra sous; the little *bôites* where we heard Damia and later the young Piaf at the height of glory, and all the other chanteuses and diseuses. . . . *C'a c'est une chose, déjà, avant nous.* . . . What songs they sang about us, how well they knew our hearts, our lives, especially Damia.

For the inevitable . . .

I was summoned to come Home, wrote evasively, did not arrive, did not arrive, and even when Aunty Nell had a serious operation and everyone gathered about her, I did not arrive.

When Aunty Nell was out of danger, it being time for Helen's seasonal descent on Paris for her spring outfits, she and my mother, after a few days shopping, came to my address in Montigny, in the forest of Fontainebleau.

They found me wearing my apron high. It was very evident that I had forgotten my Heathfield precepts and *not* stayed awake near a man. I was eight months gone with child and did not seem abashed. The scene that followed was straight out of the most lurid Victorian penny dreadful. They could not turn me out into the snow from my own house, but short of that I was spared nothing. If they had been less vehement I might have been more deeply concerned with their shock, their angry pride, or if they had shown the slightest concern for me, or asked to hear my side of the story. As it was, my mother cursed me. I would, she said, die in the gutter and so would my child. She wound up, "I forbid you ever to darken Helen's door again."

Considering that particular door was the portal to the Hell Fire Club, and remembering weekend parties at West Wycombe where most of the married couples were switching bed partners, this seemed ironic. The whole scene was so absurdly melodramatic and one-sided that I was spared having to feel for them or for myself anything but a desperate wish for them to go away.

I was alone in the house. Even my *femme de ménage,* Hélène Pinault, had gone to the market and would not be back till late. When the great operatic denunciation ceased and my family left at last to return to Paris and finish up the shopping, I was weaker and more affected than I thought. By the time Hélène got back I had started hemorrhaging and had to be taken to the clinic in Fontainebleau.

Somehow I managed to keep the baby, and in the weeks that followed I was set free from my attachment to the family, although I still felt that they must be right and I wrong. It took a long time to grow out of that guilt complex, and longer still to think of them objectively. Marriage when I got around to it later did not reconcile us. There was too much said and left unsaid between us ever since I could remember. It was only after many years and another major war, during which my mother came to me as a refugee, with

Aunty Nell and my nephew John, that the scars of what I called irreverently the Battle of the Bulge were healed.

If the course of true love "never did run smooth," the course of free love runs a good deal rougher. Love to me was first a matter of the mind, the meeting of true minds, the mystic soaring of two souls entwined. Long before the general discovery of Donne, I was steeped in him. Then another poet's deep emotional "seas between us braid hae roared." Sex was only one way of expressing love, a surprising one. I was as unprepared for it as I was for all the other prescribed challenges of a woman's life. I was full of romantic quirks and sudden reticences. I got a greater satisfaction out of shared moments at a concert, or rounding the corner of a street and coming upon some surprising scene, or reading an apt phrase together, hand in hand, lying in front of the fire, than I did out of routine sex, after too long a separation, or an exchange of querulous words, or a jarring laugh. I could not learn to turn sexual ardor on and off to fit a timetable set up by someone else.

As for marriage, considering that I was born and raised to be married and nothing else, I was absurdly ill prepared for that. I could not cook, I could not sew, I did not know how to wash a dish or sweep a floor or even dust or arrange the flowers. I had no idea of budgeting or going to the market. I had never learned biology or hygiene or simple baby care. I had no idea of anatomy. Also I felt that marriage was in itself defeat. I believed that I believed in free love.

None of this might have mattered or been insurmountable, but there were other strikes against us. It became evident that we were not "of the same song." Divorce when it came ended nothing that had not died or never come to birth.

I have often thought divorce should take place in church, with all the frills and fanfares and as many people who had witnessed the wedding gathered together to bless the liberation. I wrote a divorce service once, with prayers and hymns and God's special benediction on two people who have made a mistake and need to be freed to set it right and proceed on their journey toward Him.

Afterward there should be a reception with lots of presents and toasts and departure in two shiny cars in opposite directions for the divorcemoon.

Of course there would only be one divorce in church, and only after a long hard-working marriage, when the children were raised. Everyone would enter marriage looking forward to divorce, which would make the marriage more enduring and endurable.

I can imagine conversations like this:

"I'm afraid I can't get away that weekend. My folks are having their divorce. They've been looking forward to it for so long, I couldn't disappoint them by not being there. Give me a rain check, will you?"

"I'd prefer a simple appearance before the judge, but Mary's always wanted a big divorce with all the frills, the children want it too, and after all, it's the most important day in a woman's life, and it only happens once, so it's to be at the Church of the Disunion, at three o'clock."

"We talked it over, and decided it was important for the younger generation to have a good example set before them. Mac's getting married in the fall. We want them to see what a good marriage can be like, with a happy ending. Then they can look forward, past the years of struggle that we all go through, to a divorce like ours."

But that is yet to come. Divorce for us was a painful passage, lightened only by the humor of French frenzy over papers. One hundred and eleven couples were divorcing from the same accommodation address, appearing before the same judges. Nobody minded that, so long as the address was duly stamped and notarized with the excise stamp duly paid.

When the time came for the essential reconciliation scene, when the judge tells two people who have tried for a long time to assemble all the necessary papers to set them free, "*Reconciliez vous!*" and they not unnaturally refuse, Ernst had already left me and gone to Danzig to get a new job. I had to borrow a friend's husband to stand in for him, or wait another year for the case to come up again, with Hitler beginning to breathe down our necks. He had already declared the Poles to be subhuman, and Terry and I now had Polish Corridor passports, we were citizens of the Free State of Danzig, which, like free love, was not particularly free, and afforded no protection whatever to its adherents.

Though the judge and my lawyer had seen Ernst and me appear several times before them, nobody cared that the man who glared at me as I glared back, with beautiful theatrical gestures of "*Jamais!*" to each other, bore no resemblance to him. We were there, two of us, answering the summons, the prescribed conditions were complied with, the fees paid. "Unreconciled," the judge scrawled across our dossier, and the decree went through, giving me sole custody of Terry, in exchange for my asking for no alimony.

Paris is the place for children too. Somewhere in Terry's unconscious memory must be the things she saw and heard and found absorbing, while for me there are flashes of her, on the carrousel; running with a balloon across the Tuileries; scooped out of my startled arms by a smiling priest and borne down the aisle of Notre-Dame toward the Archbishop of Paris, making one of his rare appearances, blessing the children held up to him. We had wandered into the cathedral to get out of the sultry summer heat, unaware that such a pleasing ceremony was under way. Terry enjoyed the ride and was entranced by the Archbishop. She said so at the top of her lungs. "*T'es beau!*" she cried. Everybody beamed and no one shushed her.

I have written about Terry's life in Paris for *The New Yorker* and in

Every Month Was May and *The North Star Is Nearer*. She was two weeks old before her father saw her lying in the cherry-wood cradle that had been the King of Rome's.

"Very suitable," he said, "for your child and mine."

And I still see her, scuffling the leaves along a garden walk, looking up at him gravely, confiding, "The owl has asked me to marry him. He's handsome but I do not think I will."

"Why not?"

"He lives in a tree and that's not practical."

Terry had, at four, a good grasp of reality.

They say no woman stays a poet after childbirth, perhaps because childbirth is the supreme poem. When Terry was born I did not find a singing line come to me for six years. I was busy with survival, with earning our living in the Depression years, with the fierce undertow of life on the fringes of the world.

> Now the world whose council we ignored
> stands ready with a sword.

When I wrote again it was a novel about the underdog in Paramount, where I was working, at the Joinville studios. It came out second in an international competition sponsored by the agent A. M. Heath & Co. I was always a runner-up. I did not get the money I needed, but I did get an agent for my work and a good friend in Patience Ross, a great woman and a kind one.

When I think of how pampered I was later in my working conditions as a writer, I remember how I wrote my first novel. After working all day or all night on the set as a script girl—sometimes I was there as much as sixteen hours at a stretch—I took the métro for another hour home, and on arrival was greeted by my sister-in-law, who looked after Terry, with "No soup for you until there is a chapter." She meant it. We both knew how desperate a life lay ahead if I did not escape out of the gutter of poverty, *la misère noire*. I must sit down at a table on which there were sheets of paper and a pencil, beside a towel dipped in water to go around my head. Poems do not come that way. One novel, *Desire Spanish Version*, did.

I worked at many things through those Depression years in France. I was in the complaint department of a large store, hired to sit in a waiting room with another girl until a complaint came in. Then whichever of us was available went along to the trouble spot and took part in a scene. The *vendeuse*, the sales manager, the whoever, lit into us for being the culprit responsible for the terrible mistake, whatever it was. If Madame's dress did not fit as it should, that was because I, who couldn't thread a needle, had sewed it wrongly. If Monsieur's shoes when he got them home were the wrong size, that was because I, in the supply room, had bungled with the order and handed the wrong box to the salesman, et cetera, et cetera. Then we were expected to burst into tears and lamentations and wring our hands in apology. If the client was very put out we were fired. That always made the client feel good . . . either she interceded for us, "*Après tout, c'est la crise,*" and we were pardoned, "entirely owing to the generosity of Madame," which pleased her, or she did not intercede for us, and we were fired, without references, without a character, which pleased her if she were that sort of client. However the scene was played, the client was appeased, and when it was over we trotted back to our cubbyhole, to get on with our reading, or, in my case, my writing. Much of my second novel was written in the complaint room, in pencil in an exercise book.

Then I was assistant fitter to a gent's suiting department in another store, where my principal duty, other than holding rows of pins in my mouth, was to clap my hands together ecstatically and announce in a very exaggerated English accent that Monsieur, perhaps tubby and rotund, typically *petit bourgeois,* looked "*exactly* like the Prince of Wales!" Who also, I implied, was devoted to the same *pardessus,* or whatever article of clothing we were dealing with.

I was a typist in a garage, and then *secrétaire-traductrice* to the *administrateur-général* of Underwood Typewriters. I have written about that episode in *The New Yorker* and elsewhere. What depressed me most was the first day I spent there, typing out lists in duplicate of all my past achievements, and noting that fifteen years from then I might expect a raise of seven per cent, and also that twenty-five years of faithful service would entitle me to a certificate of honor. I had no thoughts beyond the end of the week, payday, and perhaps enough strength to go on for another week to another payday. Mercifully I was so fatigued and hungry during those months, years, I might say, that I envisaged no future. It was a matter of milk for the baby, potatoes and yesterday's bread for me, and somewhere for us to sleep.

Once, for three nights, all I could find was a métro bench, with the trains roaring in and out. It was warm, not to say stuffy, but dry, and no one bothered the sleepers until morning, when the police came to move us on. They were polite and kind. One of them told me about the free soup which was given out from every regimental barracks at 6 A.M. After that I took a bowl and stood in line for my share at the barracks which was nearest. Later, when I had a job and a one-room apartment in the Square Port Royal I continued to go for free soup. Since it was French it was palatable and, on cold mornings, hot. Sometimes it was all I had to eat for the day.

The Square Port Royal was near the Rue de la Santé, where the public executions still took place, also very early in the morning. Sometimes on my way to the soup or from it I would see a crowd around the prison wall, and know that the guillotine was set up just outside the gates. The crowd could see nothing clearly, for the guards formed a barrier between them and the condemned man, but still for some morbid reason they wanted to be there.

Later, while I was still living in the Square Port Royal, public executions were abolished.

The last man to be executed in public was the famous bluebeard, Weidmann, who murdered an American tourist, Jean De Koven, and many other women. He was executed in Versailles to scenes of revelry that shocked all France, and led to a change of law more speedily than it would have come otherwise. I remember the case well, because I used to read *Le Journal* on the way to work, and *Paris-Soir* on the way home, and the French star crime reporters were real *gens de lettres,* turning out prose of the highest, most amusing, fine writing. When Weidmann was on trial, Colette, for instance, was a special reporter for the *Paris-Soir.* The French took crime, especially *crimes passionelles,* very seriously, with the same attention they gave to great art.

I do not think I could have survived poverty and ostracism in London. Paris had compensations. To begin with, it was beautiful, wherever one might look, wherever one might step. The poor in Paris had a better life. Take Sunday. Sunday in London for the poor was a gray day of total deprivation. No shops, no cinemas, no art galleries, nothing, everything was closed, because the upper classes went for long weekends to the country. The typist stayed in her bed-sit and darned her stockings. No nylon then, to wear and throw away. In Paris, Sunday was the gayest day of the week. After Mass everybody repaired to favorite amusement places. There were gardens to walk in, the French formal kind with many paths and fountains. There were the *quais* with bookstalls to pore over, cafés where one could sit for a long time over one cup of coffee or one Bock. There were theaters and movies, and boats on the Seine, and the little *bôites* where the ancestors of crooners, who were so much better than their followers, sang bittersweet songs about our problems and made witty jokes about the dirty politicians and the scene in general. We laughed, and went home humming, ready for another grinding week.

My Paris, being the Paris of the very poor, had nothing to do with the Paris one hears of since, with Hemingway and the rich expatriates, who threw away change in the subways, and were boisterous and boorish, so we thought. The poets and the painters whom I knew were French. The musicians played in orchestras at the Châtelet and the Concerts Lamoureux and sometimes gave us tickets. I heard a great deal of music. I was there for the second performance of Stravinsky's *Sacre du Printemps,* which was dealt with more gently than the first one in 1913, but still there was derision and hostility. Not in me. I was sitting in the front row of the topmost gallery with a White Russian and two Polish law students. We had scraped and scrimped and I had gone without eating anything but free soup for many days to get these tickets. We were divided between rapture for the new, strange, fundamentally stirring, *right* sounds, and the stupid noises from the philistines, which broke into our experience. We went out from there transformed, revitalized, arms linked, to walk our Paris streets in a haze of glory. We had among us seven francs, with which we managed to procure a table at the Café des Trois Moines and share a pot of coffee. Then we went to Chez Rosalie, turned out our empty pockets, told her about the great concert, and stuffed ourselves on her good onion soup. Rosalie, who had been Renoir's model, and never forgot it herself, nor allowed the world to forget it, was a most devoted patron of the arts. If a painter, a writer, a sculptor had nothing to eat and his or her work was good —for Rosalie was firmly Women's Lib—she would feed that one free, at the same time waving away rich tourists with cries of *"C'est fermé, c'est fermé,"* even if there were empty tables. One did not abuse this largesse. When we could, we paid her, and always she received the painting, the book, the sheet of music she admired.

I have sometimes reflected on this love of the arts among hotelkeepers and restaurant managers in France. I came once to an inn in Provence, near Callian, where afterward I was to live, and feasted on local trout and wild strawberries in cream cheese. When I wrote in the guest book my name, followed by *femme de lettres,* the proprietor appeared at my side, hands clasped, saying, "Oh, Madame, my nephew has written a sonnet! If Madame would throw a blow of the eye over the sonnet, and speak to the young man about it, perhaps, or to me, I would take off ten per cent of the bill."

Elsewhere, if it is mentioned that one is a writer, not even aspiring to "woman of letters," one is apt to be asked to settle the bill in advance. That is, at any rate, the vibration one gets. But France has always loved and respected the arts, and sheltered most of the great in her tolerant care of the individual. When one considers the priority given to saving the treasures of the Louvre from the greedy grasp of German hands in 1940, the individual sacrifices and risks taken, so that Goering's cohorts of strutting boots found nothing waiting for them when they got there, and were unable during the occupation of torture and executions to discover even one of the vanished treasures, the point is proved. What does one save from the enemy? What one loves and values most.

I went to more Stravinsky firsts, to *Oedipus Rex* on May 30, 1927, to *Perséphone* on April 30, 1934. Stravinsky always seemed to come in the spring. There was one all-Stravinsky concert, in the comparatively new Salle Pleyel, for which I scrimped and saved, and heard only the applause, because I was so exhausted that I fell asleep each time the music began and was woken by the sudden bravos around me. That was a frustration I resented.

A little later I became ill and had to leave Paris. In those days before antibiotics and modern medical knowledge of tuberculosis, it was a serious thing to contract it. I was afraid for Terry in the close quarters of a one-room flat, with no sanitation and no running water except for a cold-water tap in the kitchen sink. Some royalties had wandered in a year late from an American edition of *Desire Spanish Version,* a few hundred dollars, but, with the exchange as it was, enough to last a few months if I was careful.

I gave up the apartment, sold furniture and fixings to the incoming tenants for enough to cover two one-way tickets, *en troisième,* to Marseilles.

Third class in the thirties in France meant sitting up all night on hard wooden benches which were already overoccupied, with a restless Terry on my lap, and thick garlic, cheap cigarette smoke, and the general smell of mildew and must of French *compartiments* with hermetically sealed windows to make one cough.

Nevertheless it was escape to the south. I had friends there who would help us. I went first to Cagnes-sur-Mer, to the Daniells, a painter and his wife. I had known Kent in Fontainebleau, when he was in the Gurdjieff school, and I was carrying Terry. They had children a little older, a little younger than she was. Their mother, Jessica, was English, and we had suffered through some of the same growing pains and frustrations in our growing-up. They were understanding and very kind. They helped me to find a cheap apartment in Cannes, where I installed Terry, enrolled her in the College des Jeunes Filles de France around the corner, and sent for my sister-in-law, Ilona, to come and look after her, while I went in search of health.

The treatment for tuberculosis in those pre-breakthrough times was Rest and Air. Many years later, my doctor in California, prescribing for a heart condition this time, said, "REST," then, looking at me thoughtfully, he added, "For you, Eve, that means climb the *smaller* mountain." He was right, and earlier, when I was struggling with tuberculosis, I did have an actual mountain path, to descend, to reclimb, as often as I needed food or contact with the world of any kind.

The Daniells helped me to find my home in Provence. It was a peasant *bastidon,* high above Callian, in the foothills of the Maures mountain range. They were combing the countryside for antiques, which Kent repaired and sold in the United States as a supplement to the income from his paintings. They took me in their old battered car in search of furniture and Air, and I persuaded them one day to lunch at Callian, in the village square, at the old inn where I had feasted on those fresh-caught trout from the stream that ran by the door, wild strawberries and cream cheese. The *propriétaire,* now a valued friend, came out to talk to us, and we learned that there was a little *bastidon* for sale, higher up the mountain. We went to see.

It was a small stone hut, eight feet by six, with massive walls a foot and a half thick, built by a peasant before the Revolution. There was a kitchen, a stall for the donkey, and above them a hayloft. The roof was sturdy red tile. An acre of land went with it, and water from the Roman aqueduct was turned on twice a week for a regulation number of hours. A fig tree by the door, a stone bench beside it, a magnificent view, air like wine. . . . I bought it, for a hundred dollars, which was worth more, of course, then, but still it did not seem to be excessive, although later the innkeeper told me how pained he was that I had not bargained properly and had been badly cheated. The land was worth nothing, it had not been manured for years, and Madame was badly taken in. I did not think so.

Another slice from the dwindling royalty check hired his nephew, a carpenter, and the loft was turned into a bedroom, reached by an outside stair. The donkey's stall was made into a writing room, the kitchen stayed as it was. A bucket rigged up in a tree made an adequate shower, cooking could be done on an outside stove which went with the place and probably dated to pre-Revolutionary times too. The Daniells left me, promising to look in often, Terry and Ilona were to come for weekends every fortnight. The period of Rest set in.

I have written some of the episodes, charming, hilarious, sad, that happened at this time in *Every Month Was May* and *The North Star Is Nearer*. They were fun to read in *The New Yorker,* but not fun to live through at the time. What I have never talked of was the strange, many-leveled readjustment to the Ways set before us, and the healing that came to me in that solitude on the hillside.

Twice a week I trudged down the mountain path, and up again with mail and a sackful of food. I had an old Corsican corduroy coat, with room in the back to carry a live kid. Into this I stuffed the sack, and leaning on a stick the shepherd gave me, made it up the hill, with frequent pauses to cough and gulp. There was nothing in this treatment to help tuberculosis, not even the bracing Callian air . . . famous air. There was a large state sanitarium for tubercular children near the village. Now and then one saw them, going in procession to the church.

The neighbors were friendly. After all, I was a *propriétaire,* an owner, not a renter of my land. I ranked above the wealthy tenants of large prosperous farms nearby. I was alone and ill. The *garde champêtre* kept a friendly eye on me. People brought me presents of food and wine, the herb woman gave me valuable advice and herbs for the sickness. Mostly they let me alone, with the infinite tact of those whose lives are close to the earth, the poor who know about trouble, the French who know about pride.

I spent most of the day outdoors. After the simple chores were done which kept me fed and clean, I lay in the shade or the sun and looked up at the sky. I laid aside my writing. I was working on *Summer Dust,* the story of a Polish law student in Paris in the Depression years. In the evening I read, by a candle and a small kerosene lamp, before I climbed the ladder to the loft and the long lonely nights.

Once I heard a faint sound outside, and cautiously looked out of the low door of the loft. Below me, sitting on my bench, was the shepherd with the evil eye, who grazed his sheep on other people's land by night . . . his sheep were on my field, tearing at the thyme. I could have touched his head with my hand, but I was not afraid. And when he said, without moving, "Come down," I drew on my old jacket and obeyed.

We sat together in the moonlight, companionably, watching the sheep graze. No need for words. He made me feel a valued, familiar friend. Now and then it has happened so . . . a truck driver, a farmer, a passing someone on a path, a grandson have all managed to make me feel at ease, warm, comfortable, human. So did the shepherd. People had warned me against him. "He mustn't be crossed," *Faut pas le contrarier,* with horrendous stories of what happened to those who did, or those he might not take to.

He was the shepherd without a name, who had lived all his life *en marge de la vie,* a dropout from the world into which he was born. He had never been to school, done his *service militaire,* or conformed to anything. He lived alone in a cave in the mountains, but his sheep were the best, the fattest, the most sought-after in all those parts. He was paid in silver, which he never spent. What he needed he mostly took from people's houses while they slept. I had nothing that he wanted. He had been all through what I had, to make sure, one night while I slept.

"*On est pauvre, quoi!*" he said, and then he laughed and pointed his old pipe to the sky and sniffed. His gesture said, "We have all this, the sky, and the smell of crushed thyme, and this seat, and the good air."

He told me to lie down on the crushed thyme and breathe in deeply. He said I should burn it in my house, "in a round container," for an offering. He didn't say to whom. "Healing will come," he said. Later I found that the Indians did the same with sage. In both cases it worked. I grew slowly well. Not from the thyme alone, nor the outdoor life, nor the long hours of rest, chiefly the healing came from a turning of the spirit.

I wrote to the only friend whom I thought might understand what was happening to me on the Provençal hillside, who would not think I hoped for money, or medicine or advice. Our friendship went back ten years, and survived the Fontainebleau days. In fact I had settled in Montigny when I was carrying Terry, because it was a stone's throw from Marlotte where Nancy de Croy, the second Duchesse de Croy, had her summer home and where I had stayed for weekends and longer when I was writing *The Hours of Isis* and she was working on her *Symbolism of Light.* Nancy was a student of occult subjects, from a scholarly approach. In the long hours when, according to the medical opinions of the time, an expectant mother must loll with her feet up instead of exercising, taking *any* exercise, we read and discussed Egyptology, Brahmanism and Oriental philosophy. It was a wonder that Terry didn't splash down with an ibis head, or fourteen arms in sacred gestures. Nancy had made a special study of the attitudes of the Buddha, of which there are several hundreds, with explanations of the meanings of each. Her three children thought us more than slightly mad when we went about making gestures, fingers locked together or hands outstretched: "I affirm to the earth."

A lot of it was familiar ground to me from my training in *Le Droit Humain.* Later, when I got to China and saw the Temple of the Thousand Gods, I found Nancy's explanations and descriptions lucid, helpful and correct. I do not know of another source where all this information is to be found between one set of covers.

While I was in Montigny I stumbled on a book about the Indians, called quite simply *Peaux Rouges,* published that year, 1929, by, I think, La Maison

Pavot. I do not know the author, the book has disappeared, and I have only extracts from it in a tattered notebook, but it gave me my first enlightened information on part of the Indian way of life. Nancy was interested to find that some of the signs of the Buddha were also used by Indians to communicate similar messages. Knowledge comes when the time is right, when one is already aware of the subject. Nothing in *Peaux Rouges* surprised me. It was as though someone, something, woke me from amnesia to the recall of truth grasped in childhood or in other lives. With the first joyful recognition came a great sadness. I had drifted far from the concepts of my people by aspiration, for I did not know then that they could be my people in any other way, I was convinced that I would not be able to climb to their level in this life.

In those lingering days of Victorian class-conscious hypocrisy sexual fulfillment was equated with sin, with mortal sin, except in the legal bed where frigid passivity was expected of a "nice" woman. I thought that I had broken my Masonic obligations by loving out of marriage. I was prepared to pay the psychic and spiritual penalties. Indeed, I had already paid some of them. In *Le Droit Humain* we did not believe the concealment of a few signs and symbols were the vows we had taken. They went deeper.

The cutting off of speech meant to me the departure of poetry from an unworthy poet, the lopping off of this or that human attribute meant to me a real and final loss of power. This rediscovery of the Indian way, which I had longed for instinctively and groped toward in childhood, came too late. That way was closed. But I could at least study, learn to recognize and try to follow whatever was left open. It was odd that I felt only a great and right relief at being rejected by my mother's world, a smug superiority, a willingness to pay any price exacted to be quit of all that, but possible rejection by the redskinned world filled me with sorrow.

Nancy argued with me. I had been socially foolish, the world being as it is, to flout it quite so openly, but I had not, it seemed to her, done anything fundamentally wrong in breaking what was only a man-made law, "with its roots in economics, chiefly."

"It's not what I've done or what I do, it's what I *am*. I should have put first things first."

"What things?"

"The Road to the Great Spirit."

Nancy took up the book and began to quote, translating as she went:

" 'The first thing an Indian does when he wakes is to go down to the river and bathe, and after he has purified himself, stand upright, face to the East in an ecstasy of silent contemplation.' We could still do that, only we'd have to find a private river, or wear swimming suits. 'Dreaming was more essential to the Indian than material food.' That is why the American business man never understood anything about him, and finally wiped him out. 'The rush of the spirit out of the body, the only door left open to his desire for freedom, remains prayer.' 'Each soul must be alone in the morning communion with the sun and the earth, renewed and perfumed by the great silence of the Night.' It sounds like Schuré."

Les Grands Initiés was a favorite book of ours.

"The Hindus and the early Egyptians, and peoples before them, did the same. Here it says: 'At dawn he sets out alone, completely naked, in order to present himself in humility before the Great Spirit, in the state in which it created him, free from earthly vanities. Carrying only his sacred pipe, he climbs the highest summit of the region, and presents himself to the Sun. Motionless, silent, upright in his original nudity, above the rest of the earth, reaching toward the heavens whither his soul has already fled, he remains, face to face with Guitche-Manitou, Wacondah, Yastasinane, however his tribe may name the Great Spirit, all the day, all the night, without eating, without drinking, smoking his pipe, whose sacred clouds fill him with inspiration, during which he meditates, thanking God for the happiness of being alive, without asking anything further. From his lips rises a slow chant without words, which is both an act of grace and an incantation.' I don't believe the Indians live like that now. I don't see how they can, in the modern world."

"Surely they do, some of them, somewhere."

"Even if they don't, if they never did, it's interesting. The *Peaux Rouges* and the Ancient Egyptians have a lot in common, feathers, some of the gestures, words. . . ."

It was more than that to me.

"I should have gone the Indian way."

"How could you?" she turned a page. "Listen . . . here's something touching, a woman's name . . . and this name tells us more than a long sermon about the tender fidelity of the one who bears it, 'I stay with him.' I think I shall call you that, '*Je reste avec lui*.' I wonder how it sounds in Indian. We should do some research."

"In America?" We smiled. America seemed as far off to both of us then as China, and more alien than any Buddhist country. Nancy was American-born, but fiercely expatriate, even before her marriage to a Frenchman with estates in Germany. The Duc de Croy was one of Napoleon's mediatized princes. During World War One he stayed on his estates, flying the French flag over his château beneath the Kaiser's nose, speaking nothing but French and dressing his servants in French livery, so rich and powerful that no one interfered with him. This would not have happened under Hitler. When we first met she had just divorced him and returned to France with the three children. The situation was difficult for them, being legally German, partly French, between two countries barely at peace after a bitter war. Later Charles chose Germany, Antoinette France and England, Marie-Louise the United States. Thus Nancy's grandchildren are a melting pot of family influences and backgrounds, bridging awkward chasms. When I first saw them they were three small Europeans with old-world tact and charming manners, kind to one of Maman's friends, interested, discreetly, in the coming baby.

It became apparent that *Je reste avec lui* was not to be my name, nor, for that matter, *Je reste avec elle* his. But on my lonely Provençal hillside I began to meditate on the Indian way, on the way in general. In the long hours that I lay on the earth with my face to the sky, I spoke to the Lords of karma (is it strange that they are never the Ladies?).

"I won't pretend this doesn't hurt," I said, when I felt that Someone might be listening. "It does, desperately. All right, all right, I deserve it. 'Perfect justice rules the world.' But I can't go on by myself. 'Of myself I can do nothing.' Help me, help me."

Through the long days and nights I prayed. I used the Breton fisherman's prayer: "O God, be good to me, Thy sea is so wide, and my boat is so small." I used the Indian "Father, a needy one stands before Thee. I that sing am he." I used wordless aspirations, I said *yes, yes, yes* to the will of the Great Spirit, for me and for all that lives. And I got well, to the amazement of the doctor down the hill, and those who had seen me when I came there, sick, near dying.

Now I was able to have Terry with me, without keeping her at puzzling arm's length, and I could go down to the apartment in Cannes and stay there for the winter, and even make expeditions by bus and bicycle, or go to the beach with Terry to bathe, and I could work on *Summer Dust,* and gather material for what was later to be *Pray to the Earth.*

I sat now and then for painters and sculptor friends in Cagnes-sur-Mer and Vence. Somewhere, if it survived the German occupation, there is a terra-cotta bust of me, an early work of Helen Wilson's. I look very Indian and rather smug. Later, we saw each other off and on in New York, and she was one of the few friends from the past who had known Terry as a baby who turned up at her wedding in 1949.

Then the little hoard of money gave out and we had to go back to Paris and the Depression labor market, but there went with me a core of confidence, of serenity, that was never entirely lost, though sometimes it got deeply overlaid with the material pressures of the heavy human envelope.

Part Three

I kept a diary from 1940 to 1971, so that the facts and dates to follow are accurate, but as to context, I am reminded of the challenge tossed by an earnest preacher to his gaping congregation:

"And now, brethren, the time has come for us to create the atmosphere of the loving kindness of Christ," a simple assignment which he expected them to manage instantly.

To create or re-create the atmosphere of the last thirty years would be as difficult. I can only set down glimpses of what a Lee Boo might have noticed as he whirled by in his little carriage.

When Hitler closed in on Europe I escaped from France with Terry and went to England, where I worked for a year, in London first and then in Oxford, as the Organizing Secretary of the Bodleian Appeal Committee, a job which I got through Mrs. Hoster's, and which many years later I wrote up for *The New Yorker*.

I enjoyed the time I spent in Oxford, and would have liked it to continue. I was sorry when Lord Nuffield, whose factories had ruined part of "that sweet City with her dreaming spires," gave twice as much as we were appealing for, and brought my job and other things to an end a year and a half before it was expected to be over.

Meanwhile I enjoyed my freedom of the library, being able to go on official business into Duke Humphrey's room and touch the old manuscripts and books which many hands I loved had held. I enjoyed thinking now and then that since the Bodleian stored in its stacks and subterranean streets of books originals or copies of everything that was ever written on any subject in English, and also in other languages, Latin, Greek, French, my own work would be there, in some unvisited dim corner, but there.

> Out of our urgencies we leave
> small words behind
> in corners of dim libraries
> for those to find
> who circle like ourselves

the edge of things
and disregarded have the time to read
and time to listen if a songbird sings.

Songbirds still sang in college gardens, and in smaller gardens too, especially, at night, the nightingales, which I would miss when I left Europe. Once, in Virginia, in broad daylight, I heard that pulsing, delicate trill, and stood confused for a few held breaths, thinking I was haunted, but a friend who heard it too told me that the mockingbirds had picked up the nightingale's song from a captive pair in Florida, and now you can hear it perfectly imitated, between a catbird call and a woodpecker's percussion, anywhere the mockingbirds sing. They have added it to their repertory.

I enjoyed Oxford, spoiled though it was by Lord Nuffield's cars and the uprush of population. It was still Matthew Arnold's City:

> She needs not June for beauty's heightening,
> Lovely all times she lies, lovely tonight!

Terry and I commuted from Wiltshire for a while, and then we lived in the Bardwell Court Hotel, a small quiet place, not too far from the center of the university. Every morning we walked to our work, carrying satchel and briefcase, she to Wychwood School, I to my office in the top of the Clarendon Building. We said a grave farewell at the school gates, in the language we had always spoken together, "*Travaille bien, Maman,*" "*Et toi, Chérie.*" Terry knew only French and a little Polish, and I had not thought, spoken or even dreamed in English for some years. My books were beginning to sound like translations.

Now I was back again, with English all around me, and yet not back to an England I had known. Oxford was a better, more congenial place than London or West Wycombe, not the social or the hunting set, or the gray world of the typist, but a great citadel of English literature and science, though science was more at Cambridge. While I was in Oxford a move was made to assemble all the leading scientists from every nation at a congress, where it was hoped they would band together to forswear the revelation of the new and terrible secrets they were working on to those who might misuse them, especially for military purposes. The German scientists refused to come and the project was dropped, but not before I had been sent a number of times to Cambridge, to the Cavendish Laboratory, with messages and documents from the committee.

It was my first contact with scientific procedures. I was fascinated by the Zoetrope, the Wheel of Life, set up by James Clerk Maxwell before 1869 with his own painted slides, probably the first use of moving pictures for scientific demonstration. (But the Indians had their Great Medicine Wheel long before that to explain man's position in the universe and his relationship with other living things.) I saw Maxwell's illustration of interpenetrating smoke rings, and his model, invented in 1858, I think, to show the "perturbation of a ring of satellites, for sensible image worshippers."

In 1936, Rutherford was still the Cavendish Professor, at Cambridge, working on the splitting of the atom. I was shown the apparatus he used, with Geiger, in 1908, to measure the charge carried by the alpha particles. Later, in 1957, when I was at the MacDowell Colony, struggling with my novel about the dilemma of a scientist whose lifework is used to destroy those things which as a man he values most, and which will also debase and commercialize the music to which the woman he loves has committed both of them, I drew on my memories of Oxford and Cambridge scientists. I was also at MacDowell when the astronauts gave us our first sight of the earth, hanging blue and silver in the firmament.

Rutherford died in 1937, a year after I visited his laboratory. He died convinced that the world would never be able to free the energy in the atom which he had proved was there. In *Late Interview*, adapted from the novel *I Saw My Mortal Sight*, a reporter flags down a scientist who worked once for Rutherford, and he pauses in his courteous older man's way to give the following answers:

> Yes, I was with Rutherford, in Cambridge
> when Bohr was in Gottingen and Fermi in Rome.
> They were lucky, those old giants, in
> at the beginning, not the middle
> or the end, like us.
> Rutherford's alpha particles,
> his proof that the indivisible
> could be divided
> should have prepared men's minds,
> revived a healthy dread
> of the end of the world . . .
> but then, you must remember,
> the physicists of the thirties
> were theorists, uninterested in
> the practical application of their discoveries.
> Rutherford—you must excuse me for saying this,
> but he hated reporters . . . thundered against the press
> whenever it was suggested that he and his team
> were "searching for a new source of power."
> It was not power—he said it over and over
> to those who saw clearer than he,
> or claim to, now, with hindsight—
> it was simply a search, "the urge
> and fascination of a search
> into the secrets of nature":
> Rutherford believed,
> he went to his death believing,
> that the world would never be able
> to free the energy in the atom
> which he had proved was there.
> I mean it, you may quote me,

the man whose assistant discovered the neutron
made no connection between it
and nuclear fission to come.
It was still possible
in those early days,
and even as late as 1937,
for a scientist to be blind.
None of the men Rutherford gathered about him,
Ashton—he was the one who built the spectograph,
Shimiziu—his "cloud-chamber" photographed
the paths of the atoms,
Blackett, the cartographer,
Oliphant, Cockroft, Feather,
Kapitza . . . none of them
understood what they were doing,
where they were heading,
until later, very much later,
during World War Two.
What? Thank you . . . but I was a young man then,
not in their class at all
and quite as blind as the rest.
There were times when I thought
that the first of the rockets into space
would carry symbols of our spiritual ascent,
tokens of our achievements: recorded music,
the cure for cancer, if by then we had found it,
the cure for war, if by then we had tried it,
the opening address of the first world parliament
if by then we had established that.
I thought, it seems odd now,
as the first moon whirled into its orbit
a new start might be made,
and men's minds lift together
into the age of space,
thanksgivings rise, in every language,
out of every faith,
in continuous chain reaction
following its course.
I was always too optimistic,
hopeful . . . like Rutherford. . . . Yes
I was with Rutherford. . . . Yes . . .
in Cambridge, yes. Thank you very much.

Terry got home before I did, and was waiting to welcome the tired
worker at the door of our bed-sitter. We ate at a table for two in the hotel
dining room, with grave French courtesy and polite inquiries about the
happenings of the day. I was told that some people changed from their
regular dinner hour to our earlier one just to watch our old-fashioned

formality and hear Terry's perfect French, which she lost after a few months of conscientiously twisting her mouth into the British *ows* and *ays* that passed for French at Wychwood.

She had learned her diction in the Théatre du Petit Monde in Paris, where she won the ninth place out of fourteen open in a nationwide contest for entry to the theater. For six months she performed with the company in Perrault's Fairy Tales and other children's plays, on Thursday and Sunday afternoons. The company went on tour for a month, heavily chaperoned. Terry loved every bit of it, and I was beginning to think that perhaps this was her profession. Later she would have progressed to the École des Spectacles, where all the lessons center around the stage—arithmetic, dealing with contracts and the cost of production; geography, where the theater flourishes and what sort of audiences, et cetera; history, the history of drama from the beginning. Every classroom had a stage. When children were chosen for parts in plays, their companions rehearsed with them until they were ready to join the adult cast. After the École des Spectacles, she would have entered the Comédie Française, the end of the ladder up which the winners in the Théatre du Petit Monde ascend. She could have retired at the age of twenty-one from the Comédie Française with a pension, but few do. By that time the theater is the *raison d'être,* the way of life, what the Indians call "the place" in the Medicine Wheel.

Hitler interrupted that planning for Terry's way of life. Later, there was no comparable program, in England or in the United States, for a child actor. In fact, the child actor is only to be pitied, outside of France, for an exploited, short-changed childhood. This is not so in the theater world of the French. For her brief while in the Petit Monde Terry was supremely happy. She loved everything about the theater, and went on loving it. In college she majored in drama, later she entered summer stock, became a member of Equity, acquired an agent, and then laid the theater aside for marriage, but she continued to work in Little Theater, college performances when she was invited, and anywhere else she got a chance that could be combined with a family coming first.

Terry has always been my *point de repère* with the world, an overreward for the grueling struggle at the start, a touchstone, for joy, for fun, for discernment, the sharing of people and events. Even when she was six, when we were at Oxford, there was more good Gallic sense of the worth of life in her little finger than in some of the smug and insular figures about us, completely taken in by Hitler, Ribbentrop, the Cliveden set, because they wanted to be. They behaved as though they knew nothing and cared less what might be happening across the Channel. It was the old *Daily Mail* headline again, when England, cut off from the rest of the world by a bad winter storm, announced: CONTINENT ISOLATED.

We laughed, we have always laughed together. The same things strike us as funny. The same things make us sad. We disagree madly on some things, but even then exchange our views on life with honesty and humor. "Take what you want and pay the price. . . ." Terry turned out to be the sort of human being the world needs and wants, worth any price. At six she was enchanting.

She did not like having to learn English, and long after she knew it well enough to understand, she took full advantage of being French. At the school swing she could not grasp "Your turn is over, Terry," and "No, you mustn't have any more cake" remained a mystery when she was getting A's in English composition.

When I suggested that we might someday go to Canada, she wailed, "*Non, maman!* I shall have to learn Canadian." I told her that in Canada either French or English would do, and she said, "Then I will go with you."

I did not want to leave England. It was near enough to France to make me feel that we were not permanently exiled. Also I had rejoined my Mother Lodge, Beauséant, in *Le Droit Humain*. I attended the dedication of the new headquarters and temple, a moving ceremony, with more than four hundred men and women in full regalia. Friends had built me a cottage on their grounds in Wiltshire, near Salisbury Plain, where I could spend the weekends, and look forward to living there and writing when I could make a living without an office job. They were the Pearsons, of Baynton House, in Colston, near Devizes, a famous haunted manor, where a woman murdered her baby stepbrother. The baby could be heard crying in one of the rooms in the east wing. Many people heard it, and the sound of steps, and doors opening and shutting. When I stayed there what I heard was a baby making happy noises to itself. I did not know the story and at first I thought the Pearsons had another child still in the nursery. Later I read the account of the Baynton House tragedy in *Famous English Ghosts*.

When I got back to England the first Mrs. Pearson had died, but the second Mrs. Pearson was also a friend of those days and the whole family was very kind to me and to Terry. We used to ride together over Salisbury Plain, to Stonehenge before it was fenced in and touristized, and to Salisbury Cathedral for church. Once we re-enacted the death of the last highwayman, galloping through Imber at midnight, in costume and phosphorescent paint. I loved the cottage that they built for us and longed to settle down there permanently.

But the war was drawing nearer to my un-British eyes. I decided we were not far enough away from what was obviously coming. My thoughts turned to the New World as the next stage of our flight. There Terry might have her childhood far from war and I could make a new start. I had revisited New Brunswick when I was seventeen, staying for a year with my Uncle Rob and Aunt Nellie and their family in Fredericton, where I spent my childhood summers when Grandmother Fitz Randolph was alive.

Uncle Rob was a little like Jane Austen's Sir Thomas Bertram, benevolent, kind, but formidable, with an impressive dignity that, without his wanting to, dampened and cowed the young. I was like Fanny Price, ready to be squelched. The trouble was, he had known us younger generation from birth and long ago given up expectations of intelligence from us; also the subjects suitable for family conversation had been canvassed—"carried as far as was proper." Yet I always felt he might have liked some intelligent exchange of thought, was even lonely for it. Now and then we would try, and have the effort fall flat, and give it up blushing. That at least was how I felt, and I believe my cousins too, except the youngest, Edward, born with an unquenchable disposition and a natural ability to clown and be amusing against all discouragement, which seemed to make his silent mother and his grave father dote on him. The rest of us became good listeners and kept out of the way.

Uncle Rob had a seven-seat Humber, in which he took us for Sunday-evening drives and occasional picnics along the river road. When we had driven for a while, he would stop the car. "Er-hmph . . . I think I saw a deer over there, boys. . . ."

"Girls," Aunt Nellie would say, "let's get out and pick some flowers."

We would scramble down and disappear, males to the right, females to the left, into the bushes, reappearing minutes later without flowers and with no more mention of deer, to drive solemnly on.

I have tried to imagine this scene played with different lines, the new lines of today. There is something to be said for those innocent, euphemistic times. "Hypocritical," the young would shout. Maybe so. We thought it "only polite not to mention bodily functions."

Fredericton was a sleepy little university, cathedral town, by a fine bend in the river, the beautiful river Saint John. The Fitz Randolph house was opposite the cathedral. The men of the family were churchwardens or vestrymen, the women sang in the choir. The great trees around the church were planted by my grandfather. It was a Cranford sort of place, except for the morning bustle on the river when the steamboat came and went, the *Robert E. Lee,* belching smoke. In the evenings fishermen and lovers went out in canoes.

> A green canoe, the evening lights, and soon
> stealing upon us, dear, the moon,

I wrote when I fell in love with my cousin Bob. I remembered him from childhood as a dashing cadet in Kingston, one of those who sang in the gallery, or, rather, sat in the gallery of Saint George's Church, in scarlet and gold. Bob could not sing. When we gathered around the piano for suitable songs and hymns, he produced strange contrapuntal sounds. He could not carry a tune. I admired the sounds he made and used to try to reproduce them in my Heathfield treble.

Once he kissed me on the staircase, being kind to his little cousin as Edmund Bertram was to Fanny Price, with much the same result. Edmund filled Fanny's heart, and Bob filled mine. I was afraid of what Uncle Rob and Aunt Nellie would say if they discovered my secret. Aunt Nellie would certainly disapprove. She was a wonderful housekeeper and thought I showed no aptitude for domestic things. Whenever she found me with a book she would say, "Haven't you anything to do, Eve?" and bring me some sewing or send me to help the maid wash the dishes. Fredericton was proud of being Canada's cradle of literature, with Charles G. D. Roberts, Bliss Carman, Francis Sherman, who once was engaged to my mother, and wrote some of his early poems to her, but women writers were a different thing. True there was Mrs. Ewing with her *Jackanapes,* but she was acceptable because she came from England, and was already married; moreover it was long ago, and as the Micmac said to the missionary about the crucifixion, we must hope it never happened.

Certainly Mrs. Ewing was no help to a twentieth-century girl so rash and unmaidenly as to want to write. It would be hard enough to satisfy Aunt Nellie's standards for a wife for Bob, even for the most perfectly domesticated paragon. I hadn't a chance if they discovered my secret, so I flirted with another man and got into trouble because he was engaged to the daughter of a family friend. Aunt Nellie took me aside and said that perhaps I had not noticed that I was giving signs of encouragement to a young man who could not in honor receive them and was probably very embarrassed by my bad manners. He too had kissed me several times, on the stairs and at a fancy-dress dance, with no trace of embarrassment. I did not think Aunt Nellie had the situation quite to rights, but it was almost time for me to leave and carry my memories to England.

Thinking back over these scenes I wondered if Fredericton was still peaceful and somnolent, and what the Fitz Randolph relations would have to say to a niece arriving "divorced from a no-account Polish Count" as one of them had written to another Fitz Randolph cousin in England, who passed it on to me, not to mention indiscretions I had never bothered to hide.

Still, there was no need to pause in Fredericton, or to go there at all, though I was fond of the place, and would like to show it to Terry and her to it. I could go to Montreal, or even to New York, where my cousin Connie lived and worked, though she was not there now. How she managed to escape from Fredericton and the pattern of life laid down as suitable for a Fitz Randolph daughter I could not imagine, but I liked her and counted her as more of a sister than Helen, and she and I have stayed close friends for over half a century.

While I was thinking this over, a photographer whom I had known in Paris came to visit us in Oxford, and then went back to France, after taking pictures with the new angle shots, buildings falling on their backs, slanting wildly . . . they made me nervous, looking prophetically like war. She disappeared into silence, the way friends do, then I heard that she was traveling with a circus in the Midi, and suddenly she wrote that some of the horses were being shipped to Canada and that she wanted to go with them, to photograph new things. Why not pull up stakes and come with her? The boat would sail from Marseilles to Glasgow and from there to Halifax. The passage would be cheap. We could make it cheaper by signing on as stewardesses. Europe, she added in a postscript, appeared to be doomed. I believed her. I was ready to leave.

There was only one drawback, children were not accepted. I made arrangements for Terry to sail later on the *Empress of Britain* to Saint John in New Brunswick, where I would meet her, sold everything that didn't go into one suitcase, and joined Hansena in Glasgow.

We sailed on New Year's Eve for the most uncomfortable crossing. It lasted for three weeks of bucketing across the ocean in stormy winter weather, in a dirty little tub made for the comfort of the cargo, fifteen horses, and, as an afterthought, the Captain, who shut himself up in his cabin with a case of Scotch. The rest of us fared as best we might. We were the only women and the only passengers, technically stewardesses, but there was no one to wait on but the horses, who had their own attendants.

Horses, especially trained circus horses, are valuable and must be well looked after. Horses can be seasick, but they cannot vomit. They can die from this frustration. One of our shipment did. When the roll and toss grew beyond equine bearing, barrels of oil were poured overboard . . . this was not called pollution then, it was calming down the sea, expected of a conscientious skipper. Seasick stewardesses, if they could crawl to the dining corner, could eat with the crew. If they didn't appear to eat, who cared? There was no white-coated steward with chicken soup to pamper them, as in my childhood crossings.

Halfway to Halifax, Hansena came down with chicken pox, which we had to conceal, for fear of complications when we landed, quarantine, or even repatriation. She lay miserably on a lumpy mattress, shaken and tossed about, while I tried to keep her spots from bleeding against the rough blankets which were all we had for bedding. We had brought books, but it was hard to read, and I remembered confusedly that in chicken pox or measles it was bad to use your eyes. Mostly we talked.

Hansena had a fund of psychic stories, also she had led an unusual life. She was the daughter of King Haakon of Norway and a Danish lady-in-waiting. Adopted in infancy by a rich English family, she was brought up in London, believing herself to be their child, and guiltily aware that she disliked them and their friends and detested the life they built about her. It was only when she married that the facts of her adoption came to light and lifted the burden of guilt and shame and disgust from her. When she knew they were not her parents she could feel pity, even liking, for these ogres of her childhood.

She was marrying to escape from her home, persuading herself that probably she was in love, shutting her eyes to the rather obvious attraction her husband showed toward her comfortable settlement. He was an R.A.F. pilot, a reckless, handsome devil, who led her a rough dance. "It was like this," she said, waving her hand round the sordid little cabin. After three years they divorced. She had to pay him for his compliance. Then she married again, another pilot, much like the first, only a decent fellow, with whom it would have been possible to build a good marriage, but he was killed in a plane crash before they had been married a year.

"Will you marry again?" I asked.

"Yes," she said, "and probably regret it. Meanwhile I'm going to photograph the astral planes."

"How will you do that?"

"Go to unspoiled places, where the barriers are thin, and eerie places, where there are known to be ghosts, and see."

Some of Hansena's later photographs are extraordinary, inexplicable unless, as she insisted, they do show astral scenes. She was a seeker, a student of the occult, as I was. We looked upon this journey to Canada as something more than a break with our European past. We sailed in the spirit of a pilgrimage. One of the books we had brought with us was the moving, poignant diary of Charles Miel, the Jesuit friend of Gounod, Lacordaire, Lamartine and Ravignan, the brilliant orator who represented France at Daniel O'Connell's funeral, and then suddenly abandoned the Roman Catholic Church to become, after long and painful wanderings, the Anglican rector of the French church in Philadelphia. His diary is an *apologia pro vita sua* in reverse, carrying him all the way from Rome, through Unitarianism with Emerson and Agassiz in Boston, to a church in Brooklyn, to Cincinnati, to Philadelphia, where he wrote a vision of the future which I found later in an Anglican convent in Wisconsin, and which for 1899, when it was published, startlingly foreshadowed the Aquarian Age.

We read the account of his journey to the howling of the wind and the slapping of ropes and wires. He also took three weeks to cross the ocean, but his experience was pleasanter than ours, physically, at least, for it was summer. Otherwise we shared the same "wrench of heart."

> Never, not even when I left Rome and the Roman Church, have I felt more alone in the world. Not a friend, not an acquaintance. Behind me sacrifice; before me the unknown. It is the most complete isolation. During the past two days I have been a prey to the most profound sadness, but I find myself in a solemn mood this evening and even happy in my sacrifices. The sun has just set in an immense flood of purple. The moon seems to smile at me across the cordage of the ship.

A few days later he made a friend.

> We passed our days and often part of our nights, now in intimate conversation, and again in mute contemplation, interrupted by reading or recitation of passages from our favorite authors: Shakespeare, Victor Hugo. But above all did we enjoy the meditations of Lamartine, which suited best the

state of our minds. . . . Sincerely loving the true, the good, the beautiful, we endeavored to give free flight to our souls in the field of the Infinite, and this had an ineffable charm for us.

Add seasickness, semistarvation and chicken pox to all of this and we had a journey which did separate the past from the future and prepare us for a new turn of the road. A few hours in a comfortable plane do not give time enough, change enough, to slough off the old, to be able to say with Miel:

> *Ecco nova facio omnia:* in this country where all is new to me, everything within me must become new also.

When we landed, Hansena went to Montreal where she had friends waiting for her. I went to New Brunswick to wait for Terry's boat. It was a smaller world in those days. The conductor who punched my ticket got off the train somewhere and alerted my uncle, my father's younger brother, that his niece from Europe—there were tags on my suitcase—was in the parlor car. At the next stop I found the family waiting, filing through the train to reproach me for not letting them know my plans. They tried to get me to stay with them, but I explained that I expected Terry on the *Empress of Britain,* docking in Saint John, and they let me go. They did, however, pass on the news to the Fitz Randolph relatives in Fredericton, and when the train reached the junction, there this new group was, equally reproachful. They had looked up the sailings, the *Empress* was not due for several days, meanwhile they took me to the Randolph of my childhood for an uneasy reunion after so many years. They were very kind, but I thought they seemed a little nervous lest I might be coming to lay my bones among them. They were reassured when they discovered that all I intended was to leave Terry in a boarding school—we decided on Edgehill in Nova Scotia—and find myself a job.

Terry came off the boat in a flurry of goodbyes. She had lived a great adventure, with her own stewardess to look after her, a seat at the Captain's table—to whom she said a fond farewell, but her real enthusiasm went to the cook. I gathered that she had spent most of the time in the galley, when she wasn't riding the elevator up and down. Apparently she had the family seadog legs. In the stormiest weather, when the ship rolled badly—all the *Empresses* had this fault of heavy rolling—she was riding the elevator as often as they would let her.

She had a lot of amused fans, as she had in Oxford, or in Paris, or anywhere she went. The Fitz Randolphs joined the club, and there was talk about changing Edgehill for Netherwood in New Brunswick, and my finding a job in New Brunswick. But I felt *no* to both, and decided to go on to New York. I was still raw from severing my European ties, and from life in general. I was afraid of family domination, and I thought that my father's family would be best for Terry. My last glimpse of her before I left was of a small sturdy figure climbing the great school stairway, hand in hand with tall Mildred Roechling, Headmistress of Edgehill.

"I like this school," Terry was saying earnestly.

I hoped she would. It was better than Heathfield, and not her first experience. She had known Wychwood, and before that her French *lycée*. We would spend her major holidays together, and Uncle Tim and Aunt Rita would fill in benevolently at other times, or in case of sudden crisis. It was the best that I could do, and in fact turned out pretty well. Edgehill became Terry's permanent home from home for nine years.

I arrived in New York with thirty-five dollars, a camera and a fur coat. I asked the taxi driver where he thought I ought to stay and he took me to a small hotel on Broadway in the seventies. Here I found a room for nine dollars a week, paid for two weeks, and went out to pawn the camera and the coat.

When I got back I was tired, and more than a little afraid. I lay on the bed in the stifling little cell with its grimy walls, and turned on a switch marked "radio." A grating in the wall gave forth with dance music. Then there came a pause and a man's voice said gravely: "Now for an important message."

"Here it comes," I thought. "War . . . it must be war. . . ." I braced myself in anguish for what everyone in Europe feared, expected. . . .

"Do you suffer from acid indigestion?" the grave voice asked. I could not believe what I heard. I thought perhaps my mind had given way. The strain of recent years, the journey, this exile in a foreign country . . .

There were no commercials on my radio in Europe. It was my first encounter with the never-never land of phony sell. I listened bewildered. The news when it came said nothing about war. It talked of names and people and events I could not relate to. I knew nothing about the United States except what I had gathered in my childhood. I might as well have traveled to the moon for all I knew about my new surroundings.

All my life I have been blessed and protected by friendly troglodytes. If my car breaks down on a lonely desert trail or a roaring freeway, before I have time to feel anxiety, a cheerful being arrives eager to set things straight. My first week in New York I came under the benevolent direction of a newsvendor near Grand Central Station. From the first paper that I bought there, discarding the news and keeping only the want ads, he took me in hand.

"Job hunting?"

"Yes."

"What's your line?"

"Secretary."

"Try the agencies. They take a cut, but what the hell, I figure it's worth it."

I went to several agencies. The interviews all seemed to run the same. After name, sex, age, "Where did you last work? List *all* your previous experience." If I were to do that, I thought, it would make lurid reading.

My last job was with Oxford University. "In what capacity?" "I was Organizing Secretary of the Bodleian Appeal Committee." That and what they thought was my phony English accent ended it. I never heard of an opening from any of them.

I spent two weeks like this, during which the kiosk troglodyte told me where to get the cheapest cup of coffee with a doughnut, how to travel uptown, downtown and across town for the same nickel . . . you took the el from wherever you were down to the Battery and stayed in the train until it came up on the other side . . . and how to approach an employer. "You want to smile, see? But not the cheese-cake kind."

I didn't know what he meant. I didn't know anything. I was beginning to be afraid, especially at night in my dismal little cell with the blatting radio.

Friday came. I thought, "I have an agent in New York." I would go to see her and play author for a while. This might give me courage to smile in a noncheesy way at the next interview. I took the el down to the Battery and up Third Avenue to Thirty-sixth Street, walked to Park Avenue, found number 77, which was to be the hub of my business universe for many years, and wavered into Ann Watkins' office.

"Oh yes," the receptionist said when I gave my name, "Ann is expecting you for lunch. I'll tell her you're here."

"At least I'll eat," I thought, "if she doesn't set the mistake right when she sees me."

Ann came, a dynamo with upswept reddish hair, deep-blue eyes, warm voice and overwhelming energy, said, "Come along!" and rushed me from the office round the corner to the Tuscany.

Over lunch it seemed that she had been expecting me, though why, how, was not explained. She had my name straight, and the titles of my last two books. She had just sold *Pray to the Earth* to Houghton Mifflin. She seemed to have read it too, though later I discovered her superb public-relations technique with authors, which never involved her in actually reading much of what they wrote. She got the gist of it through osmosis or smelling the pages or something, and she could be extremely convincing when she said, "On page 302 what you said about thus and so . . . it's *great*," or, more generally, "This time you've *done* it. This is an *important* book."

That day in the Tuscany she behaved like a benevolent goblin. When we reached dessert she said, "You've worked in movies, haven't you?"

"Some time ago, in Paris."

I was going on to describe the mix-up which led to my being mistaken for a script girl Paramount was expecting from Pathé-Nathan. Since I was so desperate that if they had said I was Charlie Chaplin I would have said "Naturally" and done my best to make like him, I didn't tell them I had never been a script girl. I managed to hold down the job, at first on the set and then in the translation room, for eighteen months. I wrote about it later, for *The New Yorker*, but now, as I lunched with Ann, I thought, "Hold back. There's a time and a place for funny stories against yourself."

She looked at me. Many authors quailed before that searching look, but when she smiled the most discouraged felt that after all genius could triumph over anything. They knew that they were in the right hands, which is ninety per cent of confidence.

She said, "I wonder. . . . You wouldn't consider taking a job, would you?"

I gasped, begging, crying inside, "Oh *yes,* yes, please!" While I heard my voice drawl, a note higher than normal, "Well . . . er . . . I don't know. . . . I suppose it would depend on what it meant to my writing. . . ."

"Oh, you'd have some blocks of time for that."

It was Friday. On Monday I came to work as the head of Ann Watkins' Motion Picture Department. I was not only the head, I was the whole department, in charge of selling novels to the industry. My take-home pay was $19.29 a week, my gratitude enormous, my competence zero.

On that first morning I found a copy of *Variety* on my desk with a note: "Look through this and tell me what's important. A.W."

"Nix pix fix," I read. "Zanuck rides again." And other statements as mystifying. I was worried. If I flubbed my first assignment . . . I typed out a note: "There is nothing important in *Variety* today," and put it on Ann's desk. She was out to lunch. Then I dodged out of the office and ran to my kiosk troglodyte.

"Help me," I said. "I've found a job, but I don't understand anything. Here . . ." I thrust *Variety* at him. "I'm supposed to pick out what's important, and I don't know what it means."

"Now," he said, "what's tough about *Variety?* It's a good paper."

" 'Nix pix fix.' What are they talking about?"

"Nix means no dice, pix means picture, fix means deal," and, as I still looked blank, "Look, it's saying R.C.A. ain't going to make the picture, ain't going through with the deal, it says maybe it ain't going to buy the story. This outfit of yours, what's its business?"

"It's a literary agency."

"Sells stories? To the movies?"

"I suppose so."

"Find out if it sold this one and tell your boss the deal's off. And don't panic, little lady. Just you come to me. We'll make out."

I rushed back to the office, took the note off Ann's desk, and went back to mine. Ruth Portugal, head of the Magazine Department, looked at me inquiringly. Margot Johnson, head of Books, frowned and shook her head. They had troubles with new people in the office, and especially with those who came in on a sudden hunch of Ann's.

When she got back, she found a brisk little report that in view of the deal with R.C.A. falling through—"as you already know—but now reported in *Variety*—perhaps we should offer it to Metro-Goldwyn-Mayer?"

She seemed to think I caught on fairly well. I kept the job for a year, bluffing my way along, lunching almost every day at the Algonquin with different movie buyers . . . in those days most of the properties were sold in New York, not on the coast . . . and playing them off against each other, then releasing all the galleys simultaneously, for nothing spoiled a story's chances so much as letting one company see it before the others. "Warner Brothers doesn't want it." "If there's nothing in it for Twentieth Century-Fox, we needn't bother with it." The trick was to make each of them think they were first on the list, without giving any of them that advantage, and smooth them down when they sulked. Ann was superb at this.

It was an exciting office in the forties, handling a great number of European writers. Cables and ticker tape were going constantly. There were four telephone extensions. When Ann was on the phone the rest of us were supposed to listen in so that everyone would be up to date on all the deals and able to pinch-hit for each other.

Used to the leisurely atmosphere of Oxford, where my office was on the top of the dignified Clarendon Building, without a telephone, and where I rarely wrote more than one long, well-composed letter a day, I was outclassed by the group of brilliant swift youngsters Ann had grouped around her. I bluffed my way along, as I had done at Paramount, and there were stories of my incompetence which I am sure were true. After I left they found a drawer full of letters and memos marked URGENT which I had stashed away, hoping that Ann or someone else would deal with the situations they represented before I had to ask for help. That was what usually did happen. The phone would ring, and Ann would go into action before either side discovered that she hadn't read the latest directive, hidden in my desk.

I struggled along for a year, getting more and more into debt to Terry's school, and more and more exhausted by the strain of trying to keep up with such a fast-paced group. Then one day I put on my hat—people still wore hats—and came in again as an author. "Ann," I said, "I have to have more dough."

She looked at me reflectively.

"O.K. Write an historical novel."

"How can I? I never even read them."

"What the hell's that got to do with it? Sit down! Write me an outline *now*."

I sat down obediently, but I did not have much hope or confidence in the result. Still, I did remember a rainy afternoon I had spent in the fort at Annapolis Royal in Nova Scotia, when I was waiting for Terry to get through with the dentist before I took her to Edgehill.

Uncle Tim was curator of the museum there. He showed me a series of letters about a Frenchwoman named Louise de Freneuse, written between 1702 and 1711 by several French governors. Each letter praised her or damned her in words that still came crackling off the pages. One said, "This story against Madame de Freneuse is pushed as far as hell can desire."

It might be a good idea to push it further. I wrote down what I could remember about Louise de Freneuse, that she crossed the Bay of Fundy alone in an open canoe with a small Micmac boy, that she loved the Captain of the fastest sailing vessel in the world, although she was married to two other men, that she sustained the fighting courage of a starved and defeated garrison . . . it came to about a page. Ann snatched it from the typewriter and marched out to lunch. When she got back she told me that she had sold it to Harper Brothers for an advance of a thousand dollars. "I told them I'd read half of it and that it's great so far. Now get the hell out of here. Go write it!"

A thousand dollars was immense wealth to me. I stammered thanks and remonstrances.

"Go on," she said. "I'm sick of seeing you around."

Everyone beamed assent. There was a rush of relieved goodbyes, and more cordial good wishes than I'd ever had extended to me there. Next day I caught the train for Nova Scotia. I found a little cabin in a remote fishing village, on the edge of a cliff overlooking Fundy Bay. Terry joined me for the summer and I settled down to work. I was terrified that I might not be able to write an historical novel, that I would let Ann down, that Harper would ask for the money back.

But the story about Madame de Freneuse turned out to be more exciting than I had remembered. There were my years in France to help me with the background, and New France was still a fresh experience, full of strong impressions. Moreover there were the Micmacs and the Malecites to approach for help in the Indian parts of the novel. I went to Lake Kedgimikoo-gee, where I was kindly received by two Indian families.

One of the older women made exquisite moccasins with stained quill-work for decoration. She made a pair for Terry showing a lotus or a water lily, and one for me with scarlet runner beans, because she said I was "red and hot, hot like fire, angry blood, live, live," but Terry was "cool and clear like water good, good."

Those were my first moccasins. I have had others given to me since, but none I felt so at ease with.

I wrote a chapter a day, on an old battered portable with keys that stuck and a ribbon that had to be rewound by hand because it would only go one way. The chapters were short, never more than four pages. Even so, it was a terrific strain, almost as much of a tour de force as the novel I wrote in Paris with a towel round my head.

At the end of the summer I took Terry to Edgehill and went back to New York with the manuscript of *Quietly My Captain Waits* in a suitcase. I delivered it to Ann, and went to the Henry Hudson Hotel to sit and bite my nails. There was very little of the thousand dollars left and I was worried, fatigued and depressed. I sat in the hotel and watched the waterfront from my bedroom window. Later I was there when the *Normandy* burned, and to watch the *Queen Mary* arrive, gray and drab in her war paint, and the *Queen Elizabeth* on her maiden voyage. I stayed there whenever I came to New York, until a man was murdered in the room below mine. The F.B.I.

questioned those in the rooms above, below, on either side. None of us had heard or noticed anything unusual. Yet he put up a tremendous fight for his life. It sickened me, so that I did not go back to the Henry Hudson. In these days of murders and muggings and general violence such squeamishness seems old-fashioned.

On January 31, 1940, my diary says: "Depressing letter from Harper's postponing publication day to June 6th." Evidently I thought postponement meant a lack of interest. The entry goes on:

I felt very dashed and rang up Ann who said, "It looks as though you are going places." I didn't know what she meant.

"It's a Harper Find."

Again I didn't know what she meant. "Harper has had the ms. for ages. How can they find it suddenly? I've been correcting galleys for a month."

"Read the *Publishers Weekly*."

I went to Brentano's and picked up a copy. Standing on the sidewalk I read:

"*Quietly My Captain Waits*, a romance of Canada in the days of the French and Indian Wars by Evelyn Eaton, will be promoted as a Harper Find, but the publishers expect it will build up an advance three or four times the size of that for the average Harper Find, and that, Harper says, is three or four times the advance of the average work by an unknown author. Over 1000 copies will be distributed to the trade. The advertising will be of the sort usually reserved for a Bromfield or a Maurois. Imprint postcards will be ready in time for May 1st statements and there will be four-color posters. In general the campaign will follow the lines of that put out in 1937 for *So Great a Man* which resulted in an advance sale of 28,000 copies. The ads will include full pages in the review sections and big space for all book media."

I did not know *So Great a Man,* but Bromfield and Maurois, especially Maurois, were gods to me. I could not believe that I was mentioned in the same paragraph, and still I did not understand what had happened.

On February 2 the diary says:

Odd day. Went for a stroll to return page proofs to Harper—saw jacket—liked it—went on to Ann's purely as an afterthought, to show them the jacket, and everyone fell on me with hullabaloo about Selznick wanting to see the book for Vivien Leigh and would I go to Hollywood! I had pipe dreams and nerves the rest of the day. Nothing probably will come of it but if it does . . .

Sunday February 4th 1940. I have decided, rightly or wrongly, to take out American citizenship. I do it: a) because this country has given me my big chance and I would like to return it in taxes. [I got my wish! Uncle Sam took two-thirds of all I made on *Quietly My Captain Waits.* There was no five-year stretch-out then. I was taxed as though this one bonanza were my regular annual income.] b) I want to take root and did not find my roots in Europe. c) I do believe in life, liberty and the pursuit of happiness. It seems lousy to switch in wartime, but I can help as much from here.

February 5th. Lunched with Ann. She told me Selznick had offered $2500 option for 90 days on a $25,000 sale but she had turned it down. She expects more. I think she must be insane. Oh dear! Oh dear!

February 6th. Jean Morris from the office dined with me, told me that I was "on the up and up" and that a movie sale seemed a certainty, that several enthusiastic letters had come in, notably one from Underhill.

How many times I distributed galleys of a novel to the movies, and now it was my novel circulating across the buyers' desks.

Wednesday February 7th. This is the red letter day of littul Evelyn Vernon Eaton's life; It broke in the evening. 9.20 Ann telephoned for me to get down to the office. She wouldn't tell me anything more. I got a taxi and told the driver, "For God's sake drive carefully! I'm on my way to the first bit of good luck I've had in years!" I found Ann, her husband, Roger Burlingame, and champagne. Jean arrived and after teasing me and holding out a little longer, Ann told me *Quietly My Captain Waits* sold to Warner Brothers for Bette Davis for $40,000. I got tiddly on the champagne. Roger took me home. So now success, or rather security. Seems odd. God help us in prosperity. Fun!

February 8th. Telephoned office to find out if it were true. It is! Ann said that Warner had offered an alternative $35,000 and $500 a week on a dialogue job. I turned it down in favor of the original $40,000. She thought I was right. Then I threw all my clothes on the floor and sent for the Salvation Army to take them away. No more third-hand old moldies. I kept one dress to go to Peck & Peck. Spent the morning there getting a decent outfit. Borrowed from the office to pay for it and to live on till the check comes in.

February 16th. Bought *Variety*. There was a notice: "Evelyn Eaton sold her novel Q.M.C.W. to Warner Bros." So it's true! I went with it under my arm to the kiosk troglodyte who helped me translate my first *Variety*. "See?" he said when he had read it, mouthing out each word, "Told ya, didn't I?" and we hugged each other.

February 26th. Stopped at Ralph Horgan and ordered my blue heaven, a v.8 Mercury powder-blue car with special tires, radio, etc. A dream of a car! Felt quite wicked but very determined. Got a letter from Cass Canfield saying that Walter Edmonds, whoever he may be, liked the book and said it was "a fresh and stirring story of little-known American history." I suppose they will quote him. He queried my talking of stoves, but I have authority for it.

February 29th. Discovered that Walter Edmonds is the one who wrote *Drums Along the Mohawk*. I must read it. His advance good opinion should help the book.

I seem to have felt a little uncomfortable at this torrent of what seemed to me endless good luck.

Well, February took me through the door. I'm still waiting for the check, but the sale is made, advertised, the contract signed, and E.E. unsuccessful, unknown, is E.E. what? Very grateful for this breathing space, grateful that I can now do my share, grateful that I am still young enough to enjoy the good things of life, grateful that Terry's life can be more protected, grateful for the sunlight. It is hard to walk in the sun and not remember those in the shade, in the dark, in the despair of refugees, prisoners of war, the wounded, the Jews, the miserable poor in Europe tonight—all over the world. I must try, in this disorganized world, to look after my responsibilities wisely and to build for the future. March will, I hope, see me clear of past debts and going forward. I hope not to be stingy and fearful, not to be reckless and stupid, but to complete the lessons of the past with this one of the future.

I did not know then that the movie would never be made, that most of the money from its sale would go in taxes, that I would have many more years, later, in poverty and stress, that I would come to understand fully Frost's "Provide":

> No memory of having starred
> Atones for later disregard,
> Or keeps the end from being hard.

During this heady time I was arrested for speeding in Central Park . . . on a horse. I had found a pair of jodhpurs in Peck & Peck and bought them, a sort of throwback to my hunting days. Then I discovered a riding stable near the park and hired a horse called Peggy, "a nice little plug with typical livery-stable mentality, wanting to go home, shying at papers, but good for the liver." As I was galloping round the reservoir, two policemen on horseback waved at me, I waved back, and presently they joined me in what I thought was a friendly race. They allowed me to win, and when I reined up they arrested me. It was against the law to gallop in Central Park. I must go down to City Hall and pay a fine. But at least they had let me have a run for my money.

Terry came to spend her Easter holidays with me:

We went to the circus, saw Gargantua, the giant gorilla, very formidable. Wish he and Hitler could be shut in the same cage. War news terrible. Norway and Sweden invaded. We spent a happy five hours at the circus, eating popcorn. Seemed the wise thing to do.

I did not stay in New York for publication day. I knew so little about life in these United States that it did not occur to me to ride the waves of publicity, and cash in on the brouhaha around a best seller. I went to Nova Scotia, took the same little cabin where I had written it, and settled down for a summer of work and fishing. When a telegram arrived from Clifton Fadiman asking me to appear on "Information Please" I had never heard of him, and did not know what "Information Please" was. I believe I did not even bother to answer! Small wonder then, that in face of such rudeness, which would have been even more unforgivable if he had known that I hadn't any idea of the honor he was doing me, my entry for June 11 reads:

Spent afternoon in boat trawling. Martha [Banning Thomas, poet who also had a cabin at Victoria Beach] sent clipping from Boston *Transcript* and poem. Clifton Fadiman slammed the book hard in *The New Yorker*. Terrible news, Norman Rogers killed. [Minister for War in Canada, whose wife and sons lived at Victoria Beach. His boys Mac and Alan were Terry's friends.]

During that summer of the fall of France, the little fishing village, Victoria Beach, on the edge of the Bay of Fundy, was in trouble. German submarines were fueling just off the coast, and the fishermen could not go out to make their normal living. It was a poor living at best, and to lose a summer season was disastrous. I decided this was the time to build the home I had always wanted, and make a symbolic gesture, a declaration of faith in the future of a free world, a defiance to Hitler. I thought it a hopeless stand, after Dunkirk and the fall of France, it was only a matter of time before England would be invaded, and with the loss of all her equipment in France, how could she hold out? The United States was still "neutral" and even if this changed could not get going in time. . . . Nevertheless I would build on the edge of a cliff, and for a few weeks, a month or two, give the village I had come to love a project, a substitute way of making a living.

If the Germans demanded Canada—it was one of their objectives in World War One—or if they went further than refueling their submarines and landed more than the occasional groups of saboteurs which were being picked up by the Mounties, then it would be time to decide what next. We had several landing scares. One I remember was a report that a submarine was off Green Point, and that probably there would be a landing there. The men of the village, headed by John Casey, the government pilot, hotelkeeper and veteran fisherman, ran out to the point with their rifles and prepared to spend the night there on watch to repel the landing party. The Baptist minister ran with them, carrying a lantern instead of a rifle, because he said it was his duty to hold up the light. They stayed till dawn, when news reached them that the landing had been attempted farther down the coast. The tired little party returned to the hotel for breakfast.

"Well, Jawn?" someone asked.

"Well," he said slowly, "I tell you, I wasn't planning on no Germans landing on Green Point."

I would have been sorry for any Germans who might have gone against John Casey's planning. For all his gentle ways he could be very tough.

It was a strange little ethnic group settled on that lonely strip of rocky coastline. They were Irish, with the Irish charm and touch of blarney, but they were also Baptist, with the robust faith that took them for total immersion into the icy waters of the Bay of Fundy. Baptisms were simple, moving, colorful affairs. The villagers lined up along the shore, with blankets and hot tea, and warm shawls ready for the saved. The minister, shivering in his rubber suit, stood waist deep in the swirling water, and the men and women to be baptized waded out to him. He put them skillfully under and held them there for the necessary moment to drown all their sins. One man who was very stout and had the reputation of being very sinful did not go under entirely. An inch or two of stomach rose above the waves, and it was rumored that his sins clustered there, and would be still with him. No one was too much surprised when his baptism "didn't take" and he relapsed after a fortnight of unusual virtue.

The people of Victoria Beach were slow and gentle in their motions, but fierce in their utterances.

"She tore into him savage" meant that she had perhaps said "Best not do that" to a child.

"She came down them steps same as a leppin' hound" meant that someone didn't loiter too long on the stairs.

When a funeral procession was disturbed by some hens—"Them fowl riz up like thunder and fell among the mourners"—there was perhaps a mild cluck or two, a little scattering.

Once I met a frowning friend of mine, with a crying little boy beside him, and after we exchanged the ritual "Hoi" . . . "Don't croi, say hoi to Miz Eaton . . ." I asked, "What is the matter with Woilie?"

"He ain't doing so good at school. It's that there citizenship. He don't make nawthin' out of that. So I'm going down to tell the old hag to stop fillin' up his head with citizenship, else she'll end up in the Bay. I don't want none of that there citizenship around *my* son."

They lived rugged lives, with few debilitating distractions. The village had no electric light, no running water, one store, no movies. The houses were unpainted, snugly built, but stark. Wood-burning kitchen stoves shone so that you could in fact see yourself in them. No windows faced the sea. When my house was built with an eye for the superb view over the Bay of Fundy, the villagers shook mournful heads. The sea was the Enemy. Every winter it took its cruel toll of men. In their open rowboats, hand-lining, or the larger but still rickety little trawlers, powered by old car engines, held together with string, mended with nails and even bobby pins, they challenged the strongest tide in the world, with its forty-foot drop and treacherous whirlpools. The water was so icy that a man fallen overboard would freeze to death in minutes. This was why no fisherman "bothered his time" learning how to swim, which would only prolong an agonizing death. No wonder the women waiting up for their men to come home at all hours, depending on the tides, hated the sea, and would rather look out of their kitchen windows at the more friendly road.

Everything went by the tides. I remember stopping at a gas station two hundred miles inland, and apologizing for taking the attendant from his lunch.

"That's all right," he said. "We're eating at low tide."

When Joe Casey got married, my car, the only one in the village, transported the young couple to and from the church. Watching them drive off, someone said, "Joe has a lovely day for his wedding," and I asked John Casey, "Was yours as fine?" He answered, "Well, I'll tell you. The wind was nor-noreast three points and the tide . . ." He took us through all the variations of barometer, thermometer and weather vane, for a day thirty years before. Weather was never taken lightly. Most men and some women could foretell a storm twenty-four hours before there was, to us landlubbers, any sign of it.

The treacherous waters through the gut were formidable teachers. In peacetime freighters coming in to Digby, from Saint John or Halifax or farther, used to radio ahead for a pilot. John Casey knew a week or so in advance when to expect them, and would be out in his shabby little boat, sometimes taking us along to fish while we waited for them to appear. If they came at night he would show them where to anchor and take them in the next day.

In wartime everything was different. There was no advance warning, and no radios could operate in the danger zone. Submarines were on the prowl. The big ships loomed up suddenly out of nowhere, and sent up one small flare. They came only in darkness, on moonless nights, and dared not anchor at all. He took them in at once, through the deadly reefs and submerged ranges of the narrow gut, into the landlocked harbor where they would be safe. He knew those waters, he could travel them by smell, by feel, by sixth sense. It was a specialized form of war work no younger man could do as well, but it took a toll of his health. After the long day's work he must be ready at the signal to run to the beach and launch his boat through storm or snow or sleet or turning tide or all of them together, and bring his freighter in without using a light.

Relays of watchers in the Civil Defense sat up for allotted hours with glasses trained on the sea, sweeping the horizon for that one brief flare which meant another cargo boat had slipped by the enemy and was waiting nervously at the entrance to the gut.

When we saw the flicker we would run up the hill, pound on the Caseys' door and run down again, rousing others on the way, push off, climb in and chug in the little makeshift boat toward the open sea. There were various duties to perform, feeding gas through a broken bottle neck into the sputtering engine, tending the balky motor, steering, baling the water that was always shipped. Once I remember running sleep-drugged to the beach, to push and strain and jump into the boat, only to realize when we were under way that Jawn and I were alone, that when he swung himself up the ship's ladder I would have to take his boat in to shore.

If the engine died I would not be able to restart it. I could be swept out to the bay. Even if it ran, by miracle, I would have to be in two places at once, tend to it, and steer against the tide on the turn for that ferocious rush out through the gut . . . but the freighter, with its precious wartime load, must come first. I was sick with foreboding, but it did not occur to me to mention the panic I felt. I would have to shout against the wind and we

Grandfather and Grandmother Eaton,
and Daniel Izak Vernon Eaton

Grandfather and Grandmother Fitz Randolph

Daniel Izak Vernon Eaton

Myra Eaton

Evelyn Eaton, 1922

Evelyn Eaton in
court dress, 1923

Helen, Lady Dashwood,
at West Wycombe
in the thirties

West Wycombe Park

The blue drawing room at West Wycombe

Evelyn Eaton with Chiang Kai-shek, China, 1945

The audience with Pope Pius XII at the Vatican, 1945. *Standing, left to right,* Pauline Frederick, Mary Day Wynn, Elsie McCormick, Evelyn Eaton, the papal representative, Harry Grayson, Ed Leahy, Harry Flannery, Bob Considine, Hallett Abend

Terry, aged four

Jay Te Winburn

The wedding of Terry and Dick Brengle, 1949

Evelyn Eaton in the Owens Valley, 1960

George Bruley

Evelyn Eaton with Paiute
friends Paul and Louis
recording chants near
Big Pine, 1972

Lillian Baker, a Paiute, making a cradle board out of willow

Evelyn Eaton with Paiute sculptor
Raymond Stone, 1972

Raymond Stone with one of his carved pipeheads
at his home on the Big Pine Reservation

Helen McGhee, a Paiute, with her ancestral baskets still in use, 1972

C. Robert Lee

Harihar Rao (sitar) and Paula Rao (tambula) at the Deepest Valley Theatre

Deepest Valley Theatre

Curtis Phillips

Iren Marik on the stage of the Deepest Valley Theatre

Evelyn Eaton in
Independence, 1971

Independence, California, where Evelyn Eaton now lives

were supposed to make no sound, to show no light. I steered, he attended to the balky engine. We reached the waiting boat too soon. Dimly seen faces peered overside, a rope ladder lowered, he made his spidery jump and vanished upward. The great shape moved on, leaving me alone and terrified. I tried to keep my head, to turn the boat into the heavy wake that could swamp it, and to follow the freighter through the safe channel into Digby. I would pass Victoria Beach, but I could not land there. That was always tricky, sometimes at the wharf, sometimes by the rocks, depending on the tide. Besides, I had to take the boat to Digby, so that Jawn could get back to the Beach and be on hand if another freighter should sneak in and send up a flare for help.

After two hours of terror and strain, I saw lights ahead, and a big looming shape beside the wharf. The motor sputtered for the first time. It died, but I was able to throw the rope and make fast to a stanchion, behind the freighter. I stepped ashore. Frozen and still frightened, I went to find Jawn in the Captain's cabin, comfortably settled, sharing a bottle of good Irish whiskey.

"Oh, there you are," he said as I appeared, expecting to be praised and fussed over. "Did you tie her up good?" That was that. They didn't even offer me a drink, I had to insist I needed one.

After the war, when I went back to Victoria Beach as a tourist, with Terry, Jawn helped us solicitously into the rear of his new high-powered launch, luxuriously cushioned, for a fishing cruise. "Ladies in the stern," he said, twinkling at us, and then, "Steers easier than the old one." That was all he said, but I knew that he remembered. I let him bring me a cushion and even bait my hook, as a helpless lady should.

That summer of the fall of France and the building of Fundy Tide, my moods were schizophrenic. I had spent several years straining every effort, making many sacrifices, to escape from Europe with Terry before war overwhelmed it. Many people did not realize that Dachau was built as early as 1933. In 1934 a friend of mine escaped from it. I saw him in the South of France before he died from the effects of torture. He was a violinist. Among other things done to him, his fingers had been broken, one by one, with time enough between to let him hope that if they didn't break another, he might still, perhaps, be able to play. . . . From what he told me and from what I knew about conditions in Danzig, the German-controlled Polish Corridor, I was among those forced to take Hitler's rise to power seriously. I read *Mein Kampf* and did not laugh.

During 1934 I was afraid, as I waited for the divorce which would give me and Terry a better passport. In 1936 I was advising anyone who would listen to get their children out of Europe, to Canada, to Australia, while there was still time. Why should any children go through any war? I was laughed at. It was another three years before the war broke out, in 1939, but it was building. Now that it had come, exactly step by step, as Hitler outlined it in advance for all to read, I was illogically feeling like a traitor not to be there, with the friends in England who had laughed, the friends in France who were weeping.

My respect, like most of the Western World's, went to England, the beleaguered fortress, in this "her finest hour," but my heart went to France, defeated, overrun for the third time in living memory by arrogant goose-stepping boots. I rose in the morning, I went to bed at night to the sounds and smells of the Bay of Fundy, and for the time being I could not help being flooded with a grateful bliss at the turn my life had unexpectedly taken. Then heaviness returned with the anguish of the war and the dreaded question: "What is the news today?"

All about me were reminders of France. My house was built on the ruins of an old French fort controlling the entrance to the gut. Before that it was a sacred gathering place for the Algonquins. I have a curious photograph, taken that summer, of Mr. McGraw making the picket fence. Towering above him, from a place where there was nowhere to stand, an Indian is looking on, somberly, and behind the Indian there appears to be a stone figure, Aztec in feeling, also watching the building of the fence. I took the picture and developed it myself. I know there was no chicanery, no double exposure. The Indian heads are there, not related to each other, except in ancestry. They look as though hundreds of years separated them. Their expressions are alike, not exactly hostile, not exactly friendly, watchful, waiting.

Still, it was the French, not the Indians, who spoke to me that year, everywhere I looked. The lilacs in the garden came from France. Over what had been the village dump, there was now a cluster of bushes, the dark violet kind that come from Normandy. Up and down the road, and up the valley as far as Grand Pré, were signs of French occupation, old cellar holes, more lilacs, traces of stone fences, outlines of old farms. This was Acadia, the country of Evangeline. I began to think of the Acadians, of their expulsion, as Longfellow did not dare or did not care to tell the story. I began to collect material for my next book.

I was receiving angry comments on *Quietly My Captain Waits* and *Restless Are the Sails,* for writing from the French point of view. A typical plea reached me from an old friend of Aunty Nell in Fredericton: "Please *please* write nothing further against the magnificent English!" and another note said: "It is hard to imagine that the daughter of a gallant Canadian killed at Vimy Ridge could stab England in the back in the hour of her greatest need."

I could understand the emotion. If England behaved badly in the eighteenth century, it was not the moment to talk about it now. Only for me it was. The expulsion of the Acadians was an early attempt at mass genocide, undertaken for motives of greed. It is a horrifying story of treachery, cruelty and waste of human beings. It appealed to me as being what the war was all about, what peace, when it came, must be all about. I felt that I must write the truth about the Acadian tragedy.

The title, *The Sea Is So Wide,* came from the old Breton fisherman's prayer, "O God, be good to me, Thy sea is so wide, and my boat is so small." It is the small boat, the small house, the small things that wrench the heart most when they are threatened. The Acadians were a peaceful, hard-working, frugal people who loved and understood the land they farmed. Their crime was to be prosperous, French and Catholic when England was at war with France and Governor Lawrence needed money. If he could get rid of the Acadians, representing their eviction as a necessary wartime measure, he could confiscate their lands and their cattle, and dispose of them profitably. He did.

The garden which the Acadians made from the forest and waste marsh was the work of several generations, the flowers and vegetables and orchards from Normandy, the willow trees from Touraine. The rich and flourishing farms were destroyed, as many as eight hundred burning in a day, and twelve thousand people were deported, not counting those who were killed or who took to the woods to live with the Indians. Families were separated and dumped anywhere the ships transporting them happened to be going.

When *The Sea Is So Wide* was published in 1943, I got letters from France, Louisiana, Saint Pierre, Virginia and England from people claiming to be descendants of the Comeau family, and claiming that the details about them were family traditions. The Comeaus were imaginary people, whom I had grouped together under a typical Acadian name. I was sorry to disappoint readers who thought I told the story of their ancestors, but I was pleased to have created true composites which could evoke this sort of earnest response.

For two years I lived in the skin of an Acadian, seeing what Acadians saw, feeling a deep affinity with their land, forgetting that they too had taken it away from earlier peoples who loved it and whose ancestors had been there thousands of years to the Acadians' decades, the miscalled Indians, the bronze-skinned people, whose civilizations flourished from the Bay of Fundy to the Pacific. Some of the traces of these great civilizations are now being excavated here and there by archeologists and their importance and magnitude discovered.

How brainwashed until recently we were by the history books and references in literature which children are forced to read at school! Consider the ignorant complacency with which a poet writes:

> How did you fare there, Pilgrims, Pilgrims?
> What did you build in that stubborn land?
>> We felled the forest and tilled the sod
>> Of a continent no man had trod
>> And we established there, in the Grace of God,
>> The rights whereby we stand.
>>> (Francis Brett Young: "The Island")

The Anglo-Saxon race is prone to an intolerable superiority complex for which it is beginning to pay in enforced readjustments. *A continent no man had trod,* translated, means no white man, especially no Englishman. How blind smug can one get?

I was fiercely possessive and infatuated with every blade of grass behind the picket fence at Fundy Tide. My cousin Connie Fitz Randolph came to stay with me during the first rapture. I had no guest room and put her up at the hotel, as I did all guests, on the principle that we would enjoy being together more if we had freedom from each other between meetings. Also I had to work.

One afternoon Connie came down the hill and greeted me with: "What was happening this morning? There was a lot of smoke coming from here."

"What sort of smoke?" I asked anxiously. "Ordinary smoke?"

"Oh no, it couldn't have been!"

Then I realized how absurd I was about Fundy Tide. Nothing that happened there could be ordinary. I had the Acadians' passionate attachment to my strip of land. Even the changing seasons seemed to come more dramatically in Acadia.

It is the only place I know where the fireflies and the apple blossoms come at the same time. My house was set above the gut, with all the Bay of Fundy widening below, and I could always hear the rush of the changing tide as the waters of the rip swirled through the gap to the Bay. Sometimes I was woken by the foghorn sounding on the opposite shore, the bell tolling from the little tower halfway down the cliff, to say that fog was rolling up, moving inland in strange shapes of gray mist.

Sometimes the birds woke me, singing in the apple trees, and the whole garden was full of apple blossoms and singing. Then I would get up and watch the scallop boats coming in with the first faint light of dawn. Later, around breakfasttime, an urgent, forward swishing, like the change of tide but more persistent, would be the *Princess Helene* coming in from Saint John, bringing tourists and artists and weekend guests and the mail. I always loved to watch her pass through the gap, slim proud boat, with shining black-and-white paint. During the war she was painted a dingy gray, and camouflaged to look squat.

Her passing stirred the countryside to life. Bells rang, flags rose, people waved from the fields, from the cliff, from the hotel grounds and the backyards of the fishing village. Occupations were set and timed by her; morning and evening divided into measurable periods—"before she passed the gut," "after she docked," "still at the dock," and "through the gut."

When she had gone out of sight, toward Digby, I usually took my morning walk, the same one every day, up the hill, through the village, past the wharves, across the stream by the wooden bridge, into the woods and along the cliff. From the top of the hill the village spread out below, seventeen shingled houses, a church with a broken tower, a gray shed, the school. Most of the houses had patches in front where flowers and grass struggled for supremacy and the grass won.

Nets, lobster pots and rubber boots, old trawl tubs and bits of rope lay scattered on the dilapidated porches needing paint. It was a fishing village; no one "bothered his time" with the land, good rich earth. French peasants would have cultivated every inch and terraced the hillsides to make them productive. Here they chucked in a few potatoes, some turnips, and that was all; yet they were poor, poorer than a French peasant. Few made more than eight hundred dollars a year from the fishing, mostly hand-lining and trawling. Some made as little as three hundred. On that they raised large families.

"Poor" is not meant to be a disparaging word. It seems more honest, more like the friends I knew than any of the later euphemisms, "the disadvantaged," "the underprivileged," et cetera. The Victoria Beach people were not "dis" nor "under" anything, not poor in spirit, unless in the complimentary sense of the New Testament, not greedy and not grasping. Like the Indians, who shared all they had, the Victoria Beach people helped each other.

There was no doctor in the village, no policeman, no authority of any kind. In winter, when the village was isolated for days at a time, people were sometimes buried without a death certificate. The men sat up with the sick men, did what nursing could be done, and watched over the bodies at wakes; the women did the same for the women. In between childbirth and death, which were absorbing community affairs, neighbors lent a hand to whatever daily drama might be going on.

Not that there weren't foxy fellows here and there, "coyotes, and coyote talk," the Paiutes say. There were. But by and large the people "up to the Beach" were dependably fine and always generous. During the war, when an English troopship was sunk off the coast, the village adopted the survivors. Families took them in, warmed, fed and clothed them, wrote to them when they moved on and to their families in England, a correspondence which went on for several years. It takes the poor, or, if we must, the not-too-well-advantaged, to understand basic facts of human need and living.

There was no running water in the village when I came there. I helped to put it in. The Caseys had the only telephone and they were the only ones with electricity until my house was built. Now things are different, now they "have it better."

Terry and Dick spent part of their honeymoon at the Beach, and went back in the summer of 1971 with their three teenage sons, for the first time in twenty-one years.

Terry wrote to me:

> Today fog, thick and comforting, with the Point Prim horn groaning its complaint in the old familiar way. A good day for writing. I have all sorts of impressions—the changes are phenomenal, the spirit the same as it always was. The most obvious change is one of well-being, if not affluence, all the

houses are painted, the road paved, but not spoiled, it still follows the shore-line in the same way, everyone has a car, electricity and a phone, but the names on the mailboxes [not there in my day] read Ellis, Everett, McGrath, Taylor and Hayden as firmly as ever.

A German freighter came in and we went along . . . "ladies in the stern" again, you remember? Joe's boat is a yacht compared with the old one, and Joe wears his best business suit, very mod, wide bright tie, bell bottoms, probably tailored in London, to climb the ladder these days. Such luxury and style are difficult to describe, but his spry partner gave the adventure the old-time flavor by hopping about and over the cabin roof "hollering" instructions to Joe on the ship. It's a funny blend these days of the old and the new.

The boat we crossed on, the *Princess of Acadia,* is a brand new, larger ship than the *Helene,* but with little of her charm. There are no cabins, only a vast hold for two hundred cars and campers, more speed, less quality, and a dock full of complicated lock systems and cables, just before the Digby Pines, and now there is a construction of roads to lead to such a modern contraption, so one's initial impression (after the first shock) is of giant leaps into the twentieth century.

I left Nova Scotia in 1945, and of all the homes I have bought and built and lived in since, Fundy Tide is the one that sometimes calls to me, as though we had unfinished business still. I think I left cheerful brave vibrations there for the new owners, but I had not quite lived out my quota of enjoyment . . . the war, some personal conditions of uncertainty, inner torments and outward treacheries dimmed the experience of building and living in the first home tailored to my needs, the first I came to in the New World, after struggle and strain. I drank in the feeling of being *chez moi,* and longed to have those friends trapped in France, some of whom did not survive the war, come there and sit in the garden.

I never had so individual a place again. For instance, instead of "bothering my time" with a kitchen, I had a darkroom and an oratory. Meals were brought from the hotel by Douglas, who had been a ship's boy on a sailing clipper once, used to taking his Captain's food to him in all weathers without spilling or letting it get cold. I ate wherever I happened to be and whenever I felt hungry. There was a pantry with a warming plate to keep things hot, and a place to wash the dishes before they went back to the hotel.

The house had four stone fireplaces, "with faces onto" the stones. The old mason who built them died halfway up the main chimney, not literally, but it was very evident where his fine work left off and another man finished it.

What parties went on there of wartime strangers and sojourners, and unexpected old friends, gathered in front of the great burning logs in the living room, with the sound of the sea outside, and the wind in the apple trees!

A group of Americans came every summer to the Beach, among them Martha Banning Thomas, whose sturdy cabin perched on the top of the hillside commanded the best sweep of the sea. Her strong and sensitive poems appeared in many poetry magazines and newspapers, revealing the land and the people better than anything written about that part of Nova Scotia that I have read. One in particular seems to me to *be* Victoria Beach:

COMING UP THE HILL
(Northern Shore)

First, you will see the house against the sky,
 Alone a little, maybe, waiting there;
The steep-pitched roof and ridge-pole rising high
 Above unpainted clapboards.
        Windows stare
Low-lidded, polished . . . every dark green shade
 Drawn half way down, and just a little more,
Since winter sunshine very well may fade
 The patterned oilcloth on the kitchen floor.

A clumsy cart, with four great wheels of red,
 Stands near the spot where sunflowers used to shine,
And antic calves were staked . . . and richly fed
 On unmowed clumps of ribboned grass and vine;
A pile of heavy timbers weathered gray
 As shingles on the wood-house, waits the saw;
The lilac bush is bending well away
 To windward, stripped to crooked bone and claw;

The flat and heatless look of northern light
 Makes plain things plainer than reality,
Yet, though austere, there's nothing of the blight
 Of worn-down will for living.
       It may be
You will not miss warm colors of the south
After you taste the salt wind on your mouth.

Martha and her dogs and her battered old car and gray shingled cabin were landmarks "up to the Beach." Now she is buried there, overlooking the Bay of Fundy.

An old friend of hers, Ethel Comstock Bridgman, came every summer to the hillside. She was nicknamed "Hannah" because she saved the situation in Ethel Barrymore's production of *Little Women* by going on with less than an hour's notice when the actress playing Hannah was incapacitated. Hannah was known and loved by the fishermen, because she went out with them in all weathers, caught good hauls, and always had a stock of stories and good liquor to dispense. After Fundy Tide was built she shared it with me for a joyful two years, and we were together a number of times in New York, and once for a winter in Virginia, where we rented the Market Square Tavern Kitchen in Williamsburg, before the reconstruction got so professionally organized. In those days we could roam the gardens and the houses unchaperoned or herded by ladies in crinolines and gentlemen in wigs. I was working on the Williamsburg part of *The Sea Is So Wide* that winter, still haunted by Acadians.

Hannah had known the theater world well, and her stories of New York in the thirties filled in some big blanks in my knowledge of the prewar years in the United States. She helped me to adjust to American citizenship, not taking it for granted that I knew everything. People are apt to forget how ignorant Europeans were in general about the United States. If I had suddenly become a Spaniard I would have known more about the background, politics, art, religion and general mores of the country I was adopting. It does take at least five years to make the transition, even partially. Some people never make it completely. But when we consider how absurdly little Americans knew then about other countries, even about Canada, next door to them, and things Canadian, my ignorance was not so strange.

Television has made a difference, as it may make the difference between war and peace. When war comes into the living room, justification for any sort of war goes out the window. The television generation has grown up distrusting slogans, patriotic or commercial, and knowing a lot more than we did about other countries.

Canadian friends and relatives came to the Beach, lawyers, doctors, a smattering of painters, whose names I have forgotten, but I can see us all there, coming and going about our absorbing affairs. I can hear snatches of talk. Surely that strip of hill is haunted by resolute shapes, moving up and down beneath morning mists and fog, before it burns away.

It was to Fundy Tide that my mother came, with Aunty Nell and Helen's youngest child, John, to escape the Battle of Britain. A few days before they arrived, Churchill broadcast that "as a last resort" the English government would move to Canada, and carry on from there! The Canadians, hearing this for the first time over the radio, flinched a little. And so did I when I got the family telegram to meet them eight hundred miles away, in wartime, with rationed gas and tires. But I did. And brought them back to Fundy Tide and housed them in the hotel. We met as though nothing had happened to me or to them. But of course it had. The war, for one thing. I, as a lesser breed, was expected to support the family and feel most deeply honored to be allowed to do so. I did for the summer, but when my mother said we should look for a school "most nearly approximating to Eton" for John, I said no. I couldn't afford it. I couldn't afford that sort of school for Terry, why then for John? I was remembering nights on a métro bench, days of semistarvation, years of total disinterest in anything that might be happening to Terry or to me. I would have respected them more if they had been consistent, but now that I was a best-selling author with a home of my own, their moral disapproval seemed to vanish, and I was expected to take on three relatives indefinitely. Even if I had *liked* them, or they me, if we had always "sung the same song," I could not have managed that. As it was, financing their summer wiped out my savings. I was not thanked, nor, when peace came and money could once more be sent out of England, repaid. Since England was in a jam, I and all the other good Canadians who took in refugees and looked after them through the war years were to be considered lucky to have this honor, for many of us that would be thanks enough.

Eventually the family went on to Ottawa, then to Montreal and Toronto. John did indeed go to the best Canadian boys' school. I do not know who paid for it. Mother flew back to England. She was always brave. I bought her ticket when I found that she was determined to leave.

"We have our battle stations," she said, and told me that the village had six machine guns and some weapons from the Tower of London, and that her job was to help confuse the Germans when they landed, by changing all the road signs about.

Her plane came down in Portugal, overrun at that time with desperate refugees. She talked her way onto another, for London, and sent me a telegram: DELIGHTFUL TRIP, DEAR, WILL NEVER TRAVEL ANY OTHER WAY. It was her first and last flight. She spent the rest of her life near Helen. Aunty Nell stayed for a year in Fredericton with the Fitz Randolphs, Bob and his wife, and would, I think, have stayed longer, if they or I could have afforded it. Then she too went back to West Wycombe, and so did John.

For a while I wrote to them and sent packages. Aunty Nell answered but my mother communicated only by telegram, and then it had nothing to do with the subject of my letters, it was always what the United States had done to displease her.

HOW DARE YOU MURDER OUR BOYS IN PALESTINE? was one that I received when things were not going right for England in the Middle East. Another more general condemnation ran: WHY DID YOU INTERFERE WITH GOD'S PLAN? GOD HAD PLANNED FOR ENGLAND TO RULE THE WORLD, AND YOU UPSET IT IN 1776.

I was glad that she added the date, it lessened my direct responsibility somewhat, but at that time the F.B.I. were investigating me for clearance as a war correspondent and I was afraid they would rather naturally assume these messages to be a code. Our Western Union was the local druggist. Whenever the telephone rang and I heard his apologetic voice: "I have a cablegram from England for you," my first reaction was, *someone has been killed or bombed out,* and my second, when I realized it was from my mother, a worried annoyance, about the F.B.I. and my neighbors. I was on a party line, and I could hear the clickings and sometimes sudden little snorts.

Once she cabled a more puzzling message than usual.

"DEPRECATE," the concerned voice began, "D-E-P . . ."

"Yes," I said, "I've got that. Go on."

"DEPRECATE USE OF WORD . . . er . . . BELLY . . ."

"Belly? Are you sure? That doesn't sound like my mother."

"BELLY," he repeated firmly, "ON PAGE 301. Signed MOTHER."

This time I was completely at sea. So were the listeners-in, only they were amused and I was not.

I thought that something very serious had now gone wrong with my mother. Always before it had been the old anti-American phobia that she had been brought up with and encouraged to nurture all her life. Naturally, in wartime, with England's empire waning, and unsatisfactory Evie becoming one of the hated and despised *common* Americans, and doing well in the States, these outbursts might be expected, or at least could be explained. But here was a new twist. This time surely the F.B.I. . . . I brooded for a while and then remembered that several months before, feeling that she was perhaps becoming morbid, I had sent her *Every Month Was May,* my light-hearted collection of stories from *The New Yorker,* thinking it might cheer her. I turned to the book. Sure enough, on page 301 I had written: "The mayor of the 17th arrondissement wore a tricolor sash around his belly."

The telegram to outdo all the rest arrived some years later at Terry's wedding. Her father-in-law was reading messages and wires at the reception. Suddenly he held up his hand for extra silence and attention. "We have a cablegram from Terry's grandmother," he cried, and before I could leap across the room to snatch it from him, he opened it with a flourish and read to the attentive crowd:

"ALWAYS REMEMBER, DEAR, NO MATTER WHAT, YOU ARE BRITISH. Signed GRANDMOTHER."

This to Terry, legally French, actually half Polish-Irish and half what I am, on the occasion of her marriage to a very American husband.

George Brengle, bless him, rose to the challenge.

"Terry's grandmother has such a sense of humor," he said, laughing heartily, while I signed to the orchestra to start the first dance. Champagne took care of the rest, but I did have the old familiar feeling of mortification and rage.

After that, the telegrams ceased. My mother had had the last word.

It was from Fundy Tide that I left for the "Journey to War" that was to change my inner and outer life, and it was to Fundy Tide that I returned after seeing the last of the pre-atomic world, on a mission that covered twenty countries and thirty-three thousand miles by plane and jeep.

The villagers asked me to speak to them about this experience. My diary says:

Tuesday, Nov. 6th 1945, had supper, changed into my uniform by request, drove Martha, Mrs. Everett and Evelyn Taylor to the church. Here I found myself at a Baptist evening service. We sang a hymn and listened to a reading, then I spoke. At the end I said goodbye to Victoria Beach. The soloist sang and everyone joined in "God be with you till we meet again," especially for me. It was a sweet and touching send-off and I loved it. After the war years spent together, those familiar good faces turned to me in friendship. I hoped they liked what I said to them. I found it hard to speak.

Now it is strange to be sitting here, the last night among my things. Tomorrow they go, and the next day, I. "God be with us," indeed. I feel like an Acadian, about to be transported. Perhaps I have taken on some of their sad karma.

Part Four

Nineteen forty-five was a crucial year. I was writing *Winter Reason,* which after more than a year's work and many rewritings had to be scrapped. I had taken on a book about Mother Seton, the first American-born candidate for sainthood, in collaboration with Monsignor Robert Moore of Saint Peter's Church, New York. He was to release all the material and I was to do all the work. I was recovering from an unhappy love affair. I was in debt to Ann Watkins, to the bank, and I was beginning to be desperate about finances. I had taken on a part-time job as a typist, to pay current bills. I was co-chairman of the writers' section of a sturdy and interesting club, the Pen and Brush, founded by Ida M. Tarbell, and on top of all this threshing around and overextension, there came a great turning point in my inward, and eventually outward, life.

My diary for January 24 says:

Ann put the most extraordinary proposition up to me tonight—to fly to the Pacific, which she says takes in China and India, on a two months' tour as a special correspondent, with the rank of Captain in the U.S. Army, as the guest of the U.S. Air Force, in March. The same sort of thing that Roger Burlingame, Kay Boyle and Carl Carmer are doing in Europe. (I would have loved *that* trip!) This is an exciting prospect. I have never been to India or China or the Pacific. My India is Kipling's, my China Marco Polo's. What an opportunity, *now,* when nobody can move about. I can't believe it. Why me?

Jan. 25th. Ann phoned to say trip postponed till May, and my name high on the list.

Jan. 30th. Today's paper had an account of an American family hidden in the jungle for three years among the Igorots, emerging from their hiding place and reaching the American lines. Enemy planes flew over them daily but they were never spotted. During this time they were reading one of my books! "During their Swiss Family Robinson existence, the Shaners read and reread at least four times the six books they had managed to bring along—Walt Whitman's *Leaves of Grass,* Tolstoy's *Anna Karenina, The Sun Is My Undoing, Quietly My Captain Waits, March of the Barbarians,* and *Timeless Land.* Shaner also had a set of technical books. When the day's work was done, the books were brought out and read aloud by the light of candles or coconut-oil lamps." [Frank Kelly in the New York *Herald Tribune.*] This makes me feel less futile, also when I get letters from the wounded or men on long sea convoys.

Feb. 4th. There is a strange undercurrent to my inner life, this year and part of last. It is the sad acceptance of maturity, a sort of knowingness that is calm and strong and resigned. A winding up? A letting go? Not as definite as that, but an awareness of the end, that is always with me. Perhaps another best seller would give me the illusion of solidarity—for a while.

Feb. 6th. Dynamic phone call from Ann saying that my name was up before the Board today for the Pacific thing and she *might* have news for me tonight. She is to telephone after she hears, between 6 and 7. No call, no news. But whatever way it goes I'll be content . . . try to be.

Feb. 7th. Another very bad night. I don't remember being so miserable as this for a long time. Touching letter from a sergeant, wounded, who had read *The Sea Is So Wide* in the Armed Services Edition, in the hospital. That sort of thing makes writing worthwhile. I never remember writing a book gladly, or eagerly, or anything but reluctantly prodded on. . . .

Feb. 19th. Telephone came in from Ann. She says Washington has o'kayed my papers for the Pacific trip, so if now I can only manage the timing sufficiently well, to get the shots over and get up to Canada to settle things up there, see Terry and arrange for her, also finish *Winter Reason* [a book I worked at for three years and scrapped] and get in the outline of the Mother Seton book. . . .

Feb. 27th. Mother Seton is a great trial! I have just read in her journal: "No chaste woman can read romance. Should she insist on the trial she will cease to be chaste." As a writer of romance, and trying to do a book on her, this doesn't please me much. What a book I could make if her journal and all her letters had been destroyed! As it is, I'll have to ignore as much as I can of her, humorless prig. I would have thought the Church had made her so, but she left ample evidence in her own writings that she was morbid, sanctimonious and puke-making! It will be very hard to write this book. Saw Allanah for a moment. [Friend from London and Paris days, who was temporarily refugeeing in New York. She had edited an avant-garde literary magazine in Paris.] Had my fortune told. Taking a trip, a long one, to a beautiful place, but first a short one to arrange things. Will live to be well over seventy, not that I want *that*.

March 1st. Finished the outline of Mother Seton and took it round to Ann and left it. When I got back, Elizabeth Lawrence [my editor for many years at Harper] had sent the galleys of Santha Rama Rau's book *I Went Home* [evidently a first title for *Home to India*] with a note asking me to write a comment on it. I will, with pleasure, since I think it's very good.

March 2nd. Blue all day. No particular reason. Rang up Ann about the outline. She said it was "dull," and I must redo part of it. That couldn't be enough to depress me, could it? Then bills came in, and I paid them, that *could* depress me. Then I'm lonely. After all, nothing to go home to, but work, and more work. As someone, Jan Struther, I believe, said, "I like to *have* written."

There was a special delivery letter from Henry, which made me feel better, wanted somewhere by someone, even if not the right one.

Worked on the outline until eleven. It is a tricky and tiresome thing but I must get it right if I can, by right I mean approved by Ann, chiefly. I don't know that I want to write this book, but if I don't write something, finish something soon I will have *no* money at all. Got up again and worked till 2.

Sunday March 4th. To lunch with Elizabeth Lawrence, who introduced me to Santha Rama Rau and her uncle Shivan Rau. They were both *lambs,* very real, very sweet people. He is a friend of Krishnamurti, she is a very cultured woman with a great sense of humor, no disappointment after reading her *Home to India.* I introduced them both—badly—to the Pen and Brush and they each spoke well, especially Shivan Rau who gave a very moving and I would think real picture of India. He spoke with great moderation and very telling sincerity. The pens and brushes seemed to enjoy it. I certainly did.

March 23rd. Have had my first shots, smallpox in the right leg, typhus in the left. Then to Iranian Institute for the 3rd in series on the Philippines, useful for the trip. [I took courses under Dr. Phyllis Ackermann and Dr. Upham Pope at the Institute, to help with the background for the trip.]

Ann telephoned that the 2nd chapter of the Seton outline was out, no good. I had doubts about it myself. So that means redoing that. Dear me, life is tiresome. It is odd to be middle-aged. Sun at the meridian, so little to show for it, and if no seeds before this, no garden.

March 28th. More unpleasant probings into my interior, basal metabolism, blood tests and a typhoid shot, then home to Mother Seton. Ann telephoned with two important bits of news, I am to be briefed next week, and Little Brown is greatly excited about Mother Seton (more than I am!). After briefing I shall know more about Fundy Tide, etc. I heard the news with a certain return of excitement and the feeling that at least the money for the shots will not be wasted. Wonder what I will come back with? If one were only a Mason Brown . . . his simplicity, his directness, his understanding. . . . Could I do that, could I, for the Philippines?

I hope I can make a diary of the trip, simple, real, moving. Mrs. Little People going to see what her son and husband saw, recording it.

March 31st. More typhus, more tetanus. To Rainbow Room, with Henry. Stood on the balcony for a moment, looking over all New York. An Englishwoman beside me said, "How beautiful. I didn't think it would be beautiful." (They never do. They have been told so long that New York is large and vulgar and new. I was myself, and it *is* beautiful.) Then she turned to me and said, "How vulnerable for bombs." I said, "Yes, we thought of that." The "we" made me straighten my shoulders. I have affection for Europe, but this is my home. And yet, how strangely on the rim I am.

April 6th. Viggo on the telephone to ask me to act as alternate to regional meeting, also he said that the trip might be the changing point in my life, he spoke of widened horizons and a new impetus. I have always wondered about Viggo, and have always felt he saw more than others. Perhaps because he is a priest. [The Reverend Viggo Westergaard was a fellow Co-Mason and liberal Catholic priest.]

I have just finished reading *Beloved Friend,* Tschaikovsky's biography. How strange! Renunciation or fulfillment seem equally disastrous to romance or love. Renunciation fascinates me. Once I had no patience with the idea of it, now I'm not so sure, that is, if you want a thing to remain important, more important than it is. Probably friendship and family love is best, and love of God the only exciting and enduring kind, the only adventure, because never consummated? There is always a nostalgic appeal in complete renunciation, not for salvation of self, but because the only way to *do* is to *be.*

Monday April 9th. Ann telephoned to say that General MacArthur doesn't want any women on the Pacific trip, and the whole thing may be off. Ann is to hear Thursday. I had a sort of hunch when I heard of the change of command. Nimitz had already given his o.k. Oh well, except for disappointment and some loss of face (too many people know) . . . I suppose I wouldn't mind. I *am* disappointed though. I had begun to gear all my plans and all my thinking to the trip, and felt confident about it, up to the change of command a few days ago. Since then I've felt it all recede. Maddening, just on the ground of sex!

Thursday April 12th. Dull gray morning with rain in the sky, clearing later. Worked on *Winter Reason.* Then to lunch with Putnam's Wally Hangar. Putnam's wants me to stay over in India and 1) do a book for them. They would finance my traveling, or, rather, my living expenses and my return. 2) They want a travel book of the trip. 3) They want a Canadian travel book. Then I went to the Pen and Brush and was photographed in color. Then home, and the news of the President's death met me in the elevator. I couldn't believe Scotty when he told me. I rushed to the radio and all evening long it rolled out, sorrow, tribute, regret, shock. I called Hilda and Tommy. We went for a moment to the Ascension Church. Others were there praying for him, and for Truman and the nation. This is a more shattering awakening here it seems than Pearl Harbor, more unifying.

Saturday April 14th. First I worked on *Winter Reason,* then I went for a shot of typhus—might as well keep on until we hear finally whether we get to go—then to the Memorial Service for President Roosevelt in Saint John's Cathedral. What with typhus, Empirin and emotion I felt queasy. The Cathedral was jammed, 7000 people the papers say, and the service simple and very moving. One thing bothers me, on this day hoodlums broke into the Jewish Synagogue in Brooklyn and damaged the sacred things and the place itself so badly that the Memorial Service for Roosevelt couldn't be held. Could it be beginning here? Surely we can escape Fascism here! Each country must meet its own karma, but have we that karma here?

April 16th. Listened to the new President. His voice was earnest and simple. Some of the things he said were sound. He started too soon, and I heard Speaker of the House Rayburn say, "Wait a minute, Harry, I have to present you!" and he said, "Go on." Funny little homey touch. He isn't an orator, hasn't much fire and very little originality—speaks in near-clichés, but I think he's sincere and I think he's good. So much has happened. Willkie dead, Roosevelt dead, contracts signed, more coming up, the Pacific trip mooted . . . mooting is just what they do. . . . Nice evening with Henry.

April 23rd. Saint George's day. Ann telephoned to say the trip was on. Burma, China, India, four women only, me among them. I was to telephone Washington and I just have, a Captain Ray Bonta, who told me to go ahead and get my uniform. Tropical outfit. Shall wait to get my official letter and then go over to the PX in Brooklyn and try to get it as cheaply as I can.

The lights went on again in London!! For the first time in all these dark years! I heard the people in Lambeth dancing and singing, bless their cockney hearts, and a description of how London looked in light again.

Supper with Henry and to *Carousel,* which was very moving, especially to me—good music, good songs, and colorful poignant dancing.

April 25th. Had a cholera shot, more to come. Went to Harper's and left half of *Winter Reason*. Went to lunch with Helena Kuo, charming Chinese, who gave me some addresses in China. Then to Dr. Connie Guion, who discovered that I have a streptococcus infection of the gall bladder. Must get over it before I go.

April 28th. To regional meeting of Co-Masonry in Marie Deraisme's. [Founder of *Le Droit Humain*.] I met and liked M.P.G.C. Armour 33rd and had an opportunity of talking with her. She asked me to write to her from the Pacific. I also met the Brn from the Sov. Chap. that I am to join in Baltimore when I get back, and liked them.

May 12th. There must be something wrong with any woman who at 42 finds herself so alone. Still, I am very conscious of having had a generous deal in life. "I was not ever thus," complained bitterly, in fact, when young but so much has been given me during all my middle years, and indeed right along. I've enjoyed it all, and I'm grateful. I would have liked a dear and lasting companion too, of course, but one cannot eat one's cake, etc. and I have grown too jealous of my liberty of action to be easy to live with now.

Disquieting feeling and news about Russia. Eight thousand British and American prisoners of war—some have been in German hands for five years—flown home today. I hope we don't have to fight Russia, now or at any time, but I must say they are behaving in a provoking way. I am tired tonight and will go early to bed, turning my back on *Winter Reason*. It would be fun to have an income. I used to think it despicable to live on money you hadn't earned, I still do, in theory, but in practice it is good for the stomach and the nerves. If I could make one more movie sale and get straight . . . One thing, I'm more valuable dead than alive, and if this trip is my last, the insurance will take care of Terry materially, and she is old enough, more mature and with a better start than I, to make a way for herself. Tim and Rita will help. I want to live, have lots of things to live for, but if this should be the summons, I do think I've had a good life and sometimes a good time. I've learned something, too, I hope, and that is not to snitch, not to snatch. I've also learned another thing, from an odd source, one of Dorothy Sayers' detective stories [*Gaudy Night*]: "She saw it as a holy war, with every man and woman to whom integrity of mind meant more than material gain, defenders in the keep of Man-Soul, their personal differences forgotten in the face of a common foe. *To be true to one's calling, whatever follies one might commit in one's emotional life, that was the way to spiritual peace.*"

What was my calling? Minor poet? So-so novelist? Journeyman Mason? Wanderer certainly. Human being, perhaps. That was it, nor could there be a greater, more difficult, more baffling, more alluring.

So it was that in the summer of 1945 I found myself one of five women and seven men in a party of war correspondents flying thirty-three thousand miles by Air Transport Command, over Africa, Burma, India, across the Hump to China, and back by way of Europe, Iceland and Labrador. We covered twenty countries.

For two months we shared, in concentrated form, the experience of millions overseas. We were drawn into the Army's haphazard solidarity, and shared the impact of its achievement.

It was B.A.B. (Before the Atomic Bomb). The war against Japan was growing to a climax, expected to continue for a year at least. We were preparing with great secrecy to invade the coast of China. Germany had surrendered but, if Fascism is a name for Injustice, the fight against it was settling into its stride. We watched a world stirring in deep unrest, which has been with us ever since.

It was necessarily a bird's-eye view we were being offered, but a bird sees more than is suspected from the ground. Geography and history show clearer from the air; divisions and barriers flatten. There are no frontiers to a plane, casually telescoping world landmarks thousands of miles apart into a day.

Pioneers, returning to find ourselves anachronisms, we saw the last of the pre-atomic world. The journal that I kept, of certain things glimpsed accidentally and by the way between briefings, is the haphazard account of a hurried bird, offered to more leisurely travelers. Li Po says: "Let a man of spirit venture where he pleases, and never tip his golden cup empty toward the moon." My cup was not empty, but I was. Something had happened to me. On the long plane hours of work and solitude I discovered that I had grown dusty, brittle, shallow. Poetry had sloughed me off and I had forgotten the Other. Did it begin with leaving Europe, or had it started long before that? I did not know, but this journey among strangers to far corners of the world at war came to be a painful awakening, a climbing backward and upward to the forsaken path, like Dante from his wood.

On the surface I was very ill prepared for the trip, with too many pressures and commitments to bone up for it as I should have. I did not entirely believe that it would happen. Instead of finding out who would be going with me, and what they had been and done and whom they would be representing, I made no inquiries. Instead of studying the places where we would be going, I was obsessed with finishing *Winter Reason* and spent all my working time on that. Then I had taken on the writing of the book on Mother Seton. For the first and last time I had agreed to write on a subject I did not like and did not approve of, solely for money. I had also agreed to accept a co-signer who would do none of the work. This was the low point of my writing career and I have always been ashamed of it.

I was involved in leaving Fundy Tide and Victoria Beach, where I had hoped to live for the rest of my life, and I was undergoing some strange changes in metabolism, perhaps in connection with the infected gall bladder and the treatment for it. I had suddenly grown very fat, and when I got into my uniform I was disgusted at the squat, ugly mass that I saw in the mirror.

My diary says:

May 30th. Climbed into uniform on Memorial Day for the first time. Felt self-conscious. When one is a fine figure of a woman over forty uniform is *piquante* and *scratchante*. I went to see Elizabeth Lawrence who politely said it looked well. She made popovers in celebration. We talked of a number of things. I am still upset that I am representing Putnam's instead of Harper's, because Harper's missed the bus on my credentials. I have no ties whatever with Putnam's, and Harper has published most of my books to date.

It is a strange experience to put on uniform one day and step out, seemingly part of an army, with no indoctrination to help the adjustment. When a startled WAC saluted me on Forty-second Street, both of us were taken aback, I because I didn't know how to return it, she because of the Vision that confronted her. We stared, averted our eyes and passed in a pained silence.

It showed that anyone could impersonate a WAC officer, for a short time, even with a number of incongruities. Later I found I had most insignia on upside down and back to front, and I had no papers to prove my story if I were challenged. We were to pick those up in Washington.

Meanwhile subtle changes indicated my changed estate. The porter took no tip for lugging my heavy bag, the ticket agent said, "Your furlough will be less than one single." That was Greek to me. She repeated it, adding, "You're with the Army?" "Yes," I said, and took the pink ticket. I can travel back on it three months from now, and shall keep it to do so—some sort of talisman, perhaps.

May 31 was a strange day. First of all the self-consciousness of being in uniform, so burly, in "the Nation's Capital." I went to the Pentagon, and learned from Captain Bonta that our flight was delayed twenty-four hours for visa chasing. I spent all morning getting British, Iranian and Egyptian visas. Each consulate was far from any other. Washington is beautiful in summer, green and lush and gracious, and it was a perfect day with a refreshing breeze, but my feet were in G.I. shoes. They hurt and raised a blister, a bad thing to start the trip with. It didn't appear until evening. Meanwhile I tramped back and forth, raising a smile and a nudge, front view, but startled comments of "war correspondent" side view, when they could see my shoulder patch. I had lunch at the Allied Inn, feeling silly. There were people from the British Embassy whom I recognized from those early days when I was "Lady Dashwood's sister." One of them looked at me as though he was puzzled, but of course he did not place me in that context.

Then I went back to the Pentagon for more talk with Captain Bonta, "a nervous man, who takes things hard," my diary notes. "He seems to feel he has been put upon, I hope not by me, and that some of the women have demanded impossible service, again I hope not I, and that he is going to impress upon us tomorrow that we must all be good sports. I intend to be. I know this isn't a picnic, but what an opportunity!"

On June 1 our unmilitary-looking group of men and women hurried breathlessly into the Washington airport. Some of the men wore battle dress, some coats, some pull-on visor hats. We ranged in tasteful effect all the way, as Bob Considine put it, from Brigadier-General Bruce Gould in his Saks officer's hat to "Yardbird Ed Leahy" in a battered football cap he clung to through the trip. The women too were a shock to the spruce WAC officer accompanying them, obliged to look, but not resignedly, on various travesties of her uniform.

We were breathless because in the last few days we had gathered shots against cholera, typhus, tetanus, typhoid, smallpox and yellow fever, and, almost as painfully, visas from the necessary consulates. We had been processed in the Pentagon, photographed and fingerprinted, presented with yellow cards informing the Japanese that, if captured, we must be treated with all the courtesies shown to army captains . . . a dubious distinction . . . and we had been briefed around a long, solid, severe table in the heart of the Pentagon with maps on the walls, pads and pencils before us, and a general atmosphere of hushed solemnity and mental alertness that was in itself a strain. We had met our pilot, a lovely burly Captain Barney, the crew and each other at a dinner given by Douglas Aircraft, all in our uniforms together. I looked terrible in mine. Bob Considine leaned across me. "Have you got all your weight, Honey?" I thought he was being unnecessarily rude about my shape and was about to bridle, while my heart sank at such an inauspicious start to the venture. Then it occurred to me that he was asking others, including two thin men, the same question, without the Honey. Slow as usual, I discovered that he was referring to our luggage. He wanted to put more liquor in, anywhere he could. (Later we were allowed to take as much weight as we wanted, but at first it was forty-four pounds. And we found more than plenty of liquor along the way.)

We were shepherded to a narrow projection room with four rows of chairs in front of a small screen. Ditching equipment hung in panels round the walls. In the center of the floor an inflated life raft with black-rubber sails stole the show. It was small and rakish like a pirate craft or a miniature Chinese junk, and there was an air of businesslike bravado about it. It looked like a boy's first raft, something dreamed up to sail the Spanish Main. It took the mind backward through the centuries to Leif Ericson and men like him who reached America in boats as touchingly naive. Only they had no floating radio with a yellow kite attached to it to take the aerial aloft.

The lights went out, the picture on the screen began showing the correct method of ditching. Nonchalantly, flawlessly, pilot, crew and passengers performed, but just when they were due to reach the boat a whirring click and sputtering stopped the film.

"I hope this isn't significant," someone said.

The operator, embarrassed, tinkered with his projector. After two more false starts an officer decided to explain the procedure since the movie would not work.

"In order not to delay the takeoff," he began, and step by step, saying "when" not "if," he led us through the ritual of ditching, explaining each part of the equipment.

". . . and a New Testament," he added, "for burial at sea." Nothing was overlooked. "Take it easy," he went on. "Don't lose your heads. You'll be all right."

I was remembering Aunty Nell when she asked the purser, "What shall I do if I find myself unexpectedly in the water?" and his bland, "Just be perfectly natural, Madam."

"Please come this way," a voice boomed, the first of the Metallic Voices which would direct us for the next two months, "for the takeoff."

We passed through another door to the runway. The briefing room became a Bridge of Sighs cutting us off from all we left. We had taken a long voyage in the little boat with the black-rubber sails. In front of us the shining C-54 waited impatiently, eager to rush upstairs.

We lined up for photographs. I felt nervous, shy and afraid. I had been an American citizen for only a year, and there I was, among all those streamlined, high-powered people representing A.B.C., N.B.C., New York *Times,* Chicago *Tribune, Life* magazine, *Reader's Digest.* . . .

I decided I would say I represented L.P.D. (for Laymen, Poor Devils) and try to get away with it. Later, when that cover was blown, I said whenever I was asked to identify myself, "I'm the only one here who writes fiction . . . and admits it."

Fiction was much despised, or gently tolerated, but before the tour was ended most of the newspaper people took me aside to confide, "I've always wanted to write a novel," and I assured them that I would never tell.

Then we climbed into the plane, and I took the seat which was to be my permanent home from home for the months ahead.

My diary says:

We keep the seats we started with, guarding them jealously. As far as I am concerned, until I get back, if I get back, this seat is home. I live here, I entertain here. Meyer Berger of the New York *Times* dropped into the spare beside me, confiding that he hated travel, travel of any kind, even the subway. Then what is he doing here? We munched C rations together companionably. The plane has an icebox, a hot plate, conveniences like an American Specialist, only more primitive. Great-Grandmother Eaton would never have tolerated such a rickety bucket, but most planes have none at all.

Meyer Berger wrote a plaintive story about these difficulties before they, or another something, overcame him and he dropped out from the group, to make his way back to the U.S. from Morocco. Until then he sat beside me often. He did not seem to notice my split-level daze. Perhaps he thought I had a long hangover, like some of the others. I wished it were that, but more and more I had begun to feel about the *City of Wilmington,* as the plane was called, as I used to feel and dream about the *Lusitania* . . . a Great Gray Shape, in spite of its gleaming-white exterior and white-and-rose inside. . . . A Great Gray Shape which later would be going down.

Part of me fought valiantly against this obsession, part of me said "Nonsense!" and struggled to be normal, whatever normality was. But all through the tour from the beginning I seemed to be presented with a series of il-lustrated texts, a sort of résumé test paper, on conditions of human life, re-lated to mistakes I had made, or was making, or had suffered from. It was like the first symbolical journey in the Mysteries, noise, confusion, terror, poignancy . . . doing, in fact, what was heretofore done in symbol. Only that, I had always thought, came after death.

We landed first in Bermuda, where we saw the wounded coming off lit-ters from another plane, a C-54 like ours, and here began for me the strange double focus, funneling backward, slipping into different levels that I was to meet with off and on for the rest of the trip. It came without warning, and lasted for a flash or longer, once for more than an hour. I wrote about this shifting focus in *Flight* and also in *I Saw My Mortal Sight*.

As the wounded went by, with orderlies beside them, bending to talk to them, I was back in London Bridge Station, watching other litters pass. Fog and gloom took the place of bright Bermuda sunshine. I heard the shuffling feet and saw the faces. . . .

Someone shook my arm. The group was moving forward, toward the plane. When all the wounded were out, we climbed the steps and peered inside. Like all hospital planes, it was fitted up to carry the maximum num-ber of wounded home in the quickest way. The litter cases traveled four deep, lying on blankets with a blanket under the head. The others sat on bucket seats. There was no comfort to speak of . . . comfort was sacrificed to speed.

It was a better fate than the wounded in World War One could hope for. If there had been hospital planes then, instead of hospital ships on the rough seas, torpedoed by German submarines, hundreds of men, perhaps my father among them, might have been saved.

We followed the wounded into a reception room, bright with sunshine and white paint. The litter cases were propped up on bunks fitted with back rests and were already eating soup, Spam, string beans, canned peaches, ice cream and coffee. The radio was playing swing. Nurses and Red Cross girls were sit-ting by the men, feeding those who had to be fed, joking with the others, writ-ing a letter for a litter case. All the men smoked avidly. The chaplain circulat-ing in the background said to me, "Cigarettes are the first things they want. They are twelve hours on the plane and not allowed to smoke."

I heard him through echoes, overlapping sounds, like the waves of boom-ing words receding and coming again crescendo one hears going under anaesthetics. I was bending over mutilated faces, putting cigarettes into torn mouths, in the gray chill darkness of a railway shed. In uniform then, in uniform now, part of me a shrinking child, part of me this composed woman asking:

"How long do they have here?"

"About two hours. They get their dressings changed and a hot meal and then they go on. These will be home tonight."

Dressings. Home tonight. Again the levels blurred.

It was hard to sleep that night because of the radio beam and the planes. All night they roared over or under my bed, missing me by an inch. I lay on my back, rigid, excited, tired. The last few days had no reality, they were an escapist dream. Then all that went before them and came after was the dream. There was only this infernal noise. And it was happening to me where, when? In London, in 1917? or here, wherever this was? I must somehow keep the edges of myself together, not let others see. . . .

Next day as we settled in our seats I remembered a fall I had, hunting in Berkshire. I landed on my head, but I was wearing the usual hard hunting hat, and rolled sideways, as I had been taught to fall from a horse. After a dazed while I sat up, someone caught my horse, I remounted and finished the day's run. Then I hacked home, over the border into Buckinghamshire, a good twenty miles. I had a hot bath, dressed and came down to the living room, where I began to talk to the family about the day's run, in detail . . . what had happened at the water jump, who had fallen in, who had finished up with the hounds, and though they didn't listen, as usual, after a while someone noticed that I was mentioning the names of people who were dead. I was laughing and waving my hands. They thought at first it was a poor sort of joke, typical of Evie, but when I wouldn't or couldn't stop, they got frightened and sent for the doctor. In those days doctors came when they were sent for—it was still just a few years away from when the family doctor was expected to use the back door. He said I had a severe concussion and must be kept in bed.

Perhaps what was happening to me on the plane was something like that, though I couldn't remember any fall or bang on the head. I had one obsession, nobody must find out that anything was going wrong with me, else I might be left behind, in a strange foreign place, without money or friends. While I stayed with the group I would be safe . . . and paid for. If I got separated from them . . . they had large expense accounts and big organizations behind them . . . I was on my own, representing L.P.D., Laymen, Poor Devils, with $180 to go around the world with. Whatever happened, I must stay with the group and nobody must suspect that anything unusual—more unusual than the trip itself—was happening.

Egypt revealed itself in a series of disconnected and startling color shots as the headlights on our jeeps picked out a frieze of camels bearing watermelons to market, the sleek limousine of an Egyptian potentate, a palm tree by a white wall, a veiled woman driving in a dogcart. It was the land of Osiris, god of music and medicine, who died and rose again on the third day, of Isis, his wife, and Nepthys, her twin sister, who fooled Osiris into taking her for Isis—or so he said. It was the land of Ra and of the early Pharaohs, of the Negative Confession that a man must repeat before the forty-two gods in the underworld before his heart was weighed against the Feather of Truth and he was allowed to sail through the underworld in Osiris's boat.

Since it was impossible for most men to say truthfully that they had harmed no living thing, that they had never quenched a light where it should burn, not to mention the rest of the Confession, they found themselves in quite a predicament. At first they got around it by saying, "Of course, it was never intended for a man to mean the answers he must give to the gods," it was simply necessary to be word-perfect, and if a man learned the *Book of the Dead* by heart and could repeat it perfectly he would not be flunked. Then they decided it was waste of time to learn the answers while they were still alive, that it would be better to have copies put in their tombs so that they could study at leisure after they were dead. The rich man set scribes to work copying his textbook in a pleasing style. The poor man took his chance on what he might remember. Sometimes curious incidents of spite or negligence have come to light—copies of the *Book of the Dead* in which only the first two or three pages are honestly transcribed, the rest being practice in hieroglyphs or meaningless repetition.

As we rushed toward Cairo I remembered the story of one of the Rameses, whose son died while he was still too young to study. His father had a series of scenes painted on the tomb. In the first one he is taking his son by the hand, explaining to Anubis, the custodian of the underworld, that the boy was too young to have studied the *Book of the Dead* while alive, and would probably show no aptitude for study now that he is dead. Anubis promises to prompt him and to explain matters to Isis. Pharaoh says goodbye, and in the next scene we have Isis and Anubis conniving together to get the boy through with "a thousand thousand lives, a thousand thousand felicities."

Would the tomb of a president's son be painted with detailed descriptions of how the Virgin Mary and Saint Peter wangled him through the Last Judgment? This tomb took fifty years to decorate. It was a matter of great sincerity, the outcome of the natural predicament of a man who publicly affirms the Negative Confession (or signs his name to the Declaration of Independence or the Atlantic Charter) and afterward as publicly fails to keep to it. Someone wise has said that to apprehend an ideal and not live up to it is moral suicide.

Apart from its famous terrace, Shepheard's Hotel was a dump, ramshackle, dirty, flies and jackal faces everywhere. I locked my door, but my watch was stolen in the five minutes that I left my room for one of the few and far-off bathrooms. My stockings, underwear and the insignia off my jacket were stolen too. When I complained to the management I was told, "If you can identify the man who took your watch and the exact moment it was taken, we will record your complaint." I smiled at the idea of standing, arms presumably folded, identifying a man who was taking my watch. The clerk smiled too, in anticipation of his rake-off. A gold watch would fetch a high price on the Black Market and so would the other things.

My diary says:

I made a determined effort to get to the Museum in order to see the things taken from Tutankhamen's tomb, but owing to the antics of an unco-operative and dishonest guide I missed it and was taken into a series of second-rate mosques and shops where he hoped I would buy trash from his relatives. When I finally broke from him, navigating on my own, I found the Museum was closed and would not open again until after we were gone. It was soothing to hear later that Hallett Abend's efforts to get to the Tutankhamen Collection landed him in the Museum of Medical and Social Sciences where he was led through a grim display of bottled anatomy.

Then I go into a passage in my own peculiar shorthand.

It was frightening to find myself several times today climbing steps between lions—the British Museum, shadowy, gray, but I was *there,* going toward an old fat horror behind a massive desk, waiting to insult me and *The Hours of Isis.* Each time I managed to break away, run down the steps and search for the others. Each time I caught up with them as we went into a briefing room. No one seemed to notice that I had left them, or anything odd.

Perhaps my uniformed body clumped along while my Ka wandered. It may have behaved normally, even made sense, for several times people quoted what "I" had said to them about Egypt—ancient Egypt—and according to my notebook they began to think of me as an expert on Osiris and the *Book of the Dead.* In a way I was.

When we were flying over the desert past the Suez Canal, long, narrow, straight, unimpressive from the air, a sluggish gray-green, with two boats on it, it was hard to realize that we were looking at one of the most important objectives of the war—control of a muddy ditch. Men were magnificent fools to dream up the ditch in the first place and to make it, pitiful fools to squabble and die in the dust and the mud and the sea over who should control it. From the air the world was one long unified strip of landing fields, separated by landscape flown over in order to get to them. There were no conscious divisions of nationality in the air. "If more people," I wrote then, "flew habitually, constantly, the thinking of the world would change." Now I wonder what made me think so.

We flew over the Holy Land, seeing Jerusalem and Bethlehem from the angle of the angels—targets for bombs, material for pamphlets on the "Palestinian Question"—trouble between the British, the Arabs and the Jews. Then, as now, not much change, except that there is today a place called Israel.

Yet over this land on foot or on a donkey one man passed, knowing the answers, mildly proclaiming them. People listened—people will sometimes listen—but no one through the centuries has made the full attempt to see if the answers added up to peace on earth. We have taken the things we fancy, here and there, explained away or camouflaged the rest. We have given devotion, reverence, remembrance, in long complicated rituals to the man himself, but as to living what he said, only sporadic groups have tried sporadically here and there to follow some of it.

We landed at Tel Aviv and jeeped into Jerusalem. It was an odd experience, bucketing in a jeep past camels, shepherds watching sheep beneath the cypress trees, to a town, half modern, half as old as humanity's dreams. On the whole it was a shocking experience. Oily Turkish guides asked us for chewing gum and American cigarettes in the Sepulcher, for money to turn on lights in the Sanctuary, and kept up a running stream of commercial conversation along the Stations of the Cross. A man selling mementos in the Garden of Gethsemane poked us in the ribs and showed us dirty postcards.

I was glad to get back into the jeep and drive in a cloud of dust to the plane. We were making for Abadan, the second hottest place in the world—nobody remembered where the first was, unless some Bureau of Statistics, I supposed. Everything about everything was known by someone somewhere, except the things that mattered—how to get rid of loneliness, fear, greed and hate.

Abadan when we reached it proved as hot as they said it would be. The average temperature was 126°, rising to 160°. Metal on the ground could not be touched in the daytime. A bugler must dip the mouthpiece of his instrument into cold water or he would sear his lips. A mechanic must wear asbestos gloves and work mainly at night at the temperature of around 110°.

I used this territory as part of the scenes in hell, in *Flight,* published nine years later.

It was about 135° when we took off again. The wheels of the plane had melted three inches into the runway overnight. As we sat waiting to take off it was like being fully dressed in the hottest kind of Turkish bath. As soon as the plane moved, I stuck my hand out of the window. A shower of hot air that at least was dry rushed over me. It became cooler and finally cold as we shot up. Planes were not pressurized then as they are now.

Iran was not my conception of Persia. Persian manuscripts in the British Museum, the great Persian collection arranged before the war by the Upham Popes, illustrated editions of the Persian poets, had made me think of Persia as a lush garden full of bulbuls and roses. The poet Flecker's descriptions of Ispahan did nothing to dispel the illusion, but one glance showed that, whatever might have happened to Persia, Iran was dry, hot, dusty, with only one navigable river winding through it sluggishly. The bulbuls and the roses, the poets and the princes, vanished in favor of oil experts, Russian pilots, British officers and engineers, and the American air base. Iran spells oil—not nightingales.

The courage of the men and women who stuck it out below became more apparent as we saw more of the surrounding countryside. Everywhere we landed, a piece of familiar home had been obstinately created against obstacles.

As the Romans brought baths and roads to the countries they conquered, the G.I.s brought ice water, screens, DDT, air conditioning and ingenuity—especially ingenuity—to the places they were in, even temporarily, rigging up showers out of gas drums, punkahs out of propellor blades, ice cream out of God knows where, water that was safe to drink. "Cold boiled water" might remain after the war as much a part of history as the Pax Romana was.

We passed over the Persian Gulf, blue with gray-green streaks in it, and no sign of life except for one small ship. A dhow much like it brought Marco Polo home from China 650 years ago, and Alexander the Great shipped his army from India two thousand years before that in a fleet of dhows.

In Karachi camels with bells on their forelegs were pulling carts with brand-new rubber tires on all their creaking wheels—at the height of the rubber shortage and rationing in the U.S., when even doctors had a hard time getting a tire. The camels looked superior, and well they might—no question of priority for them apparently. I noticed a little boy with a large brass jug pouring water from it over the hands of another little boy. "Wash your hands before you come to supper," Mother had evidently said. Then the procedure was reversed. They bowed to each other, separating with the same conscious virtue all little boys wear after shamelessly brief ablutions.

When we walked through the bazaar among jostling people of all castes I noticed women who spat and crossed their fingers against the evil eye as they pulled their children out of our way. I saw a man with a large snake round his neck walking through the crowd.

Our flight to Delhi was rough. Some of the men were sick. Project Officer Captain Ray Bonta lay on the floor of the plane, green-faced. When he recovered enough to be teased we reminded him of his pronouncement, "You women are on trial. If you get anything the matter with you, we'll leave you behind." He took our ribbing and our paregoric in equal doses, good-humoredly.

We were billeted in the Imperial Hotel. A flock of bearers seemed to be billeted with us. One of them insistently told Mary Day Winn as she climbed into a bunk, "No, no, *other* master belong there." Elsie McCormick said, "No *master* coming here." The chorus of bearers chanted, "Other master there, other master there," putting luggage on the bunk and pointing at the door through which the intruder was expected to arrive. When I strolled in, the bearers said Hindi "I told you so's." I was the "other master." We had become used to being called "Ma'am," now we must adjust to "Sir" in India.

We had dinner that night among the Three-Starred, Four-Starred and Five-Starred with General Merrill of the Marauders. The atmosphere was friendly and relaxed. At one point our host took Pauline Frederick and me into his room and showed us, not his etchings, but a large Nazi flag captured in Munich and sent to him by General Patton. He also played the accordion and sang some unexpurgated verses of "The Virgin of Samoa." We met General Sultan, looking very like Hughie Johnson, and British General Auchinlech. I started right away on Boswell, but that was a mistake —Boswell's Auchinlechs turned these Auchinlechs out.

It was an evening of good drinks, good talk, and every comfort. But on our way back from General Merrill's house we drove through crowded streets. Men, women and children were living on the sidewalks, their only home that part of the pavement on which they were stretched, their only worldly possessions the rags in which they were wrapped. This was the India of the Indians. The party we had just left seemed callous, and I was beginning to be aware of myself becoming hardened, brittle, out of touch with any of the levels leading to There.

Planes used the shimmering whiteness of the Taj Mahal as a landmark to orient themselves, a welcome sight to Hump-weary pilots to whom it meant a brief rest at C.I.A.D. Agra. We coasted in beside it, too, to breakfast in a long low room with bamboo walls and bamboo furniture, where we were served real milk for the first and last time on the trip. Some enterprising spirit had corraled a handful of sacred cows and kept them segregated and even more sacred, for cold fresh milk. *Breakfast in Agra* became the suggested title of a novel I was urged to write. People are always urging novelists to write this or that story, as though stories were all we needed, and could not provide for ourselves . . . never talent, time and right conditions for work. One of the editors with us was quite serious about my doing this.

He was pleased to see men who had had their share of discomfort and danger relaxing temporarily. An oasis of trim lawns bordered with flowers, air conditioning and incredible comfort had taken the place of the rough, open, dreary field on the edge of the Sind Desert where, plagued by dust storms and heavy monsoons, men at first lived under the most primitive conditions.

The soil is very fertile with plenty of water thirty feet below, so that with a little enterprise these lawns, flowers and pastures could have been developed through the centuries, as they were by the U.S. Air Force in 1942.

After interminable briefings—why the name, I always wonder, since they are never brief—we were set free to drive to the Taj Mahal, even more beautiful from the ground than from the air, rising undaunted from the shores of filthy, holy Ganges. "Serene memorial to an immortal love," the guidebooks say, but surely more moving because more precarious, a mortal, human love, entrusted to custodians who have not spared much in their stupid wars. "So long lives this, and this gives life to thee. . . ." The Bomb was still some months away, and sonic booms some years.

Things were arranged more reverently here than they had been in Jerusalem. After we had taken off our shoes and walked over the shining mosaic floor in company with a native child and a tall dark man wearing a glorified duster to guide us, we stood for a moment in the dome, looking down at the tomb, with its heaped-up treasure. There was an atmosphere of peace and detachment here as though the Beloved Empress murmured, "Stay awhile. Let us be better acquainted. Do you like this house that my husband built for me? Tell me, do they still love as we did, on the earth?"

But we had a rendezvous thousands of miles away, and I was not a good one to discuss romantic love, or perhaps too good a one, as that other Eve might have been if reporters had interviewed her after the expulsion and a few years of exile from the Garden.

We spent three days in Calcutta. On the first morning we drove out to the old jute mill by the river, Warren Hastings' summer house in the seventeenth century. After the day's briefing, during which the air-conditioning apparatus went into reverse, pumping hot air into the stifling room, so that we heard and noted figures in a fevered haze, we were glad to find ourselves for an hour on the lawn he planned for himself by the waterside.

The place had been sprayed for three miles with DDT so there were no mosquitos. For the first time in history people were able to sit under trees in the cool of the evening, watching the river boats go by, with no danger from malaria, no discomfort from scratching, and no premonition of Rachel Carson's *Silent Spring* to come. It has always been hard for me to understand that stinging insects and other "pests" have as much right on the great wheel of existence as we have. At the time DDT seemed a blessing, one for us to be proud of, and I remember that I was.

The sailboats had pink sails, but there were sailless craft. One went by with three men standing at long oars. They walked three steps backward, two forward, kicking out the right leg. Another boat went by with six men walking only one step. This was quicker. They were drifting down with the tide, hauling jute or steel, getting ready to anchor when the tide changed. American boats came down as far as Calcutta, but did not dare come farther on account of the sandbanks and the shoals. From Calcutta on everything went by plane.

The river from a distance looked gray but not as dirty as it was, muddy and full of half-charred corpses from the burning ghats nearby. The natives drank and bathed in it with no fear. They still do. Holy Hooghly, holy Ganges cannot be polluted as our mere rivers can.

When we came to the Kali Ghat, I remembered that it was one of the most holy shrines in India, in honor of the goddess Kali, the goddess of death and destruction and sacrifice, but it surpassed my preconceived ideas of what it might be like. It was filthier. At the entrance kites were tearing at the entrails of a goat that had just been sacrificed. Through the gate we came upon the sacrificial place itself with a groove for the goat to put its head, which was then cut off at one stroke. If it did not come off on the first stroke, the sacrifice was unacceptable. I like goats, I am part Capricorn (on the cusp between Sagittarius and Capricorn) and have been a scapegoat too often not to feel that most goats are better than the people or the causes for whom or for which they suffer.

We could not enter the temple itself, from which came loud harsh shouts and wailing. We walked around it between hovels and shops facing inward from the square. The gutters were strewn with rotting refuse. Kites and dogs disputed offal, children rolled and wallowed in it. Women beggars crowded round us, plucking at our clothes, shrilling like demented sheep, only instead of "baa" they said "maa."

At the end of this lugubrious tour, during which I looked into the temple sideways and saw worshippers saluting the hidden statue of Kali, we came upon the stunted Fertility Tree where wives come to be made fruitful —as if this could be necessary in India! There should be a grove of Sterility Trees instead, and not only there, all over the world. Three small girls, children, with frightened, shamed faces, were tying amulets to a branch and praying to the tree. A gray slimy ooze ran from the gutter opposite, water from the Hooghly, after it has washed over Kali's feet. This foul-smelling sewer was the place where the worshippers drank, washed and came to have their diseases cured. Where was the superior Wisdom of the East? Perhaps in the Himalayan Mountains. Perhaps in Tibet. Not here.

After the Kali Ghat we visited two more temples, walking in our stockinged feet through filth. It is hard to be a temple addict in India and remain untroubled and detached. In the gardens of the Jain Temple, comparatively modern, there were touching stylized statues of two kings riding a fat elephant and of the builder of the temple wearing a British sun helmet. There was also a naked boy to take charge of our shoes.

When we reached the Burning Ghat there were three bodies being cremated and one body waiting on a litter, covered with a cloth through which we could see its emaciation. It was probably one of the victims of starvation, of which there were many in Calcutta that summer. The wood was piled very high on one of the pyres, indicating that this corpse was a rich man. The average cost of a cremation was about ten rupees, or three dollars. Few members of the family were present. The three corpses we saw seemed unattended, although the eldest son must be present to light the fire. This was done at the head and then he walked round to light the rest. The wood was sweet sandalwood, so that the burning was surprisingly free from smell.

Smoke blew over our faces. The skulls of two of the bodies could be clearly seen. One burst as we looked and the brains spilled out. The feet of the third body stuck out, gray, unburned. Even so, it did not seem gruesome like the Kali Ghat, although the clay-colored feet moving slightly with the heat looked poignantly alive.

After the body is consumed, which takes from three to four hours, the navel, which does not burn, is gathered up, rolled in mud and dumped into the river where people are bathing and drinking a few feet away. The bodies are cremated three or four hours after death—some must be burned alive. In the old days, the widow used to throw herself on the fire. Relatives threw her on if she hesitated. The eldest son poked her in and held her down with a stick. A Red Cross guide told us that one woman had tried to throw herself on a few weeks before, but was prevented.

We contemplated this tableau of man-made superfluous misery in silence. Perhaps the widow thought a quick death by fire better than the slow, drawn-out agony of undernourishment finished off by cholera that we saw about us in all its stages on the streets. At least the woman on the pyre had the satisfaction of knowing she would not be superfluous. She would have the slave's familiar function of being used. Her husband would need her for his comfort in the afterworld. What more could a woman want?

My diary says:

When Indian women band together to answer that one, when they insist on some improvement in their status, when they see to it that their ten- and twelve-year-old married daughters do not crouch around the Fertility Tree praying abjectly to be made more fruitful—when, in short, Mother India teaches birth control, health education and equality to all her daughters and her sons, three quarters of her problem will be solved. British or no British, and whether there is a Pakistan or not, only the Hindus themselves can deal with the filth of the Kali Ghat, the implications of the Fertility Tree, the murk of Holy Ganges.

India has come a long way since I wrote those words in 1945—freedom from the British, a woman Prime Minister, a successful war and many reforms. Women, when they rule, go to war reluctantly, and as a last resort, but *if* they go to war, forced into it, in Israel, in India, they win it as soon as possible, a week, ten days, and then back to the things that matter. Not for any woman ruler would there be a planned Vietnam, a war which one must not lose and may not win! Women have, of necessity, a more logical sense of values and the cost of life than politicians, presidential candidates and Pentagons.

We left Calcutta for Assam, flying over the Brahmaputra River, over scenery like its name, to Chabua, where we were taken to quarters on the old Polo Grounds; here we had a touching reception, flowers in tin cans on our dressers, two hangers each, much appreciated, cold drinks.

Chabua is not far from Tibet or from China. It was the port of embarkation for China at the end of the longest supply route in the world with the lowest priority. To go from Calcutta to Chabua by river would have taken sixty days. We did it in a few hours.

While we dressed to meet the general—"The General is waiting!" were the first words we heard wherever we landed—a loudspeaker was calling the personnel to planes. All hours of the day and night we were to hear it shouting: "Passengers for Kunming, or Calcutta, or Chittagong, report to Despatching. Sergeant Labowski, Major Brown, Captain Polletti" . . . the melting pot.

Three hundred planes came in, we heard the swish of them at short intervals all night, giving us some idea of the Hump operations. It took three hours and fifteen minutes to make the trip to China, and there were about 1048 trips in three weeks. Once there was no need for traffic control, but with four hundred to five hundred planes in the air at one time there had to be. The control tower was thatched, which gave it an odd look. Everything was made of bamboo here, fences, roofs, partitions.

Matted grass and tea plants came to within twenty-five yards of our quarters, a paradise for snakes, of which there were many, mostly cobra and krait. "If bitten by a krait, light a cigarette. Before you have time to smoke it, you'll be dead." Cobras are fond of showers. There was one in the latrine. I backed out and gave it precedence. After a while it went away. I showered gingerly, hoping this wasn't cobra family night.

The Assam flying fields and the pipeline were part of what we had come so far to see. We saw them thoroughly. Each day, ten thousand barrels of motor fuel and high octane came from Calcutta and twelve thousand from Chittagong. There were twenty-seven stations to Calcutta and twenty stations to Chittagong with two or three men at every station. Chaplains went through once every two weeks to visit these isolated groups, cooking for themselves and fending for themselves with only black streamlined pipes and complicated engines at pump houses to look at. I was intrigued by a sign over one of the pumps, "No Smoking," in Hindustani, which since few natives can read seemed a precarious safety measure. Chiefly I was depressed at the idea of such apalling boredom, and dimly began to form the idea of hell that I used later in *Flight*.

We also saw Chinese soldiers disembarking from a C-54. Flying over the Hump there was often no oxygen for them. They would pass out in a heap on the floor of the plane and stumble down the gangway on arrival, as they were doing now, looking about twelve years old, dazed and dopey. They could have no idea of the distance they had come and often thought they were only a few miles from home. Some would go wandering off, trying to find their way back to their villages, thousands of miles away.

Next to the transport planes were the search planes of the Jungle Rescue Squadron. Two hundred men, each a specialist, worked in this Squadron. In the beginning they owned four old war-weary B-25s, one borrowed C-47 and one C-65. When we were there they had six B-25s, two C-47s, four L-55s, one L-4 for landing on sandbars, twenty-four C-64s and one helicopter en route by air lift and two expected by water. Rescue was a business with a standard procedure. We saw the type of plane which would be sent after us, with stretcher in back, painted yellow and blue, and the rescue kit.

During the briefing I sat next to a Hump pilot who told me fear was the worst hazard of the jungle. "Conquer your fear and the jungle can be negotiated," he said. By him, perhaps, big, rugged, with years of strenuous training . . . but by any of us?

We were taken to meet Lieutenant Arline, who was injured and had to bail out and who had arrived back the day before, limping, his arm in a sling. He was anxious to tell his story.

"The aircraft went into a slide and there was no time for anything. I tried to put on my chute and couldn't do it. The ship was absolutely out of control. The pilot called to put on our chutes and jump. At this time anything you did was a matter of seconds. I was very nearly resigned. Then I thought of my family. It seemed a very calm voice spoke to me, saying 'Go ahead, put on your chute. You're going to be all right.' I finally got one strap on. The Sergeant was sitting very quietly in his chair. The last look I had of the pilot he had pulled on all the power of the plane. Due to the aircraft being in a spin, it was very hard to get out. Finally I did get out and struck my right shoulder. I don't remember pulling the rip cord but I do remember a blinding flash and then I saw the chute mushroom above me. I looked down below and saw a terrific flash and that was our plane striking. I struck the ground and came to alone with my chute spread around me. It was dark. Panic seized me, but I got hold of myself, smoked a cigarette, made myself take time, rolled up my chute and went to sleep. In the morning I found I was on the edge of a drop of four hundred feet. If I had yielded to panic and started to walk or run, I would have been down it. I found my left leg was useless. The nerve was damaged and bruised so badly I couldn't do anything with it. I got my supplies together, tied up my bundle, and pushed it along in front of me. It took me from daylight to noon to make a hundred yards. Then I could see a little village, just like the Pearly Gates. I crawled forward and finally made it and rested there because I was exhausted. I left my bundle and crawled down below. Here I contacted some villagers, and the head man took me to his home for the rest of that day and the night. He sent a runner to Taga with a message to the Gurkha in charge. It was a British outpost of three hundred. In the morning the runner came back, bringing a note from Sergeant Baley: "Have the natives bring you to Taga." Next day I was carried over some of the most vicious mountain trails with grades to 160. How they got me up there I don't know. It took all day to get to Taga. Anything they could do for me, they did. They got me rice and pieces of meat. They even brought a priest and the village doctor to see me. He cooked herbs and made a poultice for my leg. I got to Taga the next morning. The Air Rescue arrived just after daylight. They hovered over and dropped supplies and DDT powder for lice and fleas. I was there approximately eight days. The Air Rescue came in every day except one when the weather was very bad. About two-thirds of the mountain peaks were covered with clouds. They sent in a ground crew and we all walked out."

Other stories were less reassuring. One man parachuted down and was caught in a tree. He pulled his shoulder straps free first by mistake and was left dangling, head downward, a foot from the ground. He struggled and managed to free one leg from the parachute. Then he put his hands on the ground to take the weight from the other leg that he was suspended by. He lifted them again quickly, completely covered with red ants. He brushed the ants off and tried to keep his arms up in an agonizing position. He poked out his gun and tried to shoot the strap of the parachute holding his leg. He fired five times and succeeded only in fraying the strap. He put the sixth bullet through his head. The Rescue Squad, helplessly witnessing his agony from a hovering plane, agreed this was the best thing he could have done. Already the red ants were on the march up the tree. It is said they take ten minutes to strip a deer of its flesh, leaving a clean skeleton.

Sobered, with the Hump flight still ahead of us, and some of the facts and figures in our heads—there had been a total of 554 lost over the Hump; 155 known dead, 137 missing, as of June 1, 1945—we were glad to turn our attention to the peaceful feature for which Siam is noted—tea.

We went to a tea planter's home to sample his special brands of tea. The house and garden were very luxurious, with velvety lawn, flowering trees, exotic flower beds, and a huge tea spread on a table, with white linen and sparkling silver, surrounded by Englishwomen in cool dresses and faint amusement. I found myself becoming more American by the minute, with the old antagonism I developed at Heathfield. After gallons of hot tea, which we drank as a token of our appreciation of the English way of life, they made a great concession and served more gallons of iced tea and iced coffee as a tribute to the American way of life. By that time our capacity for any liquid was exhausted. We left in a chorus of "Oh, but I thought you Americans loved iced things!" This trivial incident, with both sides trying so hard and arriving at so little, seemed typical of Anglo-American relations. They should not be attempted over tea, an historical stumbling block. We threw it petulantly into the harbor once. We desecrate it with paper bags and bits of fluff. "Two and a bud" is probably a closed book to Americans.

When we were due to be briefed on our coming flight over the Hump, the group assembled once again and was herded into a room to be fitted with parachutes and parapacks. This was a grim business under its forced hilarity. We knew that we would be flying the Hump at the worst season of the year, that we were losing planes daily, that it was very necessary, if to me impossible, that we master the intricacies of our heavy paraphernalia.

"When you jump, lead off with the right foot. Count ten before you pull the string. Land in a relaxed manner. Tear up your chute into strips, place them in an open space where they can be seen. Look out for leeches. Look out for snakes."

Some of us were taking notes, but I knew my limitations.

"You may come down in jungles, mountain gorges, or snow-capped ranges along the line of flight. There are wild tribes, headhunters, and Jap patrols, but your chances of walking out are pretty good if you keep your heads. And for that you must depend upon yourselves alone. There are many hundreds of square miles in which two parachutists who land more than 150 feet apart cannot hear each other's voices, no matter how loudly they shout, so impenetrable is the jungle. You may have to break your way through it for days, or even weeks. In your parapack you will find medical supplies, jungle boots, food, instructions to the natives in several tongues, a knife with which to slash the undergrowth, a compass and a book of words, beginning "So you are down." Remember Search and Rescue will co-operate to get you out if it is humanly possible. Sometimes it isn't. But the natives are mostly friendly. They will help and feed you. If you are at all ingenious, you will survive even without food. One pilot, Lieutenant Greenlow M. Collins, lived for twenty-one days on berries, bamboo shoots, locusts and butterflies, when he was found by friendly natives."

They handed us a little book, *How to Stay Alive in the Jungle.* I thumbed through it while I was waiting to be fitted to my parapack. "There is plenty of bamboo around," I read, "and that is all you need to make everything from a boat to a bunk." It wasn't all I needed. In spite of the drawings of bamboo broilers and dishes and cot, I didn't believe I would be ingenious enough to whittle any of them. I might have to eat my locusts raw, if I could catch them.

"Never sleep on the damp ground in the jungle," the book continued helpfully. "Never use the jungle grass for a mattress. Keep out of jungle grass and out of abandoned *bashas,* for here you find the mites that give you mite scrub or typhus." I would co-operate, if I could. "When lost in the trackless sections of the jungle, determine your location by the stars, the moss on the trees, or the course of a jungle stream." Probably I had better sit down on the nearest abandoned *basha,* if I could recognize one when I saw it, and *be* abandoned.

"If you are chased by a rogue elephant, your best bet is to run at right angles. The average rogue won't continue the chase long as his momentum and weight prevent his turning such sharp angles." So do my momentum and weight. And what if he isn't average? It would be just my luck to meet an exceptional rogue.

"The safest spot, if you meet a man-eating tiger, is a high tree." No doubt, but how would I get up it? "You can distinguish between the roar of the tiger and the leopard. The former makes several deep pealing growls like a bull, whereas the leopard gives three or four gurgling coughs." Oh comforting distinction! But the humorist (surely) who compiled this book reached the greatest heights in his paragraph on the chittering birds. "If you hear chittering birds high," he remarked merrily, "that is a wild animal, probably a tiger. If you hear chittering birds low, that is probably a big snake. Don't," he added helpfully, "go where you hear chittering birds."

His paragraph on leeches was very fine too. "Never pull them off. The jaws will remain behind and fester or the mouth will remain behind and continue to suck. When a leech gets up the nose, the patient should not be permitted to drink for four hours. Then hold a cup of water under the nostril. The leech may go down to the water and can then be pulled off."

And in small print: "All this may sound screwy, but it actually works."

All this did sound screwy, and screwier still was the solemn fitting to pack after pack until the right relationship was found between shapes and weights and sizes and the heavy tortoiselike contraptions on our backs. Harry Grayson sardonically informed each woman that she had never looked better as he watched us struggling to our feet under the dragging packs. This was part of whistling in the dark which expressed itself in various ways. Three of the Catholics went to Confession. Most of us packed our pockets with special little jungle comforts, which, of course, would have been lost on the way down, since the drop and the pull of parachuting was so strong that you lost your shoes and were sucked out of your slacks. Still, it was comforting to feel the pockets bulging with odds and ends as we took our places, in the drenching rain of the monsoon, and taxied off to fly the Hump.

Back in my familiar seat, with parachute, parapack and oxygen mask— a trial, since I get claustrophobia from anything over my face. There was a faint, hot rubbery smell from the mask and the odd balloon beneath my chin, blowing in and out. I did not mind it as much as taking a basal metabolism. I wasn't lying down, and I could tear it off, if I must, and pass out like the Chinese soldiers.

There was much joking from the men. The women were silent. Through our heads ran the fact that this was the worst weather and the worst time of the year to fly the Hump so far as danger was concerned. Then we were off, over the muddy little tents and tea plantations and the squelchy fields. Well up. Nothing to see but clouds and our wing against the sky. Glimpses of green land below and muddy rivers looped in squirls. It was cold. I asked for a blanket, and then I leaned back and decided to take it easy. We were flying at nineteen thousand feet, and the secret of comfort, so far as breathing went, was not to get up or put any strain on oneself. It grew bitterly cold and we plunged into an icy gray mist. I wanted to see the mountains, perhaps a Tibetan monastery, but the visibility was zero.

In the interspace was silence.

If this were the crossing of the Brig of Dread, the final journey, the take-off back to There, how appropriately planned it was . . . not on foot with Virgil, not in a death coach, nor a train, not even on a liner as in *Outward Bound* . . . no, for a twentieth-century soul it would be a plane, a plane like this, among a casual group of strangers, on their various missions, who would not know immediately that they were dead. And since all the other supernatural journeys had been made by men, why not a woman? A twentieth-century woman, intelligent, emancipated, at least from some things, flying over limbo, over hell, on, as far as she would be permitted to go. The Voice of Conscience, metallic, over the intercom. Yes, it would be like that, was like that. She would see her life funneling backward, from a new perspective.

I wrote in pencil in my notebook:

A book, or story, based on plane traveling with mixed passengers, crossing hot countries and cold, desolate, hellish and more beautiful. Pilot a mysterious individual. First stop an island like Azores, not too bad, not too good, limiting. Limbo, perhaps, or purgatory. There several disembark. Then a place like Abadan, and here three have to get out. All are kept here for a while, under wing of plane, waiting, wondering. Woman's agony. Back in plane. One man gets on. His gaunt tested figure sitting behind her . . . or beside. Their dialogue, the tenderness and comprehension that develops between them? He is expecting, rather naturally, to have to get out at the next stop. People who get on where he did cannot go far. They get out together, whenever they do, wherever it is, she might have been able to go further, but decides to stay with him. . . . *Je reste avec lui* . . . yes, of course, this must be the man . . . the Other. . . . The plane goes on, carrying the padre, or whatever more developed characters there are, toward the interspace. . . .

About 10,000 words or less. Action starts at briefing? Or in plane? Works up to suspense at landings, especially the landing in the hot, stinking verminous hell-place, where *he* gets on. The next landing, at night, so they don't know what sort of a place it will be. But they get out together, and stand close to one another in the darkness under the stars, waiting—to be met—there is a breeze and somewhere a bird sings. . . . It cannot be so very bad.

It took me nine years to live with, to write *Flight,* which turned into a full-length book, published in 1954. Sputnik was still three years away. The time was not quite ripe for *Flight,* but some reviewers gave it their blessings. "A remarkably sensitive and civilized attempt to communicate mystical experience in modern metaphor and simple language." "A long philosophical poem." Et cetera. Naturally, it sold the least well of my books to date. Two others following *Flight* sold even less well, one of them never getting out of the publisher's warehouse, owing to an editorial shake-up. When Rebecca West, passing through New York, went in person to tell that publisher that she wanted a copy of *I Saw My Mortal Sight,* and would review it, she was informed that they had never heard of it or me, two weeks after publication date! The third book, *Go Ask the River,* is still in print, but all of them together did not sell as well as the least "successful" of my historical novels.

Nevertheless, when I take the dread journey, these three books and my poems are all I would want to produce for inspection at *that* Custom House, under the heading *works.*

Meanwhile, part of me in the plane was paying perfunctory attention to details. We were flying at two hundred miles an hour. Our first sight of ground was a glimpse of terraced hillsides, brown ploughed fields, some forested spots and gorges, with a muddy foaming river. We were not far from Milkinyo, where the mountains were only five thousand feet high. The clouds were fantastically beautiful, separating now and then to show us a strange glimpse of a dark land. It was bitterly cold. The metal of the plane fixtures stung exploring fingers. Even the quality of the clouds had a cold look, *"cette implacable blancheur."* We had not reached the Hump itself yet. It was bumpy and soon we could not see anything but mist.

In *Flight* I wrote:

She stared at the heads of the passengers in front of her—alien souls, each a separate continent, the dark, unexplored, mysterious, withheld territory of another being.

Were they absorbed like her in self-examination, bewildered like her and frightened? She had a longing that they might turn into the correspondents, swapping stories and cigarettes, typing with their oxygen masks and parachutes beside them, getting ready to scoop one another and file at the next stop.

She did not want to see the faces of these fellow travelers; she had not wanted to look at them from the start. She was conscious of deliberately closing her eyes whenever one of the heads moved as though it might turn.

She did not like the faces of strangers, she did not like humanity's faces; *like* was not the right word; she feared human faces; nor was *fear* the right word; dread, horror, hatred—a mixture of these? She shrank from the human face, the shield, the mask behind which lived the disconcerting stranger, the too familiar animal, glancing out upon her now and then.

She had seen faces reflecting every emotion. She had peered at them from beneath the photographer's black cloth, through the miniature eye of the Leica, in the reflecting screen of the foolproof Rolleiflex. She had been said to have an "eye for a face," like the reporter's "nose for news," a flair for the unusual, the significant, the slant, the story.

Faces had been her stock in trade. She had made her reputation and most of her living out of faces. They crowded before her now.

There follows a description of the Kali Ghat and the Burning Ghat and then:

She had photographed the faces of the women in the "cages" of Bombay, streets of iron-barred shacks and cells where prostitutes of all ages, from grandmothers to children, shared diseases and carried on their trade. Dim light might hide the filth of the cells and the rags on the beds, but it could not hide the expression on the faces, or the smell.

Blocks of these cages belonged to wealthy and respectable owners, who pocketed the earnings, from two to eight annas a throw—less than one would dare to give a porter for carrying a suitcase. Sometimes a man owed money to the moneylender—Myra had photographed moneylenders—then he sent his daughter to the cages to work out the debt. She could not leave the 6 by 3 foot cage, after she once entered it, day or night, for any purpose. The sea was only a mile away, with its freshening breezes, but she and her working companions would not know it was there.

The sordid squalor of the cages lay in the reduction of lust to matter-of-fact function, in surroundings less alluring than a kennel or a sty. The women were clothed. There were no provocative gestures, no songs, no dances, nothing of honest sex, just rows of listless cronies, sad-eyed girls and wizened painted children, peering out apathetically, while a male madam unlocked the doors to let in customers. The customers did not look eager, furtive or satisfied —merely functional, with the expression that a man has when he spits absent-mindedly at crossroads.

My diary for Bombay goes on:

In some streets the doors were open. These were the women in the profession through heredity or from choice. In most streets the doors were locked.

We saw a few of the higher-class places, off limits to Americans, but not for the British. The venereal-disease rate among the British is proportionately higher than among the U.S. personnel. Forty thousand of these women herded into an area of two square miles!

We drove round the fashionable Malibar to think it over. The lights of the harbor twinkled pleasantly below us. Bombay is a jimcrack assembly of fifth-rate buildings, but wider streets than in Calcutta, and cleaner, fatter natives, with a smell of money modifying other smells. Opposite the Depak Mahal taken over by us, there was a promenade along the seaside in the manner of a shabby Nice. Along this promenade women in lovely saris were walking or sitting. Men in white European clothes were helping their wives from glossy cars. There is very little purdah in Bombay. How did they get these cars of American make and newest vintage? The population is predominately Parsee, richer, freer, a shade more intelligent than the average Indian I have seen or met so far—*but* there are the cages.

The next day we went on a sight-seeing tour and bought some silver and then to the radio station for a broadcast. I slipped away to the Taj Hotel, where Lady Rama Rau was waiting for me. I had promised Santha Rama Rau that I would look her mother up if I came to Bombay. I found a charming, dignified and cultured woman, with beautiful features, a high-caste Brahmin, a Nationalist. She had plausible answers for the questions I asked. The theme was let the Congress rule and immediately all would be transformed. I did not mention the cages, but I did the Kali Ghat. She said that the British would not interfere with religion, whereas the Hindus would, if they were given a chance. She said she thought that Jinna would wreck the Wavell proposition [which happened]. In spite of her charm and distinction and my admiration for her brother, Shivan Rau, I still felt India was a corrupt and evil land, and we of the naive West were short-changed on the famous "Wisdom of the East."

Cocktails with the Indian press had the unreal quality such gatherings have when everyone is grinding an axe or lying. Dinner at the Yacht Club was unreal too, because of the British this time. We had to dine behind a screen, one of the party (our hostess) not being in full formal evening dress. Our uniforms might have been condoned, but an afternoon dress never, in wartime, in 1945! When later the privileged beings from the other side of the screen emerged, old Admirals and General Blimps, it was more of a pleasure than an insult not to have dined among them. Hallett and I drove home in a gharry beneath the stars with a fresh breeze blowing. We passed another gharry with a young English naval lieutenant in it and an Indian girl, obviously lovers. Away from the cages you can see the appeal, the charm of Indian women, melting black eyes, lovely feminine clothes, graceful movements, beautiful teeth, straight out of Kipling's *Without Benefit of Clergy,* once the epitome of passionate romance.

In Delhi the weather was cooler. Three of us had a room on the ground floor overlooking a garden full of roses. We sat on the terrace, watching a bearer stroll lazily by carrying a brilliantly colored bouquet. Two of us took one of the little horse-drawn carriages, and drove, sitting backward, down the road to the Capitol.

Delhi is well laid out, with gardens, fountains, and a long artificial pond or lake, faintly reminiscent of Washington. Life for the ruling classes can be made attractive. There are beautiful horses. One American officer told me he had thirty remounts from which to choose. A groom brought them to the door whenever called upon. There are clean-looking agreeable parts of Delhi. The circles laid out on the wide streets are both modern and pleasing. So is General Merrill's house, which used to be an Indian home, built round a square black-and-white-tiled courtyard. Here, after dinner, we were shown a movie of Ernie Pyle. It was odd to look up and see the stars over the auditorium. Not planetarium stars, real ones.

Soon we were back flying over India's hot, inhospitable land. I realize I have only had a bird-in-purdah view of the country, but even a bird—even one of India's wheeling kites, land gulls—can tell where not to light. I have not seen Peshawar, the Khyber Pass, nor most of Kipling's India, nor the India-to-be. Ceylon was attractive, and the natives there, also under British rule, seemed contented and progressive. The answer must lie with the Indians. Already, even to my superficial glance, there were signs of expected birth. If only it might be Nativity and not Reincarnation! If only day might break for the common man!

I got most of the material for *Flight* from this war-correspondent tour, in the air and on the ground, particularly the long days in the plane, cut off from "normal living," compelled to face myself, to think.

I was thinking of the role of the writer, the reporter, the photographer, with growing disgust and consternation.

In *Flight* I summed up what I thought. It is still what I think of some forms of reporting and some books.

> Lose face, acquire face. . . . She had acquired numberless faces, "captured her subjects" was the phrase.
>
> They had looked at her face as she captured them, seeing the expert's hard professional appraisal, the mechanical smile; seeing her indifference to their predicaments, to their misery; seeing the calculated set-apart scrutiny of the exploiter. They had looked at her, perhaps for help, in their extremity,

in the crisis of their "human-interest stories." They had seen her concerned with obtaining the best shot, the telling effect, the marketable angle, the gimmick which would sell.

She exhibited these faces and others—victims of cholera, of famine, war casualties, survivors of Dachau—next to her portraits of American debutantes and brides in what the critics called "significant contrast." It was one of her best, most exciting exhibitions. It brought her three awards.

She had made her comfortable living out of agonies and joys which should have been sacred or shared. It had never occurred to her that she owed any part of that comfort, of that living, of the money she made, to those whose lives provided the material.

People had been her material.

The Creator took dust out of which He made people. She, and those like her, took people out of which they made dust.

But photographs like hers were justified because they aroused compassion, they startled, they informed the public, they combated indifference.

Did they do these things?

If her own compassion was not aroused on the spot of the occurrence; if she, a spectator of the actual event, had not been moved to a gesture of sympathy, of intervention, however futile; if she had not rushed forward to help, or dropped to generous knees to pray for the help she could not give, why would the casual eye looking over *Life,* or *Time,* or *Look,* or *Pic,* or any of the other markets for her work, be more moved than she?

Familiarity bred acceptance of the misery of others. Secondhand knowledge could be hardening. Her pictures had done more harm than good; her pictures had betrayed the divine, the human face.

"I hungered, I was thirsty, I was a stranger, I was naked, I was sick and in prison and ye—photographed Me."

True, Lord, and sent the circulation up.

Shallow, superficial, self-centered!

Self-centered, superficial, shallow, sinful!

Hissing words like little snakes wrapped themselves around her.

We crossed the Hump without being aware of it, except from the air pockets, the cold, our oxygen masks, and the strained expressions of pilot and co-pilot when they relieved each other and walked through to talk to us. The crossing was not so dramatic as the preparations for it. After an hour or so of unreal suspension among great clouds sitting in conference, the weather cleared enough to show us a red river, ugly gorges, a range of spiked mountains, with here and there a cultivated field. There were no towns or villages, but the valley was cultivated to the slopes of the mountains beyond. This, I realized, was China.

And in China I would find, especially in Nanning and Cheng-tu, the material for *Go Ask the River,* the life of Hung Tu, poet and Flower-in-the-mist of the T'ang Dynasty. I would also feel at home, as I only did in France, never in India or England.

We taxied past coolies under large hats, Chinese women working on the airfield. All the airfields were built by hand. We saw thousands of people tearing down a hillside with their bare hands, putting the earth in little baskets, carting it away. They worked on the gang system; whole families were engaged building up the runway with small boulders, then, eventually, pebbles broken up by hammers were added to make the surface. We saw a crashed plane that had killed a coolie. Bloody mess was drying on the ground. One ant crushed, but there were more, myriads more. It was mass production, cheaper and quicker than a bulldozer would be.

China was going straight from the rickshaw age to the plane, missing out on the railway era and, to a great extent, the car. Roads were poor and hard to make. It was less expensive to increase the airfields by the anthill way. The Chinese attitude to planes was casual and hopeful. We found them parked in barnyards or drawn up by roadsides, under trees. The contrast between primitive farming conditions, where even livestock was a rarity and most of the hauling done by human beasts, and these gleaming modern birds of the air was like other contradictions in China, full of startling charm.

Driving toward our quarters I thought the people seemed brighter than the Indians, though miserably poor. They were selling pitiful rags and bits of bread on the streets, but like their spirited, strong, willing little horses, pulling carts, all with rubber-tired wheels (why, how, with the rubber shortage?) they were energetic and eager. I saw children carried by children; women hobbling on bound feet, though the majority were unbound. The predominant color seemed to be blue. Everyone was wearing dark-blue skirts, pants or robes.

Elsie McCormick and I got hold of a command car by exerting ourselves and went into Kunming where, with the help of a Chinese soldier, we found the house of a missionary and his wife, friends of friends. They told us that the C.N.A.C. (Chinese National Air Corporation) was flying the Hump commercially once a day three times a week and that the fare was ten dollars from Kunming to Calcutta. It was cheaper, if you could manage it, to fly the Hump back and forth than it was to try to live on the ground. They spent most of their time in the air. As an example of the prices and difficulties of existence, they showed us a cake of soap, the best that could be procured and beyond the means of most people. It was a piece of hard, brown, bad-smelling grease, and its price was 1800 Chinese dollars, real dollars to them.

They gave me help about Hung Tu, and told me that in Cheng-tu I would find more. They had heard of her, but did not have any translations of her poems.

I got to the briefing somewhat pushed around and ruffled. Having got lice and fleas, with no place to wash or cope with them, I was feeling pretty tired as we drove in a jeep filled up on gas and alcohol, with only twenty-two per cent gas. This briefing was somewhat different from the general run. It was given by Chinese General Ho Ying Chin, very intelligent, very dignified, with four rows of decorations, dazzling white gloves, and a charming smile.

He was speaking of a future which is now the past, but one point he made is still debatable. He felt that China could make friends with Japan after twenty or thirty years. He added, "Certainly the Emperor of Japan is a war criminal. He should be tried and given due punishment. Japan's fate should be decided by all the United Nations, not by China alone."

I wonder what he would have thought if he could have foretold then what would happen to Japan, and what to China and Nationalist China?

General Hayden Boatner, unmilitary, wearing spectacles and very invisible stars, had a forthright manner and decided opinions. He said there was nothing consistent in China but its inconsistency. He added, "Americans do not command in this theater, though the staffs are closely integrated. The Chinese are doing all the fighting. We supply them and give them air support, but we are simply coat-holders."

This coat-holding, in Asian countries!

"Chennault was the first to see the wisdom of using gang-labor power, a thousand Chinese doing a job like ants because they have the mass, are industrious, accurate and keep on working. A few pounds of rice against one ton of gas is a good idea."

As we were on our way into Kunming we passed the wreckage of a C-46 that had crashed a few hours before, just skimming the roof of Chennault's house.

"What did they try to do that for *then?*" Chennault is reported to have asked. "They knew I was not in the house."

Everywhere we heard him affectionately or furiously referred to as "the Old Man." Deaf, rugged, enterprising, it was significant of his personality that, as we were being interviewed by General Ho, with lots of generals pontificating about, when he came in the hard-bitten newspaper people got spontaneously to their feet. No one expected us to rise, the Chinese General was still sitting. We were pulled to our feet by acknowledgment that here was a man. Chennault was the sort of figure about whom controversy floats as water breaks on a rock, and whichever side of the stream you might find yourself on, it was impossible to ignore him.

It was Chennault who told us about the pilots at Chikiang "who put in a year of missions, down on the dock day after day, hitting supply lines, locomotives, junks and sampans. They had a pick-and-shovel, milk-run business, the sort of things pilots hate, but once, in the coldest weather for thirty-four years (according to an old priest keeping records), they heard through the Chinese Intelligence that the Japanese winter uniforms, particularly the long underwear, had not come up. So they made sure it never reached the Japanese because they hammered away, day after day, at the Jap supplies. The Jap hates cold, gets sulky, and won't move from his charcoal brazier; this business of the long underwear was one of the main factors in the Japanese defeat and retirement down the Hoochich."

It was also one of the minor meannesses of war, and the sort of gloating way it was told was revealing too.

Chennault said that he was going to re-establish Chinese waterways, using barges, some with sail and some with engines. "The Chinese are excellent boatmen. A good sing-song man on a loading gang is worth his weight in gold. He keeps them laughing. It is necessary for the Chinese to laugh while they work. He sings songs, mostly obscene. They help."

In 1972 as we watched and listened to President Nixon's visit to China, crowds of silent workers, very somber, very silent, cleared the streets of snow. There was no more laughter and song at work, no good sing-song man, none of the individualistic good humor and freedom of the crowds I saw in 1945.

Later we met Wong Jung, "Seldom Wong," fifteen years old according to our calculations, sixteen by Chinese reckoning. He was a thousand-dollar-a-day man, earning a thousand Chinese dollars (about the equivalent of fifty cents) turning out three thousand dollars' worth of envelopes a day, a small, cheerful, brown-faced boy, working in a corner of Colonel Hutton's office. He made five thousand envelopes a month, using his own paste, rice paste from a secret formula. He made envelopes to specifications and was very proud of his status as an office boy. Wong was a refugee who, after losing his father, walked out of the Japanese lines with his mother. When he first came to work his mother wrote courteous Chinese notes about the great honor it was for him to work for the United States, but please would we deduct from his wage and send to her what we considered right. Wong came across the rice paddies morning and noon, without losing a day. When we saw him he was crouched in his office over a container of his secret paste. He grinned as he greeted us, and Colonel Hutton said, "I sometimes wonder what's to become of him. There are native boys, Chinese and Indian and Naga, who have attached themselves to outfits and become more than mascots. It will be a wrench to leave Wong behind."

The Chinese children seemed brave and full of high spirit, in contrast to the Indians with their unsmiling faces. Even the Chinese babies were cheerful, keen-faced and intelligent. They looked as if they agreed with their own proverb: "Life is a bamboo shoot. However often it may break into sections, it is continuous and flowers at the top."

In contrast there were the captured Japanese, sullen, sick, afraid. Most prisoners were totally ignorant of the war situation and had no news. The captured Japanese thought that he should destroy himself. After he was taken prisoner and not tortured, when food, cigarettes and a place to sleep were given to him and better treatment than in the Japanese army, the shock was too great for him to know how to behave. He was undergoing a tremendous conflict to reconcile what he experienced with what he was taught. Then he had to justify the fact that he had not committed suicide.

"They all intend to," Colonel Hutton said, "but they are treated too well; they don't get around to it. So a lot of them advance the theory that, when they are captured, they die spiritually and can never go back to Japan because they are eternally disgraced. They even hope that because they are reborn men they might become American citizens, so there is nothing they will not do to co-operate. They write leaflets—ours were old-fashioned, the Nisei's slang was dated, so the prisoners of war have been very helpful in developing language that would appeal to the present-day Japanese soldier.

"A Japanese individual prizes his family and is extremely susceptible to homesickness. We use that appeal. They gripe about their leadership, officers, food, no mail, no rotation, medical care, lack of news, and are particularly apprehensive about their lack of aircraft. Their officers usually tell them all their planes are out over the U.S. Navy, but they have heard that one before. Oddly enough, they are sensitive to the artwork in leaflets. If the illustration is not good, they reject the whole leaflet.

"A team of six Japanese prisoners was set loose to write propaganda. Their first leaflet was about their life in the American stockade and how happy they were in their newborn state, how good the coffee tasted. They had an extraordinary flair for propaganda. Three of them were old army men, sick of it all. They were headed by a lieutenant who was a university graduate. When we first asked them if they would engage in this work, they set up conditions. The first was that they were not to attack the Emperor; the second, that they would not write anything that was untrue; and third, they all wanted to be American citizens.

"The drawing for a leaflet with a speech by President Truman was done by a Nisei who used to work for Walt Disney. A hundred tons of leaflets a week were dropped in Japan itself, and about that many on occupied China. We captured two thousand prisoners of war on Sian where propaganda was used, and no prisoners at Iwo Jima where no propaganda was used."

I saw some samples of these leaflets. One showed a pretty Japanese girl in a kimona standing wistfully alone by a blossoming cherry tree, with a caption reading: "Soldiers, this year, too, the cherry trees bloom sweetly." Another contained a poem by a Japanese soldier:

MY MOTHER AT HOME

All the coins are now out of circulation
Even though all the wheat is paid out as tax
Even though no farm equipment can be bought
Even though potatoes are now rationed
Even though one has to eat grass and leaves
My mother does not know why these things have happened.

Even though you look at the sky where no eagles [planes] return
Even though three sons have died gloriously
Even though the daughter is taken away
Even though all the primary schools are closed
Even though the entire city is burnt to ruin
My mother does not know why these things have happened.

Believing all matters are government orders
She resigns herself to God
With a thought that there will be God's blessing
And without a word of complaint
She weeps in gratitude
My mother does not know why these things have happened.

I was being drawn toward another poet, in the ninth century, where the same cruelties and savageries erupted, and the same human loves and courage struggled . . . the Chinese had a great and intricate civilization when ours was a matter of mud huts. I could not wait to get to Sian and Cheng-tu, where I might dodge the briefings and find some trace of her. Meanwhile I took note of everything I could see or experience or hear of which might have remained more or less the same over centuries.

I spent a curious evening dining in a Chinese restaurant before going on to the Chinese opera. We had eaten as guests of the Chinese government at our hotels and at the houses of Chinese generals, but this was my first experience of an ordinary run-of-the-mill restaurant. It was expensive for Chinese customers. Vegetable stew, topped off with sugared peaches which were very good, came to about $2700.

While I waited at the Red Cross to be picked up, a small boy was brought in from the street to shine my shoes. He had a box over his shoulder with all the equipment in it that a shoeshine boy has in New York. He gave me a fine shine with extra elbow grease for $200. The rate of exchange was $1500 to $1.00. But it was still $1500 to the Chinese. (It rose to $3000 before we left China and then went out of sight.)

Even at these prices, Chinese families were eating around us. My progress with chopsticks was too much for the face and deportment of one of the younger Chinese. He broke down and grinned, but his older brother, about nine, scolded, then seeing it was no use expecting him to behave under such provocation, picked him up and set him firmly down with his back to me. Now and then the little black head would turn round and laughing eyes stretch into slits above wide white teeth. Up came his hand with the thumb in a friendly "*Ding hao!*" Up came mine with the chopsticks. Then his shoulders would heave and big brother look at him suspiciously.

After the meal we walked dark, crowded streets, brushed by countless shoulders—the swish of them reminded me of bats flying past. We should have called rickshaws, since Europeans lose face battling with a crowd, but the opera was near, and the man escorting us was fascinated by the "atmosphere" of China. There was nothing particularly Chinese about this part of it. It was the atmosphere of the poorer parts of any big city.

We reached the opera house and again there was color and squalor. The costumes were magnificent, the backdrop and backstage were filthy, and the performers' families, with whom we drank tea, shabby and sad. I expected to find the singing nasal and inharmonious to a Western ear, but I found instead that it exercised a subtle, penetrating influence. The whining rise and fall of human notes to a tinkling accompaniment was interesting, exciting and familiar somehow, with a pattern I had heard many times before . . . but where, but how?

I wondered whether there was opera in Hung Tu's time. I thought not, but I knew there was stylized dancing, to musical accompaniment and song. The ballet, too, was imported from India, in the T'ang dynasty.

The figures on the stage, with their painted faces and stiff, ritualistic gestures in their glowing silk robes, seemed to be inviting me to take my place among them, to perform. I knew exactly what should follow every movement, who come forward next. So did the audience, but I seemed to know it from the performer's point of view.

The audience was casual, restless, conversational. People wandered in and out with the same absent-minded courtesy that worshippers in Latin countries show at Mass, shifting chairs, greeting each other, while the show went on. Chinese Opera, I wrote in my diary, "has no sharply defined action, no scenes dependent on chorus or movement. It is an interminable traditional dialogue between two central characters, and though there are entries and exits of subsidiary figures, and changes from standing to sitting, there is no reason why you should not come in or leave at any part of the performance. The Chinese audience is familiar with the characters and the stories. They go to the opera for an hour or two, any hour or two, and out again, tomorrow there will be more of it." But tomorrow brought departure toward Nanning for me.

Hallett Abend told me on the field before we left, while we were waiting under the wings, that Nanning, which the Japanese held three weeks before, used to be a very beautiful city, but had been taken and retaken so many times that there was nothing left but rubble. Hallett knew China very well, having spent many years there as China correspondent for the New York *Times* and chief of bureau for the Far East. He had written eight books on the Far East and now was representing North American Newspaper Alliance. He was a witty, shrewd man, acid-tongued at times, but very kind to me, passing on information generously and coming to my rescue when he saw me at a loss. He and I seemed to carry the brunt of the social assignments, such as sitting either side of Chinese generals, governors, and eventually Chiang Kai-shek, Lord Louis Mountbatten, the Pope. Hallett too was getting material for a book, nonfiction, of course, but he understood my distaste for up-to-the-minute stories and military briefings which I couldn't use, and now and then we escaped together and went in search of something we wanted to see.

In Nanning, as usual, when we landed we were rushed to a briefing, and at this one I disgraced myself. It was agony to sit on a hard chair, fighting off waves of fatigue, while a colonel with what we called in my father's army a swagger stick talked his head off pointing out "facts." I struggled to take notes. My eyes closed. I was lost. The human animal sometimes cannot keep up. I was remembering as I dozed a pretty tableau in Calcutta—Harry Grayson leaning from his window beside mine utterly bemused. "Egypt," he said wearily and turned his back. I at least knew what country I was in, but that was all. In my sleep I wrote:

At present time three thousand Japs at Luchow.
Under no circumstances.
You will not touch a single piece of ammunition.
Let the Japanese have a body not a soul.
We have always left the Chinese in command of their troops.
Chang.

There was a certain martial simplicity about these lines, suggesting a poem of the new school, or an exercise in Pitman's shorthand. I had no idea who did what. The sword of my uncle is at the throat of my aunt. Chang, or possibly Selah.

Chang turned out to be Marshal Chang Fah Kwei, who received us in a house that was instantly familiar to me, spacious, clean, old, with many corridors. There was a large map of the world on the wall, with Chinese lettering in red, making familiar places look bewitched. He was forty, small, young, vigorous. He wore glasses, had a mustache and a prominent forehead. He spoke to us in Chinese. He seemed to be saying a great deal, but his interpreter gave us only:

Nanning has been captured by us for exactly one month. Your visit here today brings me great happiness."

General Li spoke. General Chang sat down. General Li was giving a résumé of tactics and positions up to that time. His Chinese seemed sharper, more vehement, less mellow than Chang Fah Kwei's.

Little Chinese cups were served, empty and beautiful.

General Li wore an embroidered ribbon, about four inches long and one wide, horizontally on his left breast, a decoration, but what? Marshal Chang kept his penetrating eyes upon us, taking notes. I was tired but awake. Their shirts looked cleaner than my ragged bush jacket, smarter.

"Four hundred Japs killed in Nanning vicinity."

General Chang had drive, sense of humor and squareness in his face, a pleasant smile, an overhanging upper lip.

Yellow watermelon was brought in, four plates of it.

"Can China defeat the Japanese without military help?"

They argued over this, the answer came: "We can positively defeat the Japs, provided we have the equipment."

Red watermelon now appeared and trays of nuts.

"Is it necessary to conserve a Japanese nation after the war?"

The lichee nuts were delicious.

Later, when I needed faces and mannerisms, the essential *Ch'i* of governors and generals and officials in Hung Tu's life, I had this frieze of Chinese figures to draw from.

We drove round Nanning, past the Catholic Bishop's house, gutted. The church was undamaged, but the army was billeted there. We went to an American general's house to pretty up for lunch . . . washing our hands in water brought to us in helmets. I stepped onto his balcony. There was a spacious garden with flowering shrubs, hibiscus mostly, enclosed in old stone walls, on the banks of the river. For an instant the levels slipped slightly. I remembered it well. I could have told Hallett where the well was, and what was round the bend of the river. I knew the house behind me, or another house before it. The balcony, courts, high ceilings and archways showed French influence, and that, I tried to tell myself, was why I felt at home, but I knew otherwise.

Nanning, one month after the enemy vacated it, was cleaner than Kunming, which was never taken. The streets were wider, the roads better. The people seemed to be running down them, men and women coolies, carrying boards for rebuilding. This too, or the spirit of it, I would use in *Go Ask the River,* though really I needed no models from the twentieth century when I came to write about Hung Tu. I had lived many lives in China.

This was the first place where we heard wind in the trees. I could have settled down comfortably here to work, to live. Nanning had missions, universities and flavor, it smelled right, there were hills. I saw small Chinese horses, larger than those in Kunming, with wooden saddles, like the T'ang pottery in museums, soldiers' mounts, flown in. The jeep I rode in was flown in. Everything came or went through the air. Too soon we were flying, sitting on our packs, over cone-shaped mountains and country like the far side of the moon, toward Chichiang, and then Chungking. As we flew south we seemed to be receding from the China that I knew. The peculiar, charged, electrical excitement with which I moved about Nanning faded. I did not get plugged in again until we reached Cheng-tu, although the high points of the Chinese experience for the others, and on this level, for me, were immediately ahead.

We arrived in Chungking grubby, disheveled and hot, suffering from dimness of vision and bagginess of trousers at the knee, to be met by movie people (there was no television then), news cameras and very spruce brass. I was helped into a command car on the wrong side so I had to be propelled in a way the photographers found irresistible. All I would have to do, I decided, to turn in a book for Putnam's, would be to show myself climbing backward down from planes, shot from below, labeled Karachi, Chungking, Rome, et cetera, and finally Washington, when I would turn and show my face.

After we had baked in the burning sun at the airport for a long half hour, we were told that if we would wait and bake some more we might have a chance of seeing the Generalissimo. His plane was parked next to ours, a new, shining silver C-47 with his wife's name, Mei Ling, across it in Chinese lettering. We waited in the car till he drove up in a closed limousine. We hadn't seen a civilian car for so long that it looked strange. His retinue followed in two Ford station wagons. A dynamic, vital man, younger than I expected, with his guards about him, advanced smiling. I remembered the meaning of Chiang Kai-shek . . . "Stands like an independent mountain" . . . as I looked at him. Small, slim, dignified, dynamic and, when he smiled, alive. There was no time for further analysis. He was very affable but obviously in a hurry, as Jimmy Wei presented us, one by one.

"*Hao, hao, hao,*" he murmured, the Chinese equivalent for "good."

Harry Grayson said reflectively, "This Generalissimo deals in generalities."

He said through his interpreter that he would see us again soon, he hoped, climbed into his plane and we went back to our truck. We watched the take-off with special interest since it was the first time Chiang Kai-shek had flown without an American crew. I got a glimpse of the young Chinese pilot's proud profile as the plane taxied past us. It was a dangerous field, with many ravines, and ticklish maneuvering necessary to get quick altitude. We watched it soar up, circle and disappear above the mountains. Then we drove to the hills that are Chungking, and turned into the Press Hostel.

The place had been bombed out, then rebuilt with a rambling charm. Large bamboo mats made efficient screens from the heat of the sun. My room was under a staircase, with a noisy and curious family behind it in an alleyway. Above me, on a balcony, someone was playing a Kate Smith recording of "God Bless America." In the courtyard a modern Chinese woman, with a skirt split to the knee and smooth rolled hair, was playing with a modern Chinese baby. White butterflies above the grass, box hedges and strange trees . . . and bugles in the distance recalling the sounds of my childhood . . . Chungking, the wartime capital.

I had hardly begun to change my shirt when two Chinese women reporters walked in. They settled themselves on the bed, smiling and asking questions in excellent English, while I dressed. They had no pencils or paper and seemed to be paying no more than polite surface attention to what I said, so I relaxed. Next day when the interviews appeared and I got them translated, I found that they had recorded every last word, and added as well a detailed description of my changing expressions as I said them. The Chinese were ahead of us with "bugging."

Pauline Frederick, whom they interviewed before me, puzzled them . . . she wasn't married. She explained airily that she was an old maid, and defined it for them, "spinster." So the next day her interview began: "Miss Pauline Frederick, an old maid and a spinster . . ."

After we had eaten we went to the Ministry of Information, in a cool room with a stone floor, wicker furniture and modern Chinese paintings. We received tea, if not much information, certainly none on what I wanted about Hung Tu, and exchanged civilities. Then we went back to the compound and to a buffet supper at General Wedemeyer's house, built high up over the Little River. There was a brilliant cosmopolitan crowd in uniform and out of it. I chiefly remember the sunset over the Yangtze, with steep hills rising opposite. There were one or two sampans on the water, one or two smaller craft, and all the Chinese crowded life on the hillside.

Then the lights came out, the edges blurred, and the distance glowed a purple mist.

We covered Chungking thoroughly the next day, looking for the Street of the Rusty Nails—there was jade among the nails—which we never found. We found a lot of other things, including the strange sight of a rickshaw with a man in it, bare to the waist, streaming with blood, his throat cut. The coolie padded placidly along. Later another rickshaw passed us with a woman dying in it, probably of cholera. Again the coolie didn't seem perturbed, nor the passers-by. Others transported scholars, pretty women, soldiers, men in robes. The rickshaws of Chungking have a parasol covering for the coolies, not only for the passengers. I saw these nowhere else.

Driving to the airfield there were circular rice paddies of a vivid green in terraced cultivation that reminded me of Corsica. But China is completely deforested. We saw few bound feet, or "golden lilies."

"Every golden lily is bought with a casket of tears." The solemn little girl inspecting our jeep and us appraisingly would not have to worry about that.

Then, flying over ranges of circular hills, blue in the distance, with lines like the Skyline Drive as I saw it later from my Virginian house, rugged country, a muddy river, I thought of Marco Polo's achievement in getting here, and mine, so unexpected and so odd, *planned,* by Someone, "if design govern in so small a thing." I thought of a book I had loved, *Messer Marco Polo,* by Donn Byrne, and how through meeting Mary Street at the Pen and Brush I was drawn to reading it again. . . . As a young rebellious girl in Richmond, she was one of the four editors of the review which first published it.

"I shall now tell you of Golden Bells, and her in the Chinese Garden. I would have you now see her as I see her, standing before Li Po, the great poet, in her green costume."

Golden Bells. Hung Tu.

Much of Marco Polo's travel book would apply today. He must have seen the same gray-stone square city walls about Sian. Those times, his times, and before them Hung Tu's, were more real to me than the wartime China I was traveling through.

There was a wedding going on at the impressive hotel where we were staying as guests of the Chinese government. The young couple were in the diplomatic service, it was a new-style wedding, so the bride wore white instead of red, but she held her head down in the traditionally modest way. She was enchanting with her painted cheeks, cherry-red mouth and sleek black hair. Golden Bells must have looked like this, and also Hung Tu.

Long tables were set for the wedding feast, which began as soon as the young couple ran out together. We sat down at ours and watched the fun. This was the first time we were living with the Chinese civilians, eating with them, sharing the same public rooms.

The essential gaiety of the Chinese became more evident as we saw more of them. In spite of all the hardships of the war, in spite of inflation and disease, in spite of the uncertainty of the future with, as they thought then, at least another year of war ahead, the people were alive with a gaiety that comes from a courageous spirit. This gaiety, this inner strength of happiness was reflected in their faces.

"Face" means much in the East, but in India it had been a sullen or obsequious countenance. The Chinese face of 1945 was full of individuality and humor. In my diary I noted:

It is impossible to conquer or keep under a people with a strongly developed sense of humor, of proportion. China has it. There is also courage and serenity. It is embarrassing to talk of courage in the face of what the Chinese have done, and are prepared to do. . . . They stood alone for more years than the British, and said a good deal less about it. When we were in Chichiang Colonel Soo reminded us that China held up 750,000 Japanese front-line troops and 20 per cent of the Japanese air force. The Chinese kept occupied forces which would otherwise have been used in the Pacific. Chinese saved American blood, he said, why was there no publicity?

A few days later we joined Chiang Kai-shek to review the graduation ceremonies of the Chinese West Point, and later traveled on his special train to the front. We got off at Cheu Sheui, and were driven in an open truck to the parade ground where the First Army was waiting to be reviewed.

These troops had seen front-line action for eight years. They were once commanded by the Gissimo himself. Now they were waiting—they had been on the parade ground since seven that morning—for his words of commendation.

They were drawn up against a dramatic backdrop of purple mountains, with, towering above them, the white thunderheads of China's fighting sky. The division commander, Major General Shu Lian Yu, of the Seventy-eighth Division, stood in front of his men with a drawn sword. He looked like an old print of a warrior against the Tartars.

The northeastern border of China was dark with smoke and dust.
To repel the savage invaders, our generals, leaving their families,
Strode forth together, looking as heroes should look.

When twenty years later I needed a model for Hung Tu's warrior Governor, Official Wei Kao, I had this man and this scene to draw on.

He had been wounded several times, so had other officers in the march-past. We could pick them out, unable to do the goose-step. Uniforms were faded, helmets battered. Equipment was pitiful. There was mule-drawn artillery, vintage 1902. I counted six bazookas among forty thousand men.

It did not seem to me that we were helping them very much with relevant supplies.

As we stood there, watching the division fall in, absolutely silently, without a word of command, coming to rest in a bunched and perfect square in front of the reviewing stand, I reflected that we were seven minutes flying time away from the Japanese, and that it might have been worth a suicide attack to net Chiang Kai-shek, his son, his First Army, and a group of Americans. Every wing that wandered by was scrutinized. We heard afterward that a Japanese plane could not warm up or turn its engine over without it being known by the Chinese Intelligence.

All the same it was a relief when the Generalissimo left. It might not have been easy for that massed multitude to escape casualties. The Japanese frequently shelled Chiang Kai-shek's train. The week before we traveled in it, the engineer and two firemen had been killed. For this reason we were not taken to the station nearest to the front. We got out some distance away and drove to Tung Kuan.

Driving may have been more dangerous. Three of us found ourselves in a sightseeing bus of uncertain age, accompanied by Chinese officers. The Generalissimo's son, Major Chang, left in charge of the party, had gone ahead to serve as guide in his jeep. Our bus got lost, and we wandered through dust gorges, into flat country by the Yellow River.

Knowing that the Japanese were on the other bank, we were a little uneasy, wobbling along very slowly in full view toward the shore. Suddenly one of the Chinese officials exclaimed:

"No . . . no . . . very dangerous. Much explosion here. Go back," and a string of Chinese expletives to the driver.

We turned and meandered back. The bus was incapable of speeding. If the Japanese had wanted to get us we were there, without so much as a pop-gun among us, in full view and within easy range. No doubt they thought anything crazy enough to be moving must be a trap or not worth shooting.

I wondered whether my yellow card requesting treatment accorded to a captain might not, after all, come in handy. But after half an hour of silence and suspense we arrived at the point where we had turned off, to find that Major Chang, anxious about us, had returned. We traveled the rest of the way in deep gorges with only a few dangerous spots where we were exposed for a few yards.

When we arrived, Harry Flannery, who had traveled ahead, said:

"Did you see those places where we were in sight of the Japs?"

We laughed, having seen more than that. Then an interpreter asked:

"Is there anything you would like the General to do for you?"

"Yes," Ed Leahy murmured beneath his football cap. "If the General has a spare moment, he might take our guide out and shoot him."

Fortunately this was not relayed. It might have embarrassed the General, or he might have embarrassed us by ordering it attended to. One must not depart from the literal in dealing with officials.

We went 150 meters along trenches to the first line. Here we could see the Japanese with no need of glasses. We were nearest them here, at 800 yards. They were quiet, but they had shelled the town the day before at the time they expected us to be there. The Chinese had circulated through the grapevine that we would arrive twenty-four hours earlier. We were amused to learn that five shells, one for each of us, had landed in the town without causing any casualties. Willkie drew a salute of twenty.

We interviewed recently captured Japanese prisoners, thin and miserable-looking. They answered our questions sullenly. One thing they said was interesting, coming at that time. No one but the war lords still thought the Emperor divine. They also agreed that they had set captured Americans to hard labor.

We took a last look at the Yellow River, which *is* yellow when it ripples, showing a queer gold gleam. Hoang-ho is its name, the second largest river in China. Li Po mentions it often:

See how the Yellow River's waters move out of heaven,
Entering the ocean, never to return.

I would cross the Yellow River, but ice chokes the ferry;
I would climb the T'ai-hang Mountains, but the sky is blind with snow.

The ferry wasn't running when we were there either, but not on account of the cold.

On the way back in the special train, we passed another train, with people clinging to the windows, riding on the roof, standing on the doorsteps, like all the pictures of refugee trains. This, however, was just an ordinary train with ordinary travelers, not necessarily refugees.

We had dinner that night with the Governor of Shensi in Sian. There was much *gambai* and many delicacies, black rice cooked for us by the Governor's wife, young and beautiful, so that when she told us she had eight children, we were baffled. But they were hers only in the Chinese sense of family relationships, in reality the adopted children of another wife, or wives.

This part of China was parched and arid, like India. We flew over the city, seeing the square stone wall again, then we took off for Marco Polo's part of China, Cheng-tu. This was the place where the poet I was to become obsessed with also lived. Her family name was Hsueh T'ao, but she is usually referred to in Chinese literary history by her style, or social name, Hung Tu. In Nanning I had heard that the grounds of her villa Pi-Chi Fang were still there, and used as a public garden. I was determined to see them if I could, and anything else that remained of hers.

It was difficult. Every moment of our time was taken up with briefings and official parties. And we were there so short a time. Driving into town to the Governor's house, where there was to be a Chinese-American celebration of the Fourth of July (my first as an American citizen), I was able to see the very green countryside, lush and fertile, and familiar to me. There were no horses or mules. Whole families were pulling carts piled high with gas drums, airplanes, food. We passed an old water wheel in a stream by the roadside. Two men were turning it on the principle of the treadmill, or like squirrels in a cage. This too I "remembered," also the large live black pigs with green leaves on their stomachs, lying on their backs on wheelbarrows covered with straw, being carried to market. Their owners sewed up their eyelids so they wouldn't try to escape. They didn't drive them because the pig might lose an ounce or two of weight. If the owner lost a few pounds it didn't matter. The hot, tired coolie, stopping at a handy stream, cooled off the pig by sprinkling water on its stomach. It didn't matter about cooling off the man.

But the Governor was waiting in a banquet hall, with loud American music, long speeches in American and Chinese, and Chinese fireworks which surpass all other fireworks in originality. These were very pretty, showing traditional Chinese scenes with Chinese lettering and flags of the allied nations. Rockets exploded in all directions, showering down on the spectators, to the great delight of the children. The children were different here. We noticed no "*ding haos*" and fewer smiles. On the way back we nearly ran down a child and were told that if we had, the Chinese procedure would be to go ahead, for if you stopped or showed concern you would have adopted the injured person. The Chinese, we learned, seldom touched the sick or injured unless they were immediate family and it was sometimes days before the immediate family discovered a patient. A man whose leg was amputated in one of our hospitals came back to it explaining, "You cut off leg, this person belong you now."

Another odd sight was the casual way airplanes were stowed in barns and backyards, side by side with the most primitive living I had seen in China, and the most attractive. The women in this part of the country seemed to be treated well. They rode on wheelbarrows pushed by the men. The children seemed happy and obviously loved. I saw a small boy singing and dancing in the dust as he herded a flock of ducks by holding a bamboo rod behind them. But the adult coolies strained and sweated, pushing and pulling heavily overloaded carts. I saw four men hauling an airplane.

Everything was made of bamboo, from the neatly plaited fences, seven to nine feet high, around the farms and compounds, to the tools and bowls and utensils of everyday life. The farms looked picturesque and prosperous, shut in behind tall trees. This was the most conservative part of China, with no great love for foreigners, practically unvisited by white people before the war, except for missionaries, because it was inaccessible, far to the north on the borders of Tibet. On clear days the Tibetan mountains can be seen.

When we reached Cheng-tu we collected an interpreter, a Mr. Vincent from the Office of War Information. He asked us what we wanted to see. I said, "The gardens of Pi-Chi Fang." The others said they wanted to go shopping.

We all started out together and I was dropped off first. I am not sure what happened. I felt a mounting awareness. I could not wait to get out of the jeep and walk through the stone gates, with bronze inscriptions on either side. There was a bench by a clump of bamboo. I sat down there, and told the interpreter I would stay there until he came back for me.

"I have some work to do," I said, "some sorting out, some thinking. . . ."

They left, and I was alone. There was no one else in the garden, a place where I had often been before, where I had planted and planned and lived. . . . I did not need to walk to the well, or to the riverbank, or to turn any corner to know what was there. I sat, slipping through the levels, funneled back into the past, the present, only time, with everything stronger, greener, freshly alive. In the end I suppose I slept.

I was dressed in long green silk, I was like a piece of jade, and the instrument I held was jeweled too. Above me a parrot swung in a cage and at my feet was a small brown dog. I was waiting in perfect contentment for the Other, the Great-heart One, to return on his spirited little Uighur horse with the gold-painted hooves, *Dragon appearing in the field, through him the world attains beauty and clarity.* But there was a waiting anguish, that he might not come, that this might not endure, that . . . that . . .

The jeep must have come for me then and taken me to join the others at a press conference, for suddenly I was there, at a long table in a circle. I was startled and confused, but I would hide it. I asked Bruce Gould, who was sitting next to me, if he had enjoyed the morning's shopping.

"Did you buy up the whole town?"

He looked at me strangely for a moment as though I'd said something unexpectedly rude.

"You didn't seem to be doing too badly," he said, and turned away. Elsie McCormick on my other side leaned forward. "Why don't we split some of the silk? You take half a sleeve and I the other? Then we'd have more patterns. I'm going to frame mine, and you said you were going to do something like that with yours."

I didn't know what she was talking about, but I said yes. Then I noticed that my musette felt heavy on my shoulder. No wonder. It was stuffed with silks, little jade animals, and a whole mandarin robe with Peiping flower stitch.

I heard later that I had borrowed $15,000 (Chinese) from Hallett Abend, carried it round in a sun helmet, made ferocious bargaining over cups of tea. . . . I had evidently spent the morning shopping with the others, while my Ka, or in this case *Ch'i,* wandered in the past.

But now we were at a press conference and the Chinese reporters were asking us some thorny questions. Mine was, being a novelist, was I writing a book on China? I heard myself answer, "No, I am not writing a book on China at the present time, but I hope to write something about China in a book. I have not been here long enough to write on China more deeply—yet." I did not want to talk to them about Hung Tu. It would have meant exposing something fragile and hidden and newly discovered to these elbow-pushers and politicians, for that was what they seemed to me to be. Their tone was aggressive as they asked if Chinese reporters were given the same treatment as others in America. Someone answered for us yes, there was no discrimination, but this was plainly disbelieved.

We got away with some perfunctory civilities and drove back to camp, before taking off for Kunming, flying at sixteen thousand feet in oxygen masks. I was glad of the interval in the familiar plane, where I could pretend to be sleeping, and try to collect my thoughts.

The next day was our last day in China. I went by jeep with some of the men to the Temple of the Thousand Gods. We went through several court-yards with gongs and bronze bells and dragons guarding them, huge figures grimacing to scare off evil spirits. Inside the temple itself, around the walls from floor to ceiling, the thousand gods, painted red, blue, gold, green, brown, with their distinctive legends, looked down on us with peaceful withdrawn expressions. They flanked an enormous Buddha in the attitude of "contemplation of Nirvana." It was a place of peace and meditation and timelessness. The others went on, but Hallett Abend and I went through to a courtyard with cloisters about it and sat down on a stone balustrade. He talked to me of China and the years he had spent there, the old China and the new China taking shape. Doves were walking round our feet, an old monk in a rusty robe watched us benevolently.

Suddenly the old monk was beside us, holding out two little strips of bamboo with lettering on them, the beautiful brushed script of Chinese ideo-grams. He handed one to Hallett, one to me, bowed and moved away before we could thank him.

Hallett sat looking at the one he held with an odd expression.

"What does it say?" I asked.

"This is very beautiful. These are the old forms of each character. *Tao ch'o hui ch'u*...." He frowned.

"What does it mean?"

"I'm not sure. I think it's a way of saying 'Goodbye, you will not come here again.' *Tao,* road, path, way, *ch'o,* step by step, *hui,* to return to or from, a turn or revolution, *ch'u,* past, gone, emptied, to remove, to get rid of, an empty vessel and cover.... That certainly finishes me up."

Past, gone, emptied, he sounded a little sad.

"Is mine the same?"

He took it from me. "No," he said, "yours is different, much more polite. *Yu,* jade, the cool vitality of life, *shih,* the will of heaven, *yun,* rhythm, harmony, *hsieh,* to write . . . setting thoughts and ideas in order in writing. . . . I would say it meant 'It is the will of heaven that you write about jade in rhythm and harmony.' Of course, it could also go, 'The will of heaven is like jade, rhythm, harmony, and thoughts and ideas in order.' "

"I like the first version better. 'Cool vitality of life' . . . I think . . . I hope it is saying that I am to write the book about Hung Tu. She was like jade, and certainly she had rhythm and harmony. . . ."

He looked at me, surprised.

"You didn't tell me you were writing about a Chinese poet."

"I didn't really know until I came here."

"Did you find something about her?"

"Yes. In spite of briefings. Did you get the material for your book?"

"Yes . . . in spite of briefings. But it won't be about jade and harmony."

"It will be a good book," I said. "Needed, full of truth and wisdom, and probably the critics won't like it."

When *Reconquest* was published in 1946 it was as I foretold, except that I had left out wit, with which it was filled. He sent me the galleys and I was amused to find that he had mentioned me, looking, he said, "like a demure wren," but, when one knew me better, "what a false impression!"

Though we were only halfway through the tour, with Ceylon, a return to India and Egypt, Carthage, Italy, Austria and Germany ahead, I thought that I had found what I had come for. The rest would be footnotes to places I already knew in Europe . . . tragic and terrible in Germany, a month after the surrender, poignant and nostalgic in Italy . . . but after we left Kunming I would be just an interested passenger, toted along with the others.

I might have known the Lords and Ladies of Karma, the Grandfathers and Grandmothers had more in store for me than that. It was a *guided* tour, not a tourist's holiday. From the start it had been a "what-think-ye-of-this?" examination, requiring answers, and not superficial ones.

In Egypt the question was, "What think ye of the Last Judgment?" At the Taj Mahal, "What think ye of romantic love?" In Rome, "What think ye of organized religion, of the Pope?"

My diary says:

I had just time to get back to the hotel and change my shirt before we set forth for the Vatican in a procession of shiny cars, preceded by motorcycle cops with screaming sirens. This is insidious. I expect to be escorted now on the most trivial errands, but this one is not trivial. We got a swift glimpse of Saint Peter's before we disappeared through the gates of the Vatican and arrived at the audience chamber. We stayed in an anteroom next to the Pope's private apartments for some time. Purple Monsignors and scarlet Cardinals went swiftly by, immersed in their affairs. Harry Grayson said, "These Cardinals run like hell." Bob Considine, his hair sleeked back like a little boy, very clean and nervous, was in charge of introducing the party. The women ganged up on me. "You were presented at court. You go first." I protested, but the door was opening and I was thrust in.

The Pope (Pius XII) was sitting at his desk, with his back to the door. He turned sideways to greet us, as we were introduced, one by one, and knelt for his blessing. When he heard that I was writing the book on Mother Seton, he gave me a special blessing, before I could tell him that I was not a Catholic, more a Pagan. When I saw that I was the only one he blessed in this particular way, though there were Catholics among us, I felt a little cheap and like an impostor. Everything to do with *Heart in Pilgrimage* has always embarrassed me. . . .

He has a radiant, gentle face, exuding serenity, but he is a far-seeing, practical, up-to-date politician, who has broken one precedent after another, and cut through swathings of red tape. He is popular with journalists because he answers questions with a twinkle and types with two fingers on a portable machine. He broke precedents this afternoon, allowing himself to be photographed informally and giving us an hour of "off the record" talk after he read us his prepared statement.

It was more or less a scolding of the press.

"What shall we say of deliberate falsehood and calumny? A lying tongue, like hands that shed innocent blood, the Lord hateth; and every just man detests a lying word. Calumny is quick-footed, as you know, especially, be it said for shame, when directed against religion and the champions of the sterner demands of Christian morality; the denial and the defense of the victim are often given no hearing or may find space after a week or so in an obscure corner of an inside page. Members of the profession who do not hesitate to smear their pages or pollute the ether with falsehood are rendering a great disservice to their fellow-men; they are aiming a mortal blow at the spirit of trust between the children of the same heavenly Father, and gravely imperil peace among nations. If competent civil authority fails, when necessity demands it, to curb such license, then civil society will most surely pay the penalty. The world shudders today to contemplate the mass of misfortune that has overwhelmed it. May it not be traced back to the flood of error and false moral standards let loose by the written and spoken word of proud, irreligious men? May God strengthen you in your purpose to serve your profession and your fellow-men in a worthy manner. . . ."

I was standing on his right, a little behind, so that I saw him in half profile. He was wearing white with a pectoral cross. He had a plain sapphire-and-diamond ring. His desk equipment made up for his personal simplicity in elaborate decoration. His golden telephone was studded with jewels, and he had a golden fly swatter. At the close of his talk he blessed rosaries and gave them to us. He then said a number of informal things, sending his "affection" to President Truman and to various cardinals and bishops. He blessed us and those dear to us at home. Then we were ushered out. We had already taken more than our due measure of his time. While we collected ourselves in the anteroom, we saw him pass to a public audience of soldiers of all faiths. Then we were rushed through the Vatican, a glimpse here and a glimpse there, ending with the Sistine Chapel. What I wanted to do was to spend a year in the library, but of course we got no peek at that.

What think ye of the Pope? As an elaborate figurehead like the British monarchy I can accept him. As the representative on earth of the Great Simplicity, the Master Jesus, *no*. I have always felt that one of the worst pangs of the Crucifixion may have been foreknowledge of what would be done by "the Church" in the name of the Prince of Peace.

We stopped for a drink with Colonel Fisher, Elsie McCormick's cousin. He told us that when he was a prisoner in the Hotel Grande he had said, "I'd like to come back as Governor of this city," which he did for one month, the first month and the worst. From prisoner to Governor, a strange reversal.

We left him to have cocktails with Ambassador Kirk in what used to be the Barberini Palace. He had "plenty to do with," which is a good thing, I suppose, though I would rather see our representative living more simply. The Italians were impressed by the style in which he lived. He had redecorated the Palace in perfect taste. Buff-colored walls rose to the frescoed Cortoni ceiling. His furniture was mostly fine museum pieces. He took Hallett Abend and me into his private suite for a few words. It was the first time and, I imagine, the last, that I have been called "a prostitute" by an Ambassador. Hallett shared the experience. Like the Pope, Kirk was saying that we should, that we must, tell the truth. If we did not or allowed ourselves to be muzzled by censorship, we were no better than prostitutes.

We went to the opera at the Caracula Baths in the open air. It was *Aïda,* a strange one to see, remembering Italy's attack on Haile Selassie, which had, in a sense, started World War Two. It was a magnificently staged performance, with a cast of three or four hundred people. The stage effects were superb, the singing smooth and good in the ensembles, though I have heard better individual voices at the Met and Covent Garden. The scene by the banks of the Nile was in a class by itself, unbelievably lovely. These people might not have clothes, especially shoes, coal, food—two of the chorus fainted from malnutrition—but they did have their opera. The open-air stadium seated thousands. The conquered and the conquerers sat together, with the same expression on their faces, enjoying the performance, united, bearing witness to the universality of music. If only we could follow the Arts, instead of politics and business!

In Naples we went to another opera, the last act of *La Bohème.* The setting was colorful and rich, with six tiers of boxes in red and gold. The audience of conquered and conquerors applauded side by side. This time there were lines of prisoners of war, guarded by G.I.s, many British in uniform and some Americans. As the last notes died away, expressions changed. The guards formed up their prisoners and marched them off, and we all came back to our various divisions. It was strange to see the French Left Quarter sung about in Italian here. Coming back from the opera, the harbor lights were shimmering, poignant as lights on water are.

In Naples I heard the first snatches of song from a flower vendor and a man going by. I saw a smartly dressed old woman carrying a pitifully little market bag; a child going to school with a dinner pail; life had resumed. The only sign of Fascism I observed was the word *Duce* stenciled on one of the houses in the poorer part of the town. On the whole there was no gaiety. We heard that the Italians did not like us, but did not want us to leave or they would starve.

Later, the Vietnamese did not, could not like us, either, but some of them did not want us to leave for the same reason. When will the pattern change?

Again the convoy of siren-blowing cars, to the Royal Palace, built as a summer residence for the Popes in the fifteenth century, full of tapestries and treasures. The chamberlain who escorted us carefully turned off each light, almost before we passed through the room. Prince Umberto, when we reached him, seemed very nervous. He was tall, thin, suave, spoke excellent English and stammered out gracious things, a prelude to another plea for coal, for food.

After this audience, as we went through the Palace gardens, a collection of war orphans met us, mutilated by mines and bombs, some of them ours, and shot at by the retreating Germans. A blind boy of five or so ran to me, chuckling and smiling, and fumbled over my dress. "Signora," he was calling out, "Signora!" Another boy, blind, with a disfigured face and both arms cut off below the elbows, was led by the director of the orphanage. This child said that he was eight, and smiled. There were other blinded children, many without an arm or a leg. We had nothing to give them, not even a stick of chocolate. We had not expected to see them. It was a carefully planned impromptu scene. The nuns in charge had gentle, sad faces.

And all over the world there are children like these.

On Monday, July 23, we flew over Anzio, over the beachhead, the harbor, the American cemetery with its nine thousand dead, along the coast. The peaceful blue of the sea contrasted with the blasted buildings everywhere. After Cassino ruins could not horrify—it was the little gaieties that seemed so pitiful. We flew along the coast, throwing our shadow over beaches with bathers and bright parasols. I was thinking of those children in the Palace grounds. More ruins, wrecked planes, wrecked tanks, ground pitted with shell holes, wrecked landing barges, everywhere the waste, and everywhere the blue serenity of sea and sky. Flocks of sheep wandering on the sand, fishermen and swimmers, war and peace, all mixed up together. The land looked parched. Southern Italy was suffering from phenomenal drought.

When we reached Florence, we were quartered at the Excelsior. I had a room with a balcony over the Arno, and no time to enjoy it. The last time I stayed in Florence it was in a modest *pensione* on the wrong side of the tracks. Luxury is insidious.

After lunch I took a car and in my pidgin Italian directed it to San Marco to see what had happened to the Fra Angelico paintings. It was closed, but an old man let me in. He told me the *Last Judgment*, the *Coronation of the Virgin*, the *Madonna della Stella* and others had not returned from the *campagna* where they were hidden from the Germans. Here as in France people risked their lives to save the national treasures. Here the Germans had been allies, in France enemies, but they robbed impartially, "liberated" was the word they used, perhaps. The old man said the paintings would soon be back. Other canvases were stacked up on the floor, without their frames, but undamaged. The cloisters, with the tree in the middle, were the same, and upstairs the cells with the frescoes in them were untouched. I went into Savonarola's and looked at the favorite one there. . . . It always surprises me that Fra Angelico should be a Dominican instead of a Franciscan as he seems in spirit.

I went to the Medici Chapel. It was closed and the statues gone, also in the *campagna,* so I went on to Fiesole, where the monks were chanting vespers in alternate rows, their tonsured heads shining in the candlelight of their dark chapel, as I had seen it in the early twenties, the cloisters where the illuminated missals were painted, the founder's cell, all exuding peace. Here was Florence, here Fiesole, serene, untarnished, with the same lovely view, only this time the land was parched by the worst drought in years. The Arno had shrunk to a muddy stream.

Later it would flood and damage paintings and frescoes, but that was still far away.

I drove back, down winding narrow roads with cypress trees, to join the group in a party at a villa—the owner was in jail. We strolled back along the Arno under the full moon, the same full moon we had been seeing, it seemed to me, everywhere. The Ponte Vecchio was not destroyed. There was very little apparent damage in Florence. People seemed better off than Romans or Neapolitans, better dressed and better fed, but Florence struck me as in a stupor. The people might be more alive than those in Naples or in Rome, the place itself wasn't. And it was obvious that we were conquerors. "They get out of the way," I thought, "they don't push and jostle, they answer questions promptly with a great show of willingness, but they don't pinch any American's behind, not even at Mass."

On Tuesday, July 24, I woke to a high-ceilinged room, with a view over the river and a mellow light on the buildings opposite. It was an unreal start to a day full of heavy vibrations. Once more we huddled on bucket seats, craning our necks to peer out of the plane. We flew along Lake Garda, across the mountains toward the Brenner Pass, where two evil men met to plan their sordid hells. My throat began to ache before I realized why. The plane was filling with deadening, heavy vibrations, the beauty we were looking at was like a painted scene, and between us lay horrible layers of dirty browns and blacks, a spiritual smog of despair. I felt sick from this miasma, which was real to me. It was nothing that I physically saw below, a green jeweled lake, a mountain river, villages, farms, a placid-looking country like Switzerland, nothing in the plane itself that was assailing me.

We landed in Salzburg and drove in Himmler's open Mercedes, collecting dirty looks from men and women as we passed in the long black cars in which they had watched their gods go by. Ten weeks after Germany's surrender, I could tell my grandchildren, I drove in Himmler's car to Hitler's stronghold, my hand on the rail that Himmler held when he stoop up to *heil*. I sat where those all-powerful German buttocks rested, and thought of what it had taken to dislodge them, to put down the mighty from that seat. Probably my grandchildren would not know or care who Himmler and Hitler were. Fortunately they would not have been compelled to know and to care.

Not long ago I overheard an English eighteen-year-old ask, idly, for information, "What did Churchill do, to have that great funeral?" It was not a malicious dig, and not a put-down. I would have felt better if it had been. It was a simple question. He just didn't know.

We climbed, through blasted country, over the road built by Yugoslavian slave labor, to the Eagle's Nest. Here was the tunnel, two hundred feet into the mountain, with an elevator shaft at the end of it. The elevator had two doors, one for Hitler and one for the S.S. to get out simultaneously at different floors. Evidently Hitler did not choose to be within reach of his trusted guards. There was no communication whatever between his part of the Nest and theirs, except by telephone.

The most striking thing about his floor was the conference room, with a long table around which twenty-six people could be seated on rough cloth chairs, and the living room with its famous window looking out upon the mountains. It was a big circular room with a stone floor, a low round table, a huge sofa before a red-granite fireplace, a large brown-and-blue carpet all in the most commonplace taste. Hitler was reported not to have been in his Nest since 1942. The last event for which it was opened was the marriage of Brigadier Leader Fegelein with a sister of Eva Braun in the autumn of 1944. Eva was there, but not Hitler. Eva was there on other occasions, we were told, privately, two-timing Hitler with a man wearing a mask.

The S.S. man still running the elevator said that he found Hitler good, kind, *sehr gemütlich*. He had never addressed him in person, but obviously had and still did hero-worship him. While we were there members of the Wehrmacht were braving capture to make what amounted to a pilgrimage to the fallen eagle's nest. It was evident, even to a quick and superficial view, that Hitler still had loyal and fanatical followers. Goering, the elevator man told us, was good too. Many times he would walk up, a feat comparable to climbing the staircase at Radio City instead of taking the elevator there.

We drove to Goering's house . . . smashed. Other Nazi Party members' houses . . . smashed. Then to Hitler's own house, totally lacking in taste, except for the view from the window, and nature provided that. Curiously, the Eagle's Nest had no sinister atmosphere, it was boringly banal, a distasteful vulgarity. This house was far more evil, especially Hitler's bedroom, like some fetid cesspool, if cesspools could sting. It was good to see it broken and shattered as he had shattered thousands and thousands of homes in Europe. The tin twisted roof flapped, creaking in the wind. I could not get away from there fast enough.

Beneath the house tunnels connected with Goering's house, Bormann's house and the administration, running far into the mountainside. They were equipped with everything, and most of it still there, bedrooms, kitchens, an operating room, a film room, with reels stacked up in hundreds, storerooms, 100,000 bottles of champagne and cognac (contents *not* still there), Eva Braun's dressing room with a bust of her on the table, a luxurious bathroom off it, a chaise-longue, still new, the wood bare, unpainted, pots of paint, and some unpainted stuff, a library. Why didn't they fight it out there as they planned? They could have held out for a time.

We left, saddened by perverted ingenuity amounting to genius. All that waste, useless, except to show to tourists through the years to come. "Except the Lord build the house . . ." Berchtesgaden was built by slave labor. Those tortured hands, that martyrdom, could have been used to transform Germany into a good land for everyman. Germany might have led Europe and the world, if she had chosen, in scientific advancement and the arts of peace. But there were too many Germans like our guide, an impudent, conceited, ex-Wehrmacht officer. It was a trial to have him eat and ride with us.

I slept that night in a German feather bed opposite the street where Mozart's house still stands. Next morning I walked to it before breakfast. The old ironwork over the gate was there, intact, above the entrance to the winding street. Men and women passed me, treading the wooden cobbles that echoed to Mozart's feet before they were defiled by Nazi processions. They looked at me with hate. They especially loathed American women in uniform, I was told later. Perhaps they thought we were like their own R.I.W.I. (their WACs).

The children were good-looking, seemed fat and well, but there were waves of longing for revenge, even from them. As our group sat in cars waiting to be driven to the airport, one mask of bitter resentment and hatred went by after another. A tall man stood near us, clenching and unclenching his hands, muttering to himself convulsively. An old crone—or perhaps a young woman, we couldn't tell from her insane face—went by seven times, unable to take herself away, yet ravaged by the sight of us.

Eighty thousand armed men had been arrested in American-occupied Austria and Germany during the few days before we arrived. It was not a place to wander as a naive tourist yet.

When we got to the airfield, we found a group of Japanese waiting with their wives and children and their mounds of luggage in new shining suitcases—no forty-four-pound limit for them—they carried luxury items, fur coats, typewriters, a child had an expensive doll—to be flown to Le Havre, where they would be transferred by boat to the United States. There were German women among them who had married these "honorary Aryans." They too were studies in desire for revenge; their collective "face" was arrogant. One man complained when he saw that the plane—a better one than ours—had no cushioned seats. His guard told him to get in or he could walk. The M.P.s watching favored them all walking. We were tempted to wish this too. It was humiliating to have to breathe the dust from their propellers, to have to cede the runway to them, and take off ourselves from a dangerous sidestrip. Their country was still at war with us. We had the Death March of Bataan to remember. This considerate preference shown them over a group of uniformed Americans visibly fed their arrogance. They thought us soft, and so we were. If the choice is between brutality and softness there is no choice, but I thought we might have done things a little differently if we wanted them to know their country had no chance to win. For example, made them wait for our plane to take off.

It was a relief to leave Austria. Flying among mountains again with their pure snows, we could forget the rats and toads on the ground. We were going back to Italy, to Venice and Lake Garda, before going on through Germany, Scotland, Iceland, Labrador and home.

We had dinner at headquarters on an island in the lake where Mussolini kept his wife during the war, while he was with his mistress on the mainland. The owners, anti-Fascists, glad to have their property restored to them, gave it to the Americans for the duration of the occupation. The three sons of this family had all been in the underground and all come through the war. The youngest, whom we met with his mother, was twelve. He had hidden many times to avoid Gestapo questioning. He knew where his brothers were and was afraid that under torture he might tell.

It was a quiet, friendly evening, in a waiting atmosphere, suspended between the changes and ravages of war, the restorations and hopes of peace.

We took the General's speedboat and went home to our more modest quarters across the way.

I swam before breakfast with Hallett Abend and a water snake. Morning light came down the hill, touched the tower of the granite church hidden among cypresses and spread upon the water in a bronze and purple mist. Afterward on my balcony I could see the sunlight through an olive tree, silver leaves in a golden haze. It was a shining day, but we had to spend it at Ghedi interviewing criminals in a dreary prison camp.

. .

The commandant of this camp, which at the time we saw it held twenty-five thousand prisoners, and had been holding a hundred thousand for the two weeks from May 14 to June 1, was Colonel Franklin P. Miller, fresh from the front line, whose brother had been killed by the Germans. He had a strong, shrewd face, a fighter's stocky build, and a determined attitude toward his prisoners. As he put it:

"We don't like them, they know it, and respect us."

We followed the proceedings from the time the prisoners arrived at the processing area to when they were shipped home to Germany, or, if they were "recalcitrants," S.S., Gestapo or other criminals, to Pisa. Recalcitrants were not repatriable.

Vehicles were taken away, they marched to the camp. Luxury items were confiscated. These included cameras, liquor, cloth, purchases of every kind—there were several large rooms stacked to the ceiling with bolts of silk looted from shops and factories—they were issued a modified B ration, composed of forty per cent American C, some K, and sixty per cent German ration, captured food. They were given no fresh vegetables, but some fresh meat, particularly hospital patients. They got no butter, no cigarettes, no coffee, but were allowed some horse meat and some sugar. All money except reichsmarks was taken away. Receipts were given. Each repatriated man received a small sum, the equivalent of fourteen dollars. During their imprisonment they got no supplies from the Red Cross. For recreation they played soccer and got up shows. They were allowed to keep musical instruments. The shows, especially the songs, were supervised very carefully.

"In general," the colonel said, "since there's no German government, they have no rank, they're all 'surrendered personnel.' We make no distinction between officers and men, except we don't tolerate German generals here, we send them to another camp."

We toured the camp, driving slowly between stockades. In some there were small, hot tents—no stockade had trees—in most, the prisoners slept on the ground. They did their own cooking. We stopped to inspect one stockade where dinner was being served. I sampled the soup. It was greasy and tasteless, no salt.

"Do they ever complain?" I asked.

"Oh yes."

"Then what happens?"

"They're brought to my office. I listen to what they have to say. Spread out on my table are photographs of what they did to our men in their prisons. I draw their attention to a few of these, then I say: 'Complaint dismissed!' "

We passed another stockade, for recalcitrants, former S.S. men and Gestapo. They were given fewer rations and were more crowded, in a hotter place.

"Screening is a big job," Colonel Miller continued. "There are the arrestable categories, the S.S. as a group. We keep them in special cages under special guards, with others wanted for war crimes. But some of them have tried, naturally, to slip into regular units. We catch them from tattoed marks on their left arms, two strikes of lightning, or blood type marked. We've picked up about two hundred in the last three weeks. We have five thousand segregated now. Then there are the displaced persons, people picked up fighting with the German army, to be returned to their countries. We allow them to go to town on passes, issue them better rations and cigarettes, and give them American clothing. This marks the difference between them and the S.S., who automatically become bastards, sitting in the sun, wondering what's to become of them." He smiled, one of his rare smiles, tight-lipped. "I recommend long-term service in North Africa under the French."

"If a man's discharged, repatriated . . . ?"

"He arrives in Munich, gets picked up by the Third Army and taken to their enclosure for a fourth screening . . . he's had three with us. If he passes that, he's turned loose, within a reasonable distance of his home, say fifty miles, given forty marks if he was an enlisted man, eighty, if an officer. He arrives home with his pack on his back, two shirts, two pairs trousers, two pairs socks, his underwear and nothing else, to take up where he left off six years ago. Men who want to go to a special area for special work, rather than home, can." He added, "Many of them do."

He turned us over to a young officer, a Captain Lehman, who asked if we would like to interview individual criminals. We said yes, and two men were called out of the rejected pen. Captain Lehman sat at a table, and the three of us who were interested sat on boxes behind him.

The first to come in was Hubner, a member of the S.A. with a Golden Party Pin, belonging to the old gang. He was a First Lieutenant in an army battalion, but he had been hiding in a labor detail till he was ferreted out. A man in his forties, with sandy hair, and sandy mustaches over a mean little mouth, shifty eyes, would-be ingratiating gestures of hands with white nails, he said he was an idealist.

"What sort of idealist?"

"Socialist—nationalist as opposed to internationalist. I believed in everything for the people, nothing for the individual."

"What were you in civilian life?"

"A grammar-school teacher in Bavaria."

"If you were free to teach again, what would you tell the German children about this war?" I asked.

He hesitated, worked his toe on the ground, stammered something.

"He doesn't know what it boils down to," Lehman interpreted, "but he would not present it in the same way as it was presented to him during the war."

"What mistakes did Hitler make?" Elsie McCormick asked.

"He felt overconfidence after the successes in France, Poland, Greece and Yugoslavia."

"Was that all?"

"No, he hoped to the last that differences between Great Britain, Russia and America would arise."

"Was that *all?*"

No answer.

"I'll put it in another way," I said. "Did you think Hitler right to start the war?"

"At the time, yes, I was completely convinced, I accepted without criticism, now, no. . . ."

"Because he lost?"

"Yes."

"No other reason?"

No answer.

"How long will it be before Germany can rise again to fight another war?"

"I think the Allies will supervise and prohibit Germany from getting strength for another war."

He was dismissed.

Obergruppen-führer Schmull took his place. He had a Golden Party Pin too, and had belonged to the party since 1932. He was fat to obesity, with pointed ears, heavy jowls, another mean little mouth, clean-shaven this time, coarse gray hair over shrewd gray eyes. He was wanted for atrocities.

"What were you in civilian life?"

"A motor vehicle expert for the city of Berlin."

"What mistakes did Hitler make?"

"He thought England would not enter the war, nor the United States. I did not think so either. I was in America in 1934, and you had not the war potential then."

"When did you know the war was lost?"

"When we made our first withdrawal in Russia, in 1941–42. I knew then we could not last to win the war, but I hoped there would not be an actual defeat."

"What do you think about the concentration camps we have uncovered?"

"I don't know. I am surprised. I don't believe the reports." He waved his hands in the same would-be ingratiating manner Hubner used, toward the two women in uniform. His arms were bandaged.

"He tried," Lehman told us in an undertone, "to commit suicide yesterday. That is, he says it was suicide, but he gave his wrists such little slashes that they wouldn't have done much harm. When we asked him why, he said it was because he felt himself humiliated in front of his men by being treated without consideration of his former rank and position. Actually, we think he did it to get out of the sun. We bandaged him and sent him back."

We asked him about the future of Germany.

He didn't know. He wasn't interested in politics.

Captain Lehman dismissed him and turned to us.

"There," he said, "that's run of the mill. That's what they're like. Those are the answers you get."

We verified this. All the German soldiers and civilians whom I interviewed here and in Munich had various answers to the question: "What mistake did Hitler make?" Not one so much as hinted it was a mistake for him to begin the war. They each had different answers too to the question: "How long will it take Germany to rise and fight again?" Some said, "Twenty years," some said, "That depends on how much of the Wehrmacht is left to organize," some said, "It will be difficult with Allied supervision." None said, "Unthinkable, she will never rise, we do not want her to." This of course was before the Bomb made the hope of rising impractical.

Questioned about atrocities, civilians and soldiers alike professed absurd surprise . . . absurd that they should take us for such dopes. Colonel Miller told us they had secured a ten-minute film of atrocities committed by the German people, and he gave us a copy of the speech made to the prisoners after they had seen it. (See Appendix.)

We followed the process to its logical end, by going to see a trainload of repatriables embark. The cars were the same kind they used for shipping prisoners and slave labor—the old forty-men eight-horse variety. But the Allies allowed the doors to be open for air, and gave the Germans C rations and facilities, such as shovels, for latrines. The Germans used to close the doors on their prisoners, and give them no facilities.

One of the guards who had been a prisoner in Germany said: "Five days after they shut us in, without food, water, air or anything, they'd open the doors and say 'Pfui! Filthy Americans!' We give them the treatment we'd give cattle we were shipping—we're responsible for their arrival in good condition, we give them the food they're entitled to, and latrine facilities, but nothing to sit on and no coddling. We get them there in good physical condition, but that's all." He straightened his shoulders as the train moved off, and grinned. We turned away.

We drove to the villa Mussolini had occupied with his mistress, while his wife was stuck on the island in the middle of Lake Garda. Mussolini's ex-valet, who was there, told us Il Duce was not completely vegetarian, that he didn't smoke, didn't drink, but he did eat a little meat. He seemed worried in his last days.

"Up to about two weeks before he died, he thought Hitler had a secret weapon that would smash down his enemies and win the war. Then he began to think the Germans wouldn't have it ready in time." This conversation took place before any of us knew of the atom bomb, still two weeks and a world's imaginings away.

"Mussolini's day," the valet went on mournfully, "was very regular. He left for his office in the morning, came back at one, had a game of tennis followed by siesta. In the evening he varied the visits of guests. . . ."

The villa was in atrocious taste, outside and in. It had a grim, depressing atmosphere. General Alexander made it his headquarters, but it got on his nerves the last time he was there, and he hadn't come to it again.

We had a chance to compare it with D'Annunzio's pretentious villa complete with phony ship and mausoleum. I thought of Duse, and felt since D'Annunzio had the wit to design his own tomb, he might have had the grace to occupy it sooner. I have never been able to bear that *pomposo* man.

After these two vulgarities, we drove through tunnels where the Germans had underground factories. Long lines of airplane engines were still stacked up and machinery of other kinds. There were seventy of these tunnels honeycombing the hills. The noise inside them when they were being worked must have been tremendous. They are strung along the edge of the lake, linked together by a road that twists and turns in a scenic drive.

Taking off for Munich, we had a dangerous and difficult experience we might have avoided if our pilot had been able to get us started when he thought it safe. We were caught in a storm, hailstones broke the "bubble" above the cockpit and cracked the windshield. Lightning flamed and crackled round us, ice formed on the wings. The noise was terrific. We dropped 2000 feet twice, and we only had 1400 feet clearance of the mountain! Fortunately our lowest and its highest didn't meet. As the plane staggered and we were thrown from our seats, nobody said anything. We sat, perfectly still, waiting for the moment when it couldn't right itself. Everybody's face was white when it was over. Barney opened the door of the cockpit and emerged, red-faced, angry. He wanted more say in when and how we flew, he told us all, since he was responsible for our safety. He was right, but we weren't the people to tell it to, we weren't the P.R.O. who decided we should stay late to tour his part of the theater, though the afternoon weather report showed a risk. We were performing seals to him and he was determined to make our act last as long as possible. He was staying on the ground, we would get through all right, he supposed, if he cared at all. Barney was furious.

We landed on a grass airstrip in Munich. As soon as we stepped out we learned that a few hours before a bomb had exploded, killing three German civilians. It was set off by someone walking over it. We might have landed near it or taxied over it—it was on the edge of the runway. One man said he had taxied near there often. Perhaps our being late was the lesser of two dangers.

Munich was dead, eighty-five per cent destroyed our figures said, a conservative estimate. The only building that seemed intact was the hotel we were billeted in. The ruin was complete. Munich was razed physically, but mentally? We drove about it, watching its people stir among the rubble. We visited the beer hall where Nazism began. A group of old men sat in the courtyard drinking beer. Chairs and tables were scattered round. Four men were playing cards resolutely, drearily in a corner.

Opposite the second beer hall, where Hitler escaped the well-intended bomb, an old woman leaned from her window, staring into space. Her ravaged face had lost all human expression, she looked, I think she was, insane. She must, from this same window, often have seen the triumphant processions of the party gods, now she looked on ruins, through a window without glass. She was there when we arrived, staring at the beer hall. She was still there when we came out, an hour later, in the same position. Hallett Abend and I walked past to glance at her more closely. She neither saw nor heard, lost in a hell of her own, in the hell that Hitler made for old women everywhere, a special hell of no future and no past that one dare dwell on without insanity.

Inside the beer hall, where the party met with Nazi pomposity, furniture and papers were scattered everywhere, records of Nazi party members, careful files of foreigners with marks against them for not being Nazi-minded, and all the humorless bureaucratic paper work of bullies. It was there, in the dirt and grime of the ruined city, where it properly belonged, taken from the files and trampled on. But the dirt and grime of the Nazi mind? I looked at the face of the old woman opposite. Did she stare, haggard, because the Nazis were defeated, or because the Nazis had existed, or because they might not rise again? Did she connect the two states of the beer hall, cause and effect, or was she, like the Germans whom we interviewed, perfectly indifferent to, unconscious of, any German guilt?

"When will you Americans rebuild Germany?" one civilian asked me on the street.

"Look what you have done to our city!"

I reminded him in my halting German and then in slow English that Germany had reaped an eagerly sown harvest.

"The people of Munich," I said once, to one very indignant civilian, commenting on the ruined city, "danced in the streets when this was done to Rotterdam, London, Coventry."

"Oh, but that was different."

"How different?"

"Well . . . not Germany."

When we entered the hotel we heard *Lilli Marlene*. Four ex-Wehrmacht men were sitting by the door of the dining room, with a saucer for pennies in front of them, singing and playing for the Americans at dinner. They didn't need to beg. There were rations for all who would work, and plenty of work clearing away the rubble of their streets. They preferred to beg, from us. They played the *Horst Wessel* song slowly and sadly, but they sang . . . for the Americans in uniform, all through our meal.

Can we imagine, ten weeks after the Japanese had won, a group of

American G.I.s or officers playing "The Star-Spangled Banner," and "Praise the Lord and Pass the Ammunition" for the Japanese while they ate? Under no compulsion, for a saucerful of cents!

The women on the streets had nylon stockings, their clothes were good, made of well-cut material, they all had hats, raincoats, good umbrellas, very good leather shoes. The men's clothes were of the same high quality, better than any we had so far seen in Europe. We saw many sports sweaters stolen from Norway. All the things we saw the people wearing were the loot of Europe, which they still enjoyed. The Italians had no such wardrobe. They had more intact buildings, but were not receivers of stolen goods, like their allies.

Rain began to fall. The general gloomy atmosphere of the ruins was accentuated by the water dripping through the shells of walls. The voices of the people were faint and tired, their faces for the most part grim. Some of the younger children laughed in the streets—we were told schools would be opening in the fall—the plump maids in the hotel giggled in the corridors. I saw two soldiers with their arms round German girls, but was spared the sight of more than two. Our Black troops passed in trucks. The Germans seemed impressed with them.

At night one or two windows showed light in otherwise ruined buildings. Whole families were living in these rooms. Now and then, as we watched, a wall collapsed, mushrooming stale dust. Ghost town, ghost people, or perhaps banshees.

It seemed that it was nearly always a Sunday when the worst tests came. On Sunday we visited Dachau. It has been described many times, in many ways, but however often written, however often read, remains indescribable, beyond and beneath even our imagined experience of horror.

To begin with the village of Dachau frightens by its normalcy. It is so pleasant and so permanent. The guards' houses are good, solid, middle-class buildings, with two-car garages and modern kitchens and bathrooms. They are built for solid family life on a middle-bracket salary. There are good-looking shops and well-kept schools for little Gretchen and Hans to attend, while father goes to his "work" less than a hundred yards away in the death factory.

Those solid, comfortable houses must have had one inconvenience—the smell. It was two and a half months since the Allies, chiefly the Americans, opened Dachau's gates, did what they could to clear it up and doused it with disinfectant. It still smelled of death. In the height of its turnover, on a hot summer day, it must have been disagreeable to Frau Nazi, little Gretchen and Hans. Papa, of course, would not notice it. His nose was used to smells, his eyes to sights, his hands to dealing death, his mind to torture, to obscenity, to a German concentration and extermination camp. Patting Hans on the head and pinching Gretchen's cheek, he would go over the way to "work" on other people's children.

He worked methodically, as our Hungarian guide was able to point out. This guide was one of the inmates rescued when Dachau fell. He was twenty-one, weighed seventy-eight pounds, had recovered without any help from typhus and pneumonia, had seen his family liquidated for belonging to the Hungarian peace party. He showed us around.

We saw first the dog cages where about 150 dogs were kept. They were fed on dead bodies. It was also good sport sometimes to feed them on living prisoners. A few yards away there was the ditch over which saboteurs were beheaded. A man was a saboteur if he paused for a moment in his work. When beheading grew monotonous or too much hard work, there was a place for five men to kneel while they were machine-gunned in the back, and there was a specially robust spruce tree for hangings. Its sturdiest branch was scored deeply by the marks of the rope.

The most usual method of the production line leading to the crematorium was the gas chamber. We inspected three. One took care of fifteen people at a time, suspended by their hands from an iron bar below the ceiling. On the door of this room a neat German notice showed the correct timing to avoid undue waste of gas: *Gasheit zu ... uhr, Auf ... uhr.* There was a place for the guards to watch. The door by which the condemned entered was plainly marked "Gas." So they knew where they were going if they hadn't been certain before.

Another gas chamber, larger, built to deal with one hundred people at a time, was arranged differently. Here there was no sign to tell the condemned their time had come, nor were they suspended from the ceiling. They were induced to group themselves conveniently and voluntarily, because they were given towels and told to take a shower. The thought of a shower, of water, of soap and towels, to verminous, fevered men, exhausted, anguished women, and lost, suffering children, must have seemed an immediate prospect of relief. They looked no further. They had been told that they were to stay in the camp for three weeks. This was the second or third day ... perhaps ... perhaps ... if it began with a chance to recover cleanliness, it would go on better ... a little better ... thus they crowded hopefully beneath the shower sprinklers in the ceiling. They did not have the time to examine these, to see that they were fakes. When all were in and grouped, the doors shut, the gas came through the walls, they died, under the eyes of peering Hans. About 160,000 people were killed in this room. Too many were gassed at one time for the crematorium to handle, so the surplus was dumped, two to a coffin, in long boxes. There were a pile of these against a wall.

It was a relief to reach the crematorium, to understand that once the production line was here, it was beyond the possibility of suffering. But the guide, speaking earnestly and softly, took this last hope away. Many people, he said, were cremated here alive.

The stretcher to shove the bodies into the furnace creaked as it was used. In a conspicuous place on the wall a typical German poster, as frightening as the permanence of the guards' houses, said: "Cleanliness is a national duty. Do not forget to wash your hands."

The cellar was filled with numbered pots or urns into which, up to 1942, ashes were dumped indiscriminately and sold to the victims' families for 1000 to 2000 marks. After 1942 this was discontinued in favor of selling the ashes more profitably in bulk, as human fertilizer. There were barrels full, addressed, waiting to be shipped to purchasers. Lying on one of the barrels was a bottle of Vermouth and there were beer bottles on shelves for the refreshment of the "packers" when they got tired of their dusty work.

Upstairs again we entered the mysterious room in which 150 bodies were found. There was blood on the walls and marks of bloody feet on the ceiling.

The people of Dachau and Munich who protested their ignorance of conditions in the extermination camps must have known what it was all about. We know that they spoke to prisoners. We know that displaced persons were threatened with Dachau if they displeased their overseers. If a slave broke down in the factory, or slowed up through ill health, he was told that a visit to Dachau would permanently cure his disability. *Also they bought the fertilizer.* There were those barrels with the damning labels. German farmers manured their fields with pulverized human bones. Germans grew fat on vegetables grown from murdered men, women and children, millions of them, produced in death factories like Dachau. The land was permeated with the ashes of victims, inextricably part of Germany forever, part of the German race who fed on them. No wonder the place gave out an atmosphere of death and of decay, a terrible spiritual stench like a pall over the land.

One wondered, would they shrink in time from the food content of their fields? One wondered, if to kiss a non-Aryan was contaminating, would not eating her be injudicious too? The countryside looked rich, the harvest promising, as we drove back to the hotel.

I was glad to leave Germany. I had not been able to eat or sleep well there, for nausea and a black, bottomless depression. I certainly would never want to go there again.

Part Five

I came back to all the problems, complications, frustrations and confusions I had left to be wafted around the world, determined to simplify life and make the rest of the way straight. I had seen what nations and races were doing to the planet, and I was filled with a sudden ardor to "co-operate with the Supreme Will in Evolution," as often before I had been set to resist It.

It was a new splashdown, as if I returned from a tour of the planes between reincarnations, and now was "restored to my personal comfort" or discomfort, to digest what I had learned.

Meanwhile nothing around me seemed to have changed, except in orientation, the needle of the compass of the heart.

I came back to the lover I call "Clive" in *Flight*. The story of the song we failed to sing together is told there, and my struggle to get free, with most of me loath to be freed, hugging the silken web.

As Millay says: " 'Tis not love's going hurts my days / But that it went in little ways," clumsy small stinging deaths.

After what I had seen at Dachau and elsewhere, I was craving innocence. But innocence is reached, if at all, at the end of life, not at the beginning, with the ignorance of childhood, nor in the middle, with its flaming autumn gold. Innocence arrives with the snow, smoothing, covering the landscape, the snow falling over the hollow bamboo.

Looking back I can see how funny my struggle must have seemed to others, to anyone bothering to watch.

It wasn't funny to me. I pained the few people who were fond of me, baffled and enraged others, alienated business partners and acquaintances who might have developed into friends, and lost whatever public image I had. Not all at once, of course. It took a number of years.

One person found my strange contradictory performance natural, "part of the condition of conversion," Father Grieg Taber, Rector of Saint Mary the Virgin, in New York, where I worshipped sporadically. Very High Church, like Heathfield, the ritual at Saint Mary's was superb (there was a rumor that acolytes from Saint Patrick's Cathedral came there surreptitiously to see how it should *really* be done, but this was probably an Anglo-Catholic joke) and the music rivaled All Saints in London, surely the best church music in the world.

Father Taber, a legend in High Church circles, was an extraordinary man, a scholar with a sense of humor; a confessor, unique in his gentle discernment and stern diagnosis of sick souls; a friend with whom there never need be concealment; a man who in his own attainment of simplicity was almost flamboyantly humble. He became my confessor in 1949 and, even after I left the church again later, remained my friend, writing me wise letters about some poems in *The Small Hour* which he liked, and *Flight,* in which he is the Father Kenelm. Loving music more than other earthly things, he died in a way that must have pleased him, alone in his box at a performance of a favorite opera. Some of his letters are scattered through my diaries and some are in the E.S.M.E. Collection in the Mugar Memorial in Boston, but I am a very minor figure in the rich tapestry of his influence on those who traveled his way, however short a time.

That he watched my gyrations with comprehension, tact and humor made me very grateful to him. When much of *Flight* began to take shape in terms of Christian ritual I found him ready to help. Later we were both mildly surprised that Orville Prescott, panning *Flight* in the New York *Times* complained that it embarrassed him "to tiptoe round some private religion" invented by the author. I did not invent Anglo-Catholicism, nor tamper with its stern and stately liturgy. If I had misquoted a word Father Taber would have set it right, probably from the pulpit, with an incisive quip, like the memorable time he announced, "We cannot serve God and Manning," when Bishop Manning, himself Low Church, wanted fewer candles and less incense at Saint Mary's.

I came back—I had never been away from her—to Terry.

Terry was to go for an extra year to Walnut Hill, before she went to Briarcliff. She had graduated well from Edgehill and could have gone straight to any college, academically speaking, but it was quite a transition from a Canadian boarding school to the more sophisticated U.S. campus, and she was very young. Another senior year in an American school might help her to make the adjustment. It was something she must handle for herself, and, I hoped, from a better start than I had, so far as being loved and wanted went.

Friday Sept. 14th 1945. There's a wistful quality about my thoughts tonight. Terry's birthday. I gave her, besides the bicycle, a string of beads, a brush and comb set, a dog, or is it a lamb? But what made the day for her was the unexpected appearance of F. who drove all the way from Saint John to see her and ask could it be as it was? No, it couldn't. Then, far more important to T., came the telegram, letter and gold identification bracelet from E. (I must say I like E. best, but there will be dozens more. She is only sixteen. Still, it must have been quite a summer in Prince Edward Island for her.) They are so lovely and so innocent in the passionate things they write and say to each other. It is poignant to realize that, and to remember, as Robert Bridges, musing over his son, says: "feet unbruised, in the ways of dark desire," and that he himself was once lovely, clean and young, and what life did to change him. "I forgive, but tell the measure/ of their crime in you, my treasure." I hope for Terry what I said in one dedication: *cuore in fronte e strada dritte*, an open heart and a straight road, and that I may not fail her. Thus far I have done some things well and some things ill, but she appears unhurt.

Before I went back to Nova Scotia to put Fundy Tide on the market, I saw and signed up for our next home, at Quaker Hill, near Pawling, New York. It was a small white farmhouse built by Quakers in the late eighteenth century. It had five acres, two brooks, and an old mill dam which could be turned into a swimming pool. Lowell Thomas, from whom I bought it, was remodeling it to make a good year-round home, and that was what I thought we needed, a year-round home, an hour from New York, with Terry's future school, Briarcliff, halfway to the city. There were friends for us both at Quaker Hill, a lake for boating and swimming, a country-club "barn" for her to dance in. What could be better? Or less simple!

I took Ann and Roger to see the house on a day when it looked lovely in the sun. They were enthusiastic, and they both told me it was perfect for me, and to go ahead. "Don't worry about finances," Ann said.

Ann was always a great promoter, even more optimistic than I was, with multiple irons in fires and telephone calls about sales in the bag, often premature. She had a heartening way of calling me early in the morning or late at night with "I've got it!" . . . a whole new story line . . . another direction . . . a terrific slant . . . "all you have to do is an outline and a few chapters. . . ."

I co-operated with some of her suggestions, writing thousands of extra words for outlines and sample chapters, and going to see a number of "key people," always sure that whatever project she launched me on would be "It." But during those crucial years it never was. I was wrong to waste the hours that I did, even though I knew I would not pay too much attention to the outline when a contract was signed. I have never worked from an outline yet. The river flows, you live the journeying experience, with a general idea of where the sea must be, but nothing static, arbitrarily decided on ahead of time. Books tied down to outlines creak.

I owe Ann a great deal, including proposing me for the 1945 tour, and before that being a sponsoring witness for my citizenship, and before that giving me a job. When in 1948 I grew desperate in the struggle to get financially straight and, wooed by another publisher who promised what I needed, I felt that I must leave Harper's because they would not or could not help me toward solvency, I decided, for her sake, not to involve Ann in the fight. I left her agency before I began the discussions, so that she would not be held responsible for what I did. This was stupid reasoning. I hurt everyone all round, myself most.

Later we patched things up somewhat. She placed *Flight* for me, I dedicated *I Saw My Mortal Sight* to her and Roger, but since I never talked it out with her, never explained why I left, it was a lost relationship. She thought me ungrateful. I thought her unsound about my predicament.

I have the Indian ingrained instinct, when things go wrong, to walk away alone, in silence, and "go behind the blanket," or, as an exasperated man who I thought had let me down badly once, complained: "She gets into one of those damn plastic bubbles and then you can't reach her any more." I like the blanket simile better, but yes I did. I do. There is the silence of the not-to-be-explained. If a thing must be explained it is already out of shape, wire broken, fuse blown. In an instant, or after long attrition, ties fray, cut, and that is that. I have been told that I expect too much from friends, overtrust them in the beginning, close my eyes in the middle, and then, forced to look at some betrayal . . . walk away.

With Ann it was no question of betrayal. It was reaction against weakness in myself. I felt, rightly or wrongly—it turned out to be wrongly—that I must leave Harper's in order to get solvent, and that she would oppose it; that I would be putty in her hands as I always was, and also, naively, that it was not fair to involve her . . . which was absurd. Ann needed no protection from anyone, certainly not from a writer. As my agent, however "ex" I tried to make it, she was involved. As an agent, if it came to a choice between a writer and a major publisher, with whom she placed many books, she must side with her bread and butter. The whole thing turned round bread and butter, hers and mine. No one foresaw the effect on fiction of the outbreak of peace, the development of television, the general public reaction against reading for recreation. I didn't know that as a nonpornographic novelist I would soon be an endangered species. I didn't know that I was entering five years of financial debacle that would wipe me out completely. That was hard to foresee when I had just begun selling stories to *The New Yorker,* when I had two contracts for books, and when constant references were being made in the press to the filming of *Quietly My Captain Waits,* with Bette Davis and Errol Flynn, Bette Davis and Paul Henreid, Bette Davis and you-name-him.

There were many references to the movie through the next three years before it was finally dropped; there were many more projects "in the bag" with prospects of "immediate dough," which did not come through. In fact, nothing that I counted on, that I really had a right to count on, from past performance and present hard work, came through.

Nothing infuriates people more than insolvency coupled with apparent extravagance, especially in the United States, where a right—respectful—attitude toward money and those who have it is the obvious, usually the only, touchstone for judging and pigeonholing people. Since it never occurred to me to explain what I was doing, as I threshed in and out of my contortions toward simplicity, people drew conclusions, most of them untrue.

I had come from a background where "the gentry" lived on overdrafts as a matter of course, a proof of status. Overdrafts indicated that you came from

234

the "top drawer," where money was not mentioned, was kept in its place. Money could not put you in that drawer to begin with. Birth and breeding mattered, who you were born, and, for a woman, sometimes, whom you married. When I tried to educate banks to this philosophy, I got nowhere. Later, most of them went beyond my teaching. They burst into commercials proclaiming "Always borrow money heedlessly from anyone who has the dust," or some such theme song, and I even had them ask me, in the early fifties, if I wouldn't like to borrow more. At the time I needed it, however, they had not started wall-to-wall carpeting and tunes to lull the customers into taking out loans at a high rate of interest.

All this on the surface. The important thing was what it always is. I had forgotten the teaching of *Le Droit Humain*, that whenever we take, however lamely, a tentative step forward, we are required to be properly prepared. Where first? "In my heart." Where next? "In a convenient room adjoining the Lodge." If we would accustom ourselves to considering the earth as a convenient antechamber to a larger, more important room in the universe, we might pass through it better. This, I discovered later, was also, in different terminology, the Indian teaching.

How prepared? We must be deprived of all metals and valuables, that is, of reliance upon money and power. The candidate who comes properly prepared comes unarmed and stripped of material possessions, unable to depend on them, or even on his own abilities and judgment, since he is in the dark. We must renounce the misuse of material goods, return to simplicity (harmlessness, nonviolence) and master our passions, including pride of possession of power. The importance, the necessity, of this freedom from the power of metals and all that they represent is stressed again at a central part of the ceremony, when the initiate is called upon to demonstrate his condition of freedom, and if he cannot, the initiation is repeated, as life repeats our initiations, over and over until we can pass.

I knew this theoretically. I taught it to many candidates entering *Le Droit Humain*, but I missed the point that now, not figuratively, not in theory, *actually* I was being prepared to take a step forward, a step that I had asked to take. Ever since the panoramic journey I had clamored to simplify my life. Several times on the journey I had turned upward, offering to cooperate with the Supreme Will in Evolution. I had recognized the first threat, to the heart, I had given up "Clives," yet I clung with all my force to "metals and valuables." I bought Two Brooks, I struggled to earn money to keep it, my diaries are full of wails of why oh why does this sale or that sale not go through? Why oh why isn't *Quietly* made into a movie? Why oh why does *The New Yorker* take so few stories? Why? Why? Why? Very simply why, I had to be taught that "of myself I can do nothing," to give up threshing about. I had to learn the interdependence of created things, and my place on the Medicine Wheel . . . a child's place, a trusting place, a humble place, a would-be candidate's place.

As happens on the Journey, too, I did not recognize the process until it was over. I was living too fully on "this" plane, the most illusory. . . . "But if it has to be an illusion," a friend complained to me once, "can't it be a pleasant one?"

Two Brooks turned out to be haunted, not gruesomely, not with horror or hatred and resentment of new owners, not with any deep grief—it was an anxious, solicitous haunting. Too solicitous. The first time that I noticed anything was when my dog, a wire-haired terrier named Cleo, who never liked to be more than a few inches from my feet, whimpered when I went into the living room, and stayed in the doorway, anxiously watching something in the room.

"Don't be silly," I said. "Come here."

But she wouldn't. She obviously wanted to join me, was unhappy about it, but she wouldn't. As long as we lived in the house Cleo would never go into the living room. She waited for me at the foot of the stairs. If I stayed too late in the evening she came to the door, clicking her toenails in reproof, wagging and ingratiating herself, but standing there, until I went to bed. It was as though someone with more authority than I told her, "No dogs in here!"

The living room was light and bright and cozy, everyone who came there loved it, but there was someone in it, someone who watched over my interests a little too closely for my comfort. I was usually alone in the house with Cleo. I am not a putter-away of things, books that I am reading, for instance. I am apt to leave them open face down on the sofa or the floor. Every morning I would find the room "redded up," the book tidily closed and on the table or the top of the bookcase.

I told myself firmly that I was getting better at picking up things, and Cleo sighed. Then one night, in the fall, with the fire dying down and Cleo waiting for me on the stairs, I stood up, stretched, and said aloud, "Well, I think I'll go to bed."

Instantly the light beside my chair went out, and the light in the hall went on. When I reached the foot of the stairs, trying to move slowly and not look back, the light in the hall went out and the light at the top of the stairs went on. I climbed them rather quickly, hoping it would stay on till I reached the switch outside my bedroom door. It went out as I reached the top step, and the light in the bedroom went on.

I was lighted all the way to my bed, Cleo climbing close beside me. Once inside the room, door closed, we both waited. Nothing further happened. I kept the light on all night, and Cleo slept on my feet, rousing now and then to look out of the window. She liked to keep tabs on the garden. Once she woke me by standing on my face, to draw my attention to seven deer crossing the lawn. Cleo had a hierarchy of values. Cows she despised and rudely chivvied. Horses she escorted in respectful silence. Deer made her ecstatic.

Next morning I tested all the bulbs and all the fixtures. The living-room lights were on a separate fuse from the hallway. The lights upstairs were on another fuse. The switches were very firm ones, requiring a little force to turn them on and off. The lamp in the living room was new, and there was nothing wrong with it. It was just that I had expressed a wish, or an intention, aloud, in the living room at Two Brooks. Whenever I did this, I would find some effort was immediately made to take care of the situation.

I tested it many times. Something was there with considerable physical power, but it would not be controlled, "pushed around," was the phrase that came to my mind. Once I said, "Please put a log on the fire." Nothing happened. A few minutes later I said, "Well, I think I'll put a log on the fire," and a small one fell out of the fire basket onto the hearth and rolled toward the chimney. It didn't quite make it, I had to put it in a better place, but still ... it was a little unnerving.

When my new chair came for the writing room, it wasn't the right height for typing. I wrestled with the very stiff mechanism for making it go up and down, and couldn't get it to the notch I thought would be right. It needed oiling and adjusting.

"Oh well," I said, "I'll do it in the morning."

In the morning it was done, and the chair was turned a little sideways, to make it easier for me to sit down.

Once my cleaning woman, Dill, when I had been there for a year, said, "It's strange about this room. I always have the feeling that someone is in here, like some little old woman, and she's anxious that I don't cheat on you; she keeps saying, 'Now do it thoroughly, don't sweep the dust under the rug.'"

"But we don't have rugs," I said.

"I know. I guess it's just her way of saying it."

Dill was part Cherokee. She had been a taxi driver, among other things, and she became chauffeur, cook, cleaner, and, after a while, when she accepted me, good friend. It was only when I had sold Two Brooks that she told me the old, the real name for Deuel Hollow was Devil Hollow and that everyone who lived in that lane had sudden and lasting bad luck.

"In what way, Dill?"

"Mostly money, but nothing goes right for them here. I'm glad you're getting away."

She also said that everyone who had lived there, as long as she could remember, loved the place and only left reluctantly when bankruptcy or suicide or other calamities forced them out.

My three years in Devil Hollow brought financial and professional disasters, a painful operation on both knees, and some heartache, but I too "loved the place" and except for being always one humiliating jump ahead of the sheriff, enjoyed the Quaker Hill experience. There were friends like the Daggs, "Bobby" (Ella Myers) and Noel, not long married, deeply happy, letting their happiness spill over to the world. Bobby was Advertising Director of General Foods, a big job for a woman, which she wore easily, with humor. She was Advertising Woman of the Year in 1948. We gave a party for her, at which she made us laugh, as only she could, over the Banquet for the Return of Tapioca given by General Foods. She had a delicious sense of fun, and it was always kind. Noel was as good as she. It was a second marriage for both of them, and they were perfectly matched, as sometimes, but so rarely, happens. *They* sang the same song, and it was a grand one, together.

The Daggs spoiled me and adopted Terry. They went to her graduation, they flanked me at her wedding, Noel brought her up the aisle. We laughed and frolicked together through two enchanted years. Another year and Bobby was dead, after a heroic fight with cancer. Then her friends knew what they had lost.

> Only the light from common water,
> Only the grace from simple stone.

But in 1948 our dance was not a Cry-Dance, and we were not dispersed.

There was the French painter, Cécile Bellé, and her husband, Ralph Carson. Cécile's galleries were in Fifty-seventh Street, she was in her landscape period, painting black-and-white cows in strange places. I remember one on a hilltop so covered with mist that it looked as though cows were browsing in the sky. Her cows were always standing knee deep in underbrush. She said it was because she couldn't draw feet, but I think it was her way of laughing at the environment. Her accent and some of her reactions made me homesick for France sometimes, but never for the hardships of my life there. I was too well pleased with Quaker Hill.

I liked the friends I made, I liked having a place with charm to invite them to, I liked it being near enough to New York for people to whirl in and out and stay for weekends, I liked the lake, especially. If I went there early in the morning, or late at night by moonlight, I often had it all to myself, or, if I had guests and felt social, there were hours when "the Hill" gathered in elegant swimsuits, as they might at a Beach Club.

I remember once when I was swimming there alone, I had a strange moment. A car drove up with a spurt, and a burly man got out, in swimming trunks, with a revolver. He stood for a moment sternly staring at me, and I wondered whether I would be used for target practice, or mistaken for a marine monster. It reminded me of a time when I was swimming off the coast of Spain, and there were shouts and wavings from a group of gaily-dressed people on the shore. I thought, "How nice of them to want me to enjoy my swim," and waved gaily back. Boom! Half the hillside fell into the water round me. They were blasting.

I was too far away to say a bright hello to this sudden menace and too startled to do anything but float and watch him. Suddenly he tucked the revolver into his holster—I had never seen trunks with holsters—opened the door of the car, and two boys tumbled out and ran into the water . . . Governor Dewey's sons, coming for the morning swim, with their special Secret Service guard.

Later we met the Deweys. Terry went swimming with them, and I remember once square dancing at "the Barn" with Governor Dewey as my partner. We were in a set getting some instruction, and he led off with the wrong foot. "Fine," I thought, "that will baffle the Russians." It was when he was running for President, and Quaker Hill was to be the next summer White House. I liked him, but I thought he was campaigning in too languid a way, almost as though he were saying, "when this tiresome formality is over, *then* . . ." I did not think that he would win, but everyone about us did. Houses were bought and sold, I remember one near mine, that had been an inn, and was now going to house the secretaries and the typists. On the fateful night I saw the bunting go up all over town with "Welcome home, President Dewey!" At 2 A.M. a little dispirited group went out to tear it down.

I liked what was happening to Terry, too. She was working in the Starlight Theater, one of the best summer-stock companies, doing well and enjoying it. She was also having fun with the young crowd on the Hill, going out with Joe, and Tom and Jack, and Jean-Philippe, and Sonny Thomas, and the Dick she eventually married.

Most of all I liked the country living at Two Brooks, the animals, deer, raccoon, beaver and egrets along the road, the snow in winter, and the silence.

I did good work there, many short stories for *The New Yorker,* most of the collection for *Every Month Was May,* and some for *The North Star Is Nearer.* I finished the book on Mother Seton, which had hung round my neck like an incubus. I gathered material for *Give Me Your Golden Hand,* which had a section on the Quakers in New York.

I went often to New York, in and out the same day. Traffic was not as it is now. I enjoyed the drive, found the city beautiful, exciting, my city. I went to concerts, necessary as breathing, to shows, to meetings of the Poetry Society, P.E.N. and the Pen and Brush Club, of which I was now the President. I liked the club for the people who used it, the friends I made, the intelligent men and women who spoke there at my invitation. My diaries are full of references to evenings at the club.

Introduced Pearl Buck, who said the problem for the writer was how to resist pressure to write what amounts to propaganda and yet make a living . . . how to keep one's integrity, in other words, and not starve. After she left I spoke a few words. I had a very warm reception from everyone.

My talk tonight went fairly well. I'm very stimulated by this whole experience of being in New York. I like the sculpture at the Pen and Brush.

A lovely late afternoon and evening at the club. Margaret Wycherly spoke like the personage she is, and everyone enjoyed it. She spoke entrancingly. She is witty and modest and brilliant and a great actress. Even though I find it a strain to introduce people, I enjoyed the whole thing.

On March 3rd 1949 *The Villager* reported: "This program followed a week of special significance at the Club, in which Dorothy Canfield Fisher spoke after a dinner given for her, and shared honors with Nancy Ross, lecturer and author of *The Left Hand Is The Dreamer*. Evelyn Eaton presided and established the mood for a fascinating discussion of the unprecedented responsibilities of the writer and creative artist in our present time, when scientific discoveries have driven far ahead of achievements in mind and spirit."

Accolade from D.C.F. [Dorothy Canfield Fisher was the Honorary President of the Pen & Brush when I was President.] I had lunch with Edith Busby [a good friend who worked in the New York Public Library] and after that to the club for reception of new poets, home to change and then quick drink with Nancy and Stanley [Stanley Young, Nancy Ross's husband, and also my editor at Farrar Straus & Young]. After that dinner, at which I presided, and after *that* Dorothy Canfield Fisher's arrival, her unexpected speaking about my book [*The North Star Is Nearer*, which was being considered for the Book of the Month, of which she was a judge]. She said nice things about the good hands in which she found the club . . . all wonderful and unexpected. Nancy's speech, which was very good, Stanley's speech, and finally D.C.F. saying suddenly to me "Let's make this real!" and kissing me on both cheeks. I was very pleased. Later I wrote her:

"Mon Général. I am as proud as any légionnaire who finds himself unexpectedly embraced upon the field of battle (knowing his deficiency) by the Field Marshal whom he loves and venerates. You said 'Let's make this real'— but you made all things real from the moment you appeared. Thank you." To which she replied:

"Well, my dear Evelyn, how you did turn into gold that contact that anybody would have thought beforehand might be so casual.

"Yes, yes, I had your note, *wonderful* to see a warm heart thus letting itself go in expressiveness! I did get your official note on Pen-and-Brush paper— many thanks. And now came your enchanting *Every Month Was May*. But what a sacrifice, to send your own copy of a book out of print! Greater love hath no author. . . . I feel guilty to keep it. But nothing would induce me to give it up. I know (and love) many of the sketches—particularly love Mère Mercredi and the ventouses, having had those used on my family many times in France . . . with just such results.

"Thanks, thanks, chère petite amie, for so you seem to your ancient, admiring, Dorothy Canfield Fisher."

I used to like to give *Every Month Was May* to people, especially if they were sick. I remember that Elizabeth Lawrence sent it once to Genevieve Taggard, who wrote to her:

> You sent me a book when I was in hospital that I read, daughter read, husband read, over which I cried and doctors gave opinions. It was utterly wonderful—the kind of book that deserves the highest and loudest and tuneful praise. And I've forgot the name and the book is gone. It was short stories and about France. Whoever the author I would feel fervent reverence. Each story a gem. But we chose different ones. I had very bad reaction to last story because it foretold the war: a night in a second-class carriage talking to two French boys, very confident of the future. Surgeon's verdict: 'Don't read any *good* books until you are stronger. Read trash!' "

This is the sort of message that makes the writing-struggle worthwhile. But how few and far between!

Went to an excellent sculptors' dinner at the Pen and Brush which made me forget my temporary troubles and perplexities for an hour or so, and probably that is what the club does for others. I thought most of those successful faces hard. "Fails the dream the dreamer, and the lute the lutanist" is often with me as I wonder whether I am written out, and whether now that all else has been taken from me, the power of working is to be taken too?

Main event today, Pauline Frederick talking at the Club about U.N. and other things. She did it very well. Elsie McCormick was there, and we all got together again, to reminisce over the tour.

One of the highest points at the club was the night that Eleanor Roosevelt spoke at the dinner given for her. I had prepared beforehand, getting extra police protection, finding a member of the club who was an old friend of hers, and arranging for them to sit together. . . . Halfway through dinner Mrs. Roosevelt turned to me and said, "Do you know that for the next three months I do not have a single evening at home? You cannot imagine how pleasant this is for me, to dine here beside an old friend!" I said that I was glad we could do something to make some part of the effort fun for her. The food was excellent, and we had about four hundred people, which bothered me, since the club was only certified as safe for three hundred. My introduction was very short. "If the world came to its senses and the united nations *were* united, we should refer to our distinguished speaker by the name given to her in many countries . . . First Lady of the World, Eleanor Roosevelt!" There were indrawn breaths from the Republicans with which the place was stuffed that night, but Mrs. Roosevelt looked very pleased. Her own speech was magnificent, warm and amusing, about the difficulties of getting the Human Rights document through U.N. The Committee had taken the American statement as a good jumping-off place, but the moment "All men are created equal" was read there were objections from the delegates. Mrs. Roosevelt had expected routine obstruction from the Russians over some of the clauses later on, but she was taken by surprise when her good friend Madame Pandit rose to protest the opening statement.

"If," Madame Pandit said, "we go back to India with the statement 'all *men* are created equal' the women of India will suffer a serious setback in their struggle for equality."

The sentence was changed to "all human beings are created equal," whereupon the Russian delegate rose frowning.

"The U.S.S.R. rejects the statement."

Pressed to elaborate, he explained, "The U.S.S.R. cannot accept the word 'created.' It supposes a creator. The enlightened Russian peoples do not accept belief in a creator."

So it was changed to read "All human beings are born equal."

The rest of the long document ran into the same sort of expected and unexpected objections and snags, down to the last period.

At the beginning and the end of her speech she said nice things about me as the President of her club—she was an honorary member—and it was *my* turn to look pleased. I had to walk home, in my long formal dress, through the dark, depressing streets between West Tenth and Peter Cooper, because I had no money, not even for a crosstown bus.

At that time I was selling my books and my spoons one by one—getting more for them that way—in order to eat, and unless people gave me a lift I had to walk everywhere.

I supported the U.N. from the start, which for me began when my brother-in-law, John Dashwood, came out to set up the British delegation in 1946, and we had a brief reunion. Later I went often to Lake Success. The most dramatic meeting I remember there was on March 22, 1948, when the Czechoslovakian Papanek pleaded the fate of his country and gave the details of the death of Jan Masaryk, murdered by the Russians, whether or not he flung himself out of the window. I listened all afternoon to that strange, grim drama. First Chile presented Papanek's letter appealing to the U.N., then Argentina and Canada proposed that he be asked to speak. The vote was nine to two. When he came forward, in the rumpled clothes he stood up in, after his flight from his country, he had to sit next to Gromyko. He made a moving and enlightening speech. Cadogan spoke next. Then the Ukrainian stooge who had already called Papanek a traitor spoke, a lot of crude propaganda, in violent and offensive language. A Czechoslovakian sitting next to me retched. It was no answer to Papanek's speech, but then what answer could there be? I remembered Jan Masaryk in London. A brave and civilized man. Papanek said quietly, "I have been called a traitor twice, once by the occupying Nazi forces, in my country, and now by a member of a *foreign* nation." He went on to describe Masaryk's last days and to accuse the Russians of murdering him. He was a brave man. His wife and family were in the Russians' hands, and, judging by Gromyko's stony face and the muscle twitching in his cheek, it was a miracle that Papanek managed to get to the U.N. alive and coherent.

I was also present, in October 1949, at the laying of the cornerstone at the permanent site by the East River.

It was a moving, hopeful, great thing. I was interested and contented to be there witnessing the beginning of the hope of the world. It was cloudy at first, gray, depressing, then the sun came out just as the stone was being unveiled, and gleamed on the one white towering wall.

In December I attended another U.N. affair.

An absolutely thrilling, soul-stirring experience, and my soul did stir . . . the U.N. celebration of the first anniversary of the Declaration of Human Rights. Margaret [Grant] took me to it. Terry and I went first to the Boston Philharmonic, and that was interesting and enchanting. I marveled that Leonard Bernstein could conduct—and *how* he conducted!—again at six, with such spirit. The program was perfectly chosen. Laurence Olivier speaking the Preamble, Copland's music to it—the Russian box was empty until after the U.N. march, written by Shostakovich, was over, and even then remained empty except for underlings. But all the rest were there. Mrs. Roosevelt spoke magnificently and so did Romulo. I was lifted into enthusiasm. It was just the right length too, timeless length, and the Beethoven Freude to end with. Even to belong to the race capable of rising to such heights of aspiration, though it has not achieved them—yet—makes me feel better.

There were others whom I enjoyed introducing to the Pen and Brush.

Raymond Massey, engaging and fun. He remembered my father in the old Ottawa and Kingston days, and placed me at once. Michele Dean, who wrote *The Four Foundation Stones of Peace*. Hélène Barland from the Resistance, with slides. She spoke movingly and it was significant to look at her and realize that she returned the Mona Lisa to the Louvre, rode on the truck that brought the picture back, also the Winged Victory, lucky young thing. Shirley Jackson, who said she was a practicing witch. Maurice Evans on the theater, Margaret Widdemer, whom I asked to direct a writers' workshop at the club, which turned into a most successful project. Margaret Cousins, seeing both sides of the author-editor syndrome. And many others, writers and non-writers.

The experience was good for me. It was at the Pen and Brush that I first learned to introduce a speaker, first made any kind of public speech, had my first experience of chairing a board meeting, of acting as a landlord, of exercising the power of decision, of planning for a group of people, and of meeting other women in the arts.

There were other things I liked about the club. The place itself, reminiscent of homes I had lived in, Dan and Mary, the club personnel, who made me remember many servants in the "old country" whom I had known and loved and could never talk to, as here I could with these over a strong cup of tea in their quarters, when I was tired from a board meeting or discouraged by what Mary called "the wicked world, the ways of them!" We talked of the old country together, the early days when they were first in service, in England, especially one house where I had been a guest.

There were fifty-two bedrooms in this house, but only one bathroom. Guests washed in their bedrooms. Two or three times a day maids appeared with large hot-water cans and emptied the slop pails. All these bedroom fittings were handsome matched sets, some of them porcelain, with flowered designs, unlike the plain ones in our bedrooms and dormitories at Heathfield, but the usage was the same. You washed in your bedroom in a basin and a hip bath which the maids emptied. You only took a bath when the bathroom was free, which happened rarely, and never at appropriate times. Gentlemen back from hunting had the first claim on it, as they had the uncontested right to warm their backsides at the fire in the chill of the evening. English country houses were cold and uncomfortable as the natural order of things, decreed, one gathered, by the Lord, who was, of course, an English gentleman.

Later, when I went back to England for the first time after the war, a wing in the house of a friend of mine in Yorkshire was being rebuilt after it had been destroyed by bombing, and I said cheerfully, "Now you will be able to put in central heating," having some hazy idea that what must have been stopping them before was the difficulty of breaking through massive stone walls.

She looked at me with English disapproval.

"Oh no, my dear," she said quietly, "I don't think we'll ever have to do that."

Not even if there were worse wars, her tone implied.

"Why not?"

"Well . . . in houses like this . . . even if one could stand the stuffiness . . . it would be dangerous. It might make the dampness come out of the walls."

I couldn't believe that she wasn't joking, but she was serious, and the subject was firmly closed.

That was where the dampness belonged. That was where it certainly was, in England, and given a chance to rebuild, you rebuilt it in the walls. Dan and Mary and I, liking our chosen country, reveled in its taken-for-granted comfort and convenience, as well as the broader companionship. In those days, and even now, when it has become the general insidious custom to blame the United States for all the ills and evils in the world, I still don't understand how anyone lucky enough to be born here, or to become a citizen, can want to give help and comfort to the enemy, any enemy, within or without its borders, by running down everything about our land, and going about with gloomy guilt-ridden apathy, instead of rolling up the sleeves, if one is old-fashioned enough to wear any, and tackling the nearest clean-up job. True, the land does not belong to those who have it now. It belongs to those who know that land cannot belong to anyone, the redskinned peoples. It is still the best land in the world, and those who don't think so should be sent to sweep the snow off Chinese streets at midnight, in silence, after a long day's work. The silence, particularly, would be good for them.

Dan and Mary were stalwart stand-bys for every event at the club. Dan was major-domo at the reception given there for Terry's wedding. As *The Villager* wrote it up:

GALA RECEPTION AT PEN AND BRUSH

The cheerful Pen and Brush Club, 16 East 10th Street, with its newly refurbished brownstone front, was the scene last Saturday afternoon of one of the prettiest wedding receptions held in the Village. One hundred and fifty guests attended to honor Mr. and Mrs. Richard Logan Brengle, née Teresa N. Eaton, daughter of the club's president, Evelyn Eaton.

Greens and white gladioli banked the mantel and outlined the arches of the club's spacious first-floor galleries where the reception was held, with guests overflowing out into the lovely garden. A four-piece stringed orchestra added to the festivities. Prior to the cutting of the three-tiered cakes, cablegrams of best wishes were read from the bride's grandmother, Mrs. D. I. V.

Eaton, widow of Colonel Eaton, Royal Canadian Horse Artillery [ALWAYS REMEMBER, DEAR, NO MATTER WHAT, YOU ARE BRITISH] and from the bride's aunt and uncle, Sir John and Lady Dashwood, West Wycombe Park, Buckinghamshire, England.

This was Terry's send-off, the "look, look well," of her launching, and though we danced, and her friends danced behind her, it was not quite like the powwow in Wyoming for the launching of the Crow Princess. Still, it was the best that I could manage, and one of my good memories of New York.

Since the word "deprived" is deliberately used of the stripping of the candidate in preparation for a step forward, it follows that one must mind the loss or feel the lack of the "valuables," the valued possessions being taken away. Perfect indifference would mean that it was not a test, that one had already passed this stage, and must face another unknown condition in another preparation. Acquiescence, joyful or resigned, with moments of stabbing nostalgia, is more usual. This I had. I minded losing Fundy Tide, I minded losing Two Brooks, I minded losing my New York apartment. I minded so much that I clung to each of them in turn, until I was dragged away, forced out:

> He shall drag me forth,
> Shrieking to the south
> And clutching to the north,

as Millay said she would face another Challenger. Worse, I went into debt to keep them, debts that it took me years to repay. Yet I had asked, importuned, offered myself to the service of the Masters, and such knocking, seeking, asking, never goes unanswered, however dense one may be about the answers at the time.

One of the ways I thought might be open to me I had been considering off and on since 1948.

In November 1948 I drove with Mary Street to the Convent of the Holy Nativity at Bay Shore to spend the weekend there. A strange metamorphosis took place. I was put in one of the Sisters' cells, since the guest ones were full up. I felt its peace, its remoteness and its rightness so strongly that I was *bouleversée*, and before I knew it, contemplating an old recurring dream of entering an order. First I would have to clear myself of debt and see Terry happily married, then there would be other things to solve and settle. But there it was, to the fore again, and this time a possibility.

The next day I walked by the sea after I had been to Mass. There was a moment of beauty, of swans on a pool. I asked Sister Anita the age limits of the order. She said forty, but an exception might be made for me. The Reverend Mother would be coming in February from the Mother House which was in Fond du Lac, Wisconsin. Then if I was interested she would "look me over." I felt a great lift and excitement in my heart "such as I have only known with the anticipation of a lover's meeting or with a *Droit Humain* degree conferred."

I came to my forty-sixth birthday more happy, calm, serene and satisfied than I had been in many years.

In the morning I got the picture Nick is giving me for Christmas, of Two Brooks, and loved it instantly. It has all the charm and romance of Two Brooks by moonlight. Mary Street came, Margaret Grant telephoned, Olga Warburton telephoned and the children gave me a dinner and many lovely presents, too lovely, too expensive, but I felt cherished. Terry came over for a moment and talked about her Dick. She gave me a photograph of herself. I had a happy day.

I might go out to Larkspur, I suppose [the headquarters of the Droit Humain, in Colorado], sometime during this period of waiting to see if I am to join the Holy Nativity Order or not. Certainly if I lived up to the Droit Humain vows and teachings and stayed in New York, fulfilling all the claims on me, I would be traveling the path, but to join a definite order and regime is more logical.

Depressed letter from X today. Nothing good comes from these personal relationships. More and more I incline to the peace and formality of the convent.

Went to lunch with Edith and to a matinée of *The Medium,* with Marie Powers, which moved me very much. Later I went to the girls' apartment and had a little time with Terry before Dick came for her, and a little time with him. I hope they are right for each other. Nothing I can do but keep hands off.

She played the piano and I sat watching the back of her head and thinking of her father, and of the long twenty years, and how they have turned out. Not too unhappily for her, so far, I think.

Anne Miller Downes was very interesting today at the club. She said that Marie Powers was on the verge of going into a convent just before she began her success this year, and Nancy Ross telephoned to say that *she* was going into a convent to do some research, in January. It turns out to be mine. We shall be gliding about under the veil together, so to speak, for a while. Strange all this urge among creative people toward convents. I heard from England that the rush to enter the Anglo-Catholic orders there, two years ago, right after the war, was so great that postulants and novices had to live in tents. It's logical. Anyone who went through the war, or even caught a glimpse of it, as I did, might be impelled that way.

Today was spent packing, assembling, sorting, and finally getting myself to the convent. I made many trips to Terry's apartment to leave various oddments and then, tired, I lay on the sofa for a quarter of an hour till the taximan came. He arrived very promptly and we drove without mishap, I remembering the way very well, considering the darkness, until I arrived just before supper. I had a very sweet affectionate welcome, and soon I had everything dragged upstairs and neatly put away. So here I am for the next three months. My cell appeals to me as much as it did before. I feel at home and I think I shall be able to work.

It rained a dismal downpour all the day. I rather like the sound of it on the tin roof. I find myself settling in here with a quiet sense of well-being. Early days yet, perhaps, but I can understand how good and happy a life this is and would be. Meanwhile it is a haven for work and *recueillement,* although strangely enough I am not doing as much meditation and reading as I did in the apartment.

I had a long talk with Sister Mary Louise, and like her more and more, but I do wonder whether the order is the answer to "Whither Eve?" I can only know by trying, I suppose.

I saw the morning star rise in the east, over the foot of my bed. Sister Anita was describing some of the things that happen at "the convent" as they describe the Mother House—this is one of the Mission Houses—and the various things one has to do and to learn. She talked of music and plainsong. I gather the convent has a great deal that the mission houses don't.

Tomorrow I must try to get the first chapter done. I don't know why this book has been so hard to do. Read *The Spiral Way* today and copied some of it.

Mass. The gray of the morning dispelled by the sun. Two swans flew by my eastern window, one by the western window last night. [Later I used these swans and the swan sounds in *Flight.*] I worked hard all day and again accomplished nothing. The start is too mannered and artificial, I think, so at the end of the day I laid it aside altogether. I love everything about the life I am at present leading except this frustration over the work, which I must do if only to pay my debts. I find that the place and the routine are becoming part of me. I could, I think, very easily give up the outside world. That would not be the trouble at all. It is more of a sacrifice to stay in it and to write and to try to remember the indwelling Presence. The religious life with all its hardships would be easier, I think.

Mass this morning aimed at me, that the Holy Nativity might grow in numbers. I prayed, meditated, and had a long talk with Sister Mary Louise. I shall see the Reverend Mother in two or three days, and make definite plans about next year. That leaves this year to finish *By Just Exchange,* to see Terry married, to sell Two Brooks, and give away furniture and belongings, and then to see. It may not be the right road—in a way I regard it as a temptation and a distraction, but less of both than life in New York can be.

The religious activities around here are so exciting, they are altogether getting in the way of the book. Talked with an intelligent woman who had been to Fond du Lac off and on for years, finally accepted for clothing, then her mother made such a fuss that she returned to the world, married and had two children, but regrets the vocation. I wish I knew! I go to Mass each day and ask for guidance. "Many roads has he fashioned, all of them lead to the light." But why in this lovely regulated place can't I get my plain duty, my obligations done? I do stick at it, but I plain *stick,* that's all.

I did not understand that *writing* the book, to pay off my debts, and because I was contracted for it and had already received the advance, was not the problem. The conflict came from my clinging to the importance of my work, as a "valuable" setting me apart, making me an exception. This is the insidious thing about a lifetime devotion to the arts as a way of life. It is a way of life, and leads most surely to the Centre of the Medicine Wheel, but it can be set up wrongly as an ego-feeding process, an idol. Randall Jarrell's Gertrude in his devastating *Pictures from an Institution* is always saying, in capitals, "As A Novelist" she should do thus and so. There is too much Gertrude in me. This un-selving . . . how hard and how essential it is! The whole point of coming to the planet, of being here, the reason for the splash-down.

The day came for my interview. Reverend Mother *is*. "There stands a winged sentry, all skillful in the wars." She has invited me to the Mother House for the month of March [later it was changed to June] and I am going. From then on it will be as the Great Spirit wills, but a gradual stripping away of inessentials, certainly. She seemed to think that writing could be used. But could I write to order, between prayer and bells? My crassness and grossness showed up every minute beside her simplicity.

Mass. Shocked at prayer for the return of the Lutherans and "European Protestants" to Holy Church! How narrow can we get? I noticed that we prayed for a "bridge" between us and Rome, but don't offer the Lutherans a bridge.

Reverend Mother left. I am impressed by her. I had a feeling I had been weighed and found wanting. But I was cheered as I stepped into my cell by its name, the first rung on the ladder.

Rose with the angelus. At 7.30 was driving in "the great silence" with Sister Christobel to the Church of Saint Thomas in Farmingdale, wherever that is. Then Mass, special blessing by the Bishop. I wish I had less self-consciousness on these occasions and had looked him in the eye. Breakfast in the basement of the church. How odd all this life is, among people I had never known and couldn't hope to know—then more church, and finally back to the convent exhausted. Mary stumped in having heard an excellent sermon by Canon Peters which set her all up, walk by the sea, got locked into the beach and had to climb out with the help of a little ladder, home to vespers and benediction, sang hymns in the evening, and so to bed utterly worn out with religion!

Got out Thornton Wilder's *Ides of March* again, simply because I couldn't think of anything else, and was once more stricken in that part of me which suffers over human love and human misery and human courage and human dignity. . . . I suppose I must be content to leave these things unsolved and turn away. A strange feeling the last few days as though I'd slipped off the Celestial Hook. I hope not. I do want to finish the book, pay the debts, and go forward to *becoming*. If only I had lived so I was free now!

After a stormy, sleepless night, rain and wind on the roof and in my heart, I woke to a wild gray day, and after Mass I was mobilized to clean the chapel, which I did, with peace and alacrity and a nostalgia for far-off Fond du Lac. In the evening I helped hang curtains and stayed up, though I was tired, for Compline. The spirit of this house is certainly of peace and strength.

No Mass today because the furnace was out. I enjoyed the extra half hour in bed. Later I began to work quite well on the book, and Roger Straus when I telephoned said they had decided to drop *Pomp and Circumstance* from *The North Star Is Nearer*, since *The New Yorker* won't get it out in time, a shame, but they are keeping "an important spot" for *By Just Exchange* on their autumn list, and wanted a long enough space between them. What a different world!

Then a letter from Mrs. Brengle inviting me to dinner on Sunday, and setting the official seal on Dick and Terry's marriage. Surely it is out of her hands or mine or anyone's but theirs.

Still no Mass. Rain, heavy rain. Devils got into me this morning, devils of resentment and self-pity. I wrote a clever synopsis of a situation I might sometime use. I wrote some of the book, but not enough.

The morning star rose properly at foot of my bed. The moon on the snow and the branches of the great tree outside my window were beautiful whenever I woke to look out.

Heavenly fine day. Mass. I wrote the fateful letter to Reverend Mother this morning.

Another fine day, not quite so fine perhaps. Mass. Took X to town. In the course of conversation her vision of the shriveled, burned-up child which has haunted her, and of which she dreamed last night, became clear. It's interesting how all the writers are hurrying into the fold, or at any rate conscious of it, a sort of "Who is on the Lord's side?" roundup at the eleventh hour. After supper tonight Nancy spoke about her war-correspondent trip, and everyone was moved. I asked her if she would speak to the club.

Five white swans have just flown by my window. What a place this is! Mass, as wonderful as usual.

Terry told me that she and Dick were going to announce the engagement on February 27th, a Sunday. He has got the ring and the wedding ring. Terry excited. Much talk of the party we'll give for it.

Nancy told me the title of her new book and her idea, some of it is based on this convent. I think she'll do a wonderful job. I do wish that I had somehow got more done so that I were free to write *The Bishop's Thumb*. In some moods it seems wonderful to go into the religious life and not write again for heaven knows how long, if ever, at other times I feel that I should stay outside and write.

Read *The Screwtape Letters*. Asked for a quiet day on Monday to prepare for first confession on Tuesday. "Prosperity knits a man to the world. He feels that he is finding his place in it, while really it is finding its place in him."

I had a harried day with correspondence. Mundane things press in. What a strange year! No settled abode and so many ideas. But I am not getting on with the first simple duty of writing *By Just Exchange*. Never did any book, except Mother Seton, resist being born so strenuously.

I wonder if one of the Kings had left an adoring woman behind? Certainly a kingdom. What a story that would make! Written from the woman's following spirit and his resting in its various stages. And when he came back from finding the Manger, he would find his own son? This place has its magic, like the fairy stories of my childhood, the same enchantment. There are the twelve white swans I saw today at the lake, six right side up, six tail up; there is the noise of their wings as they fly by my window, and the moon rising above it, or the setting sun, and there is sunlight on the sea from my window, and the rising of the morning star. There is the somewhat self-conscious goodness of all the good children, and the happiness in one's own soul.

This afternoon I had a long conference with Sister Mary Louise, who gave me books on confession. I cannot believe much of what they say, but I am willing to submit to the discipline. My fear is that in choosing Father Taber for my confessor I may put it out of court to enter the order, besides the humiliating embarrassment of confessing to a friend, whose good opinion I value. That is the trouble with the Anglo-Catholic church. There are very few confessors. But since I have been told to go to him, I will. I went to sleep, prone across the bed, and woke repeating "It is nearly ready," as of someone speaking of the thing that is I.

This time next week Terry will announce her engagement, get her ring and have her party. I will not tell her of my plans until they are final, and then I am sure she will understand that far from losing me, I shall be more hers and her family's than ever. But this is not the time. I wish I had spent these years of waiting more sensibly. But from now on the way must be clear.

My quiet day began with a most holy Mass, then breakfast at the high table. Sister Anita bounding up the stairs to say my air-mail letter had gone. An endeavor to recollect the sins of forty years, using the ten commandments, and to marshal them on paper. I did rededicate myself. If my sins automatically exclude me from entering the order, then I will have to live a dedicated life outside it. I am beginning to think it will be a relief to make a clean sweep of everything, humiliating though it is. But only to the ego, not to the immortal self. The letter from Reverend Mother arrived and was brought to me in the chapel, where I read it. She has definitely accepted me as a postulant, from October 1st. If tomorrow this decision is not advised against by Father Taber, I have only to employ the intervening time well, wind up everything, and humbly and hopefully *try*. I slipped this afternoon. Can't I ever be all of a piece?

Traveled through the rain, first by taxi, then by subway, to Saint Mary's. I was wearing my fur coat, and I arrived like some damp unpleasant animal, all bedraggled, the outer appearance matching the inner state. Here I found Father Taber waiting, a simple, just, and holy man, and probably to his embarrassment as well as mine, a friend. We had half an hour's talk before going to the church. I showed him the Mother's letter, and I told him my hopes, and then I went to the confessional and endured the agony and humiliation. There is one moment when so low you can't go lower, the liturgy restores you to a little dignity by adding to the horrible sordid pile "whatsoever thou hast done of good or endured of evil" so that the offering may be complete. My throat ached before I went in, and during, and only lifted afterward. The counsel was so right and the mercy so tender. I came out dazed, and knelt by the pillar near Our Lady for my penance. That struck home too. Then to the apartment for a time with Terry. Thinking in a general way I find myself very proud of Terry and Dick, both so good and so fine and Terry so lovely looking and Dick so handsome. I am glad that I am not their age with so many difficult years ahead. At worst I can't have more than I've had already and I hope and expect many less. Anyhow I am on the way out and they have it all ahead, but together.

Stayed in town for a tiresome board meeting at the club. Problems all the time in the club and I get very tired. Have to settle the affairs of a poor old woman, rich but senile, whose apartment hadn't been cleaned since three years ago, and who lives in a welter of disorder and dirt. What a contrast to the convent! Lately, especially this last year, the problems of lonely old age have come up again and again. Back to Bay Shore with relief. It is wonderful to know there is a dignified and growing retreat, harbor, battlefield, challenge, garden, *place* for me, where I can shed the sordidness of possessions and the worse sordidness of self, vulgar self.

Sister Mary Louise and Sister Christobel are concerned about me. I seesaw up and down, back and forth on this question of vocation. At times it seems the only important thing, and I'm in complete agreement, at times the pull of my writer's life in New York *pulls,* although when I see what difficulty I have in actually getting to work and writing I don't see why I wouldn't give it up with delight.

I have only a few more days here. It has been a growing time, whatever is ahead. Very little work on the book, but work upon myself, more important. Sister Anita's talk on the psalms most real and from an angle I had not considered. Read Damrosch's description of nuns as doing housework, embroidery and nursing the sick, while *monks* "write books, pamphlets," etc., etc. Unfair discrimination even in the religious life.

The birds have come back and have started to sing. I don't know that I can bear it. Particularly vulnerable this year to beauty, but I say that every year.

Four swans flew by as I was talking to Sister Mary Louise. Spent a sleepless night, heard all the hours strike. The thin silver sprinkling of the hours. Worked on *Flight* in my head in the night. The peace and joy of the convent is indescribable to those who have never tried it. At first it is such a tightening up of the spirit, a real recharging, that it is a strain and hard to relax, once in tune again it is peace and joy and rightness.

I got back to New York, to MacDowell, to New York again, to a very full life, crammed with pressures and happenings. This time of the start of my un-selving was as mysterious and disconcerting to me and those who happened to watch it as my surge forward toward simplicity had been.

Only one thing stayed constant, insolvency.

Down to 15 cents again, 2 grapefruit, 4 eggs and some cereal to last till the end of the month.

To dinner with Elsie and Marshall. Only food since breakfast yesterday.

To Pen and Brush for concert which was excellent and very well attended. Vernon Loggins came as my guest. Everyone enjoyed it. I'm glad I added music to the club. Walked home and spent my last ten cents on three rolls which made my supper.

Finally I gave up my apartment and took a room at the top of the Pen and Brush building for $27.50 a month, and began to look for a job, any job which would keep me in New York, where I wanted to be, and help me get free of debt.

I went for occasional weekends to Bay Shore, and I was still havering and wavering when I got a letter from the Reverend Mother.

My dear Mrs. Eaton,

This may be a great blow to you and yet it may be a relief. I have just refused a candidate of forty-six years and we have been so upset about it that I feel I must write you that it may be best if you do not try to come.

The sisters are very much opposed to anyone over age and I feel that it would be a hard six months and then rejection.

I hope this does not seem too unkind after consenting to your coming but under the present reaction I am afraid it would only result in hardship for both of us.

Affectionately,
The Mother

A sad day, full of mournful music on the radio and rain in my heart. Fasting too, which doesn't make me feel tra la. Finished the review for the *Saturday Review* on a very stupid book. Vernon Loggins telephoned he had a course for me, at the School of General Studies or something, at Columbia, starting on Tuesday night. Heaven help me, I don't know how to give a course, but I said yes.

The letter from Reverend Mother said that the sisters are very much opposed to anyone over age. Perhaps there is more in it than that, anyhow I take it as a final rejection there and it hurts more than I like to feel.

Two more letters came.

Bay Shore, May 9th 1950

Dear Mrs. Eaton,

This is just to let you know I am thinking of you and asking God to give you grace to accept the disappointment that I know The Mother's letter will cause you.

She too is, I am sure, distressed, for she is very fond of you and had looked forward to your coming.

Can't you come to us for a few days? We could have nice talks now in the garden.

This will, of course, mean adjustments and many changes of plan for you. I am *so* sorry.

With dear love and my prayers until you come,

Affectionately in Him,
Mary Louise SHN

May 20th

Dear Mrs. Eaton,

This is just to tell you that you are much in my heart and thoughts, and that I am still hoping a miracle may happen!

You, I hope, will soon be coming for the promised visit, and we can have good talks.

Dearest love and my prayers,

Aff. in Our Blessed Lord,
Mary Louise SHN

Now that the shock of being rejected by the convent is wearing off a little, I feel a distinct relief in some ways. I can settle down to being a writer and to living in New York. "And miles around they'll say that I am quite myself again." I shall always regret it, though. The death of a dream . . . but at least it's settled.

Only it wasn't.

A very strange and sad day. I drove out to Pawling, through lush green beauty, and flowering shrubs at their height of blossoming, to the Daggs' house. The maid said she had been taken back to the hospital for treatment, so I drove to the hospital and managed to get in to see her . . . in such pain. I felt a worm that I had not been to see her often, and sent more flowers . . . she is very ill, and there is nothing one can do but pray. Speaking of prayer, I had a letter from Reverend Mother today, reopening the whole question of my coming to the convent. I was very happy at first to think the decision could be reconsidered, but I had begun to adjust myself to continuing in the world, and now here we go all over again. I *think* I want to join the Sisterhood, but I wish I could have gone last year in the first flush of my, and their, enthusiasm. The long waiting, the wrestling with the book, the debts, and so on, have blunted things. I feel off the hook and swirled away. *Have* I "a call," "a serious call to the holy life," or is it merely *dégoût de ce monde* and a search for dignity, peace, etc. rather than for God?

In the meantime I had accepted the job at Sweet Briar, and it was only a year later that I was able to knock on the door of the Mother House in Fond du Lac, with the strange, exultant soaring of the spirit and frightened sinking of the heart that probably comes to everyone who stands outside a convent door asking to be admitted as a postulant.

VOCATION

Before the door where two ways meet
Amory and Division Street,
one stood in doubt.
Dare
she enter there?
One, looking out,
spied her.

Door open, she went in,
she, with her scars of sin.

The world of sin, denied,
waited outside.

Wait, world, forever,
door, reopen never,
sisters, hide her!

Woke to sun and sound of mellow gong. Mass. I was a little self-conscious, but when I get used to it I will relax. Everything seems brisk and rather staccato, except the chapel itself, and Reverend Mother, but this is only my first impression, the impression of my mundane self. There is peace in the silence and sun outside and green trees and birds singing in the trees, and I would imagine a chance, when I am rested, of doing *Flight*. I don't know whether I could stand this forever, but I am glad I came.

A month here should transform me. I am still tired from the trip and the pressures of the past year in New York. These are certainly Knights of Kadosh, stern set faces and the black and white of the degree. Perhaps that is what it has all been about. Certainly all the rest of the experiences of the time since I took that degree have been enacted in life. If I take one more, will I emerge into life, and light? I see the world as a lot of hot confusion and childishness, and yet *this* doesn't seem the solution . . . yet. A Masonic convent, if there were such a thing, or a hermitage. Here one is too self-conscious.

I worked all morning on the opening page of *Flight*. It isn't going to be an easy book, but it is one that can be written here. I went for a long walk with the Guest Mistress. She was disappointed that, even if accepted, I could not stay now. If I had no debts I could. I would be done with the world. . . . I wonder how that would feel at this time. Grim and good. An older sister, Sister Mary Kathleen, who is a Cherokee . . . how the Indians do turn up at every crucial corner . . . showed me Marya Zaturenska's book on Christina Rossetti, and told me that she had prepared her for confirmation and brought her into the Church. How strange, an American Indian and a Russian immigrant. I didn't know that when I met her at MacDowell. I wish I had. We might have discovered a basis for friendship.

At moments when I speak to the individual sisters or when I am alone in Chapel or in my sunny cell I feel that I might go through with it, but mostly when we are all assembled I am self-conscious. A sense of strain gets between me and them and the life here.

I don't think it would be any hardship to give up writing. One thing becomes obvious, I could not combine writing and the Religious Life. The Religious Life is better and higher, but perhaps not for me.

If I come here I will give up all thoughts of writing, and that way there will be peace. There's no such thing, apparently, as a convent where one could create. That would be a wonderful kind of order. But I suppose too much "vainglory" might creep in.

I wish I knew what God wants me to do about this convent. The ritual bothers me, gets between me and prayer, even while I am praying. Much would be terrible and seem like waste, to give up writing and all human relationships and sky and sea and earth and freedom and Terry and Dick and Marty . . . but no more than others have given and give, and why *shouldn't* it be hard? But then I should feel uplifted and close to Him in the saying of the offices. I don't. I pray better alone or at Saint Mary's or in the country on a long walk than I do here. It is all a puzzle. I try to think about it, to think it through, and get nowhere. Sometimes I'm sure *no,* sometimes I think *yes.* Tonight was a *yes* time unexpectedly. All I can do is to put my hand and self and life in His and say "have it your way." I do that. And I have still a year in the world to adapt.

At Mass today more peace in my heart, a better communion. I've decided not to fuss, and not to attempt to decide it, but to let the Lord bring whatever He wants to pass. I shall spend the rest of my sacred visit here trying not to waste it. I am here for some purpose, brought from the ends of the earth. If it is to enter here, then it is to enter here. If it is to expiate and draw strength and grace for a life in the world, then it is for that. The tree outside my window is a great comfort to me. I am very tired today. I have been here almost a week, a strange, ascetic, purifying week. The Novice Mistress, Sister Martha, had a talk with me in the guest parlor. She is young and full of spiritual vitality and a serious expression in her dark eyes as she pondered me. I still can't imagine that I'm here. It was so long a project, in the distance, in the background, in the foreground again.

I woke feeling well and wanting to get at the book. I hope it lasts through all the strains and services. It is another cool, sunny day with fresh blue sky, no clouds, usually there are large white thunderheads, like the Chinese skies. I get an impression of it from my window. I would spend time in the garden but the mosquitoes are terrible, fierce and legion, and hungry for something other than black robes. I am not getting down to the essentials in this book, the essentials of the life here—the blue of pictures as I follow the black-robed procession at a respectful distance down the hall—sun strikes the wall—the sound of bells and gongs and clocks. The sense of timelessness and of eternity, so that the coming of the mail is a shock and almost an outrage. I went to walk some of the fat off in the garden and ran into the Reverend Mother walking with the Guest Mistress. I retired respectfully, and now I see them there, traditional figures, "nuns in a convent garden."

Storm today. What storms they have here, violent, lickety-split, crash-bang affairs. "Straight rains and tiger-colored sky." There is something honest and forthright about them, uncompromising like the country. I think everything, sky, grass, trees and general *feel* is more abrupt and has no nonsense about it—alien to me. Exchange of a few words with Sister Alicia in the baking room. The picture that Sister Christobel gave me of this place is so unlike the reality. An interview with the Mother tonight, gracious and kind. Naturally I wonder what impression she receives. She herself is holy and consecrated and dignified.

Our service was interrupted by a knocking on the door or wall that startled me. Much kneeling and passing of notes to Mother, and sisters departing, then candles lit, and the priest strode in with white stole and took out, presumably some consecrated Hosts, and went out. Candles extinguished. I supposed at first the viaticum for one of the sisters, but apparently not, for surely we should have been exhorted to pray.

A gray day. Beset by distractions at Mass. Inconvenient and irrelevant memories and preoccupations. Then from the urgencies of the prayers for the nation I imagined something worse than usual might have happened. How peaceful it is not to know! To think that we all might live these innocent and holy lives in our families, and if we did, there would be no need for severity and austerity which now is offered by these few, these pitifully few who are living it for us. I think of Terry and Dick and Marty and pray that they may not be submerged by the dark powers of the world, the Destroyers, that they may as I have always wished for them, "grow in grace and wisdom and knowledge and love of Christ," however that growth comes, and that they may not know the sorrow I have over years of sins and wastes. I sorted altar bread today, perfect hosts engraved with different patterns, each to be the communion of somebody somewhere, perhaps my own.

Passed the whole morning before and after Terce reading the extraordinary book which Sister Mary Kathleen gave me: *Madeleine Semer*. In many ways her life was like mine, except that I went to lower depths and am not capable of the heights she reached. Nevertheless, the whole idea of the real possibilities of the Mystical Marriage should not be discarded, as I am always apt to do, as certainties for others, but for me only the plodding obedience, devotion to duty, and uncertain loyalty in the outer courts, out of a sense of duty more than of love. Love (tenderness, emotion) has always been my magnet, and I am moved and disturbed by reading or hearing of it—expressed in movements of the hands, in renunciations. Yet I have a hardened heart, hardened first by sin, then by acquiescence in its hardening, in order to avoid pain and hurt . . . so that I am not shallow, perhaps, but insensitive.

What if there is such an experience as she records, possible to me and to others? Without being brash and blasphemous, might one not *think* about it more? As an ideal and a safeguard from lesser experiences? I hear the novices practicing plainchant below. Here, in the formality and anonymity of the convent such an experience as she tells of may take place for them, may be taking place in others. At least let my thoughts not preclude it when I think of vocation. To her it came while living in the world. If I am not to return here, perhaps I can follow her example and live the dedicated life wherever I am.

It's very strange, this utterly uninteresting (to me) banal little Midwestern town, with nothing about it to arrest attention, the convent plunked down in the middle of it with no grounds, so that one hears the sound which of all others is most annoying and meaningless—children's high-pitched nasal voices . . . such stodgy children! and cars, and other noises . . . what an incongruous place to find the mysteries of the Holy Grail! Yet I know it must be right, or I wouldn't have been brought here from such other places all around the world where I might have found It or It me!

The banality extends to most of the things in the house—not all. The Fra Angelico prints, the Sisters' Refectory, are exceptions. So also the fresh air blowing through, it is always cool and airy here, no stuffiness anywhere. No doubt bitter cold in winter. So also the impression of sky and trees. Its enclosure away from the world is a thick cloak of commonplace Midwestern entourage which effectively walls off everything. But the Reality is here, on the Altar, in the life, among the Sisters . . . here and undeniable. And since the door is ajar, I will not go looking for the intellectual and spiritual delights of good taste and "culture," if I become a religious, it will be here, in Fond du Lac, where I have been welcomed so graciously and led by such seeming coincidence. The great IF. All I can do is pray and wait and try to get free of debt and then close my eyes and hurl myself into the gray waves of the cold sea of sacrifice as these so bravely, so completely, have . . . or get out of the Gardener's way and let Him work on His plants.

Later, remembering this image, I wrote:

THE GARDENER

He used me today,
I felt His hand on my life,
grip, turn, lift,

256

high,
low,
flail,
hoe,
one with Him,
tool in His light.

He left me,
propped by the trunk of this old apple tree.
I think He intended to mow the weeds round it,
but I was too dull to be used.
Ant and spider jeer,
traveling my rust,
"Where is now thy Gardener?"
I believe . . . I believe He has gone for the whetstone.
Lord, return,
take me up,
sharpen me,
cut!

I will be His,
held or discarded,
used or useless,
shining or covered with rust.
Night with its dark corrosion comes,
day with its heat,
not yet my Lord's feet.

This time, at the end of the month, the Reverend Mother accepted me as a postulant, and set the date for October 1, 1952. But when the day came, I was still an "aspirant at large." I did not present myself at Amory and Division Street to keep the engagement.

I have often thought of those eager, tugging hands, patiently hauling for so long a time the line to this exasperating sea beast, and the sisters' probable relief, when having done all and more than love and duty demanded, they saw the stubborn creature shuck itself off the hook and sink back to the sea. I would have been an awkward catch at best. Moreover, "the sea is His and He made it"—as well seek Him there as on dry land. But if Fond du Lac was only a way station, it was a blessed one:

> a house
> where all's accustomed, ceremonious. . . .
> How but in custom and in ceremony
> Are innocence and beauty born?

It was a great powerhouse of spiritual force.

I finished *Flight*. Begun in Fond du Lac, worked on at Sweet Briar, in London and on the *Queen Elizabeth* between London and New York, and finally finished in New Hampshire, at the top of the stairs in Olga Warburton's farmhouse, where I had just room for a typing table, and had to be mindful not to push the chair back and fall down them, I finished the first book which I considered to be a serious book.

December 20th 1953: Galleys of *Flight* arrived, sixteen of them, with a letter saying: "Since it was my pleasure to prepare your manuscript for the printer, I am glad of this opportunity to tell you how much I enjoyed your book. Indeed I think it is one of the most beautifully constructed and imaginative pieces of writing I have read in a long time. In my capacity as copy editor, thereby having to read many manuscripts during the course of a publishing season, it affords me great pleasure to be able to read a work of art such as yours. B. M." This from a proof editor was unusual.

Reading Elizabeth Shepley Sergeant's study of Willa Cather, I decided that to be a great writer one must have no sense of humor. Cather, James and some of the other "greats" took themselves and "their art" too seriously. That sort of approach was mashed out of me very early. But with *Flight* something had happened to me.

"There is a time in a writer's life when his 'life line' and the line of his personal endowment meet. This may come early or late, but after it occurs his work is never quite the same."

"These works of her fifties have quite another form, dimension and vibration than have her Nebraska books. Their significance tends to the religious, they seek the decisions of the world and the spirit on man's tragic fate . . . they are lifted to a level beyond manners. The agonizing problem of mortality, the oncoming of death is always present."

This is a strange reflection of the pattern happening to me. Certainly there are parallels. *Flight* is the turning point for me, as *A Lost Lady* was for Willa Cather.

A very exciting and, if one can believe half of it, amazing letter from Hiram Haydn [the editor who, at three different publishers, brought out my three best books]. He says, among other things: "Here is a bold and impressive conception executed throughout all the sections to do with death, with ingenuity, passion and depth." "You have merged quite particular and peculiarly twentieth-century concepts of artifacts with no diminution of a sense of the eternal." "You evoke the sense of wonder and terror and pity in our own idiom." He writes a friendly, concerned letter, as though he *really* liked both me and the book.

Elizabeth Bowen's comments are: "Unlike anything that has been done." "Moving, exciting." "What one hesitates to say today because reviewers have killed the word, *important*." "*Flight* is a great book, and we will toast it together in New York."

1953 has been an eventful, forward-moving year. *Flight* got finished. I have a publisher once more, Terry's son was born, John Eaton Brengle, so now there are Marty and John. My mother died. I got to England. I got to France. I signed up once more for this teaching job. I paid some debts.

Nice friendly letter from the Reverend Mother. No sad feelings.

I begin again at the start of a new spiral.

Part Six

W hen I was first displaced to the United States, I went to Columbia University to inquire whether I might go on with my interrupted studies there. I had a fairly impressive record: the Oxford Junior with Distinction in Divinity when I was thirteen; the Oxford Senior with First Class Honors in English; the Oxford Higher with First Class Honors in French; and a year at the Sorbonne.

I thought perhaps my touching precocity in Divinity might do something for me, but Divinity is not a recognized academic subject in the United States. The answer was no.

"You do not have sufficient academic qualifications."

"I have written several books. . . ."

"You have a deficiency in the physical sciences."

Unfortunately this was true, and on my record for all to read. Once I combined two elements which should not be combined, and blew out an expensive window at the Sorbonne. The phrase used then was *aucun rapport avec les sciences physiques.* Here it came again in other words.

I murmured that I had always leaned toward the Humanities, but this Tower of Pisa attitude did me no good. Sadly I took the downtown subway back to my job with Ann Watkins.

Eleven years later, with no further academic qualifications, and no deeper *rapport* with science, I received the following communication:

COLUMBIA UNIVERSITY
IN THE CITY OF NEW YORK

My dear Madam:
I have the honor to advise you that you have been appointed to be lecturer in English at Columbia University at a salary to be arranged in accordance with assignments of duties in the School of General Studies. This appointment will take effect on July 1, 1949, and is made in accordance with the provisions of the Charter, during the pleasure of the Trustees. The appointment will expire, unless renewed, on June 20th, 1950. By authority of the Trustees.

I am still, when tired, or caught off guard, apt to pay attention to words. I take *Immediate, Urgent, Road Closed, Danger,* to mean more or less what they say, instead of nothing in particular. It's a communicable—communications—disease. So for the two years I gratefully taught at Columbia, during the Trustees' pleasure, I had an uneasy feeling that since They had told me I was *ineligible* to attend my own classes, I might be defrocked for giving them. I had nightmares of a ceremony in the hollow square. I should have remembered that I had done something *else,* the first rule for success, apparently.

I had no sooner been ensconced, if that is the right word, as a member of the faculty, than I became aware that my *rapport* with academic communication was also *aucun.* Most of the time I had no idea what anything meant. I took notes, surreptitiously at first, then openly, but even when I could read them afterward, they made no sense.

What was a "floating course"? It suggested an English pudding, junket perhaps, or trifle, with lots of jam. What did it mean: "the Dean to remove a condition"? (This was when I was teaching at Sweet Briar.) I knew what the words conveyed to me, but I could not believe that the Dean would undertake to perform an abortion. What was a "variegated course in its membership" or "the effect of the complex consonants on the stability of French"? An allusion to why governments rose and fell so wildly on the Quai d'Orsay?

What did it mean to "cut across a major," or a colonel or a general? How did one "evaluate verbal intellectualism in hockey" or "recommit for formulation the experience of the initial year" or "scrutinize the modern thought in dormitory building"? How should one treat "lack of clarity of visualization, followed by student loss of momentum," poor top-heavy things, or confront those "students stronger in one area and weaker in another," unless with vitamins, or "accelerate a gifted student," unless by stepping on the gas?

The phrases at Columbia were less absurd than these, but still they had a sinister twist, suggesting dubious activities, violence done to human beings, all those dismembered poets strewn about, "units of Milton," "units of Shakespeare," "units in another field." I suppose one does have to have strong *rapport* with physical sciences, and probably with medicine too, to jaunt around those "fields" forgetting right words in order to be "language-minded."

There came a time of evaluation, "rescrutinization," a crucial time when a sheaf of papers arrived upon my desk. I took them gingerly with me into the corridor and caught the friendly arm of a passing colleague, Vernon Loggins, responsible for my being at Columbia, and whom I had known in the Greater World Outside.

"What do I do with these?" I quavered.

"Oh, just list your students alphabetically and grade them." Then, as he saw my glazed look, "It's perfectly easy, just give them all H."

He tapped me on the shoulder and went his blithe way, leaving me disconcerted that an old friend, who had never been mealy-mouthed, should feel so conscious of our academic surroundings that he couldn't come out frankly with "hell," but must disguise it under that whimsical "H."

I thought it a pity to treat the students with such trumped-up severity. They had all worked well, two of them selling stories written in the course, but if that was what he wanted, the expected procedure . . . I listed the class, gave the best students C, the rest D, and sent the papers in to the five "outlets" designated on the sheet of instructions.

Two days later the Voice of Authority called me. Had I no good students?

"Certainly," I answered, with units of indignation. "All my students are good, some of them excellent."

"Haven't they been working? If you have a problem with discipline . . ."

"Yes . . . no . . . I couldn't be more satisfied. . . ."

"Then why have you given such poor grades?"

"I thought we had to." I was taken aback. "Professor Loggins told me to give them all hell."

"He *did?* Professor Loggins told you that?"

"He was careful, of course, in front of the students, to use units of speech. What he said was, 'Give them all H.' "

"Oh," the Voice said wearily. "H is a grade, Miss Eaton, a grade which signifies—*means,*" It translated for my benefit, "that a student has not yet accomplished all his assignments for the course. It's a grade we usually associate with Creative Writing, since students enrolled in that course do not as a rule complete their assignments by midterm. When Professor Loggins told you to mark your students H he was assuming you would be conversant with the information contained in . . ." He mentioned some handbook of instruction for backward lecturers.

The Voice ceased, and after a respectful interval I too hung up, muttering, "*Papers* should be marked, not students." I felt a distinct loss of momentum following lack of clarity of visualization, leading to recommittal for units of formalization . . . until in due course I received another, inevitable, letter from Columbia University.

This time I was no longer its dear Madam, but, prosaically, "Dear Miss Eaton," and the letter began without anyone having honor or pleasure: "Because of the well-known shrinking" . . . of me, or from me, I supposed, but it turned out to be "of registration in colleges, the Administration of the School of General Studies has decided that we must reduce our offering somewhat next year."

I was the offering, that at least seemed clear.

There were episodes at Columbia I like to remember. Twenty-six veterans of World War Two were taking the class under the G.I. Bill of Rights. They were a joy to teach because they wanted to learn, they were mature, and, helped by Uncle Sam, paying for their own education. They did not try to waste their time, and incidentally mine, in the classroom. I taught the Short Story, what it is, how to read and how to write it. These men did have stories to tell and a competence in telling them. Some of them had heard of grammar as a useful tool, and used it, though there was one with a Master's

Degree who had gone through all that long process of so-called education without encountering the fact that a sentence requires a verb. He turned in strings of dangling Spanish moss, some of it quite beautiful, but hanging there helpless to move the story forward. When I told him why—there was no verb—he said, not quite as rudely as I am told students speak to elitist teachers nowadays, "What's that got to do with it?"

There were two Blacks in the class. One of them wrote very well. He sold a story to *Collier's* which he wrote in the first month as an assignment. The other had less talent but was good in class participation, asking shrewd, even brilliant, questions, doing his work ahead of time, not making the same mistakes once they were pointed out, and obviously enjoying the course, until just after midterm he changed completely in all his attitudes. He turned in his assignments late, carelessly written, and missed two completely. He took to sitting nearest to the door, came in after the class started, and left the second I stopped speaking, dashing out as though he couldn't stand to be in the room with us another moment.

I was worried. I dated the change from the time when Mr. Carrington, the *Collier's* Black, turned in an unconvincing story. It lacked the authority of his other work, and I pointed out that he didn't know either the characters or the setting. It was about an Episcopalian minister in a New England town, but it was obviously a Baptist preacher in the deep South. I explained to the class that you *must* know your characters from the inside out, and be completely sure of them, and you should know your setting with the same certainty, and be at home in it. "Sometimes," I said, "you may have an unfamiliar setting, if you make it unfamiliar to your characters too, and both of you grope together, but not to know either characters or setting is too heavy a handicap." I tried to make it general, and not a reflection on the restrictions, in those days, against Blacks. The author looked self-conscious, then mutinous.

"I don't want to write about what I know," he said. "I want to be free to write about anything and everything. . . ." *That a white man can write about* hung in the air between us.

"None of us can manage that," I said. "We are all restricted in one way or another. The thing is to make an asset out of limitations." I mentioned writers restricted because they were women, and then I repeated that one must *know*, in order to make the reader believe.

The class went on, but Mr. Brown—that was the name he gave—began his protest demonstration against what he evidently felt to be a racial slur on his colleague.

I decided to let it ride for a while, but after a fortnight, when he showed no signs of relating to us again, I decided he was too good a student to be allowed to flunk the course for such a reason, and I braced myself to have a conference with him, to try to set things straight. Before I could arrange it, while I was still thinking about it, one day before the class began, Mr. Brown came in, a transformed Mr. Brown, grinning from ear to ear.

He came straight to the point.

"I know I've been slipping. I'm sorry. I haven't done my assignments"—he shook his head—"I'll make them up . . . I'll be all right now. . . . You see . . . you see, I've just become a father!"

A human predicament, not a racial problem. Our hands went out toward each other, we grasped them, and did a little dance of triumph there in the corridor. It was a lovely moment, warm and right. We should dance on these occasions, old and young together, black, brown, green, white and red, who still do dance on some occasions, the Cry-Dance at a funeral, the renewal Sun Dance . . . blessing the four quarters of the universe, the two-legged, the four-legged, the winged peoples and all things of the world.

Mr. Brown and I did our little dance of renewal, our Sun Dance, in the corridor in front of a classroom at Columbia. I have no doubt our feet found the right step, and our hearts held the words we should have chanted, to and on behalf of that new child, "The four paths of the four Powers are your close relatives. The dawn and the sun of the day are your relatives. The Morning Star and all the stars of the sacred heavens are your relatives; always remember this!"

Another scene at Columbia, another corridor, which I was rushing through, released from class. I ran into Dick, striding in the opposite direction.

"What are you doing here?"

"I'm getting my degree. What are *you* doing here?"

"I'm on the faculty. If you wash behind your ears and brush up on your Anglo-Saxon, I might let you into my class!"

He threw a book at me. We were lucky that none of Them were passing to see a student assault an older member of the faculty. I could have explained it, I suppose: "You see, Dean, it is not a case of student-faculty relationship, this is son-in-law/mother-in-law, perfectly natural. . . ."

A few weeks before, Dick had come to me with an anxious face.

"I've something to tell you. . . ."

He seemed so grave, so disturbed, that I thought something threatened the marriage I hoped would go well for them . . . "may they sing the same song. . . ."

"What is it, dear?"

"I've left the bank."

I threw my arms round him, and we did another little dance, or I did.

"What wonderful news! I can't tell you how relieved I am not to have a *banker* in the family!"

He stared. His parents had given him a hard time, he said, and he expected me to do the same, or more so, because of Terry and the immediate poverty it would mean . . . the G.I. Bill of Rights . . . not much money to be made (in those days) in teaching, compared to the salary the bank was already giving him.

"Nonsense!" I said.

"That's what Terry says."

"You see? But what are you going to do now?"

"I've always wanted to teach English."

It seemed to me an inexplicable desire, but not so strange as working for a bank. I kissed him again, and turned back to walk with him toward his classroom.

There he was, I thought, coming up the hard, honest, long way to M.A., to Ph.D., while I, his mother-in-law, because I had written some unscholarly books and got "a name" that had nothing to do with teaching came sailing in at the top. It would be a tribute to us both if we survived this galling situation for him. It's hard enough to swim against the seas of salty jokes, caricatures, stereotyped put-downs . . . the situation of a mother-in-law is hard in itself. After twenty years of living with a child, a man you have known for a year tells you her likes and dislikes, *informs* you that Terry can't eat lobster, or doesn't like sewing, or has a gift for acting. Also he doesn't want to hear anything that happened to her in those twenty years. Life began when they met.

I once overheard Dick saying, at a party, "I've got the best mother-in-law in the world. . . ." My heart gave a little jump, but he went on, "I never can locate her." The men around him laughed.

I will try, I thought, to keep it that way, and I mostly have.

When the President of Sweet Briar—I should say, an ex-President—got married recently, to an important Bishop, a wicked witty friend of mine referred to the occasion as "the decline of the Church." He sent me a newspaper clipping which mentioned that one of her sons by a former marriage, home from his travels, or his studies in the Far East, had read a chapter of the Gospel of Saint John at his mother's wedding, in High Mandarin.

"Thoughtful of the dear boy to make the attempt," he commented. "No earthly use trying it in English." He added, "As *you* know."

I did know. I tried for ten years to communicate with the President of Sweet Briar, in English, in French, with and without gestures, and I tried harder to understand what it was she apparently felt she was communicating to me, in a flood of almost-words, structured-somethings, woolly muffle spates of utterance. We stared at each other with a wild surmise—mine was wild—and went our separate and unequal ways.

Once I got an almost clear directive from her. I could see that she was struggling to beam it outward, downward, anyhow *away,* toward my comprehension.

I had made an appointment with her to ask a specific question. "What importance does it have for the college, for the students of the Writers' Workshop, to enter national and international competitions?"

We had just won two, and placed second and third in two others. I needed to know whether this was a crime or an achievement. She leaned forward, smiling.

"We have no *serious* objections, Mrs. Eaton, to the students winning them in moderation."

There it was, for my pondering. I still don't understand it. Why should there be objections to students winning in competition with Yale, Dartmouth, Princeton, as they did in one national poetry contest? Or, more suitable to girls, perhaps, *Mademoiselle*'s guest editorship, *Vogue*'s Prix de Paris? One student in the workshop won her membership in the Poetry Society of America from an unpublished manuscript written in the class. And how do you win "in moderation"?

Once, I was told, a communication of mine made the President laugh. She was observed to be reading it, and heard to be laughing. When I learned this I said, "Perhaps . . . perhaps . . . after all, laughter relates to something, and *might* develop into communication . . ." but before I could follow this hopeful will-o'-the-wisp further, my sentence at the college came to an end. I resigned, at last, at last, hearing those goodbyes beamed at me from the start, by the administration, by my department.

The letter that made her laugh was in answer to a missive from her explaining—the Head of my department said it did—that my subject was of so little importance to the college that I must be considered part-time, and could not have a sabbatical or tenure, which had both been held out to me as attractions to my coming there, to offset my ridiculously low salary.

Since I had a teaching load of eleven hours, reaching 140 students, and there were members of the faculty with nine hours, reaching ten to fifteen students, who were considered full-time, and since two of the courses I taught were required for the degree, and I was the only member of the faculty teaching one of them, I wondered fleetingly whether the Head of my department did not understand the communication either.

After some thought I answered:

Dear President Pannell,
    Your letter of the 17th November 1954 has produced all the following symptoms in the Visiting Lecturer in Creative Writing at Sweet Briar:
        Acathasia, the dread of sitting down; and conversely,
        Basophobia, hysterical fear of standing up.
        Kakorrhaphiophobia, fear of failure.
        Oniomania, uncontrollable urge to buy.
        Sophomania, delusions of omniscience.
        Philoneism, obsessive interest in fads.
        Apierophobia, morbid dread of infinity.
        Skopophobia, paranoidal fear of spies and foreign agents.
                         Sincerely yours,
                         Evelyn Eaton

She laughed, but I was barely smiling. I did have all those symptoms at Sweet Briar. I get traces of them still when I think of the place, so beautiful, so unkind to creative people, so deadening to the short-changed young.

The President's dictionary defined "college" as "a degree-granting institution." My dictionary defined "college" as "chosen together," from the Latin *collegium,* composed of *col* meaning "with" and *lego,* "choose." "One is chosen with another." Chosen to do what? I took it for granted that a college, especially a Liberal Arts College, would be a place where people of all ages, sexes, colors, creeds, and wonderfully different backgrounds had the good fortune to be chosen together to ponder crucial questions: "What sort of a universe is this, that we are in?" "What are we supposed to do, more important, to be, while we are on the planet?" "What is a human being?" "What am I?" and to share their discoveries.

I went to my first faculty meeting, thinking, "Ah, now I shall hear some stimulating, fascinating ponderings." What I heard was whether 101 should be called 101A or 101B, but it was never put so simply.

I once had to make a commencement speech at a new college. The fuel for what I burned to say came from long captive hours at meetings, when I sat remembering the religion I founded at Heathfield to help us through similar wastes of time and energy. It had only two commandments:

I shall never allow anyone to bore me.

The second is less important, but still should be observed whenever possible:

I shall try not to bore other people.

Sometimes, I told the commencement audience, the two can be lived up to together, sometimes they conflict. Then, of course, it is the first one that counts.

What is boring? The answers differ with different persons, which makes this religion wide in its appeal.

Communism bores me, for instance, Fascism bores me, most isms bore me. The language they use about themselves, in manifestoes and so on, is so deadly dull, so humorless, so long-winded and full of clichés and bad grammar that it hurts our ears and sickens our minds. Perhaps I am not a group-integrated unit, or whatever the jargon for it is nowadays. In my day we called group-integrated units "the unimaginatives," and sometimes when our first commandment had been brutally violated by some pompous old unit or other, we called them "those bloody sheep."

We were not indiscriminate joiners. Robert Frost says:

> Don't join too many gangs. Join few, if any.
> Join the United States and join the family—
> But not much in between unless a college.

Unless a college?

What is boring? The wrong use of words is very boring. The wrong use of words by oneself is boring, because it means that one has to do that page, or that chapter, or that book, all over again, and that is drudgery. Nobody likes drudgery. Of course there is a wrong use of words that is delightful. The Hungarian pianist Iren Marik once complained that domestic life was turning her into a Household Grudge. That kind of mistake is not wrong use of language, it is wit.

The wrong use of words by others is boring because it insults our intelligence, hurts our ears and also wastes or even kills time, and time is one of the best things we have.

Consider how much time it takes to say or to listen to:

Continuance in a state of existence or the contrary, presently under consideration pending a decision by consensus, would appear to indicate that under prevailing circumstances, the former or the latter might be preferable, taking under advisement differences of opinion; the answer in the present case being of an affirmative or of a negative character, according as to whether one elects on the one hand . . . et cetera, et cetera.

When Shakespeare took the trouble to say it for us in six short words, two of them repetitions:

To be or not to be.

He added, *"that* is the question."

The question.

When Alice B. Toklas died, and was buried next to her lifelong friend Gertrude Stein in the Père-Lachaise cemetery in Paris, alongside Molière, Proust, Chopin, Delacroix and other co-religionists of the anti-boredom faith, one of the most famous passages in her book *What Is Remembered* was revived and quoted again. She was describing Gertrude Stein's deathbed.

"I sat next to her and she said to me, early in the afternoon, 'What is the answer?' I was silent. 'In that case,' she said, 'what is the question?' "

Then she died, struggling to the last with the poet's eternal obligation to get those two important matters straight.

Since this strenuous quest occupies all their powers, the poets are sometimes puzzled by lesser questions put to them, such as, "What is the position of the poet in regard to the oil lash in Saudi Arabia, or the Stalinist revisionism among tadpoles, or the multiplicity of power knowledge, or teaching in a Liberal Arts College?"

Dylan Thomas, heckled for his honest opinion on one of these absorbing sidelines—somehow one's dishonest opinion won't do—answered with simple candor:

"The position of the poet is perpendicular. Except," he added thoughtfully, "when it happens to be horizontal."

My position was that in a Liberal Arts College there must be, somewhere, a vestige of respect for liberality and for the arts, and even—this was daring —*for artists.* I took it for granted, almost to the end of my ten-year "visit" that in a Liberal Arts College the arts would be understood, would be cherished in the minds and hearts of the community. I told my students that they would get Ds if they talked or wrote of "the performing arts," as though the arts performed, instead of creative people, *artists.* "Don't leave out human be-ings. Be careful with your grammar. *In the beginning was the Word.* The Author of our being, whom the Indians call the Great Imagination, is, among other things, a poet. We, his poems, with all created things, move forward:

> That from our incoherence we
> May learn to put our trust in Thee,
> And brutal fact persuade us to
> Adventure, Art, and Peace.

"It goes without saying . . ."

It did indeed. When I got around to hearing what was actually said in that establishment, that degree-granting institution, I was amazed, incredu-lous and hurt on behalf of the short-changed young. I wrote:

IMPRESSIONS OF ACADEME

1. Of a Certain Ph.D.

You dulled, you glazed your listless students' eyes,
deadened their ears to prose, to poetry,
negated curiosity, surprise,
'and art, made tongue-tied by authority,'
mildewed their minds with muffle; pompous, taught
Shakespeare unconscious of the works he wrought,
footnotes not underfoot where they belong
but sole-important, in the place of song;
discouraged excellence, smudged under right,
led the deluded young to a Dead Sea,
launched them in riddled ships, without a light
or chart or compass to be steering by;
you, monstrous swollen mediocrity,
brought down their albatross to the flat decks to die.

2. Of a Faculty Meeting

Self-glorifying mediocrity
ascends the platform, dominating rows
of docile, disillusioned faculty,
with here and there a tenured citadel
of mutinous integrity—but those
will soon retire, or be urged to serve
on more and more committees of the kind
that sap the energy and blur the mind—
while here sit brainwashed, rot as they deserve,
the few who follow truth, who teach too well,
"rouse student interest," spur the young to hate
the shoddy, spurious, the secondrate,
and yet will not, will not, WILL NOT arise
roaring peremptory "noes!" to these sheep's ayes.

I got off to a wrong start at Sweet Briar, through my ignorance of Academe. With ill-timed flippancy, assuming that no one took such pompous nonsense seriously, that it was a necessary show put on for freshmen and parents, I said to the man I found myself beside at convocation, "I hope you're not empty, because I'm supposed to stand next to a full professor."

I was surprised when he drew himself up stiffly and turned away with a snort and sniff. Still thick-headed, I turned to the woman on my other side.

"Wouldn't it be more impressive if we *rode* in? I understand the horses here are magnificent."

Then she drew herself up—she was impressive drawn up—and turned from me with even more marked distaste than my right-hand neighbor. Later I learned that she was "Fizz Ed," to whom horses were sacred, as full professors were to him. For the rest of the year I had to stand between them. Relations generally were not improved when I was quoted that "We all marched in as usual to *Pride and Prejudice*."

A little later there was the episode of the lake. Sweet Briar had a pretty lake. In September it was still muggy and hot, and I went swimming every day. I was the only one who did. I wondered why the faculty, some of those from the North at least, didn't join me, or the students, except that these young were so obviously frail, tired . . . *taaahed* out after half an hour's exercise, exhausted after a few yards' walk across the campus. Later I realized that some of them were there for four years without entering the woods, let alone exploring the six thousand acres open to them.

Every afternoon when I came back from the wharf, I met the Head of my department, and every afternoon he asked me, "Did you have a nice swim?" Twice I met the President, and she inquired, "Did you *enjoy* your swim?"

Two weeks later I discovered that the lake was closed to all swimming "on account of excess arsenic" which was being used to clear out the algae. I brooded a little over the solicitous inquiries of President and Head of department, then I tried to put it from my mind. After all, an artist and algae . . . perhaps they didn't see much difference. . . .

Then there was the matter of the horse with racial or other prejudices. I had been riding every day through the woods and enjoying it, when the Fizz Ed Goddess of the Stables said, "Would you mind riding in the ring today?" I did mind, but I said, "Of course not." I also said I didn't mind when they changed my horse and gave me an animal that couldn't even be described as a dog. Halfway round the ring for the fifteenth time at a somnolent walk, a trap door opened beneath its feet and a little black stable boy popped up. The horse became a bronco in one flash, reared, snorted, kicked, and I fell off, landing on my back on a boulder, which had also suddenly appeared in the center of the ring.

Half an hour later we were due to assemble, capped and gowned for Founder's Day, to listen to Dr. Stringfellow Barr give an address. He talked for an hour and twenty-five minutes, and when the time came for the community to rise and sing the Sweet Briar Song, my back had "seized" and I could only sink to my knees. I was in the front row, and this devotional position mystified and irritated the V.I.P.s on the platform, but there was no help for it.

"Sweet Bra, Sweet Bra, Purity," sang the choir, while the Visiting Lecturer in Creative Writing remained kneeling, and had to be dragged out by two full professors as the procession moved off.

Naturally I acquired a reputation for exhibitionism . . . what could you expect from Creative Writing? What indeed? I tried again to explain that the phrase was a misnomer and ungrammatical, that you could have a creative writer, or dancer, or painter, but not creative writing, or dancing or painting. Grammar was not taught at college, or in the schools preparing students to arrive there. It was before Sputnik soared and scared the educators into at least considering the old three R's.

Then there was the episode of the dog, the Pekingese Wang Sun, who appears in Go Ask the River, and was honored by Marianne Moore writing lines to him after I sent her his snapshot.

"Oh to be a dragon," she wrote on a postcard:

> Oh to be a dragon—
> of milkweed silk!
> Or Siamese sealpoint
> Canadian lynx guardhair,
> May "another golden day"
> (the saying on my Chinese seal)
> be many golden days, dear Miss Eaton,
> for him and for you.
>
> M.M. June 27 1958

Like every self-respecting Pekingese, Wang would never deign to come when he was called. If he was actually coming toward you, and you made the mistake of calling him, he would stop, glare, turn around and make off in the opposite direction as fast as he could go, and that was fast. In spite of a damaged hip, he covered the ground like a race horse. Sometimes he escaped to the campus, and once I had to get him back in a hurry because I was catching a plane. There was an emergency method. When he had to take cod-liver oil I gave him a chocolate to take away the taste. He developed a passion for chocolate, but never got on to the name. To him it was cod-liver oil.

So I stood in the middle of the campus shouting "LOVELY COD-LIVER OIL!"

My students didn't turn a hair, but other passing heads shook sadly or with irritation over this confirmation of what they had always known about that woman in Creative Writing.

Looking back I can see that from the start the college tried to say goodbye to me and I was too obtuse to understand.

Relations with my own department worsened yearly. There was the little indrawn breath when, the Head of the department having asked me to sit on some committee, I answered, "Thursday? Oh no, I can't. Thursday's my *working* day." By which I meant, and took it for granted that he would approve and even sympathize, that I taught my hardest on all the other days, earning an honest living, as I must, but on Thursdays, my free day, I *wrote*.

I didn't have an inkling that this would irritate him, or anyone. I was hired as a poet and a novelist. That was my value to the college, presumably, though the monetary value they put on it was less than the salary given, apologetically, to incoming instructors with no experience. I ranked, they told me, "next to a full professor," though I couldn't be called an associate professor, but "Visiting Lecturer in Creative Writing." The visit lasted for ten years. At the end of them I emerged with a pension of $12.02 a month, which has since climbed to $19.25, from T.I.A.A. And still I didn't understand!

"Why did you stay?" people have asked.

For several reasons, I suppose. I had set up a four years' course in Creative Writing, unique in those days. Sweet Briar was unaware of what it had. In the catalogue it was described as one section of Freshman English, two of composition, and one of writers' workshop. Actually it was all one course, and at the end of it a student was prepared, I felt, to *start* on the subject. I liked teaching it, the students' response was good. They worked hard, their stories, poems, plays and even a novel won competitions and got published. The workshop hummed with life.

Then there was all that honeysuckle and magnolia, and in the first flush of enthusiasm for the place, which I thought beautiful and where I believed I would spend the rest of my life, I had built a home with Iren Marik, music room for her, writing studio for me. Terry, Dick, the family—there were three children now, Marty, John and David—were only twenty miles away. Dick taught at the rival establishment, Randolph-Macon Women's College, in Lynchburg. There was an excellent Little Theater. Terry was in many plays, winning awards as Victoria, in *Victoria Regina*, taking Helen Hayes' part, and as Laura in *The Glass Menagerie*.

Friday Feb 13th 1959. Yesterday the most moving, poignant, beautiful performance of *The Glass Menagerie*. I went prepared to be bored or repelled, having seen it in New York when it did both—and I was so moved that I cried. Moreover it came back to me in the night. Of course it is the shock of seeing Terry, fragile, crippled, lost and helpless—all the things I desperately feared for her when I was carrying her, and later when I was alone and ill and had no one to leave her to, and later when she was unhappy, the poor lamb, and I scolded her, in an attempt to help, and when I let her down before and after her marriage . . . and yet loved her as that hopeless too-possessive mother did her Laura . . . whatever the combination, it got through all armor. But how good it is that she is with this group bringing live theater at its best to people who would not see it otherwise.

Then there were high moments at the college, when, for instance, Auden's Christmas Oratorio, *For the Time Being,* was performed there, the first performance of its kind, interpreted by choreography, and the second performance of any kind. There had been one "reading" in New York, at Grace Church, I believe, before this, but the main point was that the Sweet Briar production was complete, and worthy of the poem. Bringing a great work of art to life for the first time before a perceptive audience can be shared spiritual experience of the deepest kind. It was so on December 13 and 14, 1957, for the two evenings that it lived before us.

Dr. Larry Nelson, the man who sparked the undertaking, and with consummate wile worked through the Senior Class to get it past Administration apathy and veto, managed to involve the whole community in this production of *For the Time Being*. I said no at first to what he dreamed up for me because I was abashed. He wanted me to write a poem to be used on the program. I could not imagine appearing bracketed with Auden. There is, after all, one's sense of fitness, one's "natural reticence," as Marianne Moore says. But I had something I wanted to say, that I thought was important, and this was an unexpected chance to get it said where some of the young and their parents would read it.

November 15th. Drove up to Mary Washington College somewhat later than usual, as I didn't have to teach until the evening. It was warm enough to have the top down. On the way I tried to work on the poem for the Oratorio program. "Something to do with Christmas," Larry said. It is not easy, for many reasons, and the embarrassment of being read by the community not the least. Of course I think of the 1957 carol in terms of the dead dog in the sky. Man's incredible reply to God.

November 18th. Spent the day, when not at the dentist, working on the poem. Got it finally into the form which satisfies me (as much as anything one writes can) and wrote a note to Larry.

Nov. 19th. Mailed the poem to Larry and ran into him afterward at the Post Office. Then I got a good letter from him liking it, more than liking it. I am glad, because they asked me to do it, and I accepted and came through with it on time. I am more glad of a chance to say something which should be said, where it will be heard.

CHRISTMAS
(1957)

Once above royal David's city
nearly two thousand years ago,
the cherubim, the seraphim,
sang NOEL in the night;
all the jeweled birds of God
in choirs of light
came caroling:
"Make wars throughout the worlds to cease,"
heralding
the visit of the Prince of Peace.

Dormi, dormi tu,
infant Love and Pity,
we will take care of you.

Two days ago,
"a thousand years are as a day,"
and one short night,
we sent that Visitant away.
We will return the visit by and by,
our herald now is in the sky,
to God
        from Man
one carcass of a dog, with love.
NOEL who can.

dormi, dormi tu,
bright galaxies above,
we will take care of you.

Sweet Briar College, Dept. of English. Monday noon (still)
Dear Eve,

I don't have to talk with you (though I like to do that). I'll just tell you something this way, right now.

Your poem hit me hard; it was a shock; the real thing. It *is* "stern"; but that's all right, the sternness has a setting which I can only think is *right*.

And the poem is right. It is "suitable," to use a weak word. I think it is exquisite. It is worthy of its space and place. We shall be proud to have it on our cover. And we shall print it exactly as it is. You will see proof later on. We may ask whether you want your name below or under the title. Thanks so much.

With high regard, and love from us,

                                        Larry

December 3rd. I saw the typescript of the program where the students, touching little things, have thanked me publicly for my "lovely, startling poem," sticking their necks out. Oh well, I have made enough modest disclaiming noises, and really I am very pleased that they wanted it and like it.

December 12th. Miss Stockholm [then Head of the English Department] said the poem was blasphemous. Two of my own students said they didn't understand a word of it. I explained it to them, but not to her. I said no, I was not calling Christ a dead dog, on the contrary, Christ was the Visitant, whom we sent away, by crucifying him. I told them the difference between Visitant and visitor. A Visitant comes with authority to look over a situation and report to those who sent him. I described Visitants arriving unexpectedly at monasteries and convents, staying for a month or so and then departing, with their judgments to be heard from in due course, "when the time is right," the Indians say. I asked them what they would have liked to see go up in Sputnik, representing the human race. I told them that a poem which needed so much explanation couldn't be a good poem.

"Oh no," they cried. "It was only that Miss Stockholm . . ."

"And a member of the Religion Department . . ."

"Said you were calling Christ a dead dog . . ."

"*We* think the poem is wonderful!"

Oh dear! Oh well. Larry meeting me outside the music building kissed my hand. "I've been wanting to do that ever since I read the poem," he said. It seems to have struck him deeply.

Hildegaard Flanner, who is going to write the foreword to the Sweet Briar Annual I am getting together for the fiftieth anniversary, and whose work I love, wrote from California:

"Fine and serious poem, combining as it does traditional melodies and new admonishings, and not easy to accomplish such a fusion of new things and old with just the right [unreadable word here] of shock."

Nancy Hale, up the street a piece in Charlottesville, wrote that it gave her grisly shivers and was altogether wonderful.

So much for that. All it really is, an outraged squawk from a frightened song-bird in the bushes.

December 13th. Still very cold. The Auden Oratorio. Beautiful from the start. I couldn't have believed the dancing would be so good and every single performer sincere and *right*. It was the most thrilling thing I have seen—not only at Sweet Briar, but anywhere, for a long time.

I could never have imagined that this group could do such a lovely, *high* thing as this is!—the only alive and fiery thing to have happened since I got here. I sat alone beside a young man who was yawning when he came, but sitting on the edge of his seat and deeply impressed before he left.

There were other high moments, and there were friends: Lucy Crawford, who taught philosophy in such a way that her students never forgot her, and twenty, thirty, forty years later would come back to sit at her feet and eat her own baked bread. When she died it was my privilege to help collect the material for the moving book which is her memorial at Sweet Briar. She was a warm, staunch friend, standing up to the Destroyers wherever she encountered them. Then there were Harriet Rogers, who lived at Red Top with Lucy Crawford, and John Rust, who built a house near ours, translated Lorca, and had such a passion for George Sand that he believed he was her *valet de chambre* reincarnated in these more distasteful times. I believe he may have been. There was Jovan de Rocco, the painter and architect of the house we built, an old friend from MacDowell Colony; Margaret Bannister, who wrote *Tears Are for the Living* in Charlottesville, near Nancy Hale, another friend from MacDowell days. And chief of friends, Hungarian pianist Iren Marik. I had heard her in London in the thirties when as a young prodigy she took the musical world by storm. Now here she was at Sweet Briar, incongruously brought there by Martha Lucas (Mrs. Maurice Pate of U.N.E.S.C.O.), President of Sweet Briar before Mrs. Pannell. She should, of course, have been at Oberlin, or Juilliard, or, better still, have been free to give all her time to concerts. As it was, the war disrupted everything for her, and for her family. The world's enjoyment of a great artist was limited to the times she could snatch from Academe, and she was often tired and discouraged, bewildered by attitudes she could not understand.

In 1952, when I was still not looking clearly at the degree-granting institution, I was asked to write short profiles of some of the faculty for the alumnae bulletin. About Iren I wrote:

One of the most distinguished, beloved and colorful members of our faculty from foreign countries, Iren Marik came to this country in 1946, exhausted from the hardships and privations of long years of all-out war, bombardment and the enemy occupation of her country. The war had interrupted her unusually brilliant career. She had graduated from one of the finest musical academies in Europe, the Franz Liszt Academy of Music in Budapest, she was a pupil of Imre Stefaniay, and studied with the late Bela Bartók; she had opened her musical career giving recitals in Budapest, Berlin, Munich, Vienna and Rome. Later she spent five years in London, giving frequent recitals and appearing as soloist with some of the finest orchestras in Europe. She played regularly over the London B.B.C. Critics regarded her as a fine musician on her way to becoming one of the great pianists of our time. The London press praised her unusually beautiful "singing legato tone" and her deep, sensitive interpretations.

Then came the interruptions of the war. Miss Marik gave up her profession and went home, where her duty lay, to her country and her family. There followed a time of fear, suffering, lack of food, complete cessation of the exercise of her profession as a pianist, constant helpless anxiety for the lives of people around her, to whom the presence of the enemy meant danger, humiliation, among horrible sights and sounds. Miss Marik does not mention those times, except obliquely. I heard her once say ruefully, looking at her hands, that scrubbing laundry for the Russian soldiers "did not do much to help the fingers to play Bach."

Once when a piano was needed for one of her recitals, Miss Marik went to choose one from Steinway. She had to go through a room where Myra Hess was practicing for her concert at Carnegie Hall next day. Miss Hess stopped playing, greeted Miss Marik cheerfully and called out, "One needs more than one life to learn anything about this, doesn't one?" "Yes," said Miss Marik, "I would like to have three." She is a perfectionist, like Miss Hess, a stern self-critic who is never satisfied with the quality of her playing. She practices on an average five hours a day and considers herself "lazy," but in an unguarded moment she admitted recently that she is in better hand now than ever before.

Critics everywhere always give Iren Marik unusual praise. When her records first appeared, Harold Schonberg in the New York *Times,* in 1958, said, "Miss Marik, a Hungarian-born pianist now resident in America, seldom makes an appearance in concert halls. If this disk is an adequate representation of her abilities, we have been missing much. She plays these interesting Liszt pieces with grand sweep, a very big technique and all the color they need. This kind of singing line, with such an accurate mechanism to boot is not too common nowadays. It is to be hoped that Miss Marik is heard in more Liszt—or indeed, anything she feels like playing."

The Liszt Society of London wrote, on hearing this record:

"I have just been playing it through and must congratulate you very warmly on your performances—they have both poetry and brilliance, and you always seem to get to the heart of the music! Also it is very enterprising of you to record such comparatively little-played works, especially the first version of the Vallée d'Obermann, which I have never heard anyone play in public. In some ways I prefer the later version, but it is certainly very interesting to hear this one. I hope it will be very successful in the States. . . . Humphrey Searle."

Iren made few appearances because she did not dare to give up teaching. She was helping to support her family in Hungary.

She played, during breaks and vacations, in the National Gallery in Washington, in the Guggenheim Art Gallery in New York, and toured many colleges. She also spent one summer in London, giving concerts there and at the Hague.

Not only critics' spirits soared when they heard her. Poets and other artists took fire. May Swenson, hearing her play in a studio built for her in New Hampshire, wrote a poem which appeared in *The New Yorker,* and later in her collection *Cage of Spines.* It is a recognizable glimpse of Iren at the piano, "perceptions of sound, expressed with images." It is interesting, not only because of the subject, but for the insight it gives into the making of a poem.

July 24, 1957

Dear Evelyn:

It was a pleasure to hear from you, and I am more than glad to send a copy of the poem that came from the very great thrill of hearing Iren play a Liszt concerto that day in her cabin-studio in New Hampshire. She really *gave me* this poem, with the extraordinary feeling that she put into that informal performance and that transferred itself to me. It was something very special; I feel that she is a great musician, not only technically, but spiritually —in the basic sense of that word—she infuses something much more, and more rare, than skill and intelligence into her interpretation, reaching to the deepest and most secret nerves of emotion in the hearer.

In this poem, perceptions of sound are expressed with images. Not so much the images aroused by Liszt's music, as by the interpreter's involvement with the music—as if a reflection of her inner self was revealed while she played. The visual metaphor: the woman at the piano, her arms over the keyboard like swans' necks over a lake's mirror, was the starting point of the poem. Then it tries to say what went on in her, and what rippled out to me, emotionally. Please tell Iren that I am very grateful for the experience of hearing her play. She is a powerful artist.

I'm to be at Breadloaf the last two weeks of August—will see Nancy Hale there, I believe—and after that, coming to MacDowell for six weeks, so that I'll look forward to meeting you again in September.

Many thanks for writing.

Sincerely,
May Swenson

TO HER IMAGES
for I.M.

As if the aimed
        heads of swans
        with reaching necks
        their napes curved
        came to their images
To the glozed
        the sleeping surface
        black-white-beamed
        her hands on sinuous arms
        the wrists reared dipped
Dilations of light ran
        rapid and chill
        from the high splints
        on the panel
Lower the fingers
        spanned plunged like bills
        and slower orbits began
        and opened
A kind of dawn awoke
        clean in the bone
        of the ear
        clear lake-lappings
        against the steady
        breasts of swans
Targets in the brain
        were pierced by rays
        glancing from the poises
        of those scarcely plucking
        beaks on the keys'
        reflected pinions
Then prongs ripped
        a heavy element
        strong muscled like whirlpool
        flinching the heart's drumskin
Whips of light across the eyes
        those swans
        and her body dived
In groans as of great
        stones embracing under water
        she came to her images
Then silence a long
        mirror rose upright

Warren Carrier, a different sort of poet, stranded for a semester—or was it two?—at Sweet Briar, heard Iren play, ate the good bread she made, and

279

came to spend his evenings and spare moments in her living room. He wrote, in the *Virginia Quarterly*, his impressions of an hour when she talked about the siege.

This poem too evokes Iren for those who know her.

LISZT AND THE RUSSIAN SOLDIER
for Iren Marik

Her man-strong hands that made the lovely Liszt
Sweet bread we ate, catch themselves in talk
—Or as she booms her laugh, *molto subito,*
In irony—against the new invaders:
Time, indifference, exile.
                         As we watch,
She wanders rooms in Budapest, hides
Beneath the stair with radium, neighbors' jewels,
A surgeon's instruments, against the Russian
Who, welcomed, took their watches, clocks, smashed
Glass jars, slashed a canvas on the wall
And promised to return for all the ladies
Of the house. *This one for the Captain.*

Hands clasped that but a little played
Our Liszt, or but a little washed the soldier's
Shirt, in this strange land rehearse their beauty.
Their strength will hold our enemy at bay.
In this Budapest we all are lost,
Lonely, and at home.

One summer in New Hampshire, in the studio May Swenson visited, which friends had built for Iren, on the edge of woods overlooking a hillside and a pool, there had been three years of desolate silence. All the birds were gone, after an orgy of misdirected spraying. Iren came there "on vacation," to practice, her usual five hours a day, more often seven, since she was free of teaching. The Beethoven sonatas, Liszt's *Bénédiction de Dieu dans la Solitude,* his *Saint Francis and the Birds,* Debussy, Ravel, Bartók could be heard two miles away. Presently the woods were filled with birds, madly answering. They sang so loud for certain pieces that she could hardly hear herself play. Nature responds, how gratefully, to beauty, to truth.

Humans answer too. Poets write poems, painters paint, dancers dance, gardeners garden, with renewed zest. Notes and letters and flowers and wine arrive. Iren responds. She gives parties. People look forward to her parties, avidly. They come to her home for comfort and never leave forlorn. She feeds them with gourmet Hungarian food, relaxation and laughter, then shoos them out with "Mosst you stay? Can't you go? I have to get opp early."

We have been friends and fellow fighters for the arts for twenty-three years, sharing the things that matter, music, poetry, our homes, our interests, our ups-and-downs, our fun, in a way that amazes those who know us both for very independent, sometimes hard to get along with people. I don't believe two musicians could have done it, or two writers, or two anythings too much alike, or the spoiled and pampered or the idle. Two wanderers, displaced from Europe in our middle years, done with many complications and illusions, devoted to a larger service than ourselves, we became Waysharers, "two with a light that match their steps and sing."

It is one of the great blessings of my life, for which I thank the Grandfathers. But even Iren could not keep me at Sweet Briar when the abrasions of the snubbing goodbyes became too depressing, too much a waste of spirit.

One example I remember, because it involved the students, hurt their feelings and trod on their right pride. In 1959 a history of the college was published. Under the section headed *English,* it stated: "Since 1950 there have been no changes in the English courses, except for a new section in Remedial Reading." Nineteen-fifty was the year that I arrived at Sweet Briar, set up a four-year Creative Writing course with an outstanding writers' workshop that won recognition far and wide—off campus, in the professional literary world.

This was remedial reading? I might have thought the omission was an honest mistake, the work of an editor who didn't know or care to check what had been happening at Sweet Briar during those nine years, since her day, or didn't know, and had no one to do it for her, how to glance into the catalogue or the campus newspaper, which usually mentioned the writers' workshop . . . but the report was signed by the Head of my department, the only Head of the English Department who I thought was a friend. Moreover, in case I should miss the point, my photograph appeared, without permission being asked, so that I couldn't pretend that I wasn't there, at Sweet Briar, seated among students from the workshop, teaching, presumably, remedial reading.

For a while the Sweet Briar poets and novelists and playwrights went around calling themselves Remedial Writers, but the joke wore thin and it wasn't overfunny to begin with. A chance had been lost which might have lifted their spirits in pride, pleased their parents, and given Sweet Briar a legitimate boost . . . but no. The albatross was down on the flat deck to die.

Some of them resented the intentional snub for my sake, and said so, but I was so used to two or three of this sort of thing a week that I hardly cared, except for them. I didn't like the students being hurt to get at me. I could see a growing, ugly pattern, and so after one or two more nonsenses not worth reviving here, I said the goodbye that They had been shoving me toward for so long a time, and then I was asked to "reconsider" my resignation. I saw nothing to reconsider. I would lose my home, my job, my only income, all the good work I had done and the course I had built, I would lose the garden, the dog, and what my soul fed on, Iren's music . . . but still there was nothing to reconsider.

So one fine day in 1960 I was gone and they could whistle for me. I went as far as I could get from the place, all the way to California, in a little green Corvair, with no money, no security, no plans, no prospects, and a great lifting and bubbling of the spirits.

"Baa now," I said in my best Virginian twang, "*Baa*."

The next place that I taught at—unexpectedly, for I went there as the woman who came to dinner, to give a talk, and stayed for two exciting years —was different from Sweet Briar, Mary Washington, Columbia, Ohio University, Pershing and all the other degree-granting institutions where I have worked or spoken, in the United States.

"Deep Springs, California, via Dyer Nevada," like its address in two states at once, seems on the face of it to be impossible, yet it exists, in that magic region where the Inyo-White Mountains, which the Paiutes call High Home of a Great Spirit, shoulder down into Nevada, among abandoned mines and faded trails to nowhere, in a desert valley on a high plateau, twelve miles long by four miles wide, at an elevation of 5200 feet, with a lake, mirage and alkali at one end, and an oasis, real and startling, at the other. An avenue of shade trees brought in, I was told, from Russia leads to a ring of low stone buildings. The only trees, the only buildings—Deep Springs College.

The valley has its layered history. Once there were the Paiutes, and the tribes before them, as petroglyphs and artifacts attest; then there was a boom town, with an opera house, a bank, a big hotel; then a ghost town, of ruined foundations, with only the tollgate at the pass and a station for the stagecoach left of all its glories; then a solitary cattle ranch, the Swinging T, bought to make the college founded by Lucien L. Nunn in 1917.

Mr. Nunn was ahead of his time. He has been dead for forty-seven years, but the educational world is just beginning, here and there, to discover some of his ideas.

As the student handbook says about him:

> Lucien L. Nunn was a lifelong pioneer. His energy, his vision, and his dissatisfaction with the ordinary led him into experiments which created new industries for others and a fortune for himself. . . . In 1881 he settled in Telluride, Colorado, then a prosperous mining town. Most of the mines near Telluride suffered from the high costs of transporting coal to above-timberline locations. The possibilities of alternating-current power had been considered but never tried. Direct current could not be transmitted the needed distances. Mr. Nunn, ignoring professional skepticism and his own scanty knowledge of electric-power transmission, determined to supply the mines with electricity. He encouraged George Westinghouse to build the world's first alternating-current motor at the Gold King mine, and powered it with a primitive generator at Ames, Colorado. This plant so reduced power costs that more plants were soon in demand, and not just in the mines. Long-distance transmission opened a whole new industry and was the key to the development of hydro-electric power. Mr. Nunn formed companies and built plants throughout the

country, including the first plant to tap the potential of the Niagara River at Niagara Falls. His Telluride Power Company eventually maintained plants in Colorado, Utah, Montana, Idaho, and Wyoming.

Needing the right kind of men to operate the delicate electrical machinery, he had "a vision of an education which would inspire young men to dedicate themselves to the general good and which would help them to make that dedication wise, imaginative and resourceful."

By the time he came to found Deep Springs he had come to feel that education was more important than industry, "the goal of training men to operate the power plants had become a more general one of training leaders to serve the nation. The academic emphasis shifted from engineering to the liberal arts."

By 1917 "his first concern was combating the widespread materialism and commercialism which he saw undermining society."

His way of doing this was to take twenty young men, never more, the brightest whom he could find, remove them from the pollution and confusion of any big city, place them in surroundings of majestic grandeur and rugged demands, give them three years in which to do the work of two, give them a superlative library, an excellent faculty of five, give them complete responsibility for themselves, complete autonomy—he went so far as to make the student body, that is, the students in attendance at Deep Springs at any given time, "the sole beneficiaries of a trust." They "are to be considered as the true owners of all the property . . . with the full right, power and authority of democratic self-government in accordance with the traditions and the ideals and policies of Deep Springs . . . including the full control of the conduct of its members and of the buildings used as student dormitories, and the power to veto the dismissal of any member during the school year, but not the power to dismiss any member; the right of the Student Body to maintain its organization and hold its meetings under such rules and regulations as it may adopt and with no one present but its own members except on its own invitation. . . ."

This, in 1917, was quite a constitution, even now most colleges do not legally belong to the student body. But it is when we come to the "ideals and policies" that Deep Springs is such an extraordinary place.

The student has absolutely no financial expenses. He receives a full room-board-and-tuition scholarship, but, as one student wrote, "There is nothing free about it. It may take him all his life to repay what he was given here." And another said: "As Deep Springs guards against turning out practical experts without ideals, so also it guards against producing idealists without practical ability. It aims to produce practical idealists, who will be of lasting influence in work of lasting value."

This may sound like the rhetoric of typical college bulletins. The difference is that at Deep Springs it happens to be true.

The students must work twenty hours a week on general projects. There is a ranch, with horses and a herd of cattle, which must be well maintained. "Student dairymen milk the cows, make butter and sometimes cheese. The feed man feeds the dairy cows, horses, pigs and chickens; he collects and markets eggs. In the spring he raises chicks. He is responsible for finishing, slaughtering and dressing beef and pork for ranch consumption. The water-boy maintains the pipe lines, ditches, sand traps and reservoir which bring drinking and irrigation water to the ranch. An office man helps the secretary and operates the bookstore. One student washes and irons student college laundry, etc., etc." "The student's sense of responsibility is strengthened by the fact that all jobs are necessary and must be done well for the successful functioning of the whole institution. The work program thus provides an impressive experience in community responsibility and citizenship."

And the ideals? There are mysterious hints of them in some of Mr. Nunn's letters to the student body:

> The desert has a deep personality; it has a voice; and God speaks through its personality and voice. Great leaders in all ages have sought the desert and heard its voice. You can hear it if you listen, but you cannot hear it while in the midst of uproar and strife for material things. Gentlemen, for what came ye into the wilderness? Not for conventional scholastic training; not for ranch life; not to become proficient in commercial or professional pursuits for personal gain. You came to prepare for a life of service, with the understanding that superior ability and generous purpose would be expected of you, and this expectation must be justified. Even in scholastic work, average results obtained in ordinary school will not be satisfactory. The desert speaks. Those who listen will hear the purpose, philosophy and ethics of Deep Springs. . . . Listen to the voice of the desert, and you will receive from it enthusiasm and inspiration.

The yearbook of 1961, when I was there, shows a photograph of one of the graduating seniors, looking startled, disheveled and distraught. The caption runs: "Obviously the Voice has spoken!" There was a lot of good-humored joking, under the rigid controls the students kept over themselves and each other.

There was no top-heavy administration, no red tape, no faculty committees, all we had to do—what a frustrated dream that is on other campuses—was to *teach*. When my term as first writer-in-residence at Deep Springs came to an end, I was asked to stay on as the French Department. I taught two years of college French in one, with ease, because there was no apathy among the students. I had a large class, half the student enrollment, that is, ten. After 140 at Sweet Briar, considered part-time, this was rather fun, and then they were so bright, such unusually interesting students. I was the first woman on the faculty. I am proud of both those firsts, but for me, as for the others in that strange community, it was the place and the life that caught me.

Activities, the handbook states: "The valley must be explored. Students sleep out at night in the summer with an unobstructed galaxy above them." Not only students. I did too, for many star-filled nights in the desert, smelling of crushed sage.

"The work accounts for much physical exercise at Deep Springs. Most other exercise comes from walking, hiking and riding. The Student Body controls two or three horses which are available to students at any time. Students ride herd and participate in roundups."

Once when they were shorthanded I joined them to ride herd. I had no idea of Western saddle and guiding a horse by loose reins on his neck, but I was coached and expected to catch on. I rode a sturdy brown—cob—we would have called him in England, with no manners and a mulish disposition. We grew accustomed to each other's clashes of will. I learned the rudiments of rounding up calves, and generally guiding the herd toward the corral for spring branding.

The students teased me about my "Eastern style," and took me for perilous scrambles on rocky canyon slopes. Once I dismounted and led the cob down, slipping and sliding, because, I said, "I ride for fun, and when it isn't fun, when it's an ordeal, I don't go on. . . . I don't need to *prove* anything, even to myself." Then they confessed that they were scared too, and had never ridden there before. They had just wanted to see what I would do.

During the cattle roundup the mail brought me a sudden communication from Helen, in far-off, forgotten England. She sent me a pair of shoulder-length white kid gloves. I was touched that she remembered my size, but I couldn't help wondering what would happen if, added to my Eastern seat and fancy boots, I wore shoulder-length white kid gloves to bring up the herd. I still have the gloves, unworn, a memorial to a statelier past.

"Freedom of movement is the key to a student's absorption of the environment." It was the key to mine, too. Imagine being paid for riding, for living in a place like that, for exploring, with ideal young companions, a fantastic landscape like the other side of the moon. I was in the position of the young man with the convertible who could get the prettiest girls to ride with him—I had one of the first four-wheel-drive Scouts off the assembly line. I could go anywhere I wanted to with anyone I chose to go with me. "You may drive it," I said, "but I go with the deal."

"Comparatively little time is spent in class." That was true of the French Department. We did our irregular verbs out on the mountainsides. Much practical fluency was developed, since during French hours I understood no English, and when I was driving it became necessary to be able to shout "Watch out!" "No, not *there*" and other directions in French.

"There are no dormitory hours. There are no watchful house mothers. The student is free to take a midnight walk, to sleep in the desert, or even to live in a cabin as a hermit so long as he fulfills his responsibilities."

"And in all this," Mr. Nunn wrote in *The Purpose of Deep Springs,* "the student is left to discover and achieve from within."

I do not know what Mr. Nunn would have felt about a woman writer on campus, or a woman member of the faculty, but I think, since he pioneered in so many ways, he might have in that. At any rate I shall always be grateful for my two years there. It is one of the few places left where there is still a sense of the interdependence of the two-legged, four-legged and winged people, and their relationship to the earth supporting them.

I remember talking to a group down by the lake—mostly mirage—about Boswell and Pascal Paoli and a particular discussion they once had on a subject that has fascinated human beings since the Garden of Eden.

"He has a mind fitted for philosophical speculations as well as for affairs of state," Boswell wrote in his invaluable diary. "One evening at supper he entertained us for some time with some curious reveries and conjectures as to the nature of the intelligence of beasts, with regard to which he observed human knowledge was as yet very imperfect. He in particular seemed fond of inquiring into the language of the brute creation. In different ages there have been people who pretended to understand the language of birds and beasts. 'Perhaps,' said Paoli, 'in a thousand years we may know this as well as we know things which appeared much more difficult to be known.' I have often since this conversation indulged myself in such reveries. If it were not liable to ridicule, I would say that an acquaintance with the language of beasts would be a most agreeable acquisition to man, as it would enlarge the circle of his social intercourse."

We sat there thinking about Boswell wanting to enlarge his social circle by conversing with the animals, on a day in June, when tensions ease, and we were able to stand and stare and indulge in "curious reveries."

The Accreditation Committee had come and gone—the college got its accreditation the year that I was there—the visiting trustees had come and gone, the summer break was ahead.

Where would one begin with this interchange? A start had been made, of course, with dolphins. I heard a story which I hope is true, that one dolphin being trained to assist the Navy speaks with a Southern accent because his teacher was a Southerner. Dolphins appear to have quite as good brains as we have, and to be more pleasant and more innocent, because, lacking hands, they have not been able to do so much harm as man the killer.

If Boswell, armed with a man-animal dictionary, had launched himself upon a grand tour of the West, he would probably have made directly for the High Sierra, for Inyo, the White Mountains, the Upper Deserts, this valley, to speak with remaining wild inhabitants, the endangered species, and a few enlightened two-leggeds. He would certainly have come down to this small strip of water by the withered lake to speak to a distinguished exile—*buffo exilu*—the frog in exile. There is no one like him in this country, or anywhere in the world unless some far-off part of Asia from which his forebears came.

How they got here and when, no one knows, unless he kept a record handed down to him, and would enlighten us. Why he is where he is can be grasped without the need of Boswell's dictionary. He cannot live any higher, he cannot live any lower. He must have a little water, sun and the sort of food to be found in this particular place. He is a lustrous black with distinctive markings and fringes, he is smaller than most frogs and very friendly.

While I was at Deep Springs it was feared that he might be in danger of extinction because of excessive inbreeding. An attempt was made to introduce him to a lady who lived, in similar circumstances, but a little lower in altitude. Alas, she could not live at his altitude and he could not descend to hers. The lovers died, but their relatives survived. Boswell would have sighed over this story. I am glad to report that in the spring of 1973 *buffo exilu* was flourishing, however inbred he may have become.

It was at Deep Springs that I caught my first glimpse of another threatened species, the bighorn sheep. One morning at sunrise, after a night spent on the valley floor, I saw three of them silhouetted against the horizon on the top of a steep escarpment, rising, unclimbable, above the lake.

I never have come nearer, but all about this part of the country, from Panamint through parts of Death Valley to the Coso Range, there is the record of the great herds of the past. Petroglyphs and pictographs show the importance of these sheep to the ancient peoples who lived here before the Shoshones and the Paiutes. Most of the rock drawings date from about three thousand years ago, according to the desert patina, lichen, and other means of determination. There are three periods, early, transitional and late, differing from each other in important details and easily recognizable. By the time the late period was reached it is evident that something like the cult of the buffalo by the Plains tribes had developed round the bighorn sheep. Like the buffalo the sheep was the chief supply of food, clothing, cooking fat and other useful prized objects from the horns and hooves.

The early rock carvings appear to be a form of hunter-magic, a ritualistic aid to success in capturing the sheep, like the paintings of extinct animals in the Palaeolithic caves of France and Spain. They show concentrations of thousands of bighorn, with hunters using atlatls or bows and dogs helping them. But later the human figures do not seem to be hunters. They are ceremonial figures, shaman-priests in full regalia, with horned or feathered heads, and medicine bags, minutely designed, of different shapes and patterns. Mostly they carry sticks, one in the right hand and three in the left, but no weapons for the hunt.

These figures, which Campbell Grant in his book *Rock Drawings of the Coso Range* calls "Patterned-body Anthromorphs of the Transitional and Late Periods," the Paiutes refer to more poetically, and perhaps more accurately. They are the costumed participants in the vanished Bighorn rite, like dancers participating in the Buffalo ceremonies on the plains. In one place high on a canyon wall there are several figures wearing unmistakable sheep horns, while beneath them there are stones worn smooth as though they had been used as seats from which to view a ceremony held on the valley floor. There is also a group of dancing figures, doing a step easily recognizable and still danced today.

I sat there once, on a polished stone, awed by the grandeur of the place, the solitude, the strong vibrations, wishing there were someone, sheep or man, to converse with about these mysteries. But they are gone, they have been gone for hundreds, more probably for thousands of years. Only the rocks remain, and on the rocks these innocent and joyful patterns that lift the heart and mind to the Great Imagination Who created sheep and shaman and carver.

> They are gone
> the great herds,
> the hunters,
> the dancers,
> gone.

> Weathered shapes remain
> pecked into the rock.
> As long as rock endures,
> As long as earth turns,
> men and sheep will dance
> horned ones dance
> *here*
> to Numi-na'a.

I saw no bighorn drawings near Deep Springs itself, but there were three rocks with clear pictures of the Great Medicine Wheel, the Sun and linked circles. I went sometimes to sit near them, and as in Callian in far-off France I was healed of physical illness, so at Deep Springs I was healed of a troubled mind, a sore and smarting spirit. I grew strong in the desert.

Part Seven

I did not go directly to Deep Springs from Sweet Briar. I went to the Huntington Hartford Foundation in Rustic Canyon, Pacific Palisades, where I had been granted a four-month fellowship to work on *The King Is a Witch*. It was not my first experience of foundations, or artists' colonies. I had been given several fellowships at the MacDowell Colony, beginning in the summer of 1948 when Mrs. MacDowell was still in residence, ending with two winter sessions, 1968 and 1969. MacDowell is unique in the world as a working refuge for creative people. I wrote parts of many books there, always the best parts. In the dedication of *I Saw My Mortal Sight* I wrote:

> For Ann and Roger Burlingame, and for the late Marian MacDowell in gratitude for her courage and wisdom in founding the MacDowell Colony, where writers, composers, painters and sculptors find what they need to create their best works—freedom, isolation, respect for achievement . . . dynamic peace.

Huntington Hartford was not like MacDowell in many essential ways. While I was there I always had the uneasy feeling that the Whitneys were raising horses in their canyon next door, and "Hunt" was raising artists in his, and there was no question which animal was the better investment. At MacDowell one was made to feel that achievement mattered, that we and our work were important, respected, even cherished. At Huntington Hartford we were made to feel, chiefly at meals which we took under the eye of non-creative people, that we were bankrupt freaks, and there was a sub-current of contempt . . . not so sub either, for us and our values.

Still, it was a beautiful place, at the bottom of a canyon, with exotic flowers and shrubs, and strange hillside steps, built by a Faithist colony (OAHPSE). They had meditated there, waiting for the end of the world. Their part of the place had good vibrations, a supernatural undertone of sudden rushing forces. The rest didn't.

There were some MacDowell Fellows at Huntington Hartford, to form a nucleus of mutual support, like Lee Leatherman, who wrote the superb classic book about Martha Graham. Faces brightened when Lee appeared. His sunny wit was contagious and more than once he saved us from a dreary day. There was Colin McPhee, the composer, who wrote *A House in Bali,* a nostalgic, enchanting account of early Balinese music, and who did so much to revive the classic gamelan ensembles in that country.

Colin was supposed to be a prickly pear, apt to be rude, especially to women. I was warned to steer clear of him, which made me perversely want to do the opposite. Perhaps that was all that was needed to dispel the legend. For some reason I amused him and he was gentle and charming, and let himself be teased. He took me to see his collection of Balinese instruments, which he had presented to U.C.L.A., and even let me play a gamelan in an impromptu performance.

There was Paul Earls, another composer, who wanted to make *Flight* into an opera, which over the years he did, although our contract expired in 1968 without a performance. We had hoped to put it on in the Deepest Valley Theatre, at the foot of Mount Whitney, sponsored by the Draco Foundation of California, of which we were founding members.

Blanche Dombek was at Huntington Hartford too. I had not run across her since she fell off a scaffolding at MacDowell and broke her back, a disaster for a sculptor from which she made a brave and fantastic recovery. She was working on a group of thirty-two beeswax figures which she called *The Spiritual Army.* They became the visual inspiration for *The Progression,* later performed at Oberlin, with my text and Joseph Wood's music.

Arnold Freed was there, from MacDowell days, and Jean Starr Untermeyer, with a fund of stories on literary life in the thirties and forties.

There were others, MacDowell in spirit, if not in experience. . . . Charles Rogers, the painter, with his wry humor and his Indian empathy. "I mix my paint with emulsions, buy my metaphors with grit." "Truth in a painting does not depend upon size—recognition of it often does." "A hippopotamus looks as if he might have been designed by someone with a degree in art education." "The life of an artist is like that of a captive elephant—he performs a hard task and gets a peanut for it." "Life is too short to squander it with success." "The spirit flies as a bird, the mind travels as a turtle."

Turtles are familiar Western Indian symbols. Much of Rogers' painting looks like lava outcroppings in the Inyo-Mono mountains. There was one of these that I particularly liked. "What is that?" I asked naively. "It's called 'What can you expect of a day that begins in the morning?'" he answered gravely, but there was a disconcerting, coyote sort of twinkle in his eyes. "I'm doing a companion piece, 'What can we hope from a night that ends in the evening?'"

It is hard to describe foundation, colony life to those who will never have a need for it. Who in their senses would elect to surround themselves with twenty-five temperamental geniuses, to get a piece of work underway? Yet it worked for many at MacDowell, and did at Huntington Hartford, for the brief while "Hunt" ran his imitation colony as a tax deduction.

When I first went to MacDowell and for several years after that Mrs.

MacDowell was still controlling the colony from her home nearby. A random extract from my diary says: "I got a very nice reception from everyone and worked in the library where Dika Newlin and Barbara Portland played some exciting four-handed Bach and other things. Peter Gray gave me a surreptitious highball. . . ." Surreptitious because Mrs. MacDowell, much in evidence at the colony still, disapproved of drinking and always declared that there was none at MacDowell. In the same way, ignoring or perhaps kept ignorant of many daytime goings-on, she behaved as if immorality began after 6 P.M., and if she could keep us at croquet, Ping-Pong and other traditional Mac-Dowell pursuits after supper, we would go to bed in a healthily abstemious frame of mind, ready to work hard the next day.

There was no electricity in the studios. We went to them stealthily, after the children's hour and the formal goodnights, and there by the light of obliging moons, or small discreet fires in the big stone chimneys, romance continued.

Mrs. MacDowell's surveillance made everything more magically wicked than it can be nowadays. People in the grip of a MacDowell romance spent hours crawling through the bushes with their baskets to a rendezvous for lunch. One married couple whom she had placed, one in the men's dormitory and one in the women's "Eaves," and to whom she allotted studios the length of the colony apart, said it was quite a second honeymoon, and most distracting to their work.

Distraction to someone else's work was the reason given for Mrs. Mac-Dowell's hopeful precautions. She had one anti-feminist quirk. If she learned of an affair between a man and a woman, married or unmarried, she sent away the woman. There was only one rule, besides the unwritten ones of tradition and "Mrs. MacDowell feels." That was if anyone went to another's studio *uninvited,* at any time, that person must leave MacDowell at once, and would not be permitted to return. That rule, or the spirit of that rule, with the stress on *uninvited,* remains as one of the great advantages of the colony. It means that you and you alone control your working time. Nowadays there is electricity and running water in the studios, and you are free, if the afflatus strikes, to rise and walk openly with flashlight, or to drive with headlight, to your studio, and there, lights blazing, do what you choose, with no interruption.

In Mrs. MacDowell's day no cars were allowed, no bicycles or other means of transport, within the colony gates . . . except for hers. She was liable to arrive at any moment, in early years by pony cart, later by car, breaking her own rule, to see how you were faring, to bring you wood or mail, or what she thought you might be needing. It made for some uncertainty and tension in the sanctuary of the studios. There was a wonderful drawing on a wooden shutter in one of them, of a pine tree bending down to peer in the window—with Mrs. MacDowell's face.

In one of my early summers at the colony, when a few conventions were still in force, before the days of total liberation, I was working in Sprague-Smith, which I liked, because it was a little apart from the rest, in a cul de sac less liable to be visited. It was a scorching day. I was typing with nothing on, my clothes in a heap at the far end of the room, when suddenly wheels spurted to the door. I had only time to leap toward an easel, still in place from a painter's former occupancy, and strike a Rubinesque pose near it, with my back to the door, hoping whoever came would think a painter was at work in the shadows.

I heard a little gasp, a murmur of, "Oh, I didn't know they worked from *models*," then the group of elderly ladies, "Friends of the Colony" whom Mrs. MacDowell was taking for a tour of the grounds, went away. Later that evening she came into Colony Hall for a few moments. While she was there she asked one of the fellows, "How many painters are here this summer?" They were named and numbered for her, but she still looked puzzled, her eyes straying vaguely over us.

September 2nd. The changeover of colonists. A sinking feeling to find all these new faces, and none of them particularly *sympathique*. To supper beside a scrubby little composer, evidently very "great" if greatness consists in self-boosting, eating with your mouth open, coming to table unwashed, unshaven, and being rude to everyone, especially to me (there's the rub!). Later dropped into the library after croquet and heard some interesting music, and so to bed.

Sept. 8th. With everyone else saying they have written 30,000 words or nearly finished their books, or completed their projects, I feel dismayed. I have only begun mine and here it is getting to be the end of my time here. I do not like alibis, and when I sum up accomplishment I am appalled. Several book reviews for the NY *Times* and *Saturday Review*. One story taken by *The New Yorker*. One long piece rehashed, and that is all. After lunch *heavenly* music, two-piano Bach through which some Philistines played loud pool. I have come a long way to be able to bear it, looking back on my intolerance when anyone *stirred* during music, but should one tolerate it? Pool through Bach I mean.

June 2nd 1950. What a day! Clear and sunny and full of air and a lovely noise of trees around my studio. No other studio that I've been in has this sound of trees. It reminds me of the hammocks in my childhood.

June 10. Politics even here. First brush with the enemy. Padraic Colum, whose work I've always loved, especially *Cradle Song*, is a disappointment . . . so many of us are liabilities to our own work. He and his wife have been rude and cliquey, and now he is making a drive for power to oust the present director . . . mostly because she's a woman, I think. At breakfast he announced a ballot to be taken, and I found my name on it without his asking me. I took it off, and so did three others, leaving only two, one of them Padraic. He announced the nominating committee would meet again and begin another list tonight. As dear Mr. Neagoe said: "Not vit entoosiasm is he gritted." And Margery Fischer wrote a limerick about "Colums right, and no one being bereft if Colums left!" She is a very witty woman who seems to me to talk her best work away. This sort of thing is not what I came up here for. There is enough of that in the Pen and Brush.

When I think of MacDowell I think of walking back from my studio, swinging my basket, past an open door with the sound of a flute spilling out, another with a sound of chiseling and hammering, seeing ahead of me a colonist's back, and knowing from his walk that his day has been successful. I think of great pine trees, the shadows beneath them, old stone walls, Monadnock in the distance, meals with exhilarating discussions. I think of winter sessions, being whirled to my studio in a snowmobile, the year of the great snow. I think of crackling fires. I think of a small group in Louise Talma's studio listening to her play with one hand on a tinny piano, and rap with the other on a table, a ghostlike version, a wraith of her *Time To Remember*, and suddenly before us marched the funeral procession for John F. Kennedy, raising goose pimples of remembrance, while she sang all the parts, even somehow the chorus, in her nonexistent "composer's voice," the faintest dry whispering, yet how evocative! As moving as the full performance when I heard it later in New York, with all of us in concert regalia. I think of Debby DeMoulpied in her studio among the strange floating shapes of her shell-like moving forms, the coloring, the lights . . . the whole mysterious cosmos turning there, suspended from the ceiling on black fishlines. One could have watched them forever. I think of Aspasia Voulis and her structures, about whom a MacDowell poet, Winfield Townley Scott, wrote in the *New Mexico Quarterly*, Spring 1967:

ASPASIA THE STRUCTURIST

Aspasia
Who is
Of course
Greek
Paints slabs of upson board
White.
Then she paints
Little blocks, off-square, oblong,
Yellow
Or
Blue
Or
Red
Or
Black,
Even white.
She glues them
On the board
In arrangements
And shows them to the sun,
Sometimes to us.
As the earth turns
Aspasia's mix of colored blocks

Glow
Like visible music
While their shadows
Sway slowly over.
They are alive
Yet make serious joy.
As for us
We forget despair
That we no longer find
The coal
For the snowman's
Eyes.

I think of Paul Nordoff, playing on an old upright piano in the rain, in the woods, near MacDowell's grave, to honor Mrs. MacDowell's death, and of his selfless career, composing for retarded children, helping them to perform in groups.

I think of things I learned from what people said.

"A number of points have been underlined for me this month, through Paul Nordoff a reminder of standards and of Ned Sheldon and of There. By Nancy Hale, to write out beforehand what I am to say in the next chapter, each time, so that I say it . . . *construction*. A glimpse of Thornton Wilder, reminding me of him and his works, and the first awed moment I had in Woods Studio when I found the upright desk he worked at, and his comment on the wooden board: 'Just a tired teacher.' This connection, however nebulous, with the man who wrote *The Ides of March* is a proud thing for someone who started off as I did. Then by Margaret Beck, that one must create 'with love,' and much of my book is from hate. (This also means trying to love those young things I have to teach later on.) Also from Paul Nordoff a reminder of reincarnation and karma, 'every moment you are working out the past and creating the future.' "

I think of my MacDowell "Clives" before I gave up Clives, of Henry, the first one, with his silk black hair (again an Indian!), I think of friends and enemies. The friends and enemies made at MacDowell go deep and last for life.

I think of Cid Ricketts Sumner, for whom I was asked to write a memorial when she was killed in 1970. I wrote:

I first met Cid in the summer of 1956, at the MacDowell Colony, where she was writing *Traveler in the Wilderness* and recovering from a serious operation, to which, however, she was obviously "paying no mind." She was occupying Veltin, the studio where E. A. Robinson wrote for twenty years. It suited her, with its view of Monadnock and the poet's shade for company.

"Long evenings at MacDowell," she wrote, "unless E. A. Robinson drops in. I've just seen his picture in a biography. He looked much happier this summer in Veltin, otherwise the same. No glasses, either, a hint that our physical disabilities will disappear along with the rest of the mortal coil? I know too now, having skimmed his life, why he came to *me*."

Many people came to Cid. Once when she thought she might not return to the colony she wrote:

LINES FOR ONE LEAVING MAC DOWELL
AND THINKING OF NO RETURN

I'll come no more to that enchanted wood
Where scent of fern and spice of pine are met
Where all day long I heard the hermit thrush
And dark against the sky Monadnock stood.
Some things too rare for repetition are
And closer keep when they are kept afar.

To which a disturbed colonist who saw the poem replied:

"I'll come no more to that enchanted wood,"
Chill
ran through the grove,
surprise
silenced the birds
and set a desolation in their eyes
who heard the words.
Trees, grown taller from her accolade,
stretched in the poignancy of "this, the last . . ."
argued: "because of some commitments that she made,
certain delicate spells she cast,
she will
come many times to this enchanted wood,
pass here forever part of sun and shade,
visible only to the good."

Cid is a part of MacDowell.

Playing Ping-Pong in Colony Hall with nonchalant grace and deadly precision, she nearly always won, yet no one seemed to lose.

In the library, listening to others' works, or reading from her own, or once, at a memorable Christmas party where heights of joy were reached, summing up from her center near the fire:

"When people ask us how we spent Christmas this year, murmur a little sadly, 'in the library.'"

There were whoops of appreciation as there always were when Cid chose to sum up something.

"Cid is sun-warmed rocky strength," a man said of her once. "Wisdom, wit and tenderness," a woman wrote.

Her wit was kind when she encouraged the lazy or the disheartened with an astringent word, or even a slight blow on the shoulder.

Mostly, perhaps, in passage, walking through the woods, looking beautiful, the essence of the last *grande dame*. People watching Cid underwent a sea change as they encountered *style* (sometimes for the first time).

At Scrabble, with the Ping-Pong technique, this time of mental whammy, inventing outrageous words, with absurd and combustible meanings, so the most sullen laughed . . . and the dictionary tried to back her up. Sometimes it did in footnotes, to her own surprise. No one lost against Cid.

Now that we must meet her in memory and her books, it is still Cid who finds the right, apt word. Writing of the death of an old friend, she said:

"Today a part of me withdrew. This diminution of myself . . ."

Diminution, yes. But augmentation too, a widening, a deepening of the spirit. Surely they walk a little taller who were friends and fellow colonists of Cid, of Cid Ricketts Sumner.

When I think of MacDowell, I think of the place and of people, and of music. I think of listening in the library to composers who were also performers, playing the great classics. I think of Iren Marik playing there, one weekend that she had come to New Hampshire to give a recital to the "Friends of MacDowell" on the piano where so many composers played. I think of the brilliant young Mack Schleffer, playing all of MacDowell's piano works in the evenings to anyone who cared to listen, and sometimes to me alone. I think of him later, conducting Iren with the Ridgefield Symphonette in MacDowell's Concerto No. 2. I think of replaying the tape of this performance, in the library, and also here in the California desert to groups of interested listeners who would not hear it otherwise.

I think of continuity, MacDowell continuity. . . . Joseph Wood composing *The Progression* in the studio where later I worked on *Go Ask the River,* and where I was able to play the tape of the premiere of *The Progression* in the room where it first came to birth and again in the library to a group of fellows, and later here in the desert.

And I think of Marian MacDowell, a great woman with a great vision, who lived to see the vision achieved in her lifetime and established to last after her death. Started from a small farmhouse, with a big barn and a bigger deficit, MacDowell is now a "national monument of extreme interest" to the United States and to the world.

What a legacy! From her to Edward MacDowell, to us, to the world. It was the fashion for many years to dismiss the man to whom we owe this unique memorial, as: "Edward MacDowell? Oh yes, *To a Wild Rose*." Lately there is a better appraisal of his work, especially the piano concertos. He is more often heard in concert halls in his native country. Abroad he has always been respected. Also now and for as long as concern for the arts endures, there is his colony.

I think of Mrs. MacDowell, and I am glad that I was at the colony when she was still in residence at Hillcrest, to which I was summoned to meet her as an incoming fellow, and after that, I like to think, because she wanted to talk to me. She wrote to me several letters in her own handwriting, even after she was blind, and later other letters, typed for her. They are in the Mugar Memorial Library in Boston, and in my diaries. I had a very small connection with her, but a vital one, for which I am grateful.

I spent ten magic seasons, summer and winter, at the colony, over a long period of years. The spirit of MacDowell and my experiences there encouraged me to become the endangered species that I am, a minor poet, a non-pornographic novelist. It could have been quite easy to go another way, but as Bob Kabak, the painter, another "fellow" and friend, whose own standards are high above the age, said to me once when I was depressed and discouraged, and sorely tempted by the offer of a big advance if I would write "another historical novel, with plenty of violence and sex," and give up the Chinese book, "*You know you have no choice. But not to have a choice is still a choice.*" And again, "You *know* we mustn't go back."

He slipped a little Chinese book into my lunch basket, and a pair of ground grippers for my boots . . . it was the winter of the great freeze, and walking to the studio was perilous, but I think he meant my feet not to slip on another sort of path. Dear Bob, wherever he may be, my thanks.

It was in gratitude to him, and to many others at MacDowell, and to the place itself, that I founded the Deepest Valley Theatre, in the desert, at the foot of Mount Whitney, to perform the sort of work MacDowell artists do.

In 1963 I bought a miner's hut for $350, which was all that I had in the bank, from a tax refund, and settled down to make a Californian headquarters for me, for Terry and Dick and the children, for Iren and any friends who might be able to come there and camp.

It would be camping. There was no electricity, no running water, no telephone. An outhouse, on the top of a hill, visible for a mile, painted a glaring green, was the only "improvement." There were some sweet-smelling locust trees along an irrigation stream which ran beside the house, and the house itself was built so close to the Whitney Portal Road that I felt fishbowl-naked until after a year I managed to get a high fence between me and the cars whizzing by, especially in summer.

The old miner who built the place in 1915 started with a one-room shack, and an elaborate front door with two steps up to it. Then he built on another room, leaving the front door and the two steps inside, and later another room with another front door, so that there were three front doors with steps to them inside the house, leading from one narrow little room to another, rather like a string of undersized cabooses. It was snug in winter and cool in summer, backed into a rocky cliff above a mine. The old man built it well, to last. The year of the bad flash flood when new houses in Lone Pine leaked, mine, in the center of the swirling water, stayed bone dry.

Across the road four cement steps descended to the creek below the main supply of water to the town. He put them there, and a little cement platform, for his wife, loving her enough to want to make it easier for her to haul the heavy buckets, but not enough to put in running water, which he might have done when he built. There was no Bureau of Land Management to prevent it, in 1915. That oppressive body came into being in 1948, with a high-sounding purpose and a deceptively mild manner. Individual enterprise was still encouraged in the United States. People's little houses, built sturdily in the desert, were their *homes,* not encumbrances to be bulldozed away at the fiat of some faceless bureaucrat in a far-off place. It took me three years and a lot of dollars to circumvent the accumulated red tape surrounding the passage of one small pipe through the culvert into the kitchen sink. Another year and I had a bathtub, outside at first, and then in the storage lean-to at the back of the hut. Paint inside and out and a flower garden in front of the old root house made the corner so charming that tourists often stopped to admire and take pictures. When they did I told them the purpose of the place. It was the office and operational center for the Deepest Valley Theatre, a mile and a half up the road.

There is a strange, indescribable region at the foot of Mount Whitney, known incongruously, by some whim of early miners, as the "Alabama Foothills," where enormous ancient boulders extend for several miles, fantastically shaped by millions of years of sand and wind erosion. It is Mary Austin's Land of Little Rain, about which she has said:

> Between Owens Lake and the northern end of the Alabamas, clustered all that enchanted charm of the district which people who found themselves enmeshed in it sometimes cursed as they curse the beauty of women. The Alabamas were of exceeding ancientness, and their fire-stained rocks Time sculptured into strange shapes of weirdness, between which the filmy flame of cactus flowers ran red and orange and apricot, with little patches of a more fiery green and blue pools of lupine wetted by artesian springs. The rocky core of the hills broke off somewhat abruptly just above Lone Pine, and behind that our homestead lay, looking off toward the lake and the cloud-mottle Coso country, all fawn and red and black with faint tinges of citron. The hot flat sun always "drawing water" from the lake, so that toward morning and evening, it could be seen letting down broad ladders of irised light on which, said the Indians, the children of the Rainbow came and went. Behind us in towering blocks of gray and black and white gathered the peaks of Whitney and Opapago.

But that gives only a faint idea of the grandeur and breath-taking strangeness of the place. I spent long hours driving, wandering through on foot, and camping beneath the stars. I took sculptors and painters there, for the pleasure of watching their despair. "Everything has been done." But for composers and poets it was a challenge.

In the summer of 1963 Paul Earls, who was working on the score for *Flight,* came to spend a few days with me, to talk over points in the libretto which I was writing for the operatic version we were making together. He was an exciting collaborator, because he had so many excellent visual and stage effects he wanted to try. We went roaming toward Mount Whitney, and all of a sudden we found a natural bowl, a rugged amphitheater, tucked away at the foot of three towering rocks.

We both said, "Oh . . . what a place to put on *Flight!*" Especially the scenes in limbo and in hell.

We clambered down into the center of the escarpments and the huge cliffs. Paul, who had composer's ear as well as composer's voice, but a stronger one than most, began to sing parts of the score, while I listened from this rock and that. Then I sang, and he listened. We were astounded that the slightest whisper could be heard, undistorted, and convinced that without a shell . . . the shell was there, courtesy of the Creator . . . we could produce "new and old works of excellence, orchestral and solo works, operas, drama and ballet worthy of the setting," to quote one of our early brochures.

For two years I campaigned up and down the valley, in rival towns, speaking to mystified groups of Lions, Rotarians, Chambers of Commerce, Women's clubs, P.B.W., P.T.A., and a raft of alphabetical letters. I told them about the acoustics, I told them about the projects.

"We *have* to have concerts among those rocks!" I cried.

"We do?" they said uncertainly.

"Certainly we do! The place has been waiting for us, all these millions of years. No need for a shell. Magnificent, unparalleled backdrop! This is a bowl far greater than anything anyone has known or seen, the Hollywood Bowl, Tanglewood, Aspen, are nothing to it. It could become the American Oberammergau and more, far more."

"It could?" they said. "But art and things like that are not in our frontier traditions," they suggested gently, when they liked me enough to set me straight.

"Then you don't know your own traditions. The first thing the miners did when they struck it rich was to build a grand Opery House, and get the best European and American artists there to perform, and shower them with nuggets. They got Shakespearean companies, and singers and dancers like Lola Montez. . . ."

"Oh yes," they said, "Lola Montez . . ."

A saloon keeper gave us the first twenty-five dollars, because, he explained, he had a sixteen-year-old son, "and I would like some of all this," he waved his hand, "to rub off on him."

Then he told us how, as a boy of twelve, he had helped to blow up the dam, carrying the stolen water from the valley down to Los Angeles to make the real-estate speculators in the San Fernando Valley rich on the deal that turned Owens Valley into a desert.

His contribution brought us luck. Others began to come in, from Bishop and Independence, and one from Lone Pine (but that was from a former resident of Independence and a personal friend). From the beginning, the people of Lone Pine, the town nearest to the theater, which stood to benefit the most commercially, and did benefit during the four years we were able to operate, opposed us in every way they could. We might have been proposing to establish a leper colony among them instead of a concert bowl for the best classical music, two miles away in open country that did not belong in any way to the town.

Iren came for two summers, and played benefit recitals up and down the valley, on terrible pianos, once on a shot-up upright that came from a honky-tonk bar, and made some money for the project, and a great deal of free publicity for the area.

I saw many officials and authorities and obtained a sheaf of permits to put on summer concerts among the rocks. I gave money, time—six years of professional time, during which I could not write in any sort of continuity and peace—to the project, which finally got under way in 1965.

That spring I remember taking an official of the B.L.M. and one from the Parks and Recreation Department up to the bowl, and describing to them the three weekend programs of six concerts which we were putting on that summer, also sketching the future operatic performance of *Flight*.

"Can't you imagine," I said, "the plane, with its nose pointed toward those three great rocks, and the audience seated in such a way that they will feel themselves actually inside it, taking this supernatural journey . . ."

"I'll have one there," the B.L.M. man said.

". . . and the orchestra over here, and the conductor, and we plan for a group of ballet dancers. . . ."

". . . I'll have one there, and another there . . ." Parks and Recreation said.

Presently I began to hear what they were saying.

"Have one what?" I asked. I had to ask it twice. They were too absorbed in their important topic to pay attention to a woman talking.

"Have one what?"

"Toilets."

I broke my stunned silence to object, "You can't have one *there*, that's where the conductor will be standing, nor *there*, that's where the orchestra will be, nor *there*, that's where the audience . . ."

After that I called the B.L.M. the Bowel Movement Boys, since that seemed to be, at every encounter which I had with them, the level of their thinking . . . and in the end they did flush the whole shimmering project down their bureaucratic drain.

But first there was the magic and the achievement, which cannot be taken away, and which remain in the memories of a few hundred people—those who listened and those who performed there.

Iren was program director and co-ordinator for all the performances. She started the first series off with six outstanding concerts, including a harpsichordist and an Indian performer of classical Hindu music, and wound up the season with herself and John Ranck playing Messaien's *Vision des Sept Amens*.

The third and last of the series, winding up the 1965 Deepest Valley presentations, will be Sunday September 5th, with John Ranck (whose opening recital on Friday August 27th started the whole series off on a magnificently high level), and Iren Marik, in Messaien's *Vision de l'Amen* for two pianos.

This work, which has had very few performances in this country, begins with the most complete pianissimo in the mystery of the first nebula and continues in a tremendous crescendo toward the mystery of the Light of Life.

"By joining the lives of the creatures who say Amen, because they exist," the composer explains, "I have tried to express the infinite variety of riches of the Amen in seven Musical Visions, composed for two pianos, demanding of those instruments the maximum of strength and sonority. I entrusted the first piano (played by John Ranck) with the difficult rhythms, the binding chords, everything that was speed, charm and quality of sound. I entrusted the second piano (played by Iren Marik) with the principal melody, the thematic elements, evertyhing which demands emotion and power."

It is requested there be no applause until the end of the work, after the last Amen. [See Appendix.]

About the Harihar Rao evening of Indian classical music, Aim Morhardt, local composer, painter, poet and supporter of the arts, wrote:

To preface this account of the tremendous concert of the Raos, some comment must be made about the setting in which it was given.

We have all heard of our newest theatrical site in the Alabama Hills. Most of us have shrugged it off or paid it lip service as a fine cultural project . . . for someone else. I have been around some too in Inyo county and supposed that I had sampled most of the wonders of the region, but this is one I had missed. The small amphitheater, set well apart from any distractions, is framed, like a far more ancient Stonehenge, with its incredible granite monoliths. Seated by the stage, those of us who were there early watched evening fall over the Sierra crest. A fingernail moon and its attendant evening star stayed briefly with us as the sky darkened, only to drop, before darkness, behind the dragon crest of Whitney. One by one the druid lights were lit, each in its natural rock cavity. The absolute serenity of the quiet warm night gathered us into its magic. The Polynesian lamps of the stage were lit and with a first light whisper of wind the performance began. Lacking the stage it might well have been two thousand years ago in the Khyber Pass. As an experience in today's world it was profoundly affecting.

Mr. Rao, the attendant magician, for that is how I feel about him, explained in a quiet voice some of the background of the music to be played. The sitar and tampula used turned out to be dramatically large, complex and beautiful, intricate of tuning and altogether appropriate to the Arabian Nights atmosphere. The music, as he pointed out, would also be complex and from another world most of us had never glimpsed. The microtonal system of the ragas, which employs for each piece an arbitrary selection of units from a 73-tone scale, is foreign to Western ears. The sitar must be prepared in advance for each selection by a delicate adjustment of the movable frets. It came as something of a shock to be told that his first selection would be half an hour in duration.

. . . It was, as 95 percent of classical Hindu music is, unwritten patterns handed down through the generations from teacher to gifted student, basing itself only briefly on the basic framework of the particular raga used, and from that point going off into an improvisational theme and variations on an enormously extended melodic line. It was a quiet tale at first, but as it progressed it kept on adding more and more intricate configurations.

Keeping pace with it the wind also came, whispering down around the rocks, blowing the stage lights into trails of flame which became in turn like some occult choreography sent by the djinns of our own ancient hills to keep him company. Variation piled on variation, a skein of angry words against the groundbeat of the C sharp tonic, endlessly repeated, and the susurration of the thirteen sympathetic unplayed strings which are part of the instrument. And then with a last gentle statement, it was over, and the audience came slowly back to reality.

In later years there were other great high moments, as when the Gregg Smith Choir, on the eve of its European tour, came to perform among the rocks.

Nothing like it has been heard here before, and possibly not anywhere else. . . . The singers scattered far and wide, beyond the area occupied by the audience. They clambered up to rock pinnacles as much as 30 feet above the stage level and as far as 75 feet from the stage. As they began singing the effect was indescribable. Each voice carried back to the stage clearly. They met and blended in an effect which one spectator likened to "stereo with 30 speakers, each carrying a different sound track." [See Appendix.]

In between rehearsals and performance they sat with their feet in the stream, and sang near the little house, and later, after the performance, sang under the stars, at a friend's home, halfway up the mountain road to Opapago, as they ate their supper. One does not forget such hours.

There were other choirs and orchestras, and symphonies were played, compositions premiered, and I even had the moving experience of hearing *The Small Hour* offered to those towering rocks, but I think what comes back to me mostly when I think of the theater is that first year, the first time the two great Steinway D grands came on their lumbering truck from Penny Owsley in Los Angeles. One of them was "the Rubinstein piano," the instrument Rubinstein plays when he is giving recitals in the West, and the other was as near a match to it as could be found. They came with their movers and their tuner, and parked beneath the shade of my locust trees, until it was time to take them up, over the rough, winding narrow trail into the theater. Here they were tuned and guarded until after the concerts, when they were taken out as they had come in, the sides of the truck missing boulders by inches, to drive the two hundred and seventy some miles back to Los Angeles.

Since my hut was the operational center for the project, people came dashing to it at all hours with disturbing messages:

"I think you ought to know, someone has shot up the stage again."

Vandals had poured holes into it half an hour after it was first set up, and they kept on doing so, every now and then. If we had been staging a ballet we would not have been able to go on with it for the splinters which would have slashed the dancers' feet.

"I think you ought to know the tuner has disappeared."

"Two lights are missing."

"The tickets haven't arrived from Bishop."

"The sheriff's office says there aren't any men available for tonight. We'll have to get our own night watchman."

"Thank you for telling me," I always said. I sat there "knowing," unable to do much about whatever the disaster was.

One developed a fatalistic, trusting turn of mind. I remember one time, in the Draco Art Gallery, a large upper room which I rented for artists and audiences to mingle there, in front of paintings and sculpture, after performances, I was deep in some mischance or other, when a gentle voice said in my ear:

"I'm a Buddhist and I play strange music on a wreath of leaves."

"Don't go away," I answered automatically. "I'm sure we'll be needing you in just a moment or two." I was right. It turned out that he also could paint the ceiling and wax the floors. He stayed with us for several weeks, and did play on different kinds of leaves, before he went wandering on.

I think I like to remember 1965, because none of us could have imagined then that the B.L.M., the Lone Pine Chamber of Commerce and other destroyers would savagely wipe out the shining venture four years later, when it was just getting well established, known and written-up in New York and other places, where what we were doing could be understood.

We fought the eviction "all the way to LBJ," and lost, and so the theater came to an end. The maddening part of it was that in almost every letter from the far-off authorities controlling its fate there was some remark to the effect that the Bureau of Land Management, the Department of the Interior, the other authorities involved approved of the Deepest Valley Theatre, and one went so far as to "commend" our "interest in the Deepest Valley Theatre," yet the five little houses which made its continuance possible had to be evicted within a matter of weeks, with the utmost urgency. They said that we were "standing to block the recreational development of the area, including the Deepest Valley Theatre," and that we were trespassers.

I paid rent to the B.L.M. for the little piece of land on which the theater's offices stood. A tenant is not a trespasser. At least I thought not, until then.

They were adamant. Even the most powerful intercession on our behalf in Washington drew no more than another letter commending the theater and our "interest" in it. But *we* must be evicted immediately.

There was no other place from which it could be run, and nothing to be done but let it go. When this became obvious, sadly I gathered a group of friends to sing away the spirit of the house, that there might be nothing there to be hurt by the bulldozers when they came to smash and maul at a place that had sheltered a generous shining project for the good of the area. In the five years that have passed since it was so urgent to destroy our homes and our hopes, nothing has been put in their place but a sign which looks like a urinal, stating "Alabama recreational area." All around it, where once there were flowers and pleasant patios, there are broken bottles, beer cans, trash, dying trees and garbage. For this the theater died, and five families were thrown out of their homes. No compensation. A typical B.L.M. deal. There are miners who have fared worse, losing expensive mining equipment, thousands of dollars' worth, besides a lifetime of work. All I lost was all I had, since the house could not be moved. I did manage to salvage the writing hut, and had it carted up the road to the land of a concerned friend. Here I stayed, at the foot of Opapago, in a shelter eight feet long by five feet wide.

Once I looked down the hill and saw a large yellow bulldozer making its way up the road. Suddenly I was behind the willows, shaking, sick to my stomach, starting to throw up. This strong reaction of fear and loathing surprised me, but it enlightened me too. Though I had worn a brave face I had evidently not sung away my spirit far enough to escape a brutal mauling.

Nineteen sixty-five was the year that I started going to Cry-Dances, Ceremonies and Sweat Lodges. I cannot say much about these, my tongue and my pen are bound, but I can quote what Mary Austin in a similar position has written, because she speaks the truth.

When she was frowned on for "dancing with the Indians," a phrase which can be interpreted on the surface, by those who should be left to stay on surfaces, she wrote in *Earth Horizon*:

> There are Indian episodes that are so intimately connected with my life as an artist, with what I ultimately came to understand, and stand for, in the structure and meaning of human society, that they cannot be omitted. . . . As for the other things that came to me by way of my Indian acquaintances, they are the gifts of a special grace which has been mine from the beginning, the persistence in me, perhaps, of an uncorrupted strain of ancestral primitivism, a single isolated gene of that far-off and slightly mythical Indian ancestor of whose reality I am more convinced by what happened to me among Indians than by any objective evidence.
>
> . . . I recall at Lone Pine a young wife kicked to death by a white man in a drunken fury at her resistance, and the Indian husband weeping in the broken measure of remediless despair. "My wife . . . all the same one dog." And the Ghost Dance . . . and Warner's Ranch . . . plenty of incident to set off less sensitive natures than Mary's against Christian pretense and democratic inadequacy. [Mary Austin sometimes wrote of herself in the third person.]
>
> . . . In the meantime the experience called the Practice of the Presence of God had come back to me, and a profound movement of spiritual growth *away* from the orthodox Protestant expression of it.

. . . Then there was that very real and heartrending anguish of the creative worker before the medium and method of individual expression has been mastered, which is, I suppose, always ludicrous to the onlooker not himself tormented by it.

According to orthodox Protestant Christianity, prayer was an emotional petition which you went through with as though you believed it effectual even when you knew it wasn't. Mary asked the Medicine-Man—"Do you truly *get* what you pray for?" "Surely, if you pray right." But the answer to what was "right" in the Paiute practice involved explanation. Prayer, to the Medicine-Man, had nothing to do with emotion; it was an act; an outgoing act of the inner self toward a responsive activity in the world about you, designated as the Friend-of-the-Soul-of-Man; Wakonda, the effective principle of the created universe. This inner act was to be outwardly expressed in bodily acts, in words, in music, rhythm, color, whatever medium served the immediate purpose, or all of them. Prayer so understood and instigated acted with the sureness of a chemical combination. Man is not alone nor helpless in the universe; he has toward it and it toward him an affective relation.

Once grasped and sincerely practiced, this new realization of prayer as experience . . . began as adventure and became illumination. . . . There was a part for her in Indian life. She had begun the study of Indian verse, strange and meaningful; of Indian wisdom, of Indian art. The Paiutes were basket-makers; the finest of their sort. What Mary drew from them was their naked craft, the subtle sympathies of twig and root and bark; she consorted with them; she laid herself open to the influences of the wild, the thing done, accomplished. She entered into their lives, the life of the campody, the strange secret life of the tribe, the struggle of Whiteness with Darkness, the struggle of the individual soul with the Friend-of-the-Soul-of-Man. She learned what it meant; how to prevail; how to measure her strength against it. Learning that, she learned to write.

There is a thing called the Friend-of-the-Soul-of-Man, a reality, an influence which you can call up around you. You wrap yourself in it. You are effective through it. You make use of it through rhythm; the beating of the medicine drum; the pound of feet in the medicine dance. You give way to it through rhythmic utterance. You find it expressing itself in rhythmic movement, the running of quail, the creaking of the twenty-mule team, the sweep of motion in a life-history, in a dance, a chant. You perceived that these patterns made writing; you struggled for them; won, caught, and ensnared them.

I have quoted at such length because every word of what she wrote in 1932 is true for me today, except the mule team, which has disappeared, but there are other creakings. One difference, I am not trying to "ensnare" the Indian way of life, I am ensnared by it. The friends I have made among the Indians of Owens Valley, the Paiutes, Shoshones and the Washoes, enrich my life, and will, I hope, go with me the rest of the way.

Strung out in small communities on or near the reservations scattered through the Owens Valley, remnants of the powerful tribes who once roamed a territory with probably more geographic variety than any other region in

North America, equally at home in the snows of the High Sierra or on the blistering rocks and sand dunes of Death Valley, these Paiutes, Shoshones, Washoes, live almost unnoticed, maintaining their ancient culture as far as modern conditions and the struggle against poverty permit.

They are not publicity-minded, commercially oriented or tourist greedy. For this reason, perhaps, they have been able to retain and revive some of their ancestral arts and oldtime ways of doing and living without betraying them to the marketplace. Much of the beautiful work they do is not and never will be for sale. They make it for themselves, their families and friends, to be enjoyed and used in the ancient ways.

Considering the smallness of their numbers and the hard conditions of their survival, there is a surprising and impressive tally of highly skilled artists in different media, especially among the older men and women. There is, for instance, a sculptor whose work is beginning to be widely known.

Raymond Stone—the name is appropriate—like his father Tom Stone before him, is a leader in his community. He has been called "the walking treasury of Owens Valley history" for his knowledge and love of the region. He is the pipemaker for his people, and, with the red catilin left over from his pipe heads, he carves small figures, of people, animals, birds and other symbolic pieces, with special significance for those who follow the Paiute way, but they also have a wider appeal as genuine works of art.

"They call it carving, but I call it whittling," he once said. "I started about a year ago [1970]. These carvings that I do seem like a part of me. They have a meaning of something hard to explain. As I look back I know the Great Power, as we call our Great Spirit, intended for me to do these carvings so that it would be an outlet for our people, for our way of life and our way of belief, and also maybe it will inspire some of our people throughout the valley, our Indian people, to be able to see them and do a little carving themselves. So these figures that I have carved, as long as I live they will be here with us, we'll keep them. Now and then maybe they will be taken to show some school or some other group or some museum, so that people may see them and understand they have been done by work of our own Valley Indians, and also in time our Indian people here throughout the Valley will be recognized for what they are, for their dignity and what they do and how they are."

This is also the spirit among the other artists and craftsmen, the desire to show what their people stand for, what their old ways meant and what their old people have taught them. They sell an occasional piece if and when they must, but prefer to keep, to treasure and *use* the beautiful things they make, and those handed down to them.

There is a time to gather willow, and a time to work on it. The right kind of willow is becoming difficult to find. Much of it is dying out, some has been bulldozed away, like my little house, some is contaminated with spray, and since the strands for weaving are held and passed through the mouth and must be constantly moistened, sprayed willows cannot be used. Still, although it takes longer and is harder and less rewarding, groups go out in the old companionable way to gather willow in the fall, and peel and prepare it together.

The Paiutes, as Mary Austin points out, were always noted for exceptionally fine basketry. They make baskets to hold water, to sift nuts and grain, to store things, even to wear—the distinctive small hat baskets are still in use for protection against falling sap from piñon trees. The designs woven into the baskets are those going far back to ancient times. They have a traditional meaning which the weavers know but will not discuss.

Paiute women still make cradle boards of buckskin and willow for their lucky babies. No more convenient cradle-transport has ever been devised for the comfort of a mother and a child. The baby, fastened securely to his mother's back, looks out on the interesting world, instead of only upward into an enormous human face.

Winter is the time for beadwork too, headbands, medallions and necklaces, in old authentic designs. Other arts are being revived. There is the Paiute language, with its complicated syntax and grammar. Learning it properly is an art. It is being taught in regular classes to adults and children by older women who have spoken it since childhood.

There is also a revival of music. Tape recorders are being used to preserve some of the old chants and songs. Men gather in each other's houses or on the hillside with their drums, to sing a little, talk a little, and sit together in the winter-afternoon sun. In ancient times the Paiutes did not use drums, but a divided stick, which, shaken rhythmically, tapped an accompaniment to song. Times change, now they use drums which they make for themselves of rawhide stretched over wooden frames, but the songs, the talk, the companionship remain the same.

These proud and patient people share a dream, growing slowly to a hope, that sometime, in their lifetime, perhaps *soon,* a portion of their sacred lands at Coso Range, taken over by the U.S. Navy, may be restored to them for spiritual and healing purposes, that Coso Hot Springs may be reopened for the use and benefit of all. When that happens, new life will flow through the valley and the blessing of the Great Spirit spread over the land.

As Raymond Stone put it when he acted as spokesman for a group which journeyed to Coso Hot Springs in November 1971, to meet with government officials and other authorities to discuss the situation and set forth the Indian point of view:

"This land that I talk about is one of our sources of religion. Our people years and years back used this land for healing. They came here and took the mud baths and drank the water that comes out of the hot springs, and as I look back from today to yesterday, it must be a wonderful country in there, from what I can understand from some of the older people who traveled that place. It has something that the Great Spirit has set aside for the people to use, not to sell it and not to abuse it in any way, but to go there and pray and use what is there for help on their way."

Meanwhile they wait and work, and I am privileged to wait and work with them, as Mary Austin did.

In the spring of 1966, when I was depressed and lonely, at the bottom of professional and personal oblivion, my books out of print, my pocketbook empty, my publishers and agent (not those whom I have now) indifferent, not to say rude, a letter wandered in, out of the far-off East, out of the blue:

May 5 1966

Dear Miss Eaton,

I am sure that many institutions have been in contact with you asking that they might become the repository of your manuscripts and correspondence files.

[Oh yeah? I thought sardonically. They line up on the left.]

I write to say that Boston University would be honored to establish an Evelyn Sybil Mary Eaton Collection, and to plead our particular cause for these reasons.

We are in the midst of building a magnificent new library on our Charles River Campus and we hope to make this library a center of study and research in contemporary literature. Up to the present time Boston University has been growing so rapidly as a "national" institution, that we have waited until we were ready with the proper facilities before establishing such a literary research center. With the advent of our new building we are now ready to embark upon this project.

It is our hope to collect the papers of outstanding contemporary literary figures, house and curate these materials under the optimum archival conditions, and attract to us scholars in the field of contemporary literature who would utilize our institution as a research base.

Your papers would be preserved for future generations. I do hope that you will look sympathetically upon our request. May I say personally how much I have enjoyed your published work.

Sincerely yours,
Howard B. Gotlieb
Chief of Reference and
Special Collections,
Boston University Libraries

"And God love *him*," Terry said when she saw the letter.

It was what I had always wished for, some place, some niche for what I had tried to give to the world. I was pleased and touched, profoundly moved, as much by the manner as the unexpected honor.

I wrote accepting, but explaining that much of my early work was lost in the Second World War, and that I wrote directly onto the typewriter, so that there would not be much holograph material.

Another letter arrived, with the same impressive heading.

Dear Miss Eaton,

I am delighted to have your letter of May 10, and we are honored that we shall be able to establish the Evelyn Sybil Mary Eaton Collection at this University and in this city. Your fine work is highly admired here and it is our feeling that future scholars will be studying your life and career even more avidly.

[Dear me! I thought, this Dr. Gotlieb is either an academic innocent or a naughty flatterer waving a wicked trowel. How wrong I was about both these concepts I discovered when I met that warm-hearted, clear-headed being, in his Boston.]

Thus we wish to preserve the record as complete as possible.

It is my hope that the Evelyn Sybil Mary Eaton Collection will contain the manuscripts (those not destroyed) and typescripts of all of your published and unpublished work in all states and drafts; the galleys, proofs, notes, notebooks, diaries or journals (if you have kept any), scrapbooks, photographs, tapes, inscribed copies of the published books, and correspondence relating to your life and work. In other words, everything which a future biographer would hope to find in the Evelyn Sybil Mary Eaton Collection.

You will of course retain the copyright to your papers, as will your estate after your death. You will always have access to your papers, and if the occasion occurs that you wish to borrow back certain items, this will be done. If ever you wish copies of your papers, this also will be done.

If you prefer that certain portions of your papers be restricted for a given period of time, the University will abide by your wishes. Any scholar wishing to quote or publish from the Evelyn Sybil Mary Eaton Collection will have to secure your permission through the University.

As your materials arrive here the University's official appraiser will place a tax evaluation upon the papers. You in turn will be provided with the proper documents allowing you to deduct this amount from your income tax in one year or over a period of years.

I hope that all of this information will be of some help to you. It will be a great honor to associate you with Boston University and have the Evelyn Sybil Mary Eaton Collection here.

Sincerely yours,
Howard B. Gotlieb

I smiled at the idea of future scholars avid to study my life and career, and a future biographer, but there was a warm, comfortable feeling in the pit of my stomach, like a nursery hot-water bottle to an aching spot, a discouraged anatomy. . . . I began to think of Howard Gotlieb as I used to think of Nannie . . . someone comforting out there, who maybe even cared. This concept was no more like him than the other two, except for the caring.

In October the official invitation arrived to be present at the dedication of the Mugar Memorial Library on Sunday and Monday, November 20 and 21.

I did not see how I could manage this, but friends persuaded me to make the effort. One paid for my ticket, another gave me a hat, a third found me a pocketbook and a pair of shoes. Terry offered to join me in Boston and so I decided to go.

Nov. 19th. Terry and I were walking past the bookstore in Harvard Square when I saw Marianne Moore's new book [*Tell Me, Tell Me*] which I had been wanting to buy. I rushed in saying "Tell me! Tell me!" and a nice young man said, "I'll be glad to tell you anything I *can*—what is it you want to know?" I said, "No, no, in the window . . ." and he found it for me. Afterward Terry told me he wasn't even a salesman, and then I realized how strange it must have sounded.

We watched the crowd go by, long-haired, oddly dressed, amusing faces . . . all kinds. It was the Harvard-Yale game. Coonskin coats. Then back to the hotel, rested, and finally to Dr. Gotlieb's party. There several nice things happened, first I *liked* him, even more than I thought I would. And I knew some of the other "collecteds." There were three from MacDowell, Alec Waugh, Virginia Sorensen, Jean Bothwell. Others from the Pen and Brush and other times in my life.

Nov. 20. Took a brisk walk across the bridge. The river looked bluer than I expected and the sun was fine, no smog. Saw Alec and Virginia briefly, and a glimpse of Richard Jessup who said he was looking forward to the concert for Mac somebody "sang on note." I was surprised that there was anywhere left where that could be.

Tonight was the President's reception. As we moved slowly up the stairs, a whisper ran through the crowd of the collected: "We're in cases!" It was true. Our works were lying in state in three tiers of glass coffins lining the staircase. People sidled over casually, surreptitiously, to view their remains and take a quick glance at who was buried next them.

"This is a lovely imaginative thing you are doing here," I said to the President's wife when I reached her in the line. She asked me to repeat it to her husband. Apparently no one else had thought to tell them thank you.

Monday November 21. The great day. I didn't get to the library inspection but the convocation was wonderful. I sat next to a woman who was crying. "Are you one of the collected?" "No, I'm Stephen Mugar's sister." "How proud you must be today." "Yes, but I wish our father and mother were alive to see it." The Mugars were immigrants from Armenia. Stephen Mugar was a child when they landed. He made a vow that if this new country were good to him and his family he would do something for it in return. It was very good to him. He is a millionaire. This is what he decided to do . . . a give-while-living, in which the authors join. I liked his speech.

When the orchestra played the "Pines of Rome," at one point, when the birds are singing, I saw a golden-brown light and felt that a Grandfather was there, blessing everything. Later in the evening the speeches were right. I was proud of the writing community, and the educational community, both at their best, all swords sheathed. It struck me too that I seem to have run into one person at least from every phase of my life . . . and no enemies . . . they don't seem to be here.

One nice amusing touch, James Warner Bellah stopped me on the way back to the hotel. "Are you Evelyn Eaton?" "Yes, I am." "I was in the Canadian Flying Corps in World War One. I knew your father."

I felt as though Papa had managed to get a message through to me, a tap on the shoulder, to say that he was proud of us, perhaps to repeat, "There is nothing like sticking it out to the end."

It was a magnificent Cry-Dance. The Boston Symphony played us to our rest. The eulogies were brief and brilliant, especially Martha Gellhorn's. Claude Rains was there, still able to enjoy the honor paid him. Terry went to talk to him.

And there was I, whisked through the skies to take my small, proud place near the great of my profession, the read, the quoted, the anthologized; a footnote, a tribute to them, a Lee Boo applauding from her little house while around us the trees and fields went the other way.

Appendixes

My dear Evie,

In September 1912 I first made your acquaintance. You were certainly an individual—as you have been ever since. In the earlier summer you had had a very severe attack of whooping-cough and your health was still giving some cause for anxiety. You were allowed a good deal of latitude as regards work, as it was important for you to be out-of-doors. The various members of the household, your mother, sister, the cook and myself, could be seen twice daily pursuing you across MacDonald Park, carrying a raw egg in a tea-cup, whole not beaten up, which you would hastily gulp down and disappear again with your chief ally, Bishop Bidwell's youngest daughter.

You carried on a kind of love-hate relationship with your sister Helen, four years older than yourself. At that time, no two sisters could have been more unlike. Your untidiness and general higgledy-piggledy way of life offended her very orderly well-balanced attitude, and you went out of your way to be annoying. She and several friends of her own age ran a sort of club among themselves, with a manuscript magazine of which you were fiercely jealous. They used to lock themselves in Helen's bedroom, while you made yourself a nuisance on the other side of the door until your mother or I removed you elsewhere. And yet there was no one in the world you admired more than Helen.

At Christmas we opened presents before breakfast in your parents' bedroom with a wood fire burning. Your mother was a great Christmas "fan" and though your father pretended to be scornful of the whole proceeding, he enjoyed it as much as the rest. A minor tragedy occurred later on that Christmas Day in 1912. After much searching of heart, Helen had given you her beloved French doll with her pretty china face. You were not really a "dolly" child and were rather overwhelmed by the responsibility. You were alone with your mother in her bedroom, when I heard her calling me in agonised tones. You had dropped the doll head first on the marble hearth and broken the face into atoms. I grabbed the whole disastrous remnants and retreated hastily to my own bedroom to review the situation.

I shall not forget your frightened white face as you said, "Oh, poor Helen!" Your father and I sat up half the night mending that poor face and fixing the movable eyes. Of course Helen had to be told what had happened but she never really had the shock of seeing that pretty face reduced to almost pinhead fragments. (When we were talking about old days recently she asked me if you did it on purpose. I told her that she would never have suspected that if she had seen your stricken face!)

You were rather an odd little person, not at all in the mould your mother must have expected. I remember once when she was away I made up a velvet skirt and overblouse for you in a rather rich blue and found some bright colored ribbons and velvets to make snoods. You looked so much more of a person than when you were dressed in the muslins, etc. which suited Helen so well. Mynie was quite amazed to see how much better the stronger colours suited you.

You certainly went out of your way to be as contrary as you could, especially if you could see a chance of exasperating poor Helen. She was so very innately orderly,—and still is—and you most surely were *not,* and you emphasized the difference at every opportunity just to "get a rise" out of her. You must have inherited some of your father's love of teasing.

He was a born tease and you and I were his chief victims. You used to take him seriously when he insisted that your cat would be much happier if he had its tail removed. The subject never seemed to die and you rose to his teasing every time.

Among other things you resented the fact that you just could not share all the same lessons with Helen. I should have been very ill-judged to allow it. You would have held Helen back and even worse, you'd have built your own knowledge without foundations. But I know you attended with great interest to her history lessons, when you were supposed to be doing something else!! She was really a very wide awake 14 year old. We had great fun turning French into Latin, or English into German, or French into German ad-lib, though some of our translations might have horrified the purists. I think really that Hayti [my sister's nickname] and I sharpened our brains on each other and you stood by and watched the process. I hope we all derived some benefit.

Helen's music was a joy. She had a touch which I believe was almost unique. She had been very well taught in England and was continuing her training under a local teacher in Kingston. You were supposed to be learning also, but did not evince any interest and just didn't practice.

The teacher and I came to the conclusion that it was waste of time and money for you to go on. You loved listening to Helen but I think you were just overwhelmed by the difference between you and gave up. With characteristic perversity, no sooner had the lessons stopped than you desired to try again, so the job of making you at any rate able to read simple scores devolved upon amateur me.

As Helen had a wonderful ear and an equally wonderful musical memory, she rather neglected sight-reading. The music teacher's mathematical and musical husband came to the rescue and lent us a succession of classics, Mozart symphonies, etc., arranged in duet form. Helen and I worked steadily through them all, she of course, playing brilliantly, I just enough to keep her on time so that she had to read quickly. You used to listen to us, and I wonder if the Jupiter Symphony brings back to you, as it does to me, your father's little study where the piano lived, lined with maplewood and opening by folding doors into the drawing room.

The next summer, 1913, it was decided that the house in Kingston should be let to an officer in the Indian Army who was seconded to the Royal Military College across the river, and that we should spend the summer in a wooden chalet on a farm on the lake about five miles away. We had a very healthy and happy summer. The people of the farm were Scottish and very pleasant.

Your father had to be at the barracks all day, returning in the evening on his beloved "Blue Miracle." This was a thoroughbred from a famous stud in the Blue

Mountains of Virginia. He had been badly treated by a Negro groom whom he savaged, had been looked upon as a dangerous animal and had finally arrived at a third-class circus, where your father saw him and bought him. By good treatment he became a gentle, harmless riding-horse and showed his breeding in regimental races. When he came out to the farm in the evening he was turned loose and really enjoyed himself.

Do you remember how he ate my carefully arranged table decoration of golden rod one evening when we had guests to supper on a table beside the lake? Another time he put his head over my shoulder and calmly took the apple I was eating. That shows what kindness and good training can do for a rogue horse. Dear Miracle! He died a soldier's death in France, before he lost his master.

Do you remember your wildly imagined story of men with a waggon breaking into Dr. Garrett's summer cottage about half a mile away along the lake? [One of my clairvoyant, clairaudiant experiences. No one checked, but it most probably happened either before or after I saw it.] You were quite circumstantial. They had torn down the wooden shutters over the windows to get inside and were ransacking the place. Before going to alarm the farm, I thought I had better have a look. Of course it was quiet and undisturbed. When I told your father this incident, I said, "She's certainly going to be a writer of romances," but he was quite upset. "She's going to be a regular little liar!" he said. I reassured him by telling him that children often imagine things so vividly that they do become reality and it is difficult for them to separate truth from fiction. He was such a stickler for truth "the whole truth and nothing but the truth," that he took things in rather a Puritanical way.

This is all very unchronological but I keep remembering odds and ends. I've tried to put down what may picture your background.

Francis Thompson wrote to her what may have been his last poem: "I fear to love thee, Sweet, because / Love's the ambassador of loss." The sister Viola men-

(Mrs Sowerby)
Humphrey's Homestead
Greatham
Pulborough
Sussex
Telephone: Pulborough 135

Dear Miss Eaton, — I am not in reach of any book of reference, and don't know if I should address you this, — but the reason of my writing at this moment is that — by chance I have pulled out from the shelves of my parents' — Meynell's — library a little book of your poems sent to my father in 1923 (!) by his acquaintance Miss Douglas (from the illustrious address "the White House, Tite Street, Chelsea",)

[left margin:] to Pulborough — it wd give me great pleasure to see you here. I am no longer young, so — but there are sometimes

[top margin:] other members of our family about. Yours sincerely Olivia Sowerby

tioned in the letter is the daughter to whom Francis wrote "The making of Viola" and other poems. I received the letter in August 1960.

And finding this book confirmed in me a long-held intention to send some word to you, which came to me some five or six years ago when I read aloud to my sister Viola, who was ill, your novel "Flight" and your quoting of our loved poet Coventry Patmore made us both sit up with keen awareness of a sympathetic mind.

Then a little later, in different mood, I delighted in The New Yorker account of that inheritance -- from a thrifty English king!...

Now, this is very much a letter into the unknown, but if you ever felt inclined to take a day's expedition from Victoria Station

HALLETT ABEND, representing North American Newspaper Alliance. From 1926 to 1941, China correspondent for the New York *Times* and chief of bureau for the Far East. Contributed to *Saturday Evening Post, Reader's Digest, American Mercury, Look, Cosmopolitan, MacLeans* and other magazines. Author of eight books on the Far East, including *Ramparts of the Pacific, Pacific Charter, My Life in China,* and *Treaty Ports.*

MEYER BERGER, representing The New York Times Syndicate. On the New York *Times* staff since 1926; served in London the summer of 1942 and in the Pacific the spring of 1945. His books include *The Eight Million* and *Men of Maryknoll.*

ROBERT CONSIDINE, representing International News Service. Contributor to *Collier's, Cosmopolitan, Saturday Evening Post, Reader's Digest* and others. Coauthor of *Thirty Seconds Over Tokyo* and *Where's Sammy?*

EVELYN EATON, representing G. P. Putnam's Sons, Publishers. Novelist. Her writings include *Pray to the Earth, Quietly My Captain Waits, Restless Are the Sails, The Sea Is So Wide, In What Torn Ship,* published by Harper Bros.

HARRY W. FLANNERY, representing Columbia Broadcasting System. From 1935 to 1940 he was news analyst at KMOX, St. Louis, Missouri. In 1940–41 he was Berlin correspondent for C.B.S., and wrote a book, *Assignment to Berlin.*

PAULINE FREDERICK, representing Western Newspaper Union. Became a radio and editorial associate of Baukhage of American Broadcasting Company in 1941 and has covered such stories as Pearl Harbor Day at the White House, Declaration of War in Congress, both Democratic and Republican conventions in 1944, second Quebec Conference, AFTAC at Orlando, death of President Roosevelt from Washington, and San Francisco Conference.

CHARLES BRUCE GOULD, representing *Ladies' Home Journal.* Associate editor *Saturday Evening Post,* 1934–35; editor *Ladies' Home Journal* (with his wife, Beatrice Blackmar Gould). Author of two books, *Sky Larking* and *Flying Dutchman,* two plays with his wife, *Man's Estate* and *The Terrible Turk,* and a motion picture, *Reunion.* He has contributed fiction to *Saturday Evening Post, Cosmopolitan, Liberty* and others.

HARRY GRAYSON, representing Newspaper Enterprise Association. Feature writer for the Los Angeles *Examiner* and San Francisco *Bulletin;* sports editor of the Los Angeles *Record,* New York *World Telegram* and N.E.A. Service. Author of *Florida in Wartime* and *They Played the Game.*

WILLIAM S. HOWLAND, representing *Time* Magazine. Opened the Southern news bureau for *Time* and *Life,* January 1, 1940, and has been chief ever since. From 1941 to 1944, he reported military maneuvers and training in the United States, Alaska and Mexico.

EDWIN A. LEAHEY, representing The Chicago Daily News Syndicate. For a time in 1942 he was Special Assistant to the Assistant Secretary of the Navy as labor adviser. Came to the Washington Bureau of *The News* in January 1941. His outside writing has been on labor matters for the *Saturday Evening Post, New Republic* and several Catholic magazines, including *America* and *The Sign.*

ELSIE MC CORMICK, representing *Reader's Digest.* Conducted a column for the New York *World,* "A Piece of My Mind." After three years in China, where she wrote for the Chinese Press of Shanghai, she wrote a book *The Unexpurgated Diary of a Shanghai Baby.* Her work appears in *Reader's Digest, Collier's, Saturday Evening Post, Good Housekeeping, This Week* and other magazines.

GRETTA PALMER, representing *Woman's Home Companion.* Served as foreign correspondent for the New York *World Telegram* during the Cuban Revolution of 1932, for *Town & Country Magazine* in articles on Japan and Japanese-occupied China in 1939, returned to Cuba in 1943 for *Liberty,* and went to the Mediterranean Theater in the summer of 1944 for a number of publications.

MARY DAY WINN, representing *This Week.* Staff writer and fiction editor of *This Week* and assistant to Mrs. Ogden Reid on the *Herald Tribune* Forum. She made the first eastward crossing on the *Hindenburg* for *Vogue,* toured Central and South America by air for *This Week* and *Woman's Home Companion,* and has written three books, *Marriage in the Modern Manner* (with Dr. Ira M. Wile), *Adam's Rib* and *The Macadam Trail.*

SPEECH BY POPE PIUS XII. ROME, JULY 1945

You have come a long way to Rome; and Rome is only a halfway stop on a journey which before finished will have brought you round the greater part of the globe through many climes, amid diverse peoples speaking various languages. Everywhere your quest has been for what is called today news, the latest information from all, even the remotest parts of the world, to be conveyed with the minimum of delay to an eager, impatient public. Some of you will add comments, will elaborate articles; but even they must have the element of timeliness and immediate interest. It is not an easy task; but it is an invaluable service your profession offers to society, breaking down the barriers of time and space, and assisting all members of the vast human family to share their joys and sorrows, their triumphs and disasters, their hopes and their fears. But the worthy success of your profession depends on one essential fact: your fidelity to Truth in what you write and speak.

That in the rush of routine, daily work a writer should let an error slip into his article, that he should accent information without sufficiently controlling its source, that he may even give expression to a judgment that is unfair, may often be due rather to carelessness, than to bad will. Yet he should realize that such carelessness, such heedlessness, especially in times of grave crises, may too easily have serious consequences. An editor, or writer or speaker, who is concious of his lofty vocation and its responsibilities, is always alive to the obligation he has to the thousands or millions of people who may be strongly affected by his words, to give them the truth, nothing but the truth, as far as he has been able to ascertain it.

But what shall we say of deliberate falsehood and calumny? "A lying tongue, like hands that shed innocent blood, the Lord hateth; and every just man detests a lying word." (Prov. 6, 17; 13, 5.) Calumny is quick-footed, as you know, especially, be it said for shame, when directed against religion and the champions of the sterner demands of Christian morality; the denial and the defense of the victim are often given no hearing or may find space after a week or so in an obscure corner of an inside page. Members of the profession who do not hesitate to smear their pages or pollute the ether with falsehood are rendering a great disservice to their fellow-men; they are aiming a mortal blow at the spirit between the children of the same heavenly Father, and gravely imperil peace among nations. If competent civil authority fails, when necessity demands it, to curb such license, then civil society will most surely pay the penalty. The world shudders today to contemplate the mass of misfortune that has overwhelmed it. May it not be traced back to the flood of error and false moral standards let loose by the written and spoken word of proud, irreligious men?

May God strengthen you in your purpose to serve your profession and your fellow-men in a worthy manner; may He help you to make your contribution to the sanctification of the family and the defense of human society's moral foundations. With this prayer on Our lips We bless you with the deep affection of Our heart and call down heaven's blessings on all who are near and dear to you.

You have seen here some authentic actual photographs of atrocities committed by German people. These things were done by Germans on a vast scale throughout Germany and the occupied countries of Europe as a part of a national plan to establish yourselves as the superior race in Europe and, as we now know, eventually in the entire world. These atrocities were carried out with the full knowledge and the explicit direction of Adolf Hitler and his aides, the men who promised you great things, the same men you once idolized and cheered so enthusiastically at their every appearance among you. Instead of the great glories they promised you, these men have brought you national ruin, disgrace and the hatred of the entire civilized world.

Their last acts were those of selfish cowards, when, to prolong their own evil and worthless lives, they exhorted you to fight on and on in a senseless struggle against impossible odds. Many of your cities were destroyed and hundreds of thousands of you Germans, soldiers and civilians alike, were thus needlessly killed or maimed long after those men well knew they had lost their carefully planned war of conquest. They would have you believe that you fought only to defend yourselves against us, that we were the real aggressors. On the contrary, we fought for our own freedom and for our own survival and we conquered. We knew we would, for we had to.

You Germans, especially you soldiers, always seek to excuse your participation in these things by the plea that you only obeyed the orders of your superiors. Most of you will claim that you knew nothing of these horrors which were going on in your midst for years, in fact from the very birth of your National Socialist Party and its ever present concentration camps. We in the other countries in the world heard reports of these things from time to time but preferred not to believe them. It is difficult for us to believe, however, that you Germans could have been ignorant of all this, yet you did nothing to stop it and you continued to idolize and worship the leaders of National Socialism including your former idol Hitler.

The beginning of the war and your rapid conquest of large areas of Europe was but the signal for commencement of your diabolic plan to destroy and weaken by starvation large populations of the occupied countries so that they could never again summon the strength to successfully oppose you, the Germans. Mass murders and slow deaths have been shown here.

We first began to verify these things when our Russian allies overran some of the occupied areas of Poland. There were seen for the first time some of the scientific murder factories your people had built and operated throughout the occupation. Consequently we and our western allies prepared to find similar things when our armies overran Germany. We were shocked and horrified beyond words, however, when we first saw these things with our own eyes. No doubt we were permitted to see very little of the total. The criminals responsible had doubtless succeeded in concealing much of the evidence. So fast did our armies advance, however, that they were unable to hide it all.

Many of the directly responsible have died and many will eventually die for these shocking crimes against humanity. Many more will spend long years in prison. Those of you who escape the more severe punishment I have mentioned, have already paid a part of the price for your mistakes in your lost homes, your lost comrades and the lost members of your families. You will continue to pay for years to come in the hard work of restoration of the damage caused by the war, for all of which you Germans are solely responsible. You will pay for years in the loss of respect and in the hatred of the other peoples of the world which will cease only when you have again proved yourselves fit to join the family of respectable nations of the world. It is a high tribute to our humanity that we do not make you all pay with your very lives for what you have done.

We have seen only too well what we would have suffered had we been so unfortunate as to be conquered by you. Your brutality and that of your leaders was demonstrated many times to our fighting men who faced you during the long years of combat. They observed how, when the tide turned against you, you resorted to any and every kind of dirty fighting that you could conceive of. Your mines, your booby traps, yes even your booby trapping of the bodies of your own comrades, showed the depths to which your nation had sunk. These weapons made their appearance after you knew you would henceforth be going only in one direction—back—always back, so you had little to fear in retaliation from us. They were the tactics of a rat in a corner, but you called it "total war." You used the same word to excuse the bombing of civilians in cities, a practice you began at London and for which you later paid a terrible price. We repaid you a hundred fold.

Your country has twice in the last quarter of a century plunged the world into a costly and prolonged war. We cannot allow you ever to do it again. We do not intend to. Should our resolves in this matter not materialize, you may be sure that you will fail again, in spite of everything you are taught by your leaders to believe. You are not strong enough to conquer the world and you will never be. Do not make the mistake again of believing that because a people dislike and do not want war, they will not fight ferociously and to the death if their freedoms or their homes are threatened. That applies to us Americans and to the other freedom-loving peoples of the world who have no intention of ever being ruled by you Germans.

Should you ever, in spite of our present plans, succeed in arming again and making a war on us again, the other peoples will have good reason to decide that the time has really come to exterminate you as a nation in the same manner it sometimes becomes necessary to exterminate an animal that has gone mad. There are some who have entertained the idea as a result of your actions in this war.

I predict that you will scarcely have arrived back in your own country before you will be listening to new Hitlers who will tell you most convincingly that you did not start this war, that you did not really lose it, that you must revenge yourselves upon us for the unjust peace we will impose upon you and that now after two trials you will not make again any of the mistakes made in the last two wars and the next one will surely bring victory. I hope that then you will remember some of these things I am telling you, that you will remember what such leaders brought you this time, and will again, if you persist in listening to and following them. I sincerely hope that some of you at least, become leaders on your own acacount, men who will strive to rid Germany of false leaders and dangerous thinking, who will work long and hard to restore Germany to her former place as a respected member of the family of nations. It will take a long time but the effort will be well repaid in the end.

The current series of programs in the newly-developed natural amphitheatre in the Alabama Hills near Lone Pine continues Friday Sept. 3 with a program of Liszt and Bartok by Iren Marik, well-known Hungarian-born pianist.

Miss Marik, whose powerful and sensitive interpretations have received acclaim throughout the world, is regarded as one of the finest interpreters of Liszt and Bartok of either sex to be found anywhere.

Because of her love for the region and her dedicated interest in the Deepest Valley Theatre, she has appeared on numerous occasions from Mammoth Lakes to Lone Pine, and is becoming a familiar figure in the Owens Valley, attracting enthusiastic audience response.

Born in Hungary, she was a pupil of Bartok and a professor of piano at the State Conservatory in Budapest. For the past several years she has concertized in London, Paris, New York and has recorded works of Bartok and Liszt for Draco Records, and other recording companies. Some of her records will be available for purchase after the Deepest Valley performance, at the Draco Gallery in downtown Lone Pine, opposite the fire station.

Miss Marik's program:

1. Benediction de Dieu dans la Solitude, Liszt; II. Sunrise and Allegro Barbaro, Bartok; III. Selections from the Microcosmos: Melody in the Mist, Chord study, Unison, Major seconds broken and together, Chords together and opposed, Bartok; IV. Harmonie du Soir, Liszt; V. Four old Hungarian Songs, Scherzo, Ballade, Bartok; VI. Jeux d'eau de la Villa d'Este, Liszt; VII. Vallee d'Obermann (1835), Liszt.

Liszt wrote nothing for the amateur performer; his music is difficult to play and requires the brilliance of the virtuoso performer—an Iren Marik.

Deepest Valley Theatre will feature a brilliant young harpsichordist, John Hamilton, for its fifth program in the current series, on Saturday, Sept. 4. Mr. Hamilton, a native of Washington, has studied with Wanda Landowska, Olga Samarnoff, and has concertized throughout the U.S. including a Town Hall recital and a TV series of the Goldberg Variations for KQED in San Francisco. At present he is completing his Doctor of Musical Arts Degree in performance at USC. He is also well known as one of the West Coast's finest organists.

Mr. Hamilton will bring his own specially-constructed seven-foot Challis harpsichord to the Owens Valley for the Sept. 4 performance. His program will be devoted to works of Couperin, Bach and Scarlatti:

I. Ame Ordre, François Couperin (1668–1733) 2 Aliemandes: La Raphaele, L'Ausoniene; 2 Courantes; Sarabande: L'Unique; Gavotte; Rondeau; Gigue; Passacaille; La Morinete. II. Chromatic Fantasia and Fugue, Johann Sebastian Bach (1685–1750). III. "Goldberg" Variations (excerpts), Johann Sebastian Bach. IV. 4 Sonatas, in pairs, Domenico Scarlatti (1685–1757), C. Major; K. 132, 133; D Major and Minor; K. 119, 120.

The third and last of the series, winding up the 1965 Deepest Valley Theatre presentations, will be Sunday Sept. 5, with John Ranck, (whose opening recital on Friday Aug. 27 started the whole series off on a magnificently high level) and Iren Marik, in Messiaen's Vision de l'Amen for two pianos.

This work, which has had very few performances in this country begins with the most complete pianissimo in the mystery of the first nebula and continues in a tremendous crescendo toward the mystery of the Light of Life.

"By joining the lives of the creatures who say Amen, because they exist," the composer explains "I have tried to express the infinite variety of riches of the Amen in seven Musical Visions, composed for two pianos, demanding of those instruments the maximum of strength and sonority. I entrusted the first piano (played by John Ranck) with the difficult rhythms, the binding chords, everything that was speed, charm and quality of sound. I entrusted the second piano (played by Iren Marik) with the principal melody, the thematic elements, everything which demands emotion and power."

It is requested there be no applause until the end of the work, after the last Amen.

Large audiences are anticipated for this coming weekend's programs (particularly the Sunday evening concert), therefore early arrival will be necessary to insure a choice of seating. Programs begin at 8:30 p.m. and are completed by 10 p.m. The audience is invited to the Draco Gallery in downtown Lone Pine, opposite the Fire Station on Jackson St., to meet the artists after each concert. An exhibit of San Francisco area painting and sculpture is currently on show at the Draco Gallery.

—*Inyo Register,* Aug. 28, 1965.

PROFOUND, DRAMATIC DESCRIBE

CONCERT AT VALLEY THEATRE

To preface this account of the tremendous concert of the Raos some comment must be made about the setting in which it was given.

We have all heard of our newest theatrical site in the Alabama Hills. Most of us have shrugged it off or paid it lip service as a fine cultural project . . . for someone else. I have been around some too in Inyo county and supposed that I had sampled most of the wonders of the region but this is one I had missed. The small amphitheater, set well apart from any distractions, is framed, like a far more ancient Stonehenge, with its incredible granite monoliths. Seated by the stage, those of us who were there early watched evening fall over the Sierra crest. A fingernail moon and its attendant evening star stayed briefly with us as the sky darkened, only to drop, before darkness, behind the dragon crest of Whitney. One by one the druid lights were lit, each in its natural rock cavity. The absolute serenity of the quiet warm night gathered us into its magic. The polynesian lamps of the stage were lit and with a first light whisper of wind the performance began. Lacking the stage it might well have been two thousand years ago in the Khyber Pass. As an experience in today's world it was profoundly affecting.

Mr. Rao, the attendant magician, for that is how I feel about him, explained in a quiet voice some of the background of the music to be played. The sitar and tanpula used turned out to be dramatically large, complex and beautiful: intricate of tuning and altogether appropriate to the Arabian Nights atmosphere. The music, as he pointed out, would also be complex and from another world most of us had never glimpsed. The microtonal system of the ragas, which employs, for each piece, an arbitrary selection of units from a 73 tone scale, is foreign to western ears. The sitar must be prepared in advance for each selection by a delicate adjustment of the moveable frets. It came as something of a shock to be told that his first selection would be a half hour in duration. First he played us the scale and then, with his young American wife Paula (who, by the way, is an elementary teacher in Altadena) seated impassively behind him to play the drone bass of the tanpula, we were literally off into another world.

It was, as 95 percent of classical Hindu music is, unwritten patterns handed down through the generations from teacher to gifted student, basing itself only briefly on the basic framework of the particular raga used, and from that point going off into an improvisational theme and variations on an enormously extended melodic line. It was a quiet tale at first, but as it progressed it kept on adding more and more intricate configurations. Keeping pace with it, the wind also came, whispering down around the rocks, blowing the stage lights into trails of flame which became in turn like some occult choreography sent by the djinns of our own ancient hills to keep him company. Variation piled on variation, a skein of angry words against the groundbeat of the C sharp tonic, endlessly repeated, and the susurration of the 13 'sympathetic' unplayed strings which are part of the instrument. And then, with a last gentle statement, it was over, and the audience came slowly back to reality.

This then, was the first half of the program and the second was like unto it, except that the instruments were two drums, quite unlike ours or any we know and understand, each head having multiple sounds built into different concentric rings, which varied from an illusion of dropped silver coins, to a muffled call. The combination of effects produced was beyond description, especially so, as, in addition, Rao chanted the rhythmic patterns in all their frightening complexity, thus adding the human voice to what would in any case have been an implausible experience. As he explained it, the tabla solo he played was based on a 16 beat cycle, but hardly in terms of the four-four rhythm we would have assigned it. Rather, the broad framework was broken into unequal units, and these, in turn, further subdivided into as many as five beats for each of the 16. Adding to this the many possible sounds of each drum-tap and the result was an assault on one's credulity. He mildly remarked that such patterns had to be memorized into the sub-conscious over 15 or 20 years before improvisation could take place. I believe that such knowledge could only be, in part, at least, atavistic, built over generations into the individual. In any case, it was something to marvel at.

Mr. Rao is here on a Fulbright and will shortly return to India. He is presently instructing jazz musicians in the Los Angeles area in the rudiments of this most complex system. I deeply sympathize with anyone who attempts to master it. When asked, after the concert, if there were many people in his country who could perform as he does, he remarked that few were proficient on both the sitar and the drums. It would be surprising if any were since the physical dexterity alone in either medium is so enormous.

His performance added depth to our possibly provincial concept of artistic culture as practiced in the West. It was a rare privilege to hear him in such surroundings as the Deepest Valley Theatre affords. Once again our thanks to Evelyn Eaton for the driving force that has made it possible. For you who love music, drama or just sheer magic, may I suggest that you go to at least one performance in the Deepest Valley Theatre this next weekend. It is an experience I can guarantee you will never forget! —Aim Morhardt, *Progress Citizen*, Aug. 28, 1965.

Perhaps someone should conduct a little research into the acoustical properties of decomposing granite.

The Gregg Smith Singers, who performed among the time-eroded rocks of Deepest Valley Theatre last weekend, demonstrated that for the transmission of sound there is nothing to equal the way the pure tones of vocalists were reflected off the weirdly-shaped boulders which surround the theater area.

Nothing like it has been heard here before, and possibly not anywhere else.

Smith sprang a few surprises on the audience (which was entirely too small considering the quality of the concert.) Saturday afternoon he put his artists through a grueling four hours of rehearsal under the hot sun in the Alabama Hills.

He tried placing them in various positions to extract the most from their excellent voices. The time spent in selecting precisely the right locations was well justified.

In the second third of the program the singers scattered far and wide, beyond the area occupied by the audience. They clambered up to rock pinnacles as much as 30 feet above the stage level and as far as 75 feet from the stage. As they began singing, the effect was indescribable. Each voice carried back to the stage area clearly. They met and blended in an effect which one spectator likened to "stereo with 30 speakers, each carrying a different sound track."

Smith has used this technique before—but indoors where the confining walls set up reverberations which did not exist here in Deepest Valley. The audience was held spellbound. The Singers will simply have to return to Deepest Valley next year, and anyone who misses their artistry then can dam well stay home and listen to rock and roll.

Last week's performance was indicative of the quality of concerts that Draco Foundation has booked for the amphitheater in the Alabama Hills. This weekend's programs will be equally exciting. Saturday night the Los Angeles String Quartet (and you can imagine the effect those stringed instruments will produce in the clear night air.) On Sunday Miss Iren Marik will display her piano artistry again, and there's no question this will be well received since she's already proved her attraction for DV audiences. —John Wintersteen, *Inyo Independent,* Aug. 25, 1967.

BOOKS BY EVELYN EATON

NOVELS

The Encircling Mist, 1925
Desire Spanish Version, 1934
Summer Dust, 1936
Pray to the Earth, 1939
Quietly My Captain Waits, 1940
Restless Are the Sails, 1942
The Sea Is So Wide, 1943
In What Torn Ship, 1945
Give Me Your Golden Hand, 1950
Flight, 1954
I Saw My Mortal Sight, 1959
The King Is a Witch, 1965
Go Ask the River, 1969

NONFICTION

The Hours of Isis, 1925
Every Month Was May, 1946
The North Star Is Nearer, 1949

POETRY

The Interpreter, 1923
The Small Hour, 1954
Love Is Recognition, 1971

CHILDREN'S BOOKS

John Film Star, 1937
Canadian Circus, 1938

Index

Index